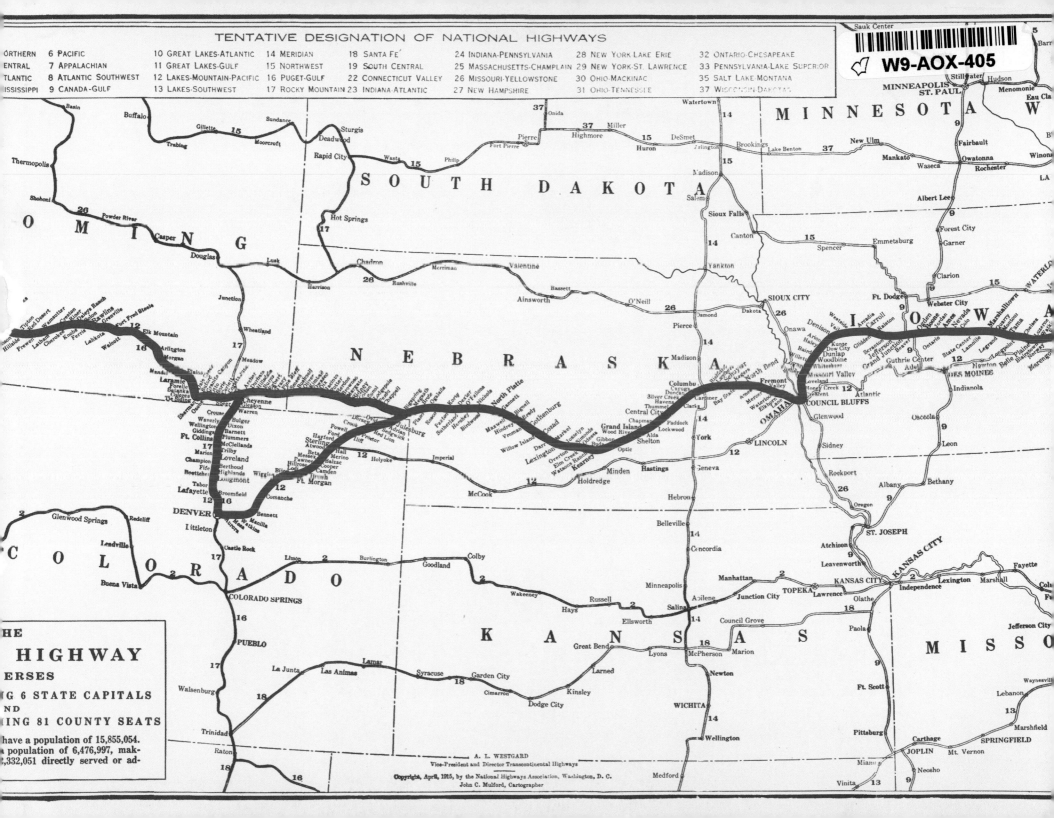

Greetings from the

Lincoln Highway

America's First Coast-to-Coast Road

Brian Butko

STACKPOLE BOOKS

Copyright ©2005 by Stackpole Books

Published by
STACKPOLE BOOKS
5067 Ritter Road
Mechanicsburg, PA 17055
www.stackpolebooks.com

For our friend Jackie Bachinsky

Printed in China

10 9 8 7 6 5 4 3 2 1

FIRST EDITION

EDITOR: *Kyle Weaver*
DESIGNER: *Beth Oberholtzer*

Photos by the author and illustrations from the author's collection, unless otherwise noted

Endpapers: Map of the Lincoln Highway as the main transcontinental route, issued by the National Highways Association in 1918. Some of the towns on the route, such as Camden, New Jersey, had been removed from the Lincoln years before. THE LINCOLN MUSUEM, FORT WAYNE, INDIANA (#4593)

Title page: While driving a new 1916 model Packard Twin Six, left, from Detroit to San Francisco in June 1915, LHA president Henry Joy, LHA secretary and publicity director Austin Bement, and Packard mechanic Ernie Eisenhut met another transcontinental touring party in an Indianapolis-made Pathfinder near Austin, Nevada. HENRY BOURNE JOY COLLECTION, BENTLEY HISTORICAL LIBRARY, UNIVERSITY OF MICHIGAN

Library of Congress Cataloging-in-Publication Data

Butko, Brian.
    Greetings from the Lincoln Highway : America's first coast-to-coast road / Brian Butko.
      p.   cm.
    Includes bibliographical references and index.
    ISBN 0-8117-0128-X (hardcover : alk. paper)
    1. Lincoln Highway—History. 2. Automobile travel—United States. 3. United States—Description and travel. I. Title.

HE356.L7B87   2005
917.304'91—dc22

                         2004022294

Contents

Acknowledgments

Here are some folks who helped with this project, with apologies for any omissions. Editor Kyle Weaver was a constant, dependable resource, advocate, and good friend in every aspect of this project—my endless thanks go to him. Also helping behind the scenes were copyeditor Joyce Bond, paginator Kerry Jean Handel, sales director Patrick Moran, designer Beth Oberholtzer, specialty accounts manager Donna Pope, art director Caroline Stover, and many others at Stackpole Books.

Kevin Patrick masterminded the maps for this book and was always ready to discuss the highway and the many vexing, conflicting parts of its history and routing.

My wife Sarah and children Andrew, Nikolas, and Natalie were also continual sources of assistance, knowledge, and inspiration.

Many friends and fellow researchers shared their time and expertise, including Carol Ahlgren, Wib and Margie Albright, Lynn Asp, Bob and Joyce Ausberger, John Baeder, Jay Banta, Michael A. "Bert" Bedeau, Charles Biddle, Frank Brusca, Michael Buettner, Merry Bush, Kevin and Lori Butko, Jim Cassler, Hallie Chatfield, Joe Ciccarelli, Dave Cole, Jim Conkle, Dan Cupper, Kathleen Dow, Karen Fetter, Sherrie Flick, Ruth and Clare Frantz, Gregory Franzwa, Clara Gardner, Mike Gassmann, Peter Genovese, Kerry Glenn, Amanda Gillen, David Halaas, John Harman, Craig Harmon, Mella Harmon, Maureen Harper, Bernie Heisey, Lyell Henry, Olga Herbert, Dan Hershberger, Lora Hershey, Drake Hokanson, Cy Hosmer, Carol Ingald, Sue Jacobson, Jamie Jensen, Jerry Keyser, Jeff Kitsko, Kevin Kutz, Philip Langdon, Bob Lichty, J. R. Manning, John Margolies, D. Lowell Nissley, Doug Pappas, Jesse Petersen, Chris Plummer, James Powell, Walter Powell, Michael Pratt, Lyn Protteau, Bob Puschendorf, Bernard and Esther Queneau, Angie Quinn, Jim Ranniger, Russell Rein, Norman Root, Rosemary Rubin, Beth Savage, Leon Schegg, Keith Sculle, Rick Sebak, Paul J. Sestak, Susan Shearer, Rebecca Shiffer, Jan Shupert-Arick, John Skarstad, Richard L. Smith, Rollin Southwell, Alan Stockland, Howard Stovall, Mark Tabbert, Carolyn Texley, Douglas Towne, Megan Tressler, Cindy Van Horn, Randy Wagner, Michael Wallis, Michael Weigler, Richard Weingroff, Mark Wolfe, and Andrew Wood.

In my family is a 1926 Model T coupe, black enamel, upright windshield, and hand-crank start. Its care has been given over to me, a joyous task. Since it sits most of the time, getting it started sometimes takes priming, fiddling, some swearing, and considerable cranking. Once it starts, and I've played with the spark and throttle enough to know it will stay running, there comes a moment of magic.

The little car stands at attention, vibrating, rocking with kinetic potential. In that few seconds before I release the brake and step on the low-gear pedal, I briefly relive the start of every road journey I've ever taken, the beginning of every great automobile trip there ever was. I marvel at the machine, its marriage to the road, and co-joined, their nuptial promise of adventure "—somewhere west of Laramie," of keen experiences that would put Walt Whitman to writing a dozen new verses to "Song of the Open Road."

Every auto journey should start with excitement like this, and those that Brian Butko writes about in this volume all did. The first thirty years of the twentieth century were a singular era in American history, a time when automobiles first allowed millions to find a little relief from the isolation of farm, factory, or high-society life, and discover a bit of their own country through mud-spattered windshields on highways that had lyric names but few improvements or markings. For a short while, before giant interchanges and coast-to-coast fast food, the adventure quotient ran high, and anybody who was able took an auto trip to see the country firsthand.

Of course, it couldn't last. In a country so bent on improving itself, the road and the automobile soon evolved into the sprawling and usually efficient system we take for granted today. As Butko points out, the Lincoln Highway aficionados who attend the annual convention usually get there by four-lane interstate highways, if they drive at all. And I, for one, would not give up my fuel-efficient, stereo-enhanced sedan and the wide four-lanes I drive to work.

In the 1980s, when I was on the road for long weeks photographing and digging deep in research libraries for my own book on the Lincoln Highway, I found myself constantly thinking about the early "autoists" and their experiences while crossing the nation on this road. Certainly things like bridges, route markings, concrete, federal legislation, and early Lincoln Highway Association correspondence were vital to the book, but I found myself returning to the stories of those who went early and wrote about what they found.

Through my own often mud-splattered windshield, I looked out on the likes of the Ship Hotel in the mountains of Pennsylvania and the tiny oasis of Fish Springs in the Utah desert and thought, What did they think of this place? What tiny but memorable part of their lives did they live here? When my book was finished, I knew there was a lot more to be discovered and to be written about in the tales of the travelers and where they camped, turned the wrong way, got stuck, broke down, ate, bought gas and where they sailed along with a sense of liberation that few have felt before or since.

Effie Gladding, who crossed on the Lincoln Highway in 1914, understood it. She dedicated her book to the adventurous auto travelers of her time. Now Brian Butko has written the book for modern adventurers—take it with you in the minivan or the Honda and become one of Gladding's "lovers of the open road and the flying wheel."

Drake Hokanson

The Good, The Bad, and the Muddy

An Introduction to the Lincoln Highway

In May 1911, Henry Joy, president of Packard Motor Car Company, drove west from Detroit in a new automobile. He was wealthy enough that he need never have left the office, but Joy was a hands-on guy. He and his chief engineer figured a cross-country drive would be a good test of the company's new model. At Omaha–not even halfway across the country–Joy asked a Packard dealer for directions to continue west.

"Follow me and I'll show you," came the reply.

The dealer got in a car and led the men to a wire ranch fence.

"Just take down the fence and drive on and when you come to the next fence, take that down and go on again."

"A little farther," said Joy, "and there were no fences, no fields, nothing but two ruts across the prairie."

Less than a century ago, there was no road across the United States. There were wagon trails in the West and decaying turnpikes in the East. A few people had envisioned and even named cross-country routes. One, the Transcontinental Road, traced a line much like the Lincoln Highway would adopt in 1913. But it wasn't a real road, just someone's conception of trails that could be hooked together between the coasts.

That was essentially the Lincoln Highway at first, too. Famed pathfinder A. L. Westgard told potential tourists that they'd find the road enjoyable, if they were "fond of changing tires and digging a car out of sand pits and mud holes." Henry Ostermann, who would become the Lincoln Highway Association (LHA) field secretary, estimated in 1908 that a cross-country trip would take sixty days–ninety if difficulties were encountered. But it could be done. It had been done, starting with the first cross-country drive in 1903. What made the Lincoln different than other vaguely routed paths is that it was the first and most concerted effort to improve, mark, and promote a road across the United States. It succeeded because it gave disparate groups–motorists, manufacturers, farmers, and politicians–a common rallying point.

It became a crusade for the men involved in its founding. They were determined to get America out of the mud as well as build the greatest monument possible to the martyred president, Abraham Lincoln. No mere statue or building would do. The proclamation of the route, released September 14, 1913, hammered home that the establishment and improvement of the highway was the patriotic burden of every person. Their later writings and speeches were infused with a desire to make this road a perpetual memorial. In 1914, two years after he conceived of the highway, Carl Fisher declared: "The Lincoln Highway is to be something more than a road. It will be a road with personality, a distinctive work of which the Americans of future generations can point with pride–an economic but also artistic triumph." It didn't hurt that the road could help sell more of the cars and accessories that these men made their everyday business.

In the nine decades following the Lincoln Highway's establishment, it went from a red line on a map to the best-known highway ever; the term "America's Main Street" was used to describe the Lincoln as early as the 1918 LHA guide. It then slipped into obscurity, being overshadowed by Route 66, though it predated that highway by more than a decade.

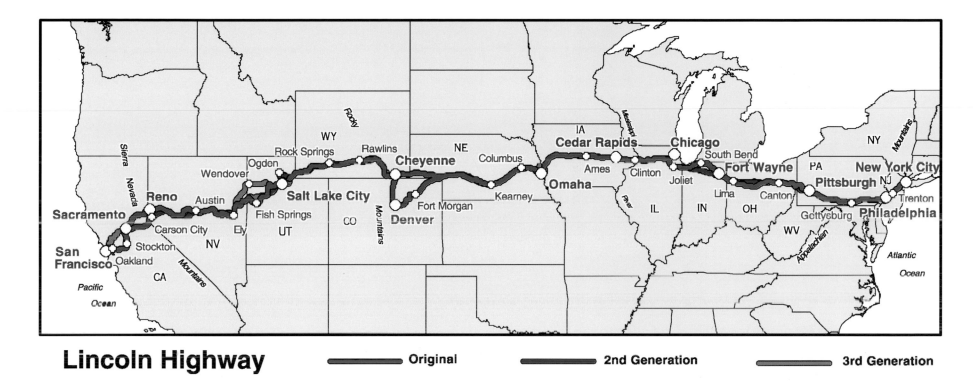

Lincoln Highway

━━━ Original ━━━ 2nd Generation ━━━ 3rd Generation

Road improvements that once were cutting-edge have been dug up, paved over, or simply left to wither. A 1928 photo taken east of Schellsburg, Pennsylvania, shows the original Lincoln and an adjacent improved version with guardrails and a modern culvert. They could be there today and might be fun to drive. But a third generation–straighter and hard-surfaced–bypassed both roads long ago, and in 1940, the Pennsylvania Turnpike became the ultimate bypass. The original two roads have become faint traces in the woods, their secrets fading into the bramble.

Such stories, however, are able to surface because the Lincoln Highway did not die after all. Just as the last of the old-time boosters were passing on, it was rediscovered. Drake Hokan-

son's engaging 1988 book inspired a new generation to hit the roads and archives in search of the road and its story. A new Lincoln Highway Association began spreading the word with a quarterly magazine and yearly conference.

For fifteen years, I considered writing a book about what's along the road, but I didn't want to just cobble together photos of neon signs and quaint cabin courts. There's much more fascinating history and geography to be learned from the road. A number of books have been published lately–painstakingly detailed state guides, notably a series by Gregory Franzwa; adventures such as Bill Roe's bicycle journey; Pete Davies's absorbing tales of the First Transcontinental Army Truck Convoy–but no general guides to the route.

I'm also intrigued by what traveling the road might have been like, and nothing captures the tribulations of early motoring better than the words of those who lived it. A number of memoirs published between 1910 and 1930 recount trips that followed at least part of the Lincoln Highway. Postcard messages likewise captured the immediacy of traveling. On a postcard showing the highway at Point of Rocks, Wyoming, Len wrote to Sweeps, "There plenty of nothing out here for sure, this is the way it looks for sure. Everything is okay." The landscape was the main feature to Len, moving him to say no more.

That's not to say that early motorists were above brief flirtations with nostalgia. In *Excuse My Dust*, Bellamy Partridge wrote: "There was

You can learn a lot about travel habits and road conditions from old postcards.

Hotel Crary,
Only Hotel on the Lincoln Highway,
Boone, Iowa.

Tarry at the Crary.

a gaity to motoring in those days, a vacation spirit, a *camaraderie* of the highway that is almost unbelievable today. Nobody could have believed that so simple a pleasure would, in a single generation, grow into a monster

called Traffic." And he was writing in 1943! I'll bet the 1903 transcontinentalists would have traded a few miles of concrete for some traffic.

And so I wrote this book to help me figure out what's where, and I hope it helps you too. It includes a mix of geography and history, with no particular goal of retelling every town's history or every gas station's lineage. It supplies directions to explain the route, but you'll need more detailed guides for navigating. I was lucky to find so many vintage photos, and friends generously loaned their rare postcards. The book also incorporates many quotes that describe life on the road. But take them for what they're worth; as James Montgomery Flagg wrote in *Boulevards All the Way—Maybe*, "Most Americans can tell the truth about something. Motoring is the one topic about which they all lie."

The Memoirs

One of the earliest auto trip narratives is *Two Thousand Miles on an Automobile*, penned anonymously by "Chauffeur" in 1902. The author didn't give the make of his car, but it was an American-made, one-cylinder vehicle rated at eight and a half horsepower. He captured a world that was quite different from our own:

> A man with a white elephant could probably travel from New York to San Francisco without disbursing a penny for the keeping of his animal. . . . It is a good deal also with an automobile; it is still sufficiently a curiosity to command respect and attention. The farmer is glad to have it stop in front of his door or put up in his shed; he will supply it with oil and water. The blacksmith would rather have it stop at his shop for repair than at his rival's—it

gives him a little notoriety, something to talk about. So it is with the liveryman at night; he is, as a rule, only too glad to have the novelty under his roof, and takes pride in showing it to the visiting townsfolk. They do not know what to charge, and therefore charge nothing.

But not all were so happy to encounter his car: "Why the hoodlums who stand about the street corners should be animated by a seemingly irresistible desire to hurl stones and brickbats—as well as epithets—at passing automobiles is a mystery."

The ride was jarring, too: "Going at twenty or twenty-five miles an hour in a machine with thirty-two-inch wheels and short wheelbase gives about the same exercise one gets on a horse; one is lifted from the seat and thrown from side to side. . . . It is trying on the nerves and the temper."

Horns were not yet a staple of the road: "In the country the horn is not so good for attracting attention as a loud gong. The horn is mistaken for dinner-horns and distant sounds of farmyard life." Gongs were more familiar, as they were used by policemen, firemen, and trolley lines.

A decade later, autos were familiar to most people, and writers concentrated more on the road and landscape. By the end of the 1920s, 90 percent of all cars were enclosed, the inverse of a decade earlier. Frederic Van de Water was an exception, as he noted in 1927:

> We are one of the few remaining families in this hemisphere who consider a top a nuisance and an obstruction unless it is actually raining. . . . But all our highway mates traveled beneath a low roof . . . which, to our abnormal minds, ranks a little lower in pleasure than riding in a railroad coach.

Though many memoirists were elite, one exception was Theodore Dreiser, who published *A Hoosier Holiday* in 1916. His account of returning to his childhood haunts in Indiana covers little of the Lincoln Highway, but it stands out as beautiful writing and one of the few narratives that embrace the working class. Dreiser also left a tantalizing mystery for Lincoln Highway researchers. His friend's chauffeur, and the driver for this trip, was called "Speed." The book never reveals his real name but describes him as "a blond, lithe, gangling youth with an eerie farmer-like look and smile. . . . He seemed half-mechanic, half street-car conductor, half mentor, guide and friend." He was said to be "one of the chauffeurs who led the procession of cars from New York over the Alleghenies and Rockies to the coast, laying out the Lincoln Highway," and Dreiser wrote that he saw testimonials and autographed plates proving it. Which trip was that? Who *was* Speed?

The writings of the other memoir writers you'll meet in these pages vary widely in style and focus. Many noted specifics about flowers, aromas, and the clarity of the air; they were driving open cars at low speeds and really absorbing the landscape. Today one can cross three states in the time it took them to go between two towns.

On June 9, 1909, twenty-two-year-old Alice Ramsey left New York City in a dark green Maxwell 30 touring car with friend Hermine Jans and sisters-in-law Nettie Powell and Margaret Atwood. In *Veil, Duster, and Tire Iron*, she recalled how they left their homes and husbands (except bachelorette Hermine) in Hackensack, New Jersey, and arrived in San Francisco fifty-nine days later, making Alice the first woman to drive across the United States. She had been challenged by a sales manager for the Maxwell-Briscoe Company, which sponsored and publicized the trip to convince the American public that cars were here to stay.

Ramsey did not reach the future Lincoln Highway until Ligonier, Indiana, but from there she almost always stuck to the soon-to-be transcontinental route. In fact, she wrote, "I almost feel as if I were the 'Mother' of it! And believe me, the labor pangs prior to its birth were terrific. It is still a lusty and worthy offspring—even if its name is now obscured and desecrated by its unromantic designation as Route 30!" Ramsey would cross the country more than thirty times in the next seventy years. For the first trip's ninetieth anniversary, two women retraced Ramsey's tracks in a Mercedes Benz sedan.

In her 1911 memoir, *A Woman's World Tour in a Motor*, Harriet White Fisher told of her ten-thousand-mile journey around the globe in a forty-horsepower Locomobile roadster. She had been widowed in 1903 and, in a rare turn for the times, personally took control of her late husband's Eagle Anvil Company in Trenton. On the trip, the forty-two-year-old took along a servant for cooking and secretarial duties and a maid; her nephew Harold did the driving. It was an amazing feat, just one year after the famous New York–to–Paris race that had left many cars far short of the goal. She and her entourage were abroad almost a year, arriving in San Francisco on June 17, 1910. They reached New York City two months later.

In *Fill 'er Up!*, Bellamy Partridge described his trip across the country in August 1912. His recollection, four decades later, was that news

Alice Ramsey repairs a flat near Rochelle, Illinois. Note the cover on the rear oil lamp next to the luggage.

of the Lincoln Highway had inspired the trip, so perhaps he was thinking of 1913. Much of Partridge's book was a chronicle of the American Automobile Association (he was invited to join by Robert Bruce, who would later write a book about the Lincoln Highway in Pennsylvania). Partridge recalled that the first resolution passed after AAA's formation in 1902 "was in favor of a transcontinental highway from New York to San Francisco, and yet so lacking was the public interest in roads that after some ten years of effort not even the route had been decided upon."

Effie Gladding had just returned from three years touring the world when she departed from San Francisco on April 21, 1914. She and her husband, Thomas, first drove the El Camino Real six hundred miles south before turning and meeting the Lincoln at Stockton. In a 262-page book titled *Across the Continent by the Lincoln Highway*, she doesn't

reach the focus of her title until page 108, then detours off it for another 47 pages near the end, skipping most of Ohio and Pennsylvania. Still, it was the first full-size hardback to discuss transcontinental travel, as well as the first to mention the Lincoln Highway:

> We were now to traverse the Lincoln Highway and were to be guided by the red, white, and blue marks; sometimes painted on telephone poles, sometimes put up by way of advertisement over garage doors or swinging on hotel signboards; sometimes painted on little stakes, like croquet goals, scattered along over the great spaces of the desert. We learned to love the red, white, and blue, and the familiar big L which told us that we were on the right road.

After her return, Gladding wrote the foreword to the LHA's first road guide, directing it to women motorists.

Thornton Round recalled his family's 1914 trip from Cleveland to the Pacific in *The Good of It All*. His parents, brother, and sisters made the trip in a Winton Six and a Ford Model T Runabout to carry the baggage. Though Round was writing from memory more than forty years later, he had clear recollections, plus he uncovered reports his dad had sent back and published in the local AAA magazine. The family used a Blue Book to navigate, but found its directions ended at Salt Lake City. After that, the book advised using a compass to head west.

Emily Post was divorced and was writing for money (including romantic serials of high society), when *Collier's* magazine commissioned her to cross the United States and write about it. Her son Edwin drove, and an unnamed family member joined them. Her story was published in 1916 as a book, *By Motor to the Golden Gate*. Her fame came later in 1922, with the publication of an etiquette book. In 1961, her son wrote her biography, with one part recounting the transcontinental drive.

In the 1920 book *A Frenchwoman's Impressions of America*, Comtesse Madeleine de Bryas wrote of a trip across the country in 1918 with her sister. They traveled for six months, giving more than two hundred lectures to solicit aid for French war relief. She noted Americans' love of their cars: "'The house was a luxury, but the car a necessity.' And truly they live in them, sleep in them, and finally go camping with their dearly beloved motor-cars."

Beatrice Massey wrote in *It Might Have Been Worse*, that she had been inspired by Emily Post's book: "After talking and planning for three years, we actually decided to go in ten minutes." Massey, her husband, and another couple departed from New York on July 19, 1919. They came back well satisfied with their twin-six Packard touring car.

In *A Long Way from Boston*, Beth O'Shea and her friend Kit crossed the country in the early 1920s on a more modest budget. They drove a black 1918 Model T roadster that looked "like what those early cars really were—a carriage that had mislaid its horse."

Frederic Van de Water's 1927 book, *The Family Flivvers to Frisco*, is one of the most consistently funny accounts, and it is insightful too. He set off with his wife, whom he referred to only as the Commodore, and young son whom he called the Supercargo. He began by describing the reaction of their friends to the idea of a cross-country journey:

Fences

Fences may seem an unlikely part of the Lincoln Highway story, but early motorists would disagree. Western stretches of the road typically crossed ranches that were fenced in; motorists had to go through or around.

Thornton Round recalled in *The Good of It All* that when his family drove west in 1914, they ran into fences, literally. They were hurrying toward Denver on the Colorado Loop at dusk when Thornton's car hit a barbed-wire fence stretched across the road, pulling the post from the ground. "When it hit it took the headlights and radiator clean off the car," he wrote. They plugged the radiator holes to the engine with sagebrush roots and steamed onward.

Gates and fences even showed up in guides such as the Cheyenne to Reno *Auto Log*; at thirty miles west of Medicine Bow, travelers were instructed to "open gate into ranch," drive around sheds, and go "thru gate out of ranch yd." Two miles east of Lyman, it informed motorists that they would go through two fences and a gate. In Packard's 1913 *Lincoln Highway Route Road Conditions and Directions*, the road from Laramie and Rawlins, Wyoming, had eighteen gates at which motorists had to stop, open, pass through, stop again, and close.

In *A Woman's World Tour in a Motor*, however, Harriet White Fisher wrote that as they approached Ely, Nevada, from the southwest, they were "obliged to travel four or five miles around over rough stubble and sagebrush. . . . These fenced-in places generally contained a notice that any one caught trespassing would be shot without further notice."

While driving cross-country, Lester Whitman found that fences were even more dangerous at night, as recorded by Curt McConnell in *Coast to Coast by Automobile*:

> All through Nebraska and Wyoming barb wire fences and barb wire gates will be encountered across the trail. If running at night the greatest precautions will be necessary, for no matter how powerful the searchlight it fails to pick up a wire fence until too late to apply the brakes, and somebody gets badly cut by the flying wires as the auto crashes through.

Also reported in *Coast to Coast by Automobile*, Jacob Murdock found during his family's 1908 trip that some fences did not even have gates: "In many places, where the roads had originally been good, they were unavailable on account of the erection of fences around new ranches. This necessitated detours and the making of new trails through the sage brush and over the washouts."

Alice Ramsey and her party had to deal with gates as they encountered cattle and sheep ranches: "Our highway ran directly through some of this privately-owned property. To keep the cattle in, there were gates we had to open and close behind us as we passed through. No matter how inconvenient it was, no one would think of neglecting this little chore in return for the right to pass."

These held that if adults wished to penetrate the sinister and savage wilderness which every New Yorker knows lies beyond Pittsburgh, that was their own affair. But to take a poor little innocent six-and-a-half-year-old boy along! . . . it was evident that they felt the case should be referred to the S.P.C.C. [Society for the Prevention of Cruelty to Children].

They traveled forty-five hundred miles across the continent in thirty-seven days. Their expenses amounted to $247.83.

In his 1928 book, *The Better Country*, Dallas Lore Sharp and his wife, Daphne, were in their fifties with four boys in college. Sharp told of how they took a trip to find out if "a better country" existed out there. After a harrowing incident in Iowa gumbo, he dreamed of the day when concrete roads would cover the land, although he could not completely quash his sense of adventure: "But let us pray that the detour may occur even then occasionally, if not to stall us, at least to slow us down." Sharp also wrote a number of nature books, but this may have been his last; he passed away in 1929.

This sign west of Walcott, Wyoming, shows that fences were still a concern in 1915.

You may be familiar with the movie called *The Long, Long Trailer*, starring Lucille Ball and Desi Arnaz, but the book it's based on, by Clinton Twiss, is even funnier. In the book, it's Clinton who is mesmerized by the aluminum gleam. Before he and his wife had even left, he'd spent $11,001.95 for the trailer, car, furnishings, and other gadgets, wrecking their budget of $2,000. Desi Arnaz tried to acquire the rights, but MGM outbid him. A friend at the studio nonetheless asked the couple to star in the movie. The rest of MGM meanwhile wondered who would pay to see actors they could watch for free on TV. The movie was filmed in June and July 1953. Lucy and Desi, television's most popular performers, earned $250,000, combined.

Although the highway was named for Lincoln, the Great Emancipator, a number of memoir writers wrote with words that now are decidedly unacceptable. Beatrice Massey, James Montgomery Flagg, and Bellamy Partridge belittled blacks and Native Americans. Racism is the dark side of roadside nostalgia that rarely lifts its head. After encountering postcards that claim "exclusive clientele," it becomes obvious why minorities hold a much less romantic view of the mid-twentieth century roadside. Such treatment led to a series of travelers' guides called the *Negro Motorist Green Book*. Beginning in 1936, the guide listed businesses that accepted African American travelers. "Carry your Green Book with you," warned the covers. "You may need it." *A Travel Guide of Negro Hotels*, published in 1942, and *Bronze American National Travel Guide*, 1961–62, likewise listed places that accommodated blacks.

In his 1965 book, *This Is My Country Too*, John A. Williams wrote, "I do not believe white travelers have any idea of how much nerve and courage it requires for a Negro to drive coast to coast in America." He did it by carrying a "rifle and shotgun, a road atlas and *Travelguide*, a listing of places in America where Negroes can stay without being embarrassed, insulted, or worse."

A Rural Landscape

The Good Roads movement began with agitation from bicyclists. Col. Albert A. Pope, a bicycle manufacturer in Connecticut, led the charge. (The "Father of Good Roads" later advocated for Memorial Miles to honor fallen soldiers.) Bicycling reached the level of a national craze between 1890 and 1910, mainly because of the introduction of the low-wheeler with rubber tires—less expensive—and much easier for amateurs than the high-wheeler. Young people especially yearned to hit the road to reach new amusements, such as trolley parks and picnic groves. New Jersey led the way with an appropriation of $75,000 in 1891 for road building. The state was also home to one of the inevitable anti-bicycle groups, aghast at the speeds and the way that female cyclists dressed. The bicycle business was centered in Michigan and Ohio; as the industry peaked and then declined, some makers survived by turning to automobiles.

In 1903, as Horatio Nelson Jackson and Sewall Crocker headed east to settle a $50 bet that a car could not cross the country, two other teams were hot on their wheels. The other teams were sponsored by automakers—Packard and Oldsmobile—which would be the norm for the next few years, as car companies tempted potential customers by sponsoring long-distance treks, then publishing ads, pamphlets, and books that pointed out the superiority of their product over others. Many of these early drives crossed the country from west to east. They wanted to put the hard part behind them first, the wind was with them, and some even believed the slopes were easier heading east, or maybe they were just thinking of the publicity bonanza as they arrived triumphantly in New York City. Either way, by 1905, the first transcontinental round-trip was completed—it took ten months.

As early as 1906, a juvenile novel series called "The Motor Boys" was being published. Imitators followed, such as "The Motor Maids" series, which included *The Motor Maids Across the Continent* in 1911; and "The Automobile Girls," by Laura Dent Crane, a set of six beginning in 1910. Even "The Outdoor Girls" series, by Laura Lee Hope, offered *The Outdoor Girls In a Motor Car* in 1913.

In *The Longest Auto Race*, George Schuster recalled the 1908 New York–to–Paris race. He was the mechanic for the sole American entry, a 1907 Thomas auto, and later became the driver. Much of the route the six cars followed across the United States later became the Lincoln Highway (two never even made it to San Francisco). A photo shows the Thomas in a blizzard crossing a trestle between Goshen and South Bend, Indiana.

> In the morning we went on [from Goshen] toward Elkhart. The Indiana Railway, an interurban trolley line, ran from there to South Bend, Indiana, and we got permission to drive over its right of way. We were on our way over the ties in the morning, thankful that their snowplows had kept this road open.
>
> Beyond South Bend we bargained with farmers, and, with the help of six or some-

times eight horses which wallowed in the drifts and exhausted themselves trying to keep on their feet, we finally reached New Carlisle. Eighty dollars had been this day's expense for team hire, and we had covered a distance from South Bend of scarcely 15 miles.

At Cheyenne, they gave a ride to a thirteen-year-old who had come from Berthoud, Colorado, to see the racers. Floyd Clymer, who went on to fame as a publisher of automobile books, had already been selling cars for two years and thereupon became a dealer for Thomas too.

The race was parodied six decades later in *The Great Race*, starring Tony Curtis as the hero, Jack Lemmon as his nemesis, and Natalie Wood as a suffragette reporter. The original race was honored in 1968 with the Transcontinental Reliability Tour, in which thirty-six pre-1914 cars went from Times Square to San Francisco. The 1907 Thomas Flyer was trailered and displayed each night, then returned to its home at William Harrah's Automobile Collection in Reno. Schuster, ninety-five, was finally awarded the $1,000 winning prize, sixty years late.

As a few people began crossing the country on their own, a surprising number were women, perhaps testing the waters of their increasing independence. Regardless of whether they were men or women, most of the transcontinental adventurers were white, upper-class professionals who had sufficient salaries and vacation time. They celebrated the diversity they found on the road, but really, they were just meeting different versions of their own type.

Emily Post squarely fit the definition of high society. Her friends were aghast that she and her party would attempt to cross the country without a chauffeur or mechanic or servants. She had already motored "across Europe again and again" and "gone from the Baltic to the Adriatic in one of the few first motor-cars ever sold to a private individual." As she herself admitted, "The majority looked upon our undertaking with typical New York apathy. Why do anything so dreary?"

A cross-country trip would have been quite a task, if not dreary. Every part of a trip that we take for granted today could be perilous then, or at least time-consuming. Starting a car meant cranking, which was backbreaking and risky, or waiting for the steam boiler to heat. Gasoline was ladled from barrels at hardware stores and blacksmith shops. In *Fill 'er Up!* Bellamy Partridge even recalled buying gasoline at a popcorn stand. Automobiles ran rough and had primitive steering and brakes. Open cars were completely exposed to the elements; goggles and leather were required to go any farther than across town. Even after people began ordering cars with tops, rain and snow could penetrate a horizontally split windshield or side curtains.

Tires were a constant hassle. Many were entirely smooth, providing no traction on slippery roads. As John B. Rae observed in *The American Automobile*, "In those days, a familiar sight on the highways of America was sweating motorists laboriously and profanely removing tires, patching them, pumping them manually to their sixty pounds pressure, and wrestling them on the wheels again." Bellamy Partridge listed the many possible troubles: "leaky valves, nail punctures, rim cuts, tube pinches, and innumerable sand blisters." When his party left Ogden, Utah, in 1912,

Stuck in the Fallon Sink between Fallon and Frenchman's Station, Nevada.

they had four new tires and tubes, but, he wrote, "they were pretty well worn out when we reached San Francisco." Thornton Round wrote in *The Good of It All* that he had to fix flats caused by square horseshoe nails and upholsterer's tacks.

Likewise, the infrastructure we take for granted did not yet exist: no roads, parking lots, gas stations, maps, standardized parts, mechanics, directional signs, traffic signals, or smooth, hard pavement. Bellamy Partridge wrote that when he drove from New York to San Francisco in 1912, he saw only one outdoor filling station: "It was in a suburb of Chicago, and was so great a novelty and curiosity that, although our tanks were well supplied, we drove in to be 'serviced'—a new and rather comical word regarded by the professors as about as barbarous as being 'burglarized.' Indeed the two terms had quite a little in common."

Tourist facilities were few, and even when free camps developed in the teens, these were usually just open fields that perhaps had running water. Some road guides were available, and the Automobile Club of Southern California was an early advocate of road mapping and sign posting, but it wasn't until the 1920s that gas stations widely circulated free maps, and not until 1924 that Rand McNally issued its first national road atlas.

Roads existed, but they were wagon trails connecting farms to markets. The few that had been improved as turnpike were eclipsed by railroads in the mid-nineteenth century and left to decline. Competition between rail lines kept rates so low that the coming of cars and trucks did nothing to inspire a need for passenger or freight transport by road. In fact, roads were worse by 1900 than they'd been in 1850.

Farmers could not yet see the value of cars, and worse, the few rich drivers who came through their towns seemed ostentatious or at least uncaring, running over chickens and other farm animals at an alarming rate. In *The Automobile Girls in Chicago*, a 1912 young adult novel by Laura Dent Crane, one girl, Ruth, runs down a cow, then nonchalantly comments that it was probably just a glancing blow, "for I barely felt the jar." As if the farmer said, "I told you so," it wasn't too many pages later that the five "Automobile Girls" were lying senseless in shattered glass and twisted metal.

Farmers had many methods of getting back at motorists, from scattering tacks to repainting their houses, rendering Blue Books useless with their "turn right at yellow house" directions.

Cowboys also disliked the auto and were known to threaten speeding motorists with guns. In his *History of Wyoming*, T. A. Larson

recalled a 1909 state bill that, had it passed, "would have required [motorists] to stop their machines on public roads in the presence of frightened horses and to give their names and addresses to anyone on demand." But autos slowly gained acceptance, and as Larson recalled, members of Good Roads clubs "carried sacks of gravel on their running boards, prepared to stop and dump the gravel into the first mudhole." The ranchers came to understand the benefits of having roads connect them to the outside world.

Not all rural folks were against the car; in *The Good of It All*, Thornton Round recalled that many farm families showed kindness, letting them camp for free, giving them milk, even feeding them, and would not accept payment. When he and his family bogged down in mud ten miles west of Kearney, Nebraska, a rancher pulled them out at no charge, as he felt it was his fault for flooding the road while working on a drain outlet. In return, the Rounds delivered a message for him on their return drive eastward, telling a hatchery in Kearney that he really needed his order of turkeys. Bellamy Partridge similarly noted that farmers repeatedly rescued them from midwestern mud: "The farmers were always willing to help, almost too willing, and they refused curtly my offers to pay."

In 1908, Ford produced its first Model T and General Motors was formed, but numerous automobiles had been available before, including some popularly priced makes such as the Curved Dash Olds. Even the Ford Model A (the original, not the 1929 version) had become the farmer's best friend and was adopted for everything from hauling animals to sawing wood. The Model T was intro-

duced on October 1, 1908, as a 1909 model. More than fifteen million were produced over the next nineteen years. Henry Ford had finally found what he'd been aiming for: a vehicle that was low-priced, easy to operate and repair, and durable. Rural people who had found the auto a bother now sensed a source of income as they hitched their teams to drag cars from local quagmires. Or they could buy their own car and for a few hundred dollars, convert it to plow their fields, and then drive it to town. Owners also adapted them to other tasks, such as pulling stumps, transporting hay, or filling silos.

One of the Model T's interesting quirks was having the gas tank beneath the front seat so that gravity could draw fuel to the carburetor. On steep hills, the carb became higher than the tank, forcing the driver to turn around and climb in reverse. The gear ratio also was lower for reverse than for low gear, adding power.

The Dawn of Highways

The Yellowstone Trail has been called "America's Oldest Organized Highway," and it's true that its origins can be traced back before the existence of the Lincoln Highway, but claims of its being the first transcontinental highway are unfounded. Still, it was one of the few major named routes with an organizational structure that promoted the road's improvement.

The Twin Cities–Aberdeen–Yellowstone Park Trail Association was founded on October 9, 1912, at Lemmon, South Dakota, and incorporated on February 17, 1913. Even at this later meeting, according to the recent concise history of the road by Alice and John

Ridge, the group's aim still was to "establish and map a route from Minneapolis/St. Paul to Yellowstone Park," as well as to "promote a vision of a nation webbed with roads." Not until 1914 did the group seriously begin considering a coast-to-coast route. The group's name was shortened to Yellowstone Trail Association (YTA) in 1915, but it still only connected Chicago to Seattle. In February 1916, the road was extended from Chicago to Plymouth Rock. That September, according to the Ridges, the YTA challenged the Lincoln Highway Association to an ocean-to-ocean race. The challenge was not accepted, but the YTA still made its 3,673-mile run in just over 121 hours using sixty-four relay cars.

The YTA's slogan "A Good Road from Plymouth Rock to Puget Sound" debuted in 1916, but it was not until January 14, 1917, that the group announced that it had reached that goal with an article and a map in the Aberdeen newspaper. It also produced folders, promoted improvements, and encouraged tourism.

On their 1919 trip, Beatrice Massey and her party, by then three, took the Yellowstone Trail from Chicago to St. Paul, Minnesota. They had no trouble following it: "At every turn, right or left, the yellow disk is in plain sight," she wrote. But she was less enthusiastic about the road's "Good Road" tag line: "The trusting soul who wrote that alluring statement has never been over the entire trail, or I am greatly mistaken."

The National Old Trails Association was also formed in 1912 to create a cross-country highway from New York City to Los Angeles. The group connected the National Road from Maryland through Illinois to Boonslick

Road in Missouri, then followed the Santa Fe Trail to New Mexico or the Oregon Trail to the Pacific Ocean. Like the Lincoln, it was marked with red, white, and blue stripes.

That same year, AAA published a map titled "Three Transcontinental Routes to Be Surveyed, Mapped and Standardized by A. L. Westgard during 1912 for the American Automobile Association." Its "Northwest Trail" resembled the future Yellowstone Trail, going through Chicago to Seattle. Its "Midland Trail" roughly followed the National Road and the future U.S. Route 40 until Utah, then headed to Ely and Los Angeles. The third, a middle route, labeled "Overland Trail," closely followed the future Lincoln Highway, with two exceptions: It chose Buffalo and Cleveland over Pennsylvania, and it went north of the Great Salt Lake (but still dipped south to Ely). It even included its own Colorado Loop.

This middle route was sometimes called the Transcontinental Road. It's mentioned in Estella M. Copeland's *Overland by Auto in 1913*. The introduction tells us that "Guy Copeland, an Indiana farmer returning home after a disillusioning year attempting to settle in California, packed up his mother, his wife, and their young family—two little boys, aged eleven and eight—into a 1910 Mitchell, purchased secondhand the previous fall." Early in 1913, Copeland's brother-in-law relayed advice from a Mr. Dunlap of Lawton, Oklahoma, said to be familiar with the nation's roads. He enclosed a U.S. map with a central and southern path marked:

If you come the central which he says is much the best road and best scenery out take the *Transcontinental road*, which leads from San Francisco to Eley [sic], Salt Lake

City, Cheyenne, Denver, Colorado Springs, Pueblo. . . . [At] Salt Lake City he says you will find numerous ranch houses where you can put up at night and will always find good accommodations, can get gasolene [sic] or any thing you need. The longest stretch between ranch houses now is 52 miles, that is just west of Salt Lake in the Alkali desert, he says don't tackle that unless it is dry. . . . Mr. Dunlap says if you will mention his name that most of those ranchers know him.

Carl Fisher was involved in numerous auto-related ventures. He had formed a partnership to manufacture an automobile, the Empire, in 1909. But three of the four Indianapolis businessmen also decided to build a racetrack. What would become the Indianapolis Motor Speedway took most of their time, leaving the car to languish. After a disaster at the opening of the new track, Fisher decided to pave it in brick. In December 1909, after the last ceremonial brick was placed, the first car to ride the new racetrack was an Empire, the first one off the line. As the *Standard Catalog of America Cars* noted, "This was probably the most attention its builders ever paid the car," and they sold the company in 1911.

Fisher had also struck gold with his Prest-O-Lite Company, maker of practical headlights. Previously, drivers had to light kerosene lamps or use carbide gas. Now, compressed gas did the job, and refueling required only an exchange of cylinders. Fisher, meanwhile, reached an agreement to sell Prest-O-Lite to Union Carbide. Electric lamps were making his product obsolete, but the buyer wanted Prest-O-Lite for its cylinders, which could be used in the growing fields of welding and

In many places there had been fresh oil used on the roads, which spattered over everything, and this oil also eats the tires, and, when dry, must make a very disagreeable dust for the traveller to inhale.

—Harriet White Fisher,
A Woman's World Tour
in a Motor (1911)

Carl Fisher takes a break from hard driving during a 1915 trip, most likely in Elkhart, Indiana.

medicine. That made the plants and distribution system equally attractive. Fisher got more than half of the $9 million selling price.

It was in this milieu that Carl Fisher gathered like-minded industrialists on September 10, 1912, in Indianapolis at Das Deutsche Haus (The German House, renamed the Athenaeum in response to anti-German sentiment during World War I). These were wealthy men who had seen Europe, who had taken steamship vacations. The next great adventure lay right at their doorstep—America. The Great Plains, Indians, cowboys, desert lands, the Pacific coast, all called out to their sense of adventure. As drivers themselves, they knew how poor the roads were, especially outside of cities; Fisher wooed them with visions of good roads linking East and West.

Fisher called his plan the Coast-to-Coast Rock Highway, with the plea, "Let's build it before we're too old to enjoy it." He proposed that each auto manufacturer, dealer,

Carl Fisher signed this July 1913 letter as chairman of the Temporary Committee and vice president of the Lincoln Highway Association, but it was still on Coast-to-Coast Rock Highway letterhead.

and maker of accessories pledge one-third of 1 percent of their company's gross receipts for three years, or one-fifth for five years. Fisher thought at least $10 million could be raised, which would be used to buy materials and to contract with states and counties to construct the road. No route was chosen; that would be left to a committee to determine later. He hoped that all the pledges would be signed by January 1, 1913, and the work completed by May 1, 1915, in time for the opening of the Panama-Pacific International Exposition in San Francisco. Individual memberships were also available at the $5 or $100 level. Goodyear's Frank Seiberling pledged $300,000 of his company's money that very night. Within a month, $1 million was raised.

The September 11, 1912, issue of *Horseless Age* lauded the plan to raise $10 million as "one of the most practical and rational yet suggested in the good roads field." More interesting, the article said that arrangements were being considered with phone companies along the chosen route to have facilities between towns for motorist in trouble to call for help.

Fisher had written to all the auto industry executives, but he had not heard from Henry Ford. Fisher sought him out, and Ford reportedly agreed at first, then changed his mind. A note came on September 18, 1912, via James Couzens, secretary and treasurer of Ford Motor Company, saying that the board would consider it but that acceptance was unlikely, "because as long as private interests

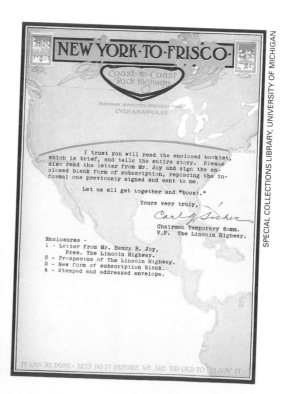

are willing to build good roads for the general public, the general public will not be very much interested in building good roads for itself." Couzens sent a formal rejection on October 25. Among the board's reasons: "We believe it is better to spend our money in making the price of the cars low, as this will have the beneficial effect of putting more cars in use, and the more cars there are in use, the greater demand there will be for the government building Good Roads."

Packard president Henry Joy is usually credited with bringing Lincoln's name to the road. Joy's father had been a friend of the sixteenth president. In December 1912, Joy wrote to Carl Fisher suggesting that his group protest to Congress that funds scheduled for the Lincoln Memorial would be better spent on roads that served the public. In January 1913, a congressman wrote to Fisher suggesting that his road would have more patriotic appeal if his group used a name such as Lincoln. Fisher also was a Lincoln enthusiast, later giving the main boulevard in his Miami Beach the name of Lincoln Avenue, and calling his first public accommodations on it the Lincoln Hotel. Whoever suggested it first, Fisher and Joy both agreed it was the perfect name.

Fisher's goal of $10 million in pledges by January 1, 1913, was not nearly reached. Packard pledged $150,000, and Hudson Motor Company signed up for $100,000 later that month. Fisher wrote to Ford again on February 7, but to no avail. (Edsel Ford, however, later supported the LHA, joining the board in 1920 and contributing $5,000 toward the group's operating expenses in 1923, 1924, and 1925.) In March 1913, Lehigh Portland Cement Company president A. Y. Gowen,

who became a regular LHA supporter and director, offered to contribute 1.5 million barrels or more of cement.

On April 14, Fisher called a meeting in Joy's office to organize. The group decided to incorporate, with Joy as president. Their headquarters would be in Detroit, and their route would be named for Lincoln. The Lincoln Highway Association was incorporated at the first meeting of its directors in Detroit on July 1, 1913. Henry Joy, his attorney Henry Bodman, Hudson Motor Car Company president Roy Chapin, Detroit banker Emory Clark, and Good Roads advocate Arthur Pardington met in the Dime Savings Bank Building.

At almost the same hour, Carl Fisher and more than seventy men in seventeen cars plus two supply trucks were leaving Indianapolis on the Hoosier Tour, a four-week trip across the nation to promote Indiana-made automobiles and the Lincoln Highway. Although

he worried that the tour might be mistaken for a route-finding expedition, he knew that the publicity would help the cause. Indeed, every town the tour visited took it as a sign that it would be on the route, and almost every city across the country's midsection campaigned for inclusion, from Baltimore to Cleveland to Los Angeles.

On the tour, Fisher was invited to the upcoming Conference of Governors at Colorado Springs that August, where he thought he might obtain some immediate financing. A year after the idea's launch, he had only $4.2 million, still less than half of his $10 million goal. He knew the attendees would want to see a route, so he persuaded the LHA board to hammer one out. Henry Joy had already spent three weeks in May and June exploring the possibilities. As western communities began writing to the LHA to get on the route, a standard reply went out explaining the desired attributes: directness, points of scenic and historical interest, centers of population between these points, and the character and volume of support from communities.

The LHA board prepared a map with a red line to indicate the proposed route, and Joy, Fisher, and the other LHA vice president, Arthur Pardington, took it with them to the Conference of Governors. They gave a speech, which they called "An Appeal to Patriots," explaining the route and its rationale. The response was positive except from Kansas and Colorado, which had come to believe from the Hoosier Tour that the Lincoln Highway would pass through their states. Feeling pressure from their host, the LHA made an exception for Colorado, creating a dogleg to Denver.

On the train returning home, the men drafted a public announcement. It went out on September 14, 1913, proclaiming the LHA's aim "to immediately promote and procure the establishment of a continuous improved highway from the Atlantic to the Pacific, open to all lawful traffic of all descriptions, without toll charges and to be of concrete wherever practicable. This highway is to be known, in memory of Abraham Lincoln, as 'the Lincoln Highway.'" The most anticipated announcement was of the route itself, but the "Proclamation Route" was perhaps more a list of cities than an actual route. Those familiar with the first LHA road guide from 1915 may be surprised to see Camden, New Jersey, and Marion, Ohio, listed. Within a few weeks, Marionites found themselves removed from the route. Camden was removed soon after, but while the New Jersey city apparently did not protest, things were quite different in Mar-

ion, which vehemently protested the perceived slighting. Other towns fought to be on the route, and many that weren't claimed to be. In *Fill 'er Up!*, Bellamy Partridge recalled hearing that the town of Linton, Indiana, offered to change its name to Lincoln if the highway would be routed through it.

Business leaders from Washington and Baltimore kept pushing to reroute the highway, and in the spring of 1914, they won President Woodrow Wilson to their side. Wilson had been the first member to join the Lincoln Highway Association, having sent a $5 check to Henry B. Joy dated September 11, 1913. Wilson wrote to Joy in June 1914 asking that the route divert from Philadelphia to Washington, D.C., and then to Gettysburg. Joy replied with a telegram on July 29 that this would add seventeen miles (somehow it seems much longer), and that the communities in Pennsylvania had already put forth a lot of effort and had renamed streets. Most of all, "devious windings . . . would insure its failure as a permanent useful memorial way." But, as researcher Craig Harmon has uncovered, Joy reversed his decision a year later.

Many years ago, Kevin Patrick found an ad for a Lincoln Highway Garage in Chester, Pennsylvania, fifteen miles south of the original route, indicating that at some time the Lincoln Highway was planned for, or actually passed through, the town. Paul Sestak had likewise discovered references to the Lincoln Highway in Delaware, writing to me: "I have several articles that refer to this section of road as the Lincoln Highway including an article on its construction and construction contracts. The words Lincoln Highway also appear on several early subdivision plans."

What Harmon found was hundreds of articles from *The Washington Post* detailing the efforts of businessmen and boosters from Washington and Baltimore to have their cities put on the Lincoln Highway. Ultimately, a feeder route was approved in 1915 from Philadelphia to Chester, Wilmington, Elkton, Havre de Grace, Belair, Baltimore, and Laurel. It entered Washington via Maryland Avenue, went through Potomac Park and around the Lincoln Memorial, then to Massachusetts Avenue and west on Rockville Pike, and continued through Rockville, Gaithersburg, Damascus, Ridgeville, Frederick, Thurmont, and Emmitsburg to Gettysburg. Two huge signs, ten-by-fifty feet each, announced the route, one sign five miles north of Phildelphia, the other at Gettysburg. Despite the intensive campaigning by those along the route, it was still only a feeder road—one article even called it a detour—and therefore was marked with red-white-red signs. There were reportedly hundreds of such official Lincoln Highway feeders across the country to cities that were just off the main route, though the only ones to be noted and called that in LHA guidebooks were a set of three into Chicago.

Researcher Russell Rein says, "Maybe this explains the Lincoln Highway postcard I have of Laurel, Md., and the token I saw for the Lincoln Highway Seafood Co. in Baltimore."

Even more interesting was a heretofore unknown attempt to add Los Angeles to the route. Fred Baker of that city became the Southern California consul in 1919, which the 1935 LHA official history chalked up to a special circumstance. A possible explanation can be found in a *San Francisco Chronicle* article of September 30, 1923, about LHA field secretary Gael Hoag's comments at a conference of San Francisco–area chamber representatives, hotel owners, the state auto association, and state officials. Hoag said he was going to the LHA board immediately to recommend that Los Angeles be named an alternate terminus because of the lack of support from San Francisco. And in a blurb titled "Lincoln Highway Ultimatum" in *Motor West*, Hoag told San Francisco leaders that he would urge the LHA to cease efforts at improving the road from Salt Lake City to San Francisco, and instead work toward Los Angeles, by either the Midland Trail or Arrowhead Trail. This was part of a larger fight that had been brewing for years over the western routing.

In Placerville, a proclamation was rushed by the El Dorado County Chamber of Commerce on October 2, 1923, appealing to "central and northern California and central Nevada to unite" to halt the rerouting of the Lincoln Highway between Salt Lake City and San Francisco. Chambers and newspapers were urged to call on the LHA to keep the original alignment.

A few articles even mentioned Hawaii as being the true western terminus of the Lincoln Highway, specifically Nuuanu Pali, a precipice six miles above Honolulu. The thinking was that many drivers who motored across the country continued on to the islands (which would not be a state for forty-six more years). The 1935 LHA history does say that the state had a consul in the early years as one of the "special circumstances" for "points not on the route."

Most realignments were done to straighten the route, but another leading reason was to eliminate railroad crossings. A day's drive of a couple hundred miles often included dozens. Ten miles east of Salt Lake City, for example, the 1913 *Lincoln Highway Route Road Conditions and Directions* listed ten crossings in less than three miles. Lack of crossing gates, engine noise in the era before mufflers, and window curtains that could be cloudy all made accidents far too common. Worst of all were the steep grades on each side of the tracks. These were hard to run up to and cross, and the tilt could cause carburetors to starve and engines to die right as the vehicles got on the tracks.

The April 1902 *Automobile Magazine* described the railroad crossings in Wilkinsburg, Pennsylvania:

> There are ten tracks to be crossed, almost a continuous passing of trains, some of them express trains going at a very high speed, no gates, and only infrequently a watchman. The track crossings are extremely rough, making it necessary to run slowly over them if one is to avoid chancing a breakdown directly on the railroad. The tracks curve in both directions from the crossing and there are usually several freight cars massed on the unused outer ones, which very thoroughly limit even what small view there is. . . . The road continues to and through Wilkinsburg center over the vilest brick pavement that the automobile mind can conceive.

No wonder the town celebrated the elimination of its rail crossings in 1916 with a huge celebration, capped by the dedication of a Lincoln statue. Even in the late 1920s, Frederic Van de Water wrote in *The Family Flivvers to Frisco* of coming upon a crossing accident at Clarks, Nebraska, that left only a

SPECIAL COLLECTIONS LIBRARY, UNIVERSITY OF MICHIGAN

baby alive from a family of four. "Peril," he wrote, "has not been wiped out entirely from transcontinental pilgrimages."

Rise to Fame

October 31, 1913—Halloween—was pronounced a day of celebration. Ceremonies started just after midnight in Council Bluffs, Iowa, with the sounding of sirens and factory whistles. Across the river in Omaha, the Union Pacific Railroad donated three train car loads of railroad ties and had one of the largest fires in the nation, reportedly attended by ten thousand people. The Union Pacific also lit blazes along three hundred miles of track, from Omaha to Grand Island. Fireworks, cannon fire, and dances marked the event in other towns. In Indiana, farmers put jack-o'-lanterns on their fence posts. In Carroll, Iowa, thousands of cars lined up for a parade. The gov-

Perhaps proof that the LHA was serious about moving the western terminus, a crew from the Automobile Club of Southern California posts signs on the Midland Trail between Fly and Tonapah, Nevada. Duckwater Indian Reservation is about twenty miles north of the road (now U.S. Route 6), and the Hot Creek Mountain Range is about twenty miles west.

ernors of Nebraska, Wyoming, and Nevada proclaimed it Lincoln Highway Day.

By 1914, however, Henry Joy felt that pursuing $10 million in pledges was a wasted effort, and instead proposed "Seedling Miles" of concrete to stimulate interest in areas where the quality of the roads was most poor. The LHA would provide cement for a mile-long, sixteen-foot-wide road if a community would pay for the labor and materials to build the subgrade and drainage and promise maintenance for a reasonable period. The thinking was that once locals experienced the change from quagmire to concrete, they would become Good Roads advocates too. The first Seedling Mile was built west of DeKalb, Illinois, in late 1914. Engineers from around the world lauded the efforts of the LHA.

The first guide to the Lincoln Highway was a little-known folder sponsored by Packard titled *Lincoln Highway Route Road Conditions and Directions*, copyrighted in October 1913.

Cartoonists were quick to grasp the significance of a road connecting the coasts, as they did with the first transcontinental railroad half a century earlier. The *San Francisco Examiner* ran this one on October 31, 1913, the Lincoln Highway's official day of celebration.

Effie Gladding used it as she crossed the country in the summer of 1914. It gave directions such as "turn left across fields," "straight ahead across sage brush mesa," "go through gate and Indian farm," "across creek (no bridge)," and a couple more zingers. About fifteen miles east of Rawlins, it directed, "Pass in front of saloon buildings and turn to left around shearing pens, then to right and westerly over the hill." And between Eureka and Austin, Nevada, "fill each ditch with brush before crossing."

In 1914, the LHA issued *Hints to Transcontinental Tourists*, written by F. H. Trego, the group's chief engineer. It consisted of six pages of suggestions such as things to do (carry yellow goggles), things not to do ("don't carry good clothes–ship them"), and instructions on how to get out of a mud hole and how to sleep on the ground (dig a trench for the hips). It also gave tips on how to estimate costs and time, and listed two pages' worth of needed equipment. The advice was expanded for the first LHA guide, *The Complete Official Road Guide of the Lincoln Highway*, published on March 30, 1915, which was essentially a listing of towns with descriptions, not directions.

Conversely, guides such as the Cheyenne to Reno *Auto Log* gave excruciating detail at a time when a farm lane could look more like a main road than the real main road. Such entries were necessary in a world that lacked directional signs and required drivers to patch together a through route from pieces of local paths. This is from western Wyoming:

78.7–LYMAN. Straight ahead; cross covered ditch.
79.1–Turn R.
79.3–End road; white house on R.; turn L. with poles.

79.9–Four corners; turn R.; still follow phone poles; pass general store on L. (81.9).
82.6–Beyond covered ditch, keep R., crossing several wooden bridges; follow poles to end of road.
84.4–Fort Bridger.
84.7–R.-H. road; turn R., follow ford through fort; jog L. (85.1), then R., entering lane (85.5).

By 1915, a B. F. Goodrich guide from Kearney to Cheyenne noted the places where the highway's colored stripes could be found on poles . . . or trees.

The Lincoln Highway publicity machine also approved a number of products, including Lincoln Highway cigars, a tin service station toy (manufactured by Marx), a board game, gas pumps, and tires. A stage play called "The Lincoln Highwayman" in 1917 became a movie two years later. "The Lincoln Highway March," a song by George B. Lutz, also came on a piano roll played by Osborne and Howe in 1922:

From the land of William Penn on
    a highway firm and true;
Girded by the mountain peaks, lakes
    and plains, and the sky so blue,
As we journey miles and miles thru
    the Lincoln land of smiles . . .

Decades later, C. W. McCall (of "Convoy" fame) penned "Old 30":

It was 3,000 miles of rockin' rollin'
    highway,
a million memories long and two
    lanes wide.
It was known to all the truckers as
    the Mighty Lincoln Highway,
but to me it's still ol' 30 all the way.

There was even a line of automobiles called the Lincoln Highway, made by the Lincoln Motor Car Company in 1914. Most notable was the interior: a folding seat up front and the steering wheel in the rear seat.

The LHA's big year was 1915. Not only would the Panama-Pacific Exposition opening in San Francisco be a draw, but there were numerous other events. One of the most significant and profitable was a motion picture caravan to document the Lincoln Highway, creating seven thousand feet of film. Towns along the route contributed funds to ensure that they would be included in the film, then went out of their way to welcome the crew and spruce up for what they saw as their big chance at fame. East Liverpool, Ohio, went so far as to cover an old glass house kiln with pottery and blow it up. The caravan ended in San Francisco, with a huge celebration of Lincoln Highway Day in front of the Palace of Transportation, home to a 365-foot-long Lincoln Highway map. LHA secretary Arthur Pardington had dreamed up the film, but passed away just as it was nearing completion. At Pardington's death, Henry Joy proclaimed that the Lincoln Highway was "more his work than that of any other man. Thousands have given dollars to the cause. PARDINGTON GAVE HIMSELF."

A photographer accompanied the film caravan, and some of those photos appear in this book courtesy of the National Heritage Museum in Lexington, Massachusetts. A scrapbook of the pictures, along with a commemorative plate made in East Liverpool, Ohio, was donated to the museum by the family of Jacob "Jake" Meinzinger, a racer and carburetor engineer who developed the

"NH" carb used in some Ford Model Ts starting in 1920. Another set was located by former LHA director Leon Schegg.

In late May 1915, Henry Joy drove west to the expo with new LHA secretary Austin Bement and Packard mechanic Ernie Eisenhut in a new Packard 1-35 Twin Six, the first twelve-cylinder production car. His comprehensive photo album, with hundreds of photos from the muddy 2,885-mile journey, can be found at the University of Michigan's Bentley Library. They averaged thirty-five miles per hour, arriving back on June 18. The captions themselves are often entertaining: "Nearing Tama, Iowa, our rear wheels threw gumbo higher than the telephone poles." "The natives took reserved seats to watch us work their roads." "Four hours were needed to dislodge us from the Lincoln Highway east of Marshaltown." "He pulled us out for $3.00 and a drink of whiskey."

In 1919, the army organized its own trip across the Lincoln Highway with almost three hundred men in eighty-one vehicles. It had no formal name that can be discerned and so shall be referred to in this book as the First Transcontinental Army Truck Convoy. (A medal awarded to soldiers upon its completion was worded First Trans-Continental Motor Transport Convoy.) The convoy was sponsored by the War Department to demonstrate the practicality of transcontinental motoring. It started in Washington, D.C., with the unveiling of the Zero Milestone on the ellipse, in back of the White House, from which all U.S. mileages were to be measured. That milestone was temporary; the current one was dedicated on July 4, 1923. The west face of the permanent milestone was inscribed

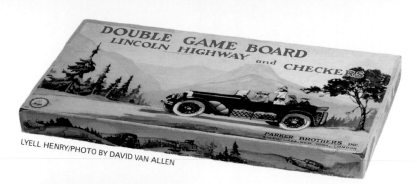

The Lincoln Highway board game actually had players follow numerous named highways across a U.S. map.

Guides like this Auto Log helped drivers in the era before maps by giving directions in tenth-mile increment. This one invokes the Lincoln name and follows the Lincoln Highway as far west as Ogden, but then directed "autoists" north around the Great Salt Lake and along the Humboldt River through Nevada.

Gasoline pumps were another novel method of promoting the highway's identity. This ad appeared in the 1918 LHA road guide.

Filming the Lincoln Highway in 1915.

Henry Joy struggles through Iowa's famed gumbo mud in June 1915. The LHA president had left Detroit on May 27, bound for the Panama-Pacific Exposition in San Francisco, with Austin Bement and Ernie Eisenhut.

Meeting the locals during the Lincoln Highway Association 1915 movie film caravan.

to note the 1919 tour: "Starting Point of First Transcontinental Motor Convoy over the Lincoln Highway, July 7, 1919."

One of the speakers was Charles Lathrop Pack, president of the American Forestry Association, who, like Col. Albert Pope, advocated the planting of memorial trees along the growing network of roads. "Call them Roads of Remembrance," he said. "For no finer memorial can be erected in honor of men who fought for world freedom." One of the best known of these sections was along the Lincoln Highway near York, Pennsylvania.

The caravan, led by LHA field secretary Henry Ostermann in the LHA Packard, covered some thirty-three hundred miles in sixty-two days. Dwight D. Eisenhower's experience in the convoy—he was then a young officer—left indelible impressions: "[U]ntil 1916," Ike said of the Army in *At Ease*, it was "pretty much tied to the mule and horse." But times were changing and the Army was realizing the military advantages of motorized speed and mobility, not to mention the tactical advantages to be gained from trucks and tanks. Still, Ike said the changeover was difficult:

All drivers had claimed lengthy experience in driving trucks; some of them, it turned out, had never handled anything more advanced than a Model T. Most colored the air with expressions in starting and stopping that indicated a longer association with teams of horses than with internal combustion engines.

Ike admitted that the convoy "started me thinking about good, two-lane highways." This coupled with his experiencing Germany's autobahns during World War II led him to campaign for broad superhighways, which became the U.S. interstate system.

The convoy also had more immediate results. LHA directors believed it helped with the passage of the Townsend Federal Highway Act in 1921, which allotted $75 million in matching funds to states. The LHA saw it as vindication of its efforts.

The LHA had long wanted to build a stretch of road incorporating leading innovations, an ultimate seeding mile where the change from rural road to pavement would be most appreciated. After much planning, they built what they called the Ideal Section between Schererville and Dyer, Indiana, near the Illinois border. Completed by 1923, the Ideal Section was actually a mile and a half long. The concrete was forty feet wide and ten inches thick, with steel reinforcing rods, and included one bridge and one culvert. It was also one of the first urban roadways to be lighted, if not *the* first. Motorists were awestruck that they could drive at night without headlights.

The ten millionth Model T rolled off the line on June 4, 1924. It was an amazing feat. The one millionth T was produced in December 1915, and the five millionth T in May 1921. That had taken more than twelve years from the first Model T in 1908, but it took only another three years for that count to double. That ten millionth Model T made a cross-country tour along the Lincoln Highway. It left Times Square on June 16, driven by racecar driver Frank Kulick and sent off by

The October 1, 1919, LHA *Forum* celebrated the army's arrival on the west coast: "The convoy was met at the California State Line on the south shore of beautiful Lake Tahoe by representatives of all the Chambers of Commerce on the Lincoln Highway cities between Nevada and the coast and a barbecue was staged in connection with a rodeo as a welcome to the State of California."

LHA president J. Newton Gunn, arriving in San Francisco on August 1. A film crew went along, and today clips can be found in the National Archives. By 1924, two-thirds of all cars registered in the United States were Fords, all Model Ts.

Many of the Model T drivers became "tin can tourists," eating their food from cans while camping or putting up in tourist camps nightly. Near Clinton, Iowa, Beth O'Shea had to ask the driver of a parked car if a large field along the Mississippi was a tourist camp. "'Sure, it's a tourist camp,' he told us. 'Anythin's a tourist camp what has water and no no-trespass signs. All the towns has got 'em now. They figure they give you a place where you can pitch your tent and you'll buy food and stuff at their stores.'"

Municipal camps also grew because tin can tourists were ravaging farmers' fields and leaving their trash. Even Effie Gladding noticed: "As we drive along, we constantly see the remains of former camps by the roadside. Old tin teakettles, pieces of worn-out campstools, piles of tin cans." Frederic Van de Water wrote that camps in the West charged a fee to keep

With Edsel Ford's help, the Ten-Millionth Model T became a promotional tool for the Lincoln Highway too. Racecar driver Frank Kulick left New York City on June 16, 1924, and took the Lincoln Highway to San Francisco. He carried a letter from Mayor John Hylan to Mayor James Rolph Jr.

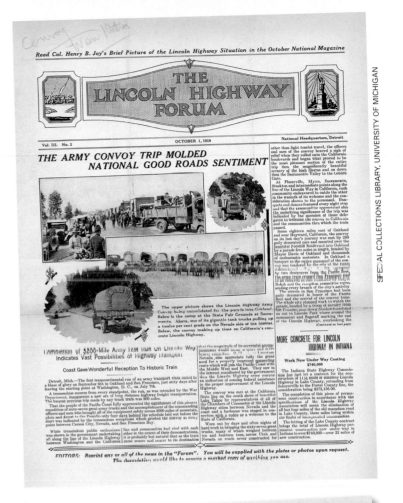

THE FIRST AND TEN-MILLIONTH FORD.

out transients: "West of the Mississippi, roads swarm with auto tramps, folk who have started out motor camping and have not been able to stop. They are a sinister, frowzy, none too honest lot and the half dollar keeps camps free from these undesirables." He and his wife learned to choose privately operated camps, which were better run. "Local patriotism may be a powerful force but hope of personal profit is stronger."

Perhaps the most memorable part of staying at a tourist camp was the nightly gathering of "road liars," whose egos inflated their drives into wild adventures. Van de Water described them: "Thus, every road he has traveled becomes, in retrospect, an ordeal through which he brought his car safely only by the possession and exercise of abilities such as few men own. . . . And the more he talks, the worse they become." It took him a while to realize that veteran campers paid little heed, discounting their statements by "at least 75 per cent." He disdained those who went motor camping and then wrote about it "as though it were an art that only a chosen few can command. The secret it this: Any one can do it. It's a cinch."

Proprietors began to build cabins for those who didn't carry tents and to lure those who

CRAIG HARMON

An early-1920s annual report of the Koehring Company, makers of concrete mixers, promoted the road-building material as "the magic medium of modern empire builders."

did. The trend was booming in 1927, when Van de Water wrote, "Cabins are a godsend to automobile parties that come rolling in late, with the complicated process of camp making still before them." Appearing in all shapes, sizes, and motifs, but often just as a plain cottage, cabins were the first step toward motels.

A Fading, Fraying Line

In 1924, the fifth edition of the LHA guidebook was published. Filled with ads and extra information, it would be the last. The next year, the Association of American Highway Officials proposed a numbering system for interstate roads. The flowering of highway boosters and associations led to a confusing mix of named roads with their colored bands on phone poles. In addition to the previously mentioned Yellowstone and National Old Trails highways, other transcontinental routes included Bankhead Highway (Washington, D.C., to San Diego), Old Spanish Trail (St. Augustine to San Diego), and the Theodore Roosevelt International Highway (Portland, Maine, to Portland, Oregon). Like the Lincoln, the Victory Highway (via St. Louis and Denver) and the Pikes Peak Ocean to Ocean Highway (via Indianapolis and Colorado Springs) both connected New York to San Francisco.

The named highways were intentionally not marked as one continuous federal route, but were split among many different numbered routes. In general, the Lincoln Highway was made part of U.S. Route 1 from New York City to Philadelphia; U.S. Route 30 to Granger, Wyoming; U.S Route 40 in Utah; and U.S. Route 50 in Nevada and California.

Meanwhile, the Lincoln's route continued to be improved and shortened. The biggest

obstacles to road betterment came in the West, particularly Utah and Nevada, with the sparsest populations on the corridor. These states found it hard to justify spending large amounts of money on roads that outsiders could use simply to speed across. Locals were quite content with the condition of their roads. The Utah dispute became especially caustic. The LHA finally relented to state pressure in 1927, forsaking its Goodyear Cutoff and instead adopting the route of the Victory Highway to Wendover. Even as late as 1935, when the LHA published its history, the front and back maps were not of the road they'd worked so hard to build, but of the disputed routes west of Salt Lake City.

The LHA was relentless in trimming miles from the route. Here are the figures from the Packard and LHA guides:

1913	3,388.6*
1915	3,384.0
1916	3,331.0
1918	3,323.5
1921	3,305.0
1924	3,142.6**

* Includes Camden, NJ, and Marion, OH, but not Ogden.
** 14 miles longer if via Donner Pass, which had become less preferred than the Pioneer Branch.

At the end of 1927, the LHA ceased active operations, but it was agreed to mark the route a final time. On September 1, 1928, Boy Scouts across the country planted concrete posts along the highway. Their locations had been plotted months before by LHA secretary Gael Hoag, who produced a typewritten log, noting the type and orientation of each post. Although about four thousand pole-mounted signs were placed on city streets, it's the concrete posts that are remembered, sought out, and occasionally stolen. The seven-foot poles, half of which went underground, were cast concrete with steel reinforcement rods. Researcher Russell Rein has transcribed Hoag's log, counting 2,437 markers between Elizabeth, New Jersey, and Lincoln Park, San Francisco. The markers, however, add another layer to the Lincoln Highway routing confusion, for the route they mark differs from the final LHA guide in 1924. Changes came later, too; for example, when U.S. Route 30 bypassed Omaha, Nebraska, the markers were moved to follow the new road from Missouri Valley, Iowa, to Blair, Nebraska, though the LHA had disbanded years before.

In advance of the marking, four Boy Scouts traveled for a month along the Lincoln Highway from New York to San Francisco. The National Safety Council cosponsored a Highway Safety Program, which included first-aid and American Red Cross lifesaving demonstrations. The Boy Scouts of America had just been established in 1920, so the trip was also intended to help increase membership and start new troops. Scout leaders hoped the programs would introduce camping and hiking as alternatives to more dangerous play in the streets. But promoting the marking of the Lincoln Highway was of at least equal importance.

The scouts rode in the back of a Reo Speed Wagon, a truck body specially fitted for this trip with a top resembling a Conestoga wagon. In the back also were duffel bags, blankets, and cooking utensils. Bernard Queneau especially remembered the harsh seats: "They were just benches. We didn't have any

soft cushions." Flaps in the sides of the canvas let the scouts see out, but with only a small opening at the front of the canvas, they couldn't see the road ahead very well. Queneau and the other three scouts making the trip were fifteen years old, but in an interesting twist, each one was in a different school grade. Queneau, who had already graduated from high school, recorded his adventures in a little journal, writing about a page a day, noting stops they made and people they saw. His observations were succinct. From western Ohio he wrote: "We again ate fine in Lima, the hotel being great for such a town. Ohio is full of pigs, cattle, bad roads, and rain."

John T. Faris must qualify as the pioneer in a long line of "blue highway" writers. In his 1931 *Roaming American Highways*, he looked back on nine of the named, long-distance highways. He marveled at the changes since they had been established two decades previously. In the sixty-one-page chapter on the Lincoln Highway, he noted that this road, which had carried perhaps 150 cross-country drivers the year of its founding, now saw hundreds of thousands of motorists.

A 1933 fourth grade geography book, *Our Neighbors Near and Far*, followed the Lincoln Highway for twenty-eight pages. In 1935, the LHA published its own history, *The Lincoln Highway: The Story of a Crusade That Made Transportation History*, a detailed but incomplete account. The author remained a mystery until Craig Harmon found this inscription on the copy at the Oakland Public Library: "Ten months, plus 55 cases of letters and documents, plus much sweat went into this book. Text is mine; biographical sketches by Gael Hoag. D. R. Lane." David Lane was a reporter

Numbered highways replaced names in the 1920s. Scotchlite produced this card that showed off its reflective U.S. Route 30 billboards.

and writer. Harmon followed up with Lane's daughter, who had two of her dad's notebooks and the correspondence.

A six-mile stretch just west of Buffalo Bill Cody's Scout's Rest Ranch in North Platte—dedicated on November 5, 1935—was said to be the last portion to be hard-surfaced. But that doesn't count the segments that had been bypassed. And a congratulatory telegram from President Roosevelt called it the last paved link in U.S. Route 30, which is not at all the Lincoln.

In July 1938, the Lincoln Highway Association celebrated the twenty-fifth anniversary of its founding by holding a ceremony in conjunction with those honoring the seventy-fifth anniversary of the Battle of Gettysburg. The events included the lighting of the eternal flame by President Franklin Roosevelt. As few veterans of the war remained, so too were the ranks of LHA founders thinning. Henry Joy had passed away in 1936. Fisher would die in 1939, but his highway continued to garner attention.

The finale of *Babes in Arms*, a 1939 Busby Berkeley film starring Mickey Rooney and Judy Garland, featured the gang singing "God's Country":

Hi there, neighbor, Goin' my way
East or West on the Lincoln Highway?
Hi there, Yankee, Give out with a great
    big thank-ee,
You're in God's Country

Also that year, world's fairs were held in both New York and San Francisco. The latter's Golden Gate International Exposition designated July 1 as Lincoln Highway Day. A program on Treasure Island honored LHA officers and regional leaders. A period article said, "Ceremonies will be brief and a major part of the day will be devoted to reunions among pioneer members of the Association." Texaco joined in by producing ads, maps, and little strip-map booklets of the road. One map was produced specifically for the fair. LHA vice president Austin Bement drove a new Hupp Skylark across the country, taking a letter from New York's mayor to San Francisco's mayor. He was said to be "making an official inspection tour of the Lincoln Highway, the 3000-mile connecting link between 1939's two world fairs."

On July 2, 1939, three years after his death, a monument was dedicated to Henry B. Joy in Wyoming. He had camped near the site in 1915, on the Continental Divide, under what he thought was the most beautiful sunset ever, and had asked to be buried there. He was buried elsewhere, but a stone tablet and eight concrete LHA posts were set here. Western historian Randy Wagner found that the ceremony was at 5:00 P.M., when Joy would have made camp for the evening.

The next year, the Lincoln Highway radio show debuted on NBC. Sponsored by Shinola Shoe Polish, the melodramas lasted through 1942. That year, Keystone View Company—the world's leading manufacturer of stereoview cards—published two sets of Lincoln Highway images, twenty-five in each, split at the Mississippi River. The images were available as either stereo cards or lantern slides. "From Omaha East on the Lincoln Highway" was Geography Series Unit #17, numbered 401 to 425 west from New York City. "From Omaha West on the Lincoln Highway" was Geography Series Unit #18, numbered 601 to 625 west from Omaha. Not every image was of the Lincoln Highway, or even of a town on the route, such as one of Lincoln, Nebraska.

In *The Steel Mirror*, a 1948 novel by Donald Hamilton, a young doctor is traveling the Lincoln Highway in Illinois when his car breaks down and he hooks up with a woman who's being followed. The Lincoln highway is not the focus, but it was nonetheless referenced, despite being overshadowed by numbered highways two decades earlier.

The next year, the highway's identity was still strong enough that *Collier's* sent a writer in search of stories from the route, much as it had done with Emily Post in 1915. John Kord Lagemann's two-part "The Glory Road" is breezy but insightful. The author realistically recalls the hazards of early motoring, describes the advances (or not—"most of the hotels and tourist courts exclude Negroes"), and marvels at, while bemoaning, the coming superhighways ("completely detaches you from the countryside").

In 1951, when NBC presented a special episode on its Sunday afternoon program,

"The Eternal Light Radio Show," called "The Lincoln Highway." The February 12, 1951, installment was part of the national observance of Lincoln's Birthday. The program used the geography of the Lincoln to tie together fourteen poems by Carl Sandburg about American people and places. The highway was mentioned early in the show: "Lincoln's memory is kept on a living arterial highway moving across state lines from coast to coast, to the murmur, 'be good to each other sisters,' 'don't fight brothers.'"

The Federal Highway Act of 1956, which established limited-access interstate highways, made even the thirty-year-old federal routes seem obsolete. The old named trails were forgotten in the era of tailfins and cloverleafs, but even as they faded, interest in roadside

Dr. Alan Hathaway prepares to head west from Pittsburgh in 1996 in what he believes is the famed Ten-Millionth Model T.

culture and highway history was growing. John Baeder's *Diners* (1978) and *Gas, Food, and Lodging* (1982) inspired readers to search out old roadside haunts. Drake Hokanson's 1988 book sparked renewed interest in the Lincoln Highway, and in March 1991, Iowa State University organized an exhibit of his photos and a symposium exploring the design and conservation of the road. I was just one of many attending who spoke of a day when a national group might help preserve and document the Lincoln Highway. Little did we know that in the audience were a couple who would turn our words into action.

Bob and Joyce Ausberger were concerned about a proposed widening of the Lincoln near their Iowa farm, especially as U.S. 30 is a modern roadway just a mile away. They hooked up with overland trails historian Gregory Franzwa, and by the following October, the new LHA was founded. Driving tours, publications, and state and local chapters have helped the organization grow to twelve hundred members and ignited countless preservation and documentation projects. In the past decade, two state heritage corridors have been formed, decaying landmarks have been restored, and new songs and books celebrating every aspect of the road have appeared.

In 2000, Congress even directed the National Park Service to evaluate the significance of the Lincoln Highway, resulting in comprehensive maps, a catalog of sites, and a summary report. Though the study found the road to be historically important, its conclusion that the entire corridor does not retain a high degree of integrity has inspired further debate about how to preserve and protect the highway.

The most prolific painter of Lincoln Highway scenes is Kevin Kutz. In the fifty-by-seventy-inch folding *Fanfare for Common Man*, Dunklo's Gulf in Bedford, Pennsylvania, anchors various on-the-road attractions.

Indeed, so much of early motoring is romanticized that we often forget that real people faced unimaginable obstacles in those days. The idea of locating a bypassed piece of original concrete roadway can be exciting, but the *cla-clunk* rhythm that driving on it produced could be pretty tiresome after a thousand miles in a period car. Clinton Twiss noted it in his 1951 book, *The Long, Long Trailer*: "From Indiana to Wyoming the roadbed is concrete, with expansion joints that met only occasionally. Just often enough to create a sickening, rocking motion that could be overcome only by slowing down to twenty-five miles per hour." That's why, as members attend LHA conferences or chapter meetings today, a fair share drive the interstates (or fly) to get there. As John B. Rae wrote in *The Road and the Car in American Life*:

The flaws in the Interstates are minor when they are set against the advantages. The motorist . . . who crosses Wyoming on I-80 and has had experience of doing the same thing on two-lane stretches of Route 30, with unending lines of heavy trucks in each direction, will unhesitatingly agree that the change has definitely been for the better.

So enjoy the armchair trip, and if you have a chance, seek out some of the old Lincoln Highway. There are lots of places to explore. Many bypassed sections of the Lincoln Highway are now on private land, however, and some may not be posted. Ask if you're not sure.

By telling people you're following the Lincoln Highway, you'll be surprised at the new information and adventures that will follow. As Emily Post wrote in her 1916 book, *By Motor to the Golden Gate*, "It is your troubles on the road, your bad meals in queer places, your unexpected stops at people's houses; in short, your misadventures that afterwards become your most treasured memories."

Greetings from
New York

The Lincoln Highway needed to start somewhere, and where better than the symbolic center of New York City, the "Crossroads of the World," Times Square. Not really square, the term encompasses the lively area around the convergence of Broadway, 42nd Street, and Seventh Avenue. Though the Lincoln Highway had a western end too, Times Square was and is thought of as the beginning point; a Lincoln Highway trip was looked upon as a journey into western America.

The Lincoln Highway had little impact in cities, where the streets were already paved

	NEW YORK	U.S.
Population in 1910	9,113,614	92,228,496
Population in 2000	18,976,457	281,421,906
Persons per square mile in 2000	401.9	79.6
New York County in 1910	2,762,522	
New York County in 2000	1,537,195	
Approximate miles of Lincoln Highway	1	3,389

and marked and used daily by thousands of locals. The 1913 Packard guide to the route, which gave directions by the tenth of the mile out west, relegated directions here to "we ferry over to Jersey City," then the next two towns listed are Newark and Trenton, sixty-seven miles away.

When San Francisco considered having a statue of an Indian on a horse, called *The End of the Trail*, placed at its end, New York discussed placing something similar here. Nothing came of it, and the eastern terminus remains unmarked nearly a century later. But if the new transcontinental highway meant little to New Yorkers, it did mean something to the rest of the country. Persons heading west who lived at all nearby made Times Square the ceremonial beginning of their journey. Lots of drivers would also dip their wheels in the Atlantic Ocean, hoping to do so again at the Pacific.

The Lincoln Highway perhaps was less celebrated here because it was less meaningful than the region's other transportation enhancements. Easy access to water via its harbor, the Hudson River, and later the Erie Canal led to Manhattan's early dominance as a manufacturing center. When railroads arrived in the nineteenth century, most ended on the New Jersey side of the Hudson, luring industries to relocate there, where they also had room for spread-out, more efficient plants. The rise of motor transport somewhat equalized the field, but the lack of bridges across the Hudson was still an impediment. Much of the freight handling moved over to the Hackensack Meadows, convenient to the growing network of roads in New Jersey. New York City retained a lot of small manufacturing, served by the flow of immigrants arriving at Ellis Island, but the city grew mostly as a financial center, broadening its international connections. Arriving in this milieu, the Lincoln Highway was simply another name for a street that already had one.

Places to See for the History-Minded

When Henry Hudson came ashore in 1609, the Lenni-Lenape already had organized villages. The Indian name for the big island was Man-a-hat-ta, meaning "heavenly land." When the

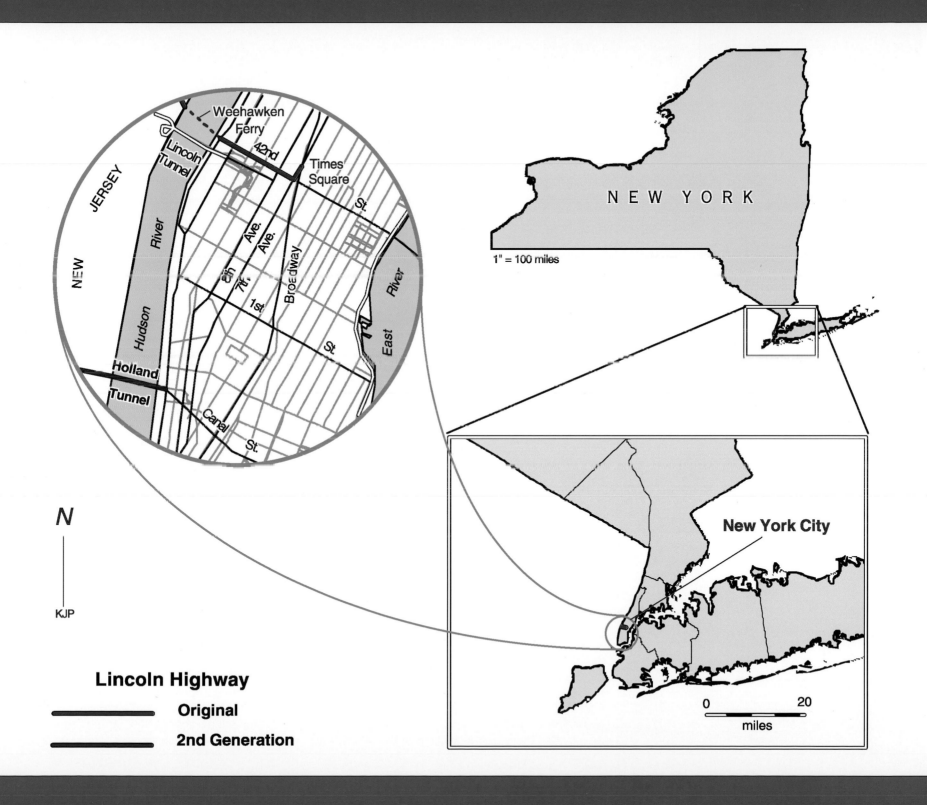

N

KJP

Lincoln Highway

———————— Original

———————— 2nd Generation

Weehawken
Ferry

Lincoln
Tunnel

42nd

Times
Square

St.

NEW JERSEY

Hudson River

8th Ave.

7th Ave.

Broadway

1st

St.

East River

Holland

Tunnel

Canal

St.

NEW YORK

1" = 100 miles

New York City

0   20

miles

Shirley Woolfitt revels in the excitement of Times Square. She and her husband, Bob, are about to depart in their 1934 Packard sedan on the 2003 Lincoln Highway Anniversary Cross Country Tour.

New York–Paris Auto Race. Times Square. New York.

Thomas (American Car), waiting for signal February 12, 1908.

natives made the infamous trade in 1826 of Manhattan for $24 worth of trinkets, the crime was not the price, but that they thought they were turning over only the right to use the land, not its ownership. It was also an indication that the Dutch were interested in more than just trading furs.

At the southern end of Manhattan, a log wall was built in 1653 by slaves of the Dutch to protect from attack by the former inhabitants. It lasted only a few decades, but its legacy survives as Wall Street.

The British wanted the island too, finally taking control in 1664 and renaming the colony for their duke of York. Manhattan became the name of one of New York City's five boroughs; the others are Bronx, Queens, Brooklyn (formally the rarely heard Kings), and Staten Island (formally Richmond).

Across from the southern tip of Manhattan, two smaller islands are home to the Statue of Liberty and the Ellis Island Immigration Museum. Farther south, overlooking the Atlantic Ocean from Brooklyn, sit Brighton Beach and Coney Island, which retains a number of old rides, such as the 1920 Wonder Wheel, the 1927 Cyclone coaster, and a 1932 carousel (spelled Caroussell here), where you can reach out as in decades past and try to grab a metal ring.

Back in Manhattan, at 233 Broadway (just east of the World Trade Center site), you'll find a building completed about the time the Lincoln Highway was set here: the 792-foot Woolworth Building, opened in 1913. It was the world's tallest until the Chrysler Building topped it in 1930. Across from it is City Hall Park, home to the 1812 City Hall and the 1872 Old New York County Courthouse.

Just north of that, a colonial-era cemetery was unearthed in 1991 during construction of the federal building at 290 Broadway. Span-

Times Square was the launching point for car races as well as the symbolic start of the Lincoln Highway. Here, George Schuster and Monty Roberts, the American team, await the start of the 1908 New York–to–Paris race on Lincoln's Birthday. Schuster, who took over as driver at Cheyenne, won 169 days later.

ning about five blocks, it held an estimated twenty thousand graves.

Several parks strung along the Hudson River waterfront offer an amazing variety, including the New York branch of the Smithsonian's National Museum of the American Indian in the 1907 Beaux Arts Customs House building and the Museum of Jewish Heritage. Near North Cove Yacht Harbor (and just west of the World Trade Center site), a metal railing has two quotes inscribed. One is a poem by Walt Whitman; the other, by Frank O'Hara, nicely sums up how different New York is from the Lincoln Highway you'll experience farther west: "One need never leave the confines of New York to get all the greenery one wishes—I can't even enjoy a blade of grass unless I know there's a subway handy, or a record store or some other sign that people do not totally regret life."

North from there, Hudson River Park has gardens, cafés, and other entertainments all the way to 59th Street. At Piers 25 and 40, you can fish or rent outdoor games. Pier 25 also has a miniature golf course, and Pier 26 has a boathouse offering free kayaking. Nearby are Chinatown, Little Italy, and Greenwich Village. There are a surprising number of old buildings, even a few taverns dating to the eighteenth and nineteenth centuries.

Some blocks east of Times Square on Howard Street are a couple longtime businesses: E. Vogel is in its fourth generation making footware, and a few doors down, Putnam Rolling Ladder Company is in its third generation producing the sliding library ladder. On 38th Street just past 6th Avenue, Tinsel Trading, selling ribbons and garment trims since the 1930s, is run by the founder's granddaughter. East of Times Square, right on 42nd Street, is the New York Public Library. Stretching north from East 42nd at Park Avenue is Grand Central Terminal, opened in 1913.

North of Times Square on 46th Street, "Restaurant Row" offers every kind of food imaginable. On 52nd, the Museum of Television and Radio holds more than fifty thousand items, and on 53rd is MoMA, the Museum of Modern Art.

Stretching from 59th Street to 110th Street is Central Park. Overlooking the greenery at 72nd is the Dakota Apartments, built in 1884, just eight years after the park. Along with its infamy as the site of John Lennon's assassination and the filming of *Rosemary's Baby*, it played a prominent role in the history-drenched time-travel novel by Jack Finney, *Time and Again*.

Times Square and West on 42nd Street

The ceremonial eastern terminus at Broadway, 42nd Street, and 7th Avenue was originally called Longacre Square; it was renamed in 1904 when the *New York Times* moved its offices here. That's also when the annual New Year's Eve celebrations began. The twenty-five-story, triangular building cost sixty-eight times its estimate. Today it is mainly valued as a billboard, but at the time it was north of the city's commercial district. The arrival of the *Times* and a subway station attracted businesses and cultural attractions, especially theaters. The 5-cent subway delivered people around the clock, bringing vice to the area too. Author James Traub wrote in *The Devil's Playground* that "Times Square was already the sex capital of New York by the early years of

the twentieth century," and the trend only accelerated: "The Times Square of 1915 would have been practically unrecognizable to the denizen of 1905. The rules of self-restraint and delayed gratification—that is to say, the Protestant ethic—that had been drilled into generations of Americans had been lifted, if not quite obliterated." The change in the area can be perhaps attributed to the rise of cabarets, which encouraged drinking and dancing.

Broadway was already known as the Great White Way for the glare of its electric signage, and the triangle of Times Square was well suited for "spectaculars," or giant signs. International corporations now spar to have the largest, liveliest signs imaginable, such as the NBC-Panasonic Astrovision TV, which measures twenty-six by thirty-four and a half feet. A scale model of a Concorde looms above the Times Square Brewery. The Times Square Visitors Center, in the restored Embassy Theatre on Broadway between 46th and 47th Streets, is open daily.

The change from trashy to trendy has not been without turmoil. In *Down 42nd Street*, Marc Eliot wrote, "By 1980, the city's fabled Manhattan crossroads had become ground zero for the manufacture, exhibition, and distribution of pornography, drug dealing, pedophilia, prostitution, and violent street crime." James Traub reported that in 1993, "Times Square alone had forty-seven 'adult' stores, even though many of those on 42nd Street had been closed down by the process of condemnation." By then, politicians and developers were struggling to revamp the entire area. Today, the barrage of signs and lights draws camera-toting tourists during the day and crowds to theaters and restaurants at

BERNIE HEISEY

night, though some New Yorkers find the new corporate-dominated entertainment zone as disconcerting as the old.

Vintage roadside relics are few, but the Howard Johnson's at Broadway and West 46th is a throwback to the years when the chain dominated America's highways and toll roads such as the Pennsylvania Turnpike. The 1959

Times Square about 1930; by then, few cross-country motorists would have bothered to start here

Looking east on 42nd Street to the Times Square Brewery.

31

A Lincoln Highway sign marked the route on 42nd Street. Note the Times building at left.

eatery retains its original decor while serving cocktails. Reports that it's about to close come about once a year, but it hangs on. In *The Devil's Playground*, Traub explains that the land is worth far more than the restaurant, but the "footprint" of the space may be too shallow to find a ready buyer. Until that time comes, Traub calls HoJo's an "outpost not so much of nostalgia as of pathos."

Heading west from Times Square, West 42nd Street also has been redeveloped in the past decade. This was once and is again "theater row" and is now home to nine venues, including the New Victory, the Times Square, and Loew's. Most notable is the New Amsterdam Theater, built in 1903 for $1.5 million and host to famed performers of the era, such as Will Rogers and W. C. Fields. It was converted to cinema in 1937, but the area was changing, and by World War II, the street had become home to risqué theaters showing such fare as *Sins of Youth* and *Wayward Girls*. The Amsterdam closed in 1982, but Disney

The Lincoln Highway film crew at New York City's 42nd Street ferry terminal, 1915.

restored it for $34 million and reopened it in 1997 (rechristening it "New") as the home to *The Lion King* and other live musicals.

A block north of the route, at 11th Avenue and 43rd Street, is the Market Diner, a 1962 DeRaffele-brand diner. It was nearly destroyed recently when the rent was hiked, but a last-minute change of heart by the landowner kept this fututistic-looking diner humming around the clock. A less happy fate awaited the River Diner, a 1930s Kullman at 11th and 37th, remodeled in 2004 into a rental store.

Within a half dozen blocks, the Lincoln Highway meets the Hudson River. For the earliest drivers, the only choice was a ferry; in the decades following 1913, motorists had a variety of options in crossing to New Jersey.

Ferries and Bridges

The Hudson River has long been an impediment to travel from the island settlement to the interior lands. A tunnel was first suggested in 1806 by Col. John Stevens, a Hoboken inventor and engineer who planned to lay a wooden tube along the riverbed; he never found backers. Robert Fulton's steamboat ferry, begun in 1812, finally connected New

York City and Jersey City. A century later, Lincoln Highway travelers likewise crossed by ferry.

The principal ferry in 1913 departed 42nd Street and crossed the river diagonally to a slip at Weehawken. In his 1925 book *Boulevards All the Way—Maybe*, James Montgomery Flagg wrote: "One misses the old time hollow reverberations of the horses' hoofs on the shredded floors of the ferries. The stench of burnt gas has taken its place, but the poignant smell of the wharf water is still there."

A 1920s AAA tour book listed it running around the clock—every ten minutes overnight, every seven minutes during regular hours, and every five minutes during rush hours. According to John T. Cunningham in *New Jersey: America's Main Road*, as late as 1926, 13.7 million vehicles were crossing the Hudson annually, each one by ferry. By 1932, that had dropped to 11.6 million ferry rides; the rest were taking the Holland Tunnel (11.4 million) or the George Washington Bridge (5.5 million). Still, the Weehawken Ferry lasted into the 1950s.

The spiritual replacement of the 42nd Street Ferry, begun in the 1980s, departs from

LHA field secretary Gael Hoag with the organization's Packard at the 42nd Street ferry, 1924.

Midtown Station at 38th Street and docks at Port Imperial in Weehawken, New Jersey. A one-way trip is $5, with boats running at least every fifteen minutes from 6 A.M. until midnight. Many tourists opt to take the ferry and tour New York City on foot; with almost a million vehicles trying to enter the city each day, drivers have little patience for sightseers on the road.

When the Lincoln Highway was marked for the last time in 1928, a sign was posted at the western exit of the Holland Tunnel, putting it on the transcontinental route. No markings were recorded in New York City, if indeed the LHA would have even bothered.

Bored beneath the Hudson River at a cost topping $48 million, the Holland Tunnel became the first underwater vehicular tunnel in the United States when it opened on November 13, 1927. The first year, 8.7 million vehicles used the tunnel at 50¢ a trip. Connecting Manhattan with Jersey City, it was soon joined with the Pulaski Skyway to give drivers a speedy route into central New Jersey.

The Lincoln Tunnel, opened in 1937, more closely approximates the original route of the Lincoln Highway, and its name leads one to consider it a replacement, but it was never part of the Lincoln Highway. Still, you can take it today by driving west on 39th Street toward the tunnel and I-495; then upon exiting, take Boulevard East north to the top of hill. There, Pershing Road is the Lincoln Highway; to the right, it descends back to the Weehawken Ferry, and to the left is Jersey City.

After 1931, another option from New York City to New Jersey was the George Washington Bridge, but its location 136 blocks north of Times Square would have lured few drivers following the Lincoln Highway.

Looking east to the New York City skyline from the Weehawken Ferry, which again transports cars and people across the Hudson River.

In his 1916 book *A Hoosier Holiday*, Theodore Dreiser described the departure for his trip westward:

> Finally we were off—up Eighth Avenue and across Fortysecond Street to the West Fortysecond Street Ferry, while we talked of non-skid chains and Silvertown tires and the durability of the machines in general—this one in particular. It proved to be a handsome sixty-horsepower Pathfinder, only recently purchased, very presentable and shiny.
>
> As we crossed the West Fortysecond Street Ferry I stood out on the front deck till we landed, looking at the refreshing scene the river presented. The day was fine, nearly mid-August, with a sky as blue as weak indigo. Flocks of gulls that frequent the North River were dipping and wheeling.

Beatrice Massey had similar sentiments as her party departed by ferry in 1919: "With a last look at the wonderful sky-line of the city, and the hum and whirl of the great throbbing metropolis, lessening in the swirl of the Hudson River, we were really started; with our faces turned to the setting sun, and the vast, wonderful West before us."

Once the Holland Tunnel was open, drivers quickly took to it, and the LHA eventually sanctioned this route.

Greetings from New Jersey

The Lincoln Highway angles across central New Jersey in a southwesterly direction. This road through Newark and Trenton was perhaps the country's busiest corridor when the Lincoln Highway adopted it, but traffic volume was not the only factor in determining the route.

Motorists leaving New York City had three choices to reach Ohio: a series of toll-charging turnpikes and radiator-boiling hills across southern Pennsylvania; a hilly, zigzag course of unimproved roads across central Pennsylvania; or the fairly level Hudson and Mohawk valleys across New York State. Most drivers took the New York route to avoid the mountains, reassured that there were fine

hotels in cities like Buffalo and Cleveland; it's the route taken by Bellamy Partridge in 1912 and Emily Post in 1915. When Lincoln Highway planners faced the same question, the choice would likewise seem obvious, but the founders of the Lincoln wanted the straightest route possible. The most direct, most improved way west—until I-80 was built a half century later—was via southern Pennsylvania. New Jersey's course was thus set.

Many of New Jersey's roads, including much of the Lincoln Highway, follow paths carved by the Dutch in the 1600s. The Lenni-Lenape Indians were already there, and a few of their village names survive; some along the Lincoln Highway include Hackensack, Metuchen, Passaic, Rahway, and Raritan. When Peter Stuyvesant arrived in 1647 to oversee the Dutch settlement of New Amsterdam, he directed the scattered settlers to band together and was responsible for founding the first village—Bergen, now Jersey City—in 1660. A ferry was started the next year to connect nearby Communipaw with Manhattan. But the English also laid claim to these lands, and in 1664, when their ships arrived at New

Amsterdam, Stuyvesant surrendered peacefully. After the fleet commander changed the colony's name to honor the duke of York, the duke granted the land to two men; one of them, Sir George Carteret, had previously defended the Isle of Jersey for the royal family, inspiring the duke to name this portion New Jersey as a nod to him.

Though the Lincoln stretches only sixty-some miles across the state, the northern and southern ends of the route are vastly different, reflecting the colonial Dutch heritage of New York City and the Quaker roots of the Philadelphia region. The path between the two cities became a major trade route, and the arrival of the auto only intensified the traffic. Neither of these major cities is actually in New Jersey, which is why it is known as the "corridor state."

Just as William Penn is said to have considered the east bank of the Delaware before placing Philadelphia on the west, so did Lincoln Highway planners first stick to the New Jersey side in that region. Camden was included in the LHA's Proclamation Route, the September 1913 listing of towns along the highway.

	NEW JERSEY	U.S.
Population in 1910	2,537,167	92,228,496
Population in 2000	8,414,350	281,421,906
Persons per square mile in 2000	1,134.4	79.6
Approximate miles of Lincoln Highway	64	3,389

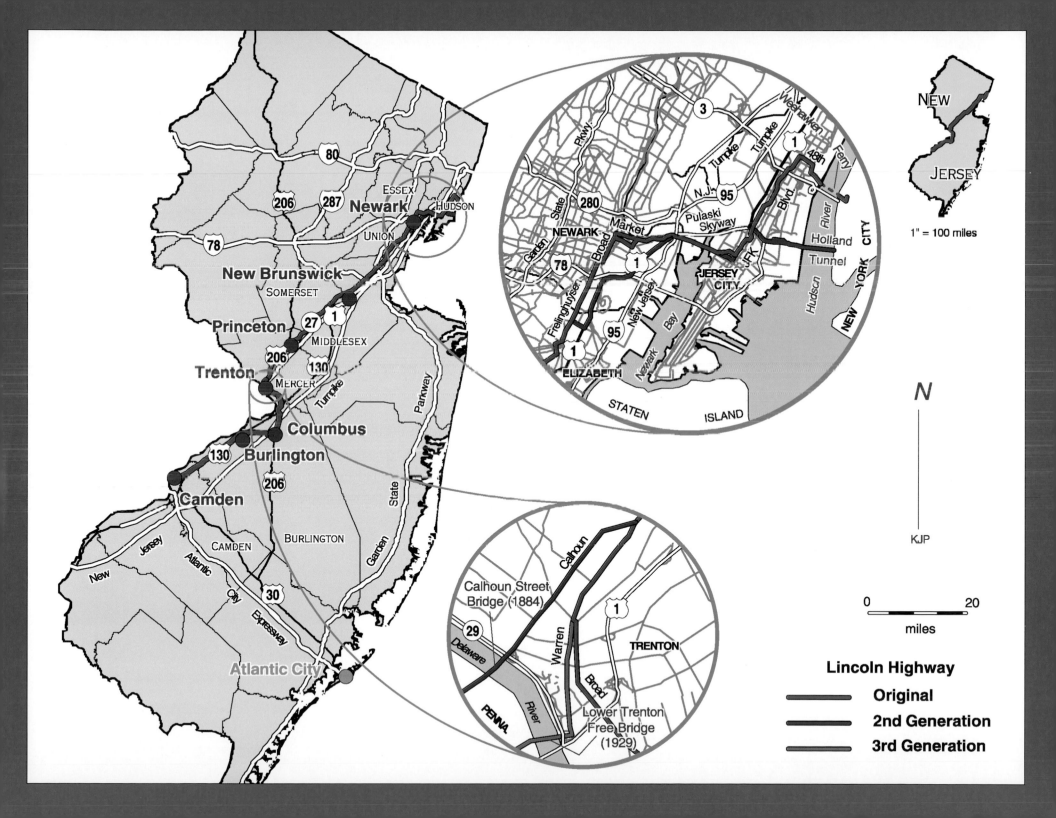

N

KJP

1" = 100 miles

0   20

miles

Lincoln Highway

Original

2nd Generation

3rd Generation

Breathtaking views of the Hudson River and New York City await at the top of Pershing Road and along John F. Kennedy Boulevard East.

Before autos and the Lincoln Highway, trolleys and pedestrians were the main users of Hillside Road (now Pershing Road).

Hillside Road from 42nd St. Ferry, Weehawken, N. J.

BERNIE HEISEY

The city is also listed in the 1913 *Lincoln Highway Route Road Conditions and Directions*, but period maps and newspapers of Camden and Trenton do not mention this routing or its having been eliminated. The Camden route is mapped here along a logical course via Burlington (though a 1915 National Highway Association map instead placed Mount Holly on the Camden route). As in New York City, the Lincoln Highway meant much less in congested urban areas, and chances are that Camden's commercial and passenger traffic was less desirable than Philadelphia's suburbs. This book will not try to retrace this undetermined part of the route in the text.

New Jersey is said to be the most densely populated state, and much of the northern part of the route is intensely urban. In the late 1920s, while western states had only dirt trails for the Lincoln Highway, New Jersey was already replacing it with the construction of U.S. Route 1. With even more drivers on the road today, tensions run high and horns blow constantly.

West from Weehawken

Upon crossing the Hudson River by ferry from New York, motorists disembarked at **Weehawken**. With thirty-three hundred miles ahead of them, cross-country travelers first had to climb the Palisades on Pershing Road. Until about 2000, the cobblestones leading to Pershing could be seen in the ferry parking lot.

Theodore Dreiser noted his party's disembarking from the ferry in *A Hoosier Holiday*: "We were off again, Speed obviously holding in the machine out of respect for officers who appeared at intervals, even in Weehawken, to wave us on or back. I could not help feeling

KYLE WEAVER

Note the "coast to coast" claim at Chicken Galore, 606 Kennedy Boulevard, Union City.

as I looked at them how rapidly the passion for regulating street traffic had grown in the last few years." And that was in 1915.

Like so much of the route in urban areas, the town at the top of the hill has changed a lot. Called West Hoboken at the time of the Lincoln Highway, it's now a separate town called **Union City**. It is home to many of the immigrants who arrive in the United States through New York City. The population is more than three-fourths Hispanic, making it home to the second-largest Cuban population (after Miami) outside of the island nation. Businesses and homes are densely packed; it is said to be the state's most urbanized area.

The road overlooking the Hudson River and New York City was East Boulevard; it's now John F. Kennedy Boulevard East. A nearby monument honors founding father Alexander Hamilton, killed by U.S. vice president Aaron Burr in an 1804 duel at the bottom of the hill near today's small Weehawken Park. Descendants reenacted the duel on its bicentennial in 2004, the first time in forty years.

After arriving at the top of Pershing Road, our route crosses JFK East and jogs over to 48th (originally 5th) Street. After about a half dozen blocks, it turns left (south) on JFK West/NJ Route 501. To Lincoln Highway drivers, this was Hudson Boulevard, laid out in the 1890s as a City Beautiful parkway in contrast to parallel but congested city streets. It has become just as urban, and U.S. Route 1 now runs parallel a few blocks to the west. Follow JFK West heading south toward Jersey City, the state's second-largest city.

At 30th Street, JFK passes under I-495. About a dozen blocks past 1st Street is Leonard J. Gordon Park, named for the creator of Jersey City's free public library system. Established in 1912 and running to the corner of Manhattan Avenue, it has statues of a buffalo, lion, bear, and soldier. A couple blocks right on Manhattan, at the corner of Tonnelle Avenue/U.S. Route 1, is the round-front White Mana, a late-1930s Paramount-brand diner, opened here in 1946. The circular counter is designed so that the cook never has to take more than three steps to make food, get drinks, and serve customers. It has an ongoing rivalry with the White Manna in Hackensack over which really came from the 1939 World's Fair in Queens. Current owner Mario Costa sold the diner and lot to Dunkin' Donuts in 1996, but repurchased them when he learned the diner would be remodeled.

Back on JFK/NJ Route 501, a few blocks south, the Lincoln passes under the connector of the Holland Tunnel to the Pulaski Skyway. (A few blocks west, on Business U.S. Route 1, a Muffler Man turned rug-holding guy stands in the shadow of the Skyway at Wilson's Carpet, 220 Broadway.)

The Pulaski Skyway, though never marked as the Lincoln Highway, was meant to bypass it. The cantilever and truss structure, completed in 1932, was dedicated to Casimir Pulaski, a Polish-born hero of the American Revolution. Just 3.5 miles long, it cost $20 million.

Bellamy Partridge wrote in *Fill 'er Up!* that he was able to cross the country in the 1940s "without breakdown, mechanical adjustment or tire trouble . . . the only place where we went

This converted "Muffler Man" looms over Wilson's Carpet, located beneath the Pulaski Skyway.

The Pulaski Skyway, connecting Jersey City and Newark, also made it easy for eastbound drivers to access the Holland Tunnel to New York City. It now serves sixty thousand vehicles per day.

astray was on the Pulaski Skyway in New Jersey, in plain sight of the Empire State Building."

In his 1951 book, *The Long, Long Trailer*, Clinton Twiss and his wife, Merle, approached New York City from New Jersey. His main concern was not ending up in a tunnel where the trailer would get stuck. Approaching the Skyway, they weren't sure they had to follow the truck route, so they instead chose the ramp for passenger cars.

> I was positive of two things: We had to get *on* the Pulaski Skyway, and we had to make a *left turn* to get off it and onto Tonnelle Avenue. . . .
>
> A sign, "No Left Turn," stunned me.
>
> I had scarcely recovered from this shock when another sign appeared, "No Right Turn." This was followed almost immediately by "No U Turn." There was no *anything*. I was becoming panicked. . . .
>
> Another sign appeared. Merle read it. "Holland Tunnel—Straight Ahead." . . .

Directional signs in Jersey City, 1918, erected by the Auto Club of Hudson County.

Just then Merle gave me the clutching hand and said, "I thought you didn't want to go through the Holland Tunnel."

I gritted my teeth. "*I don't!*" I shouted.

"Then why–?"

"I don't *know* why!! I'm *lost!*"

I had shouted so loud I attracted the attention of the occupants of the car alongside us. They gave me a sickly smile. "The rats," I thought. "Building a trap like this for a trailer."

Approaching the tollgates, Twiss screeched to a halt and leaped out. A police officer, "shaking and mopping his brow," listened as Twiss held him by the arm to plead his story. Turning away, the officer muttered, "Another gawddamn trailer," then the officer stopped traffic, had Twiss circle around, and pointed him to the correct turn.

The Lincoln Highway continues on JFK into **Jersey City** and Journal Square. The 1918

The Stanley Theater, 2932 John F. Kennedy Boulevard, on the eastbound lanes of Journal Square, Jersey City.

LHA guide listed the control point here as the Lincoln Way Garage, 3422–24 Hudson Boulevard. Like Times Square, its New York City counterpart, Journal Square became the transportation crossroads and cultural hub of Jersey City, but not until the 1920s. The Pulaski Skyway was built partly to bypass this congested area. After decades of typical urban decline, the area is rebounding, and $7 million recently was spent to landscape the area. The Jersey Loew's Theater, built by MGM in 1929 as its three thousand-seat flagship in northern New Jersey, showed movies and held live shows featuring the big names of the day–Duke Ellington, Bing Crosby, Jean Harlow, George Burns and Gracie Allen, Bill Robinson, Jack Benny, Bob Hope, Cab Calloway–but malls and multiplexes lured away customers. Loew's closed in 1986 and was set to be demolished, but locals rallied for it, and in 1993, the the-

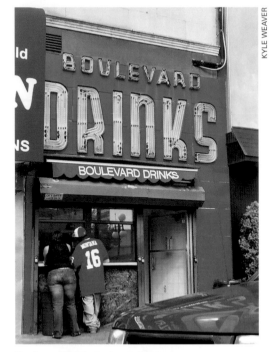

Boulevard Drinks in Journal Square.

January 1914. It has been renamed again to Communipaw Avenue and also serves as the truck route for U.S. Routes 1 and 9.

Back on JFK, a few blocks past Fraser's Lincoln statue, the road intersects Communipaw. The Lincoln Highway turns right at a Walgreen's. The road has to cross the Passaic and Hackensack Rivers, both waterways branching north from Newark Bay. The surrounding marshland from Perth Amboy to Hackensack has become well-known as the Jersey Meadows, or the Meadowlands. It was long a dumping ground for garbage, but the name is familiar to outsiders for its sports stadiums (north of our route) or its reputation as a final resting place for enemies of the mob. More recently, it's become a transfer point for shipping containers from freighters to trucks. At the Port of New York

This monument to Lincoln, in front of the courthouse in Newark, was sculpted by Gutzon Borglum, creator of Mount Rushmore.

ater was purchased by Jersey City. With continued help from the Friends of the Loew's, the theater again hosts films and live acts. Not only does it have state-of-the-art equipment, but it also retains a circa 1929 sound-on-disk Vitaphone projector and a restored 1954 Perspecta Stereo sound integrator.

Across the street, the Stanley Theater serves as a Jehovah's Witness assembly hall. Also in the square is a statue of Jackie Robinson commemorating his first professional baseball game, which took place in 1946 at nearby (but now demolished) Roosevelt Stadium.

An interesting Lincoln Highway connection is that Jersey City was briefly the center of America's ceramics industry, until two of its workers moved to East Liverpool, Ohio. The potteries they established there began the shift of the industry from Jersey City to the

area around East Liverpool and across the Ohio River in Chester, West Virginia, both on the Lincoln Highway.

JFK Boulevard makes an S-curve out of Journal Square and continues south. Coming down Bergen Hill, on the right at Belmont Avenue is Lincoln Park. Sitting just inside is a 1929 statue of President Lincoln designed by James Earl Fraser, a sculptor, designer of monuments, and perhaps best known for designing the Indian head–buffalo nickel. The Lincoln Highway originally entered here; the 1923 *Automobile Green Book* directed drivers to turn right (on today's Belmont) into West Side Park (the original name), past a fountain, a circle, and a concrete barn, then turn south to the Lincoln Highway/Plank Road. That road was named Essex-Hudson Lincoln Highway when it was upgraded and reopened in

The Winfield Scott Hotel was a landmark along the Lincoln Highway (North Broad Street) in Elizabeth.

HOTEL WINFIELD SCOTT, ON LINCOLN HIGHWAY,

NORTH BROAD STREET, ELIZABETH, N. J.

BERNIE HEISEY

tury, Market was called the busiest roadway in America. Today, Market is one-way eastbound, and merges into Ferry Street. At the cloverleaf, follow signs to the left for Newark; the road forks, but as Ferry Street is also one-way eastbound, take Raymond Boulevard (old Passaic Avenue) westbound, which eventually bumps into Market, and cut over.

Brewing was a major industry here by 1850, Germans coming into the area fueling the demand. This coincidentally made the state one of the leading glass producers.

Just before Penn Station, you'll jog left (follow signs for the station and Market Street). On East Market, you'll dip under the train station and railroad tracks, then pass the Paramount Theater. The Lincoln turned left (south) at Broad Street, but a block ahead, in front of the Essex County Courthouse, is a

The White Diamond Diner, 510 East Saint Georges Avenue, Linden, is small but keeps busy with breakfast customers plus take-out orders during the day.

statue of a seated, hatless Abraham Lincoln, which was always mentioned in LHA guidebooks. It was created in 1911 by Gutzon Borglum, best known as the sculptor of Mount Rushmore. The statue is commonly called the "Children's Lincoln," because its inviting style attracts so many young ones to climb on it. Borglum was a lifelong admirer of the

and New Jersey, about four thousand containers arrive daily.

To cross the rivers, drivers must contend with a pair of drawbridges. Local traffic and trucks (banned from the Pulaski Skyway since the 1950s) cause congestion. The Pulaski Skyway can be seen to the north, 135 feet in the air. Once you cross the first bridge into South Kearny (also Hudson City), just to the right on Hackensack Avenue is the Truck Stop Diner, a circa 1946 Kullman-brand diner. At the end of the second bridge is a cloverleaf with the New Jersey Turnpike.

The Lincoln took Ferry Street to Fleming Avenue to Market Street into **Newark**, the state's largest city. Early in the twentieth cen-

sixteenth president and read all he could about him. He even named his son Lincoln, who also became a sculptor and oversaw the day-to-day work on Mount Rushmore. The elder Borglum also carved a marble bust of Lincoln for the rotunda of the nation's capitol, but the seated statue was his favorite. A reproduction of the seated Lincoln is on display at the Borglum Historical Center near Mount Rushmore.

The "four corners" intersection at Broad and Market was said to be the country's third busiest, and by 1924, the Lincoln Highway was rerouted to avoid it via Jackson and Lafayette Streets. Claims such as "most urban area" and "busiest intersection" are questionable, but they do indicate that this has long been a congested region. In fact, the 1928 log of Lincoln Highway markers said that the road followed the U.S. Route 1 bypass around Newark to North Avenue in Elizabeth, which went back west to the original route.

One of the noted Lincoln Highway–era hotels was the Robert Treat, opened in May 1916. The hotel was named for Newark's founder on the city's 250th anniversary and featured 300 rooms and 275 baths starting at $1.50.

The Skyway ended in Newark and connected to U.S. Route 1, which replaced the Lincoln Highway. U.S. Route 1 was made for quick travel and is not considered part of the Lincoln; in fact, the country's first cloverleaf interchange was built on this highway near Woodbridge in 1928. The 1941 guidebook *America's Fascinating Highways*, described U.S. 1 south from here as an "express highway."

In the early eighteenth century, the stagecoach trip from Newark to Philadelphia took a

week. By the 1770s, road improvements and competition cut the time to thirty-six hours. The road was lined by inns, though few remain. From New Brunswick, two roads headed south. The "lower road" became George's Road. The "upper road" became the King's Highway and later the Lincoln Highway.

Although the Lincoln turned left at Broad, turns here are no longer allowed, so continue straight on Market, then take a left on Halsey Street, another left on Branford Place, and a right on Broad. A mile and a half later, Broad ends at a ramp to join NJ Route 21; turn right on Poinier Street, then left on Frelinghuysen Avenue/NJ Route 27. A decaying 1920s gas station with pyramidal roof sits on Frelinghuysen at Meeker Avenue.

Two miles later, at **Elizabeth**, the road becomes Newark Avenue. Elizabeth was the state's first English settlement, purchased from Indians by settlers from Long Island in 1664. It was named for the wife of Sir George Carteret, one of the state's founders. The Lincoln Highway follows NJ Route 27 through town, which puts you on Rahway Avenue. Then, entering **Roselle**, the road becomes East St. Georges Avenue.

At 510 East St. Georges Avenue, on the southeast corner with Roselle Street in **Linden**, is the White Diamond Diner. This tiny Mountain View–brand eatery serves up good meals; locals use it for take-out. Other than a wall at front and center that blocks the grill, the diner retains its classic style.

Enter **Rahway**, a Lenni-Lenape Indian name that has been changed in other places to Rockaway. The 1924 LHA guide reported that in 1919, the road from Rahway south to Menlo Park had been completely relocated to

Newly poured concrete near Metuchen, 1921.

Linwood Grove offered camping, a cider mill, swings, dancing, and other diversions.

Edison Tower marks the location of the inventor's famed Menlo Park laboratory, moved long ago to Henry Ford's Greenfield Village. The 129-foot tower is topped by a bulb almost fifteen-feet tall itself.

Looking southwest from Highland Park to New Brunswick as the Raritan River Bridge between them was being widened in 1924. Sharing the span are cars, trucks, trolleys, and horse-drawn vehicles.

Looking west on the Lincoln Highway's new forty-foot-wide concrete, one and a half miles west of Highland Park, 1927.

the west side of the Pennsylvania Railroad main line, eliminating fourteen sharp curves, a four-track crossing at Iselin, and a dangerous underpass at Menlo Park. Workers from the state reform school and state prison rebuilt this and much of the road to Trenton.

Metuchen is another Lenni-Lenape name. The Metuchen Inn has served travelers for more than two centuries. The 1918 LHA guide carried an ad for the Hotel Pines east of town, a dining place specializing in "French Fresh Mushroom or Shore Dinner."

The Lincoln Highway becomes Middlesex Avenue, but the route is now blocked by I-287, so turn left on Lake Avenue; it curves around and becomes Lincoln Highway, passing beneath the interstate.

The road name remains Lincoln Highway through **Colonia** and **Iselin**, one of the state's

The Mack Diner sits abandoned in New Brunswick.

oldest municipalities, formed in 1669. Iselin is a Swiss name, one of many variations that also produced the surname Isaly, the family branch that opened Isaly's dairy stores and invented the Klondike ice cream bar.

Raritan Township was renamed **Edison Township** in 1954 to honor its famous former resident Thomas Edison. **Menlo Park**

Just down the block in New Brunswick, at French Street and Jersey Avenue, is this stunning Art Deco clock.

was home to the laboratory where Edison invented the incandescent light bulb and phonograph. It was essentially the world's first industrial research center. The site is marked by a tall cut-stone tower just off the highway; turn right on Christie Street, and it's two blocks to the tiny Edison State Park.

Edison moved here from Newark in 1876; he wanted a secluded spot where he could get back to the "invention business." He got it on this pasture overlooking the rail line and hoped his lab would produce "a minor invention every ten days and a big thing every six months or so." The veil of mystery, as well as the curious lights and sounds emanating from the place, led to his nickname the Wizard of Menlo Park. With his wife's death in 1884, and having outgrown the lab, Edison moved to West Orange, where he built a facility ten times larger. The Menlo Park lab was condemned but saved by being moved to Greenfield Village in Michigan. The 131-foot-

tall Edison Memorial Tower was built in 1936. It's topped by the world's largest lightbulb, formed from 153 pieces of two-inch-thick Pyrex glass. An adjacent museum has a kinetoscope, phonographs, and memorabilia.

A side note to automotive history: Thomas Edison Jr. was one of the first in the state to buy an automobile, a steamer, in 1899. At the time of his purchase, New Jersey required steam car drivers to have a man walk one hundred yards ahead of the car waving a flag.

NJ Route 27 becomes Raritan Avenue, passes through **Highland Park**, and crosses the Raritan River, a water connection to New York City and Philadelphia, on the multiple-span, masonry-arch Albany Street Bridge. On the far side, it enters **New Brunswick**, named for King George I, duke of Brunswick. Raritan changes to Albany Street and climbs through the town and past the campus of Rutgers University, chartered by King George III in 1766. The route then becomes French Street. At the top of a hill, the neighborhood is predominantly hispanic. The Mack Diner, a 1941 Fodero at 150 French Street, recently was home to the All Ears Records shop but has been shuttered for some time. Just ahead, an Art Deco clock uses the letters of New Brunswick in place of numerals.

As it enters **Franklin Park**, the route is again posted as Lincoln Highway. Coming downhill in **Kingston**, the original route branches to the left into the Delaware and

A monument in Princeton commemorating George Washington's efforts during the Revolutionary War.

The original Lincoln Highway branches off from NJ Route 27, over the stone-arch Kingston Bridge to an old mill, and dead-ends, all part of the Delaware and Raritan Canal State Park. Nearby is lock number 8, the locktender's house and station, and access to two miles of towpath along Carnegie Lake.

Interurban tracks paralleled the Lincoln Highway in Mercer County. Note the LHA emblem on the sign on the tree: "New York is 60½ miles ahead; San Francisco is 3,329 miles behind you."

SPECIAL COLLECTIONS LIBRARY, UNIVERSITY OF MICHIGAN

As in many towns, Trenton leaders eagerly embraced the Lincoln Highway idea.

CRAIG HARMON

for the lake is the state's last surviving 1928 concrete marker. As of 2004, it had been temporarily removed during road construction.

Driving under a canopy of high trees, you enter Princeton's ritzy business district. **Princeton**, or Prince's Town, because of its proximity to what was once Kings Town, served as the U.S. capital in 1783, but is best known for Princeton University, founded in 1746. The first intercollegiate football game was played here in 1869, against Rutgers. In the middle of the campus, where NJ Route 27 and U.S. Route 206 meet, is the fifty-foot-tall limestone Princeton Battle Monument, showing George Washington leading the troops in his 1777 victory over the British.

Washington performed one of his epic feats at this junction. As his troops headed north toward Morristown along what is now U.S. Route 206, he had soldiers on horseback drag branches along the current Lincoln Highway toward New Brunswick, tricking the British into thinking that was the way his troops were escaping.

Bear left at the monument onto U.S. Route 206/Stockton Street. Two historic bridges are on the Lincoln Highway here: the 1790 masonry-arch Stony Brook Bridge and the wooden-deck Shipetaukin Creek Pony Truss Bridge, which has been bypassed and closed to traffic. U.S. Route 206 continues to **Lawrenceville**. About ten miles past Princeton, as you approach **Trenton**, turn right onto Princeton Avenue/County Road 583. This is the northern limit for sailing vessels coming from Philadelphia because of a series of rapids on the river called the "falls" of the Delaware, making it an important transfer point.

Raritan Canal State Park. This segment, bypassed in 1969, crosses two small timber bridges (rebuilt in the 1990s) and the 1798 masonry-arch Millstone River Bridge. The canal was opened in 1834; surviving is a canal lock, the lock tender's house, and the Kingston Mill. At the end of the stone bridge, the road would have met the current road, now above on an embankment.

The body of water seen from both the stone and modern bridges is Lake Carnegie (or Carnegie Lake), the world's largest artificial lake when built. It's accessible by a small park up ahead. NJ Route 27 has become Princeton Pike. Across from the parking lot

On Christmas night 1776, Washington's troops crossed the Delaware River about seven miles north of here and surprised the Hessian mercenaries, who were sleeping off their holiday cheer. Much of the battle took place on today's Warren and Broad Streets, later to be included as part of the Lincoln Highway. The Trenton Battle Monument was dedicated at the corner in 1893. The city also served as the U.S. capital in 1784.

A mile farther, turn right onto Calhoun Street/County Road 653. At NJ Route 29, stay left to take the Calhoun Street Bridge across the Delaware River. The route originally entered Pennsylvania across this 1884

Fritz's Diner, Trenton.

bridge. Its predecessor had been destroyed by fire that year. The current iron bridge opened that October 20 atop the old stone masonry piers and abutments; the first day's count was sixteen two-horse vehicles, seven one-horse vehicles, and 175 pedestrians. It was listed on the National Register of Historic Places in 1975 and still carries traffic, but its metal-grate surface compels a speed limit of fifteen miles per hour.

In 1924, the Lincoln Highway was rerouted to Warren Street and over the Lower Trenton "Free" Bridge to avoid tolls. That bridge was replaced in 1928 by the current span, called the "Trenton Makes" Bridge for the sign on its side. Both bridges were placed on stone masonry piers and abutments first built there for a river crossing in 1874.

"Trenton Makes, the World Takes" was once very true of this and other northern industrial cities that really did supply the world with steel, glass, rubber, wire rope, pottery, rubbery, tools, watches, clothing, and hundreds of other products. In 1910, the Trenton chamber of commerce held a contest for a phrase that would capture the city's manufacturing vitality. S. Roy Heath's winning phrase was actually "The World Takes, Trenton Makes"—that's what radio station WTTM is named for. By 1911, a wooden version hung on the bridge connecting Trenton to Morrisville. In 1917, it was upgraded using twenty-four hundred light bulbs, ten-foot-tall letters, and a blinking American flag. The sign migrated when the current five-arch span replaced the bridge in 1928, and 1935 saw a new neon sign longer than a football field. New letters were installed in 1980, but because of troubles with neon combined with the bridge's restoration, plans as of spring 2004 included replacing the lights with LEDs.

The Delaware River Joint Toll Bridge Commission operates both of the current bridges and charges tolls. In all, it oversees twenty bridges; the seven that charge tolls pay for the entire system. Both bridges into Morrisville are considered part of the Lincoln Highway.

The "Trenton Makes" bridge, connecting Trenton, New Jersey, on the right with Morrisville, Pennsylvania, on the left.

Greetings from
Pennsylvania

Once the Lincoln Highway was set to cross Pennylvania, the logical course was to follow long-established roads along the southern tier. A string of turnpikes between Philadelphia and Pittsburgh called the Pennsylvania Road passed through Lancaster, Harrisburg, Chambersburg, Bedford, and Greensburg. The Lincoln Highway followed most of this route but went through York and Gettysburg instead of Harrisburg. Not only was this path more direct, with an easier connection to Washington, D.C., but it was unthinkable to not include Gettysburg, a shrine to Abraham Lincoln.

In the east, these turnpikes were relatively flat and straight, but halfway across the state, drivers encountered the Allegheny Mountains, the first major ridges since leaving the coast. West of Gettysburg, South Mountain was barely felt, but after Fort Loudon, Tuscarora Mountain suddenly loomed. From there, drivers crossed a series of ridges and valleys: down into McConnellsburg, then over Scrub Ridge; through Harrisonville, then over Sideling Hill to Breezewood; through gaps in Tussey Mountain and Evitts Mountain to Bedford; over Bald Knob Summit, through Stoystown, and over Laurel Hill; through Ligonier and a gap in Chestnut Ridge. Travelers would not see such climbs again until the other end of the country.

In *The Family Flivvers to Frisco*, Frederic Van de Water wrote that figuring out how far they could drive in a day had been easy until they reached central Pennsylvania: "In our calculations we overlooked the considerable matter of the Alleghenies. All day long we boiled and wheezed up them and scorched our brake bands sliding down their further slopes, ascending and descending with the regularity of an office building elevator."

It was the Alleghenies that inspired the building of the Pennsylvania Turnpike in the late 1930s. Its route from Carlisle (west of Harrisburg) to Irwin (east of Pittsburgh) followed much of the cleared, but never used, bed of the South Penn Railroad. Such a long-distance, limited-access roadway was a gamble, but drivers, particularly truckers, took to it immediately when it opened in 1940. It was said to save nine thousand feet of vertical climb compared to the Lincoln Highway. Citing a Brookings Institute study, John B. Rae's *The Road and the Car in American Life* said that a truck taking the turnpike used only half the fuel that it would on the adjacent Lincoln Highway, and made the trip in less than half the time.

West of Pittsburgh, the Lincoln Highway was aiming for Chicago, and a number of roads across central Ohio could be joined to accomplish this. But how to reach it? The Steubenville Pike went too far south, and the road to Cleveland strayed too far north. The solution was to take the road to Cleveland down the Ohio River to Beaver, then turn west toward that central Ohio corridor. Two

	PENNSYLVANIA	U.S.
Population in 1910	7,665,111	92,228,496
Population in 2000	12,281,054	281,421,906
Persons per square mile in 2000	274.0	79.6
Approximate miles of Lincoln Highway	350	3,389

roads went west from Beaver; one was bad and the other worse. The Lincoln Highway followed the longer, but better, of the two roads.

Across the Delaware River

Just as early drivers did, today's Lincoln Highway tourists can cross the Delaware River to enter Pennsylvania via the multiple-span Calhoun Street Bridge. Overlooking the Pennsylvania end is an iron marker denoting the state border and the ends of the Lincoln Highway. These were produced in 1917 by the Lebanon Machine Company for each Lincoln Highway state border; this is the last one in place. The best place to park is to the left along the levee, but no left turns are allowed, so if you want to stop, you must proceed straight and double back.

The Calhoun Street Bridge drops travelers onto Trenton Avenue in **Morrisville**. This makes a fairly straight shot through the north edge of town. The 1920s reroute via the Lower Trenton "Free" Bridge (later replaced by the "Trenton Makes" bridge) went through downtown Morrisville on Bridge Street. The Transit Diner, a 1946 Silk City diner, has been converted to a fishing bait store. The two generations of roads meet at **Lincoln Point** and pass beneath the Pennsylvania Railroad tracks into **Fallsington**. A nearby overpass takes traffic across the railroad close to the spot where the original route crossed at grade.

West of the underpass, the route turns right on Business U.S. Route 1/Lincoln Highway. On the left is the Lincoln Garage, with a profile of President Lincoln and the slogan "Don't Cuss, Call Us." Ahead, across from a stone house, is the former entrance to the U.S. 1 North Drive-In Theater. Farther ahead is

Sesame Place, a Sesame Street–themed amusement and water park operated by Anheuser Busch. This area is known as **Oxford Valley**.

Continuing straight, the Lincoln enters **Langhorne Gardens**. The road divides, and two generations of Lincoln Highway head toward Philadelphia: the original route through Langhorne and a later one through Penndel.

The original route takes PA Route 213 south. The road becomes Maple Avenue in **Langhorne**. The 1915 LHA guide listed here what is perhaps the lowest automobile speed limit ever—four miles per hour. At Bellevue Avenue is the circa 1704 Langhorne Hotel, Tavern, and Restaurant. The route then bears left onto Old Lincoln Highway; after a few miles, it goes downhill past some homes and dead-ends. At one time, the road went straight, but by the Lincoln Highway era, it turned left and crossed the railroad tracks at **Janney Station**; stone bridge abutments remain where it crossed. An adjacent four-lane U.S. Route 1 bridge now dominates the view. To continue

The Interstate Glass House Restaurant, Morrisville, Pa.

The Glass House on U.S. Route 1 was operated by the Interstate Company of Chicago as part of an early attempt at standardized road food.

on this alignment, you can backtrack a couple blocks, get on U.S. Route 1, and then quickly exit at **Neshaminy**. There it is joined by the later route that went through Penndel.

The Lincoln Highway switched to that later route in 1923. Today, back at Langhorne Gardens, you can follow it by taking Business

The U.S. 1 North Drive-In Theater lay in ruins by the time this photo was snapped in the winter of 1991.

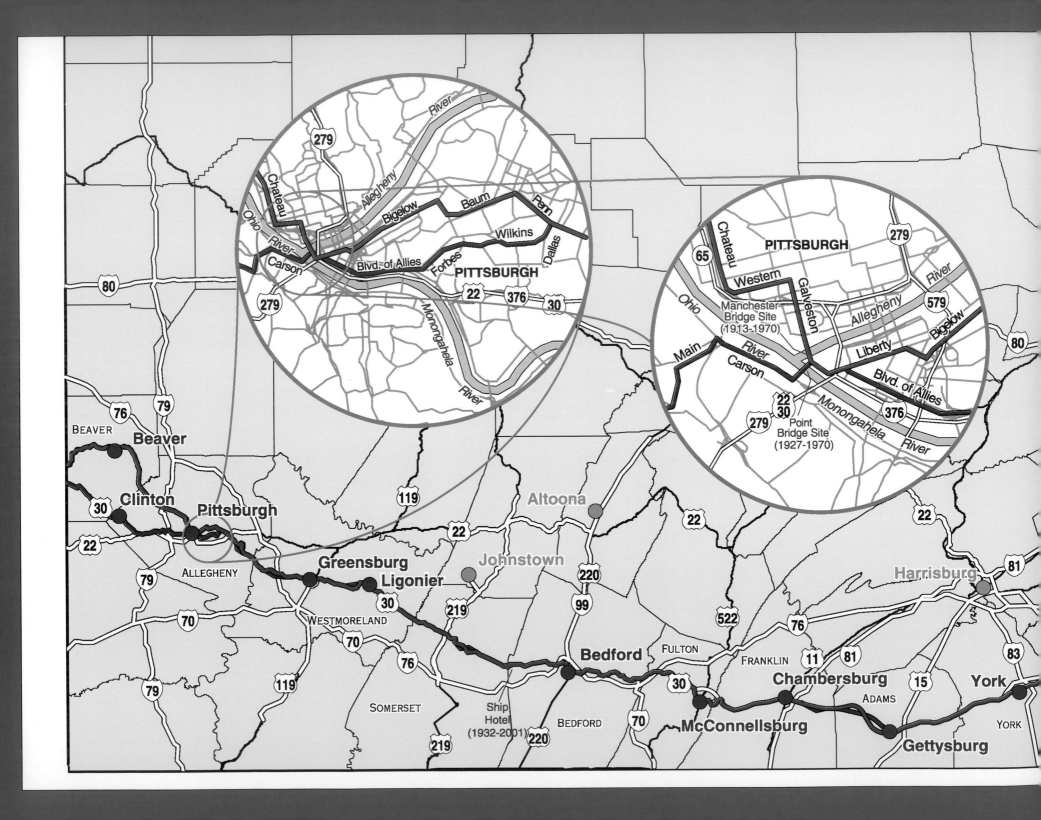

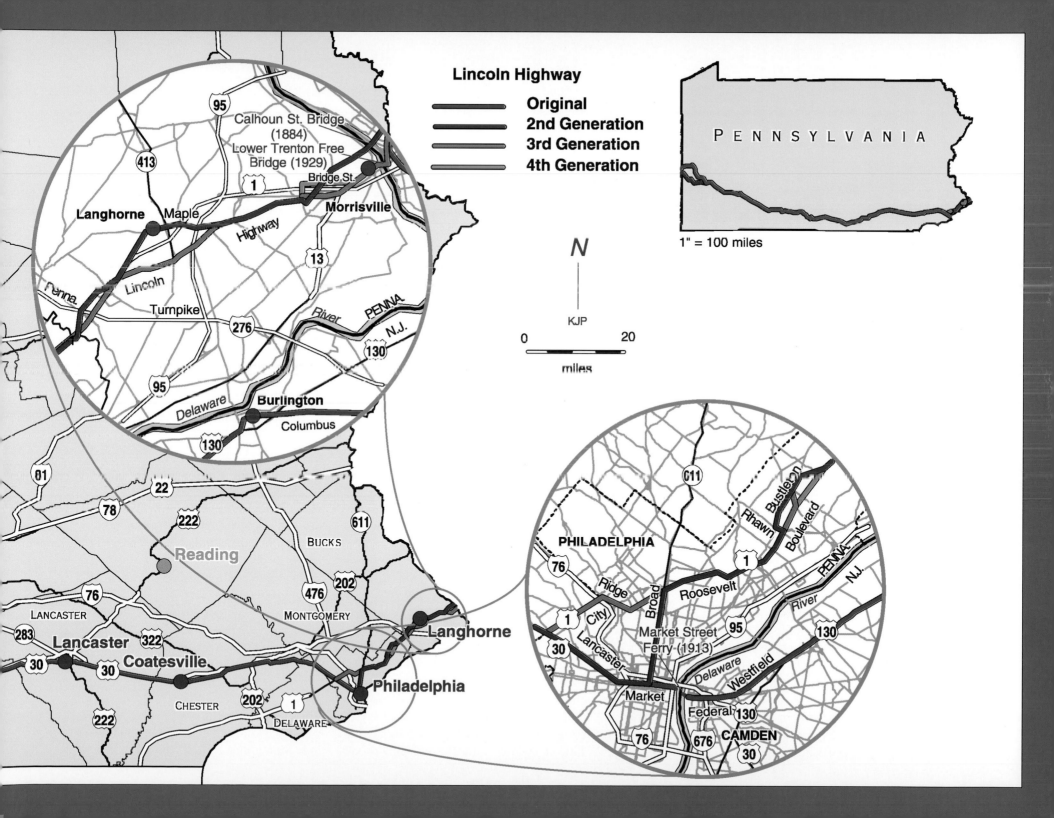

Lincoln Highway

Original
2nd Generation
3rd Generation
4th Generation

PENNSYLVANIA

1" = 100 miles

N

KJP

0   20

miles

Calhoun St. Bridge
(1884)
Lower Trenton Free
Bridge (1929)

Bridge St.

95

413

1

Langhorne   Maple

Highway

Morrisville

13

Lincoln

Penna.

Turnpike

276

River

PENNA.

N.J.

130

95

Delaware

Burlington

130

Columbus

81

22

78

222

611

Reading

BUCKS

202

476

202

MONTGOMERY

76

LANCASTER

283

Lancaster   322

Coatesville

30   30

CHESTER

202

1

222

DELAWARE

Langhorne

Philadelphia

611

PHILADELPHIA

76

Rhawn

Bustleton

Boulevard

1

Ridge

Broad

Roosevelt

1

95

River

PENNA.

N.J.

130

City

Market Street
Ferry (1913)

30

Lancaster

Delaware

Westfield

Market

Federal   130

76   676

CAMDEN

30

This stunning Atlantic service station graced the major intersection of Broad Street and Hunting Park Avenue just south of Roosevelt Boulevard. *National Petroleum News* reported in 1918 that "fifteen attendants are on duty here till 11 p.m."

Route 1. Much of this stretch is lined with sprawl, though a small office at a used-car lot on the right looks to be the old Poplar's Inn store and restaurant pictured in many circa 1920 postcards. Past it on the right is Reedman Car Truck World Center, at 150 acres perhaps the world's largest car dealership. Across from it, a shopping plaza has taken the place of Langhorne Speedway, fondly remembered for the many local and national heroes that raced there. (Local race fans also had the Trenton Speedway at the New Jersey State Fairgrounds.)

At **Penndel**, you'll see a big sign for Skyline Car Wash and Diner. The diner is a 1950 Paramount, now covered in red brick. It sits closed and surrounded by a fence. A cottage-style gas station can be found on each side of the road; then, on the left, an Amoco mini-mart at Durham Road marks the spot of the Airplane Family Restaurant and Diner. A 1954 Lockheed Super G Constellation propeller airplane, brought here in 1967, sat atop

the restaurant, dominating the intersection. The plane closed about 1990, but the restaurant beneath operated until 1995. The plane was hauled away and the restaurant was bulldozed; the only clue to its existence is an airplane model atop the Amoco sign.

A sign for "Old Lincoln Highway next right" alerts you that you're rejoining the original route. The westbound lanes go under U.S. Route 1; to the right are the Janney Station bridge abutments. The lanes above, which bypassed both routes in 1933, were touted as a four-lane "superhighway."

Ahead on the old road, the Lincoln Highway crossed Neshaminy Creek on a covered bridge, long gone except for some abutments. The road still crosses on a concrete bridge built to replace the wooden span in 1921.

Oakford is just north, but continue straight and uphill. At the top of the rise to the right is Penn Valley Terrace mobile home park, once the location of Penn Valley Park, the self-proclaimed "largest free amusement park in the world." Old postcards show it as a tourist camp with rides. The park closed around 1934, though a swimming pool hung on longer. Ahead, the area to the right is known as Linconia, perhaps a derivation of the Lincoln Highway name. The road intersects U.S. Route 1; a business park on the corner was the site of Ridge Farm Tourist Camp and later, Liberty Bell Deluxe Cottages.

Old Lincoln Highway crosses U.S. Route 1 and seemingly ends, but beyond the blocked road is the best segment of the old highway in the area. It was originally part of the Byberry and Bensalem Turnpike, which now runs behind the Lincoln Motel. It served as the Lincoln Highway until 1921, when Roosevelt

Boulevard was extended north to here. Walking the old trail, you immediately cross a masonry-arch bridge over Poquessing Creek, marking the border of Philadelphia and Bucks Counties. Built in 1805, it was widened in 1917 to handle Lincoln Highway traffic. Today it's crumbling into the water below. The path is not long, but becomes too overgrown even to walk on.

The Lincoln rejoins and generally follows U.S. Route 1/Roosevelt Boulevard, with a few sidetracks. Roosevelt was conceived as a landscaped City Beautiful parkway. Renamed in 1918 for Theodore Roosevelt, it was originally Northeast Boulevard. Its extension from Broad Street eastward to the city line began in 1913 and was certainly a main factor in routing the Lincoln Highway here instead of through Camden, New Jersey. It was finished in stages starting north of downtown, with parallel suburban streets carrying the traffic until each segment opened. The first leg northeast from Broad Street stopped at Rhawn Street just before Pennypack Circle. It was extended a couple miles to Welsh Street in 1920, and in 1923 the road reached the city line, spurring the new alignment through Penndel that year. Though retaining some of its parkway atmosphere, Roosevelt has become a congested semifreeway.

Only a few early roadside businesses remain. At Red Lion Road, the Kona Kai Polynesian Restaurant was the former Red Lion Inn tavern. Stone duplexes line the road at times. A twelve-lane bridge crosses Pennypack Creek; in Pennypack Park below, you can see how the original circa 1920 span was widened. Near Pennypack Circle is the closed Jolly Mon miniature golf course.

Oxford Circle is hard to recognize, now that through lanes tunnel beneath it, and the crossroads have been reshaped to look like any other intersection. At Adams Avenue, a rooftop neon sign announces the Great Wall Chinese restaurant, which is in the former Seven Stars Tavern. Then, on the left is Regan's Bar, with a neon sign indicating the former "Ladies Entrance." Two miles ahead, you must make a choice in passing through Philadelphia.

At Broad Street, the Lincoln originally turned south toward downtown **Philadelphia**. The 1924 LHA guide called this major crossroad "The Circle." The intersection has changed greatly over the years, and technically, the two streets no longer intersect; Roosevelt becomes Route 1 and goes underneath Broad. If you're in a hurry, you can take U.S. Route 1 to Exit 339, City Line Avenue, to reach U.S. Route 30 west of town. When the Lincoln Highway was marked one last time in 1928, it went west via Hunting Park Avenue. This route, through a sometimes faded part of town, nonetheless has some interesting roadside architecture.

At the intersection of Broad Street and Hunting Park Avenue was a grand Beaux Arts–style Atlantic service station shaped as an oval temple ringed by columns, with a backlit terra-cotta signboard. A quick look at Hunting Park Avenue today finds the Eastern Casket Company in a possible Lincoln Garage at 2245. At 2450 is the beautiful Philadelphia plant of the Budd Company, which specializes in the stamping and assembly of body components for cars and trucks. At 2801, the Tastykake bakery is a five-story buff-colored building with funky blue and aluminum trim

and capped by a little clock on its rooftop billboard. A right on Ridge Avenue takes you to U.S. Route 1 South/City Avenue. Also called City Line Avenue, this busy road continues to Overbrook, where it meets U.S. Route 30/Lancaster Avenue.

If you're a Lincoln Highway purist, turn south from Roosevelt onto Broad Street, where you'll be rewarded with numerous vintage auto showrooms and garages along the city's "automobile row." Among the onetime tenants was the Seiberling Rubber Company, founded by longtime LHA president Frank Seiberling in 1921 after he was forced from Goodyear, which he had cofounded. At Lehigh Avenue was a 1914 Ford assembly plant, one of two dozen regional factories that received knock-down chassis from Detroit and produced finished Model Ts. Just south of Potts Street on the left is the 1916 Roman Building, with a flying spoked wheel in relief on the facade. At 317 North Broad Street is the 1910 Packard Building designed by Albert Kahn, now housing luxury condos.

Hotels have survived too, notably the huge 1898 Lorraine at Ridge Avenue and the 1902 Bellevue-Stratford, now known as the Park Hyatt Philadelphia at the Bellevue, just south of City Hall at Walnut Street.

The 1918 LHA guide noted that Philadelphia had a horn at every street intersection, a noisy form of traffic control before signals.

Broad Street runs to Penn Square, which encircles the 695-room City Hall. About ten blocks east is Independence National Historical Park, which includes Independence Hall, Carpenter's Hall, and the Liberty Bell at the new Liberty Bell Center. The signing of the Declaration of Independence took place here

on July 4, 1776, as did the adoption of the U.S. Constitution in 1787. Philadelphia also served as the nation's capital from 1790 to 1800.

Boy Scout Bernard Queneau came through the city on July 7, 1928, on a cross-country safety tour: "Left fairly early and went and saw Liberty Hall and Betsy Ross's house. On Broad Street we went over 45! And how!"

Multiple traffic lanes circle and branch from Penn Square. In his 1925 book, *Boulevards All the Way—Maybe*, James Montgomery Flagg wrote, "Getting thro Phildelphia is a bore, as you always lose your way near the City Hall, and go around it dizzily several times before you can find a street to break away from it—and the cops are all surly and arrogant."

Lincoln Highway drivers would have circled right one-quarter of the way and headed west on Market Street. Today that is one-way

Looking north on Broad Street at Lehigh Avenue, Philadelphia. The building on the left opened in 1914 as a Ford assembly plant. "Knocked down" Model Ts were shipped by rail from Detroit and finished here for local distribution. Between 1914 and 1927, the plant produced 625,949 vehicles. Botany 500 was later headquartered here.

eastbound, so you take John F. Kennedy (originally Pennsylvania) Boulevard to 20th Street, then drop south to Market and proceed west. Some eight blocks later, the Lincoln crosses the Schuylkill River on the 1920s Market Street Bridge, a spread-eagle statue at each corner. On the far side, Amtrak's grand 30th Street Station sits to the north. The Lincoln cuts through the campuses of Drexel University and the University of Pennsylvania, then bears right (now via 36th Street) on Lancaster Avenue.

An alternate route west used the one-way pair of Walnut and Chestnut Streets just south of Market. These reached Lancaster Avenue via 63rd Street, which even had a Lincoln Highway Garage, now a dry cleaner. Travelers could also go north through Fairmount Park, which became easier with the opening of the Benjamin Franklin Parkway in 1920, or take Ridge Avenue northwest from city center.

The famous Guernsey Cow at the Exton crossroads has been refurbished by a bank.

West from Philadelphia

Lancaster Avenue was the most direct route west from town, following the old Lancaster Turnpike. A Lincoln Highway Garage was located at 4854, where a white horse sign now hangs next to the Union Tabernacle Baptist Church. The Ace Diner, a circa 1940 Silk City, is hidden behind a sidewalk-to-sky mansard roof. Anna's Pizza is in a 1954 Fodero-brand diner originally called the Overbrook Diner.

On the northwest corner of Overbrook Avenue are the Lincoln Court Apartments and Dining Room. At City Line Avenue, the Overbrook Presbyterian Church remains on the northeast corner. It's obvious you've reached **Overbrook**. The northwest corner once had a tollhouse when this was the Lancaster Pike. More than a century later, motorists still found numerous tollgates to Lancaster and beyond. The LHA campaigned for their end, and the last section of toll road (not counting bridges) along the thirty-three-hundred-mile route was freed in 1917, when the state highway department acquired the Lancaster Pike for $165,000. A number of small Lancaster Pike milestones remain, indicating the mileage to Philadelphia.

The road passes through numerous suburbs along the Main Line of the Pennsylvania Railroad. The highway mostly keeps to Lancaster Avenue, except for an occasional old bend that can be discerned by roads branching off with names such as Old Lancaster Pike. It's slow going, though not exactly congested. In **Ardmore**, the Chung Sing Restaurant is in the former Dean's Diner, a 1952 Fodero. The town was also home to Autocar, a leading supporter of the LHA. Founded in Pittsburgh, the company moved to Ardmore in 1900 and switched to trucks-only in 1911.

In 1920, Autocar donated two trucks and paid their operating costs for marking the Lincoln Highway with enameled steel markers from New York to Omaha. Today Ardmore is perhaps best known for Suburban Square, one of the country's first department store–anchored shopping centers when it opened in 1928. Just as pioneering, Ardmore was the site of the first-ever Sunoco station, opened in 1920. Old photos of the station show the cross street as Lehigh Avenue, but no Lehigh exists today; it apparently was an earlier name for Woodside Road, where a modern Sunoco sits.

On the right at **Bryn Mawr** is the former Bryn Mawr Garage, with its name and a winged wheel on the facade of brick with inlaid blue tiles. The road goes downhill through the **Rosemont** business district, levels and passes Villanova University, established in 1843, then heads through **Radnor** and **St. Davids** and into the **Wayne** business section. Until 2001, the China Buddha restaurant was in the former Wayne Diner, but this 1955 Mountain View–brand diner was hauled away and restored as the Lake Effect Diner in Buffalo. Still in town is the circa 1910 Tudor-style Wayne Hotel and the Art Deco Anthony Wayne Theater. Another diner, Minella's Main Line Diner, a 1964 Fodero, was hauled away in 2003 to Lake City, Florida. A new DeRaffele diner replaced it.

About five miles north of this area is Valley Forge National Historic Park, site of the Continental Army's encampment during the winter of 1777–78. U.S. Route 30 enters **Strafford**. At 629 West Lancaster Avenue, John Harvard's Brewhouse is in the old Covered Wagon Inn. The Devon Square Business Center is on the site of the former Main Line Drive-In Theater.

To the right, Old Lancaster Road branches off under the Main Line. At the corner is a 1920s gas station, the only remaining English cottage–style Pure Oil station on the Lincoln Highway in the state. The Lincoln Highway follows Old Lancaster Road. A large house at Valley Forge Road is the former Lamb Tavern, built in 1805 to serve turnpike travelers at **Devon**. A block west is the Devon Tea Room, a 1912 log house where Main Liners dined while their servants took their cars to the adjacent garage to be cleaned and serviced. Old Lancaster Road rejoins U.S. Route 30 a mile from where it departed.

Just west is the **Berwyn** train station, then Old Lancaster Road again turns right across the tracks and runs to near the **Daylesford** station. On U.S. Route 30, a pizza shop on the left occupies the site of the former Twaddell's Diner, the first diner built by the Swingle company in 1958. Ahead, **Paoli** was the site of a notorious Revolutionary War battle in which the British attacked the Continental Army under Gen. Anthony Wayne at night. The town was named for Corsican patriot and general Pasquale Paoli. Roadside fans will want to visit Matthews Sales, the oldest Ford dealer in the state, a franchise since 1921.

The original Lincoln Highway branched left on King Road to **Malvern**, but before reaching the business district, the route turned right and went under the railroad tracks at Green Tree Station. The station is long gone, and the underpass was filled in and blocked by a wooden fence fronting the Rusticraft fence company. To reach the other side, pro-

ceed west into Malvern and turn north on Bridge Street to cross the tracks and meet Old Lincoln Highway. Backtracking east, a 1928 concrete marker points to the now-gone underpass and station.

Turn around and head west on Old Lincoln Highway; going downhill, turn left on Old Lancaster Avenue, the original Lincoln Highway. The General Warren Inn here dates to the Lancaster Pike era. Next to it, another filled-in underpass marks the original route of the Lincoln Highway beneath the Pennsylvania Railroad. The road from here back through Malvern was bypassed by the current U.S. Route 30 in the 1930s.

Route 30 rises into **Frazer** and past the Frazer Diner, a late 1930s, streamline moderne style O'Mahony. Recent changes ahead have been erasing similar roadside relics. Past Lincoln Court Shopping Center is the former site of the Quaker Motel on the right, opened in 1948 by Mr. and Mrs. Henry Eyden. For half a century, the seven-unit motel had no telephones, but it had beautiful knotty pine walls and furniture, plus reading lamps with deer-hoof bases. After the owners retired in 1996, it fell into disrepair, then was cleared for development.

Across the road, the Malvern Meeting House cabins are gone, and the main restaurant is scheduled for demolition. Near the hilltop, the former Hillcrest Cabins were replaced in the late 1990s by a day-care center. West of Planebrook Road, however, a few cabins remain behind a roadhouse on the right, remnants of Swayne's Cabins. Robert Swayne said his dad started a store and campground in 1922 with a single Texaco pump, then added the first of a dozen cabins in 1928.

Frazer Diner in 2000, before cloth awnings were installed.

At the top of the next hill in **Glenloch** ("Lake of the Glen" in Scottish) is the Sheraton Great Valley hotel, built around a circa 1760 eight-bay-wide stone house. Across the street is what remains of a six hundred-acre estate centered around the original Glen Loch, an 1867 Swiss Gothic mansion now barely visible with the encroachment of chain stores. Just past it is the intersection of U.S. Route 202 and the Exton U.S. Route 30 bypass.

At Ship Road is the Ship Inn, a 1796 tavern, then the road enters **Exton**. A string of cabins and a defunct 1937 filling station and restaurant mark the former Williams Deluxe Cabins. The complex is listed on the National Register of Historic Places, though it has been converted to other uses. In front of the Exton Square Mall is a bank in the former Guernsey Cow restaurant, best known for its thirty-five-foot-tall cow billboard erected across the road in 1945. Next to the bank, the former Sleepy Hollow Hall, a circa 1685 stone house, which was expanded in 1740 and 1820, has also been saved.

The intersection with PA Route 100—Exton Crossroads—has become completely developed over the decades. The Valley

CIRCA 1960
The Quaker Motel, Malvern, Pennsylvania

Really nothing Quaker about this except the name & location.

Hi Doty

BERNIE HEISEY

The twenty-four-hour Downingtown Diner specialized in homemade pies, but is famous as the diner attacked by the Blob.

KYLE WEAVER

The Gap Diner is in the heart of Pennsylvania Dutch Country.

Creek Coffee Shop was long a welcome respite for travelers. Even the 1924 LHA guide noted it as a good spot for camping, but it is long gone.

The road heads west into **Downingtown**. To the right at Kerr Park is the circa 1701 Downingtown Log House, then the road crosses the east branch of Brandywine Creek on a 1921 concrete arch bridge.

Business U.S. Route 30 heads west from Downingtown and passes the former Downingtown Diner, a circa 1962 Silk City best known for its role in the 1957 movie *The Blob*. Well, it was an earlier diner on the site that was engulfed by the Blob, but that one was bulldozed decades ago; this replacement has at times traded on that legacy, sometimes spurning it, mostly embracing it.

A big hole was left in local hearts, and the ground, when the Ingleside Diner was pulled out from **Thorndale** in 2003. The 1956 Fodero-brand diner was founded as Zinn's. It was the family's third diner in the area, the first being the Town Diner in Coatesville at 823 East Lincoln Highway.

As the Lincoln Highway approaches **Coatesville**, the road crosses over railroad tracks on the Caln Bridge. At its west end is the V.I.P. Diner, a 1948 Paramount. In town, the Lincoln Highway Inn on the east end was one of six hotels in town; it was advertised in the 1915 LHA guide as "homelike" and "artistic"; by the next year, that had been changed to "select."

Leaving town, the West Branch of Brandywine Creek is spanned by a 1914 masonry bridge with a milestone embedded in the middle. Surrounding this are the mills of Bethlehem Steel, formerly Luken's, the world's largest steel plate rolling mill when built. The Lincoln Diner once sat between Church Street and Brandywine Creek in an area now fenced for parking. The diner was a reconditioned O'Mahony purchased in 1935 and operated by Robert "Stan" Viguers Sr. His son Bob said his dad considered O'Mahony the "Cadillac of diners."

The road climbs and crosses the Ben Weaver Bridge; at the far end, a short piece of Old Lincoln Highway breaks briefly to the south. The road continues climbing and the landscape becomes more rural. A 1799 eight-bay inn with two front gables, formerly the **Sadsburyville** Hotel, is now Harry's Restaurant. Downhill, past Lincoln Crest Mobile Homes Park, are the remains of Drake's Spanish Court motel. The word "office" is barely legible above a corner door.

The U.S. Route 30 bypass rejoins our road. The Keystone restaurant and motel are to the left. To the right is the Cackleberry Farm Antique Mall, in a long red building on a former poultry farm. About half a mile later, a garage and gas pump island help locate the former Olga's Restaurant, now a residence.

The road climbs another hill, and the Brass Eagle Family Restaurant is to the right. Next door are scattered remnants of the Queen Oak Camp, and across the road are the remains of the Edgewood Camp. Heading downhill, the old Lincoln weaves right and left of U.S. Route 30 and then rejoins it before the road enters **Gap**, named for its location at a break in the mountain ridge. On the southwest corner of the U.S. Route 41/Newport Pike intersection is the Gap Diner, a remodeled 1959 Kullman-brand diner announcing "Local Dutch-Amer. Cooking."

As the road climbs west, traffic increases; this stretch has been examined for years for possible widening or bypass. Lined with hundreds of historic structures and farms, it's been designated as one of the "10 Most Endangered Scenic Byways" by Scenic America, a Washington-based national conservation group. The small Oh! Shaw Motel on the left, named for the motel's founder, has changed little over the years. Ahead are the Stage Coach, Paradise Hills, and Lucky 7 motels. At the tiny town of **Kinzer**, a sign points south to Red Caboose Motel where guests spend the night in old train cabooses.

The Lincoln Highway enters **Vintage**, home to the National Christmas Center in the former Dutch Town and Country Inn. Over another rise, a huge lumberyard on the left was the site of Rosey's Auto Graveyard. Two historic bridges ahead may not last long; the Eshleman Run Bridge, built in 1929 with distinctive balustrade-rail beams, was widened in 1935 when the paralleling interurban line

KYLE WEAVER

Dutch Haven is one of the few surviving examples of early auto tourism east of Lancaster.

that also used it was abandoned. The similar Pequea Creek Bridge is west in Paradise.

The road rises to cross railroad tracks; when a steel-arched bridge was replaced in 2000, a concrete Lincoln Highway marker was moved from the rise to a road immediately west and south of it. Coincidentally, this road appears to be the original Lincoln Highway, predating the first bridge here from 1923. The road can be followed to the tracks, where it once crossed at grade.

To the west are **Leaman Place** and then **Paradise**, settled about 1800 by Dunkards and Mennonites, both German Anabaptists. After the Pequea Creek Bridge, at 3063 Lin-coln Highway is the 1740 Historic Revere Tavern and Best Western Revere Motor Inn.

Traffic continues to increase, and the Lincoln finally reaches the edge of Lancaster's eastern strip at **Soudersburg**. The best survivors from midcentury are across from each other. Dutch Haven, identifiable by its tall windmill, dates to the 1940s. A Pennsylvania Dutch–style restaurant inside has closed, but in its place are crafts, collectibles, and Amish pine furniture. You can also still buy shoo-fly pie, a traditional Pennsylvania Dutch dessert made with white flour, brown sugar, cinnamon, refiner's syrup, and other ingredients that make for a gooey pie. They're shipped all over the world; as they don't contain raisins or any other fruit, they have a long shelf life. Every visitor gets a free warm sample topped with whipped cream.

Dutch Haven grew to include other buildings and attractions, but all have changed through the years. The wackiest now is The Outhouse, a country store full of silly gag gifts. Behind the buildings is a small area for performing pigs and goats; the show is free, but donations are welcome.

Across the road is the Soudersburg Motel, now in the third generation of the Stauffer family, but retaining its 1950s stone decor. A few doors down is Miller's Smorgasbord, started in 1929 as a filling station and truck stop.

Ahead in **Ronks** and to the left, a Sunoco minimart was the site of Hart's U.S. 30 Diner, a 1957 Kullman. Just across the road, Jennie's Diner still packs them into a small 1959 Silk City. A vestibule recently added to the front is the only major change from its factory-fresh look. A nice "Air Conditioned" sign at the roofline and a vertical neon sign by the road still glow.

The intersection with PA Route 896 has changed from quiet to all-out crazy since the arrival of outlet malls about 1990. On the southeast corner, the Robert Fulton Steamboat Inn is a hotel in a full-size replica of a boat. Just northeast, on PA Route 896/Eastbrook Road, the Weathervane Motor Court is a family-run motel.

Ahead, the American Music Theatre replaced the Willows Restaurant and Motel in 1998. The Willows was founded by the Neuber family in 1931 and became *the* place to eat on the city's rural east end. Among its Pennsylvania Dutch specialties were sauerbraten (pickled beef pot roast), schticker kolb flaysch (Dutch-style veal cutlet), roe grumberie poonkucke (raw potato pancake), and gebocka gedatt siesz welschkann (baked dried sweet corn). The building had thirteen guest rooms plus cabins in back. In 1956, son Adolph

KYLE WEAVER

Jennie's Diner is surrounded by farmland, though development is rampant just to the west.

A 1960s view of the Wally the Whale boat ride at Dutch Wonderland fantasy park, a few miles east of Lancaster.

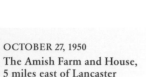

OCTOBER 27, 1950
**The Amish Farm and House,
5 miles east of Lancaster**

Dear Vera,
Please cancel my luncheon
reservation on the 12th!—
we are in this lovely Penna.
Dutch Country so restful—
Regards to you &
Maurice—

Myrtle & Arthur

Neuber built the adjacent Amish Farm and House, the first large-scale facility here devoted to serving tourists, as it still does.

The strip ahead is increasingly modernized; remaining on the hilltop is Italian Villa East, a Rodeway Inn centered around an old five-bay home that also serves as the motel office. Nearby is the nineteen-unit, family-run Garden Spot Motel, and across the road on the left is the Congress Inn, with a cool capitol dome sign.

Dutch Wonderland amusement park can be spotted by its huge castle facade and monorail ride. The park was opened in 1963 by motel operator Earl Clark, who was looking to keep guests in the area longer. It was bought in 2001 by the company that runs nearby Hersheypark. Clark was also responsible for the adjacent Lancaster County History Museum (until recently, the Wax Museum of

Lancaster County), which features thirty-two historical scenes and 172 lifesize figures.

After more strip businesses, U.S. Route 30 bypasses the city, while the Lincoln Highway becomes PA Route 462 and passes through Lancaster and York. Following the

original route, at 1687 Lincoln Highway East is the Lincoln Haus Inn, an Amish-owned bed and breakfast in a 1915 white stucco house. At Conestoga Woods, you cross the Conestoga River on a 1932 concrete bridge, which replaced the notable Witmer's Bridge, built in 1799–1800. Incorporated into the current railing is a stone tablet from the original, which names builder Abraham Witmer and gives the mileage: "61 M to P, 1 M to L." At the western end is the Conestoga Bar and Restaurant, built in 1789 as the Sign of the Pennsylvania Arms.

The road heads uphill, past an old brick garage. At the top to the left is the Lancaster County Hospital and Alms House. The Lincoln went straight through **Lancaster** on King Street, but that's now one-way eastbound, so follow PA Route 462 to East Walnut Street, which is one-way westbound. The street is lined with old row houses. At Queen Street, the town center, Penn Square, is one

Trolleys dominate Lancaster's Penn Square, February 18, 1925.

block south at Queen and King Streets. The square, laid out in 1730, also features a Soldiers and Sailors Monument from 1874 and Central Market, the country's oldest publicly owned, continuously operated farmers' market. The current red brick structure was built in 1889. Nearby, at 114 East King Street, is Demuth Tobacco Shop, the country's oldest tobacco store, established in 1770. Next door is the Charles Demuth Museum in the former home and studio of the world famous artist. Demuth (1883–1935), best known for the paintings *My Egypt* and *The Figure 5 in Gold*, lived and worked here most of his life.

The Lincoln heads west again on Walnut, then drops down to PA Route 462/Columbia Avenue. There you'll find directional signs for Wheatland, the home of James Buchanan, the state's only native-born president. The estate is named for the nearby wheatfields.

Farther on are the old Maple Grove mill and, past that, a McDonald's restaurant sign with a single big golden arch sporting a pair of coats of arms. Five miles from downtown is the Cozee Court motel, then the road passes through **Mountville**.

Roadfans will find both a diner and drive-in theater east of **Columbia**. The Prospect Diner, a 1955 Kullman, was built at the dawn of the space age, most realized by its flared overhanging roof. The 1957 Columbia Drive-In Theater has been rumored as a site for a shopping center but it continues showing outdoor movies. A turnpike milestone between the two gives the distances to three towns: P71, L8, C2, for Philadelphia, Lancaster, and Columbia.

PA Route 462 descends into Columbia. An ad for the Lincoln Highway Garage at Sixth Street noted its curb service. The Lincoln Highway originally crossed the Susquehanna on a steel truss bridge built by the Pennsylvania Railroad in 1897. Problem was, the railroad still used it, so when a train was approaching, traffic had to be stopped on both ends of the mile-long span. Faulty signals also could allow a car or horse-drawn wagon to proceed onto the bridge as a train approached. It was replaced in 1930 by the Veterans Memorial (or Columbia-Wrightsville or Lancaster-York Intercounty) Bridge, the longest multiple-arch, reinforced concrete bridge in the world at the time. A new state historical marker at the eastern end honors the Lincoln Highway. The railroad bridge was demolished in 1964, but the stone piers remain. The four-lane U.S. Route 30 bypass to the north uses the 1970 Wright's Ferry Bridge.

A 1931 project planted red roses along the Lincoln Highway from the Susquehanna River to Lancaster, and white roses from the river to York. This tradition, being attempted again today, derives from the English royal houses of Lancaster and York and their families' badges. A white rose symbolized the Yorks, a red the Lancasters, hence the fifteenth-century "War of the Roses." You'll often see references to the White Rose or Red Rose city or county.

The Veterans Memorial Bridge reaches **Wrightsville**. As the road climbs, to the left at 8th Street is one of two Road of Remembrance markers. (The other marker is near the 81 Diner between York and Abbottstown.) They were erected in 1922, one at each end of York County, as part of a program to honor local sons and daughters who fought in World War I by planting trees along the

The Art Deco Columbia Bridge replaced the trestle at center, which served both cars and trains.

highway. The Women's Club of the United States undertook the planting of trees along the full length of the Lincoln Highway; for $2.50, local participants could choose a tree of their liking, elms, oaks, and maples being the most popular. Each tree had a metal tag shaped like a federal highway shield, with information about the soldier.

Heading west, the road passes Jim Mack's Ice Cream, a 1950s drive-in restaurant that also has a tiny zoo, miniature golf course, basketball hoops, arcade, pirate ship, and picnic area.

Across from the Hellam Municipal Building is a 1928 concrete Lincoln Highway marker. The road soon enters the borough of **Hallam**. (The borough is spelled Hallam, the township Hellam.) The street is lined with houses, little garages, and other businesses.

West of town at Shoe House Road, a right turn takes drivers to the twenty-five-foot-tall Shoe House, the zany dream of "shoe wizard" Mahlon Haines. In 1948, he built the

Haines Shoe House, built along the Lincoln Highway, now sits closer to the U.S. Route 30 bypass.

Shoe House as a promotional gimmick for his chain of forty retail shoe stores. It overlooked the Lincoln Highway, but the U.S. Route 30 bypass now cuts much closer.

The Shoe House is actually modeled on a high-top work boot, and it even has a stained-glass window of Haines holding up a pair of them. Its five levels are forty-eight feet long and seventeen feet wide. Haines offered his odd-shaped house to elderly couples, providing food, clothes, a car, even a servant. Later, he offered it to honeymooners, who could register in his stores. The stores closed after his death in 1962, and the Shoe House fell into disrepair. About 1990, his granddaughter purchased it and began restoration. New owners Carleen and Ronald Farabaugh are likewise working to restore its luster. They run an ice cream parlor and charge $3 for a tour.

By the 1960s, the Lincoln Highway Garage was selling mostly Esso products but still carried its own Sportsman's Special gasoline.

A few older businesses have survived east of York, including the brick Chateau Motel, the Flamingo Motel (at the sign of the pink flamingo), Barnhart's Motel, and the Modernaire Motel, sporting a great neon sign and rounded corner entrance. It's run by Deb and Robert Straw; Deb's parents bought the place in 1966, and the Straws have run it since 1985.

The stretch ahead that is now a strip of malls was once filled with businesses that have been erased over the past two decades. In 1962, a new mall and road widening displaced Ye Olde Valley Inn (also called the Olde York Inn). The 1738 tavern was saved and moved to Susquehanna Memorial Gardens, a cemetery to the southeast near Dallastown, where today it holds offices. Past this spot is a Coca-Cola bottling plant with the company's famous script name carved in relief and "1942" below that.

Many other businesses have been lost, a fate that recently befell the city's best-known roadside landmark, the Lincoln Highway Garage. Stewart Lehman opened a small garage at 1242 East Market Street in 1921. He also operated a Rickenbacker car dealership there, as well as selling fishing and hunting supplies. The garage offered as many as thirteen different brands and even formulated a couple of its own, including Sportsman's Special in 1957. It was operated in recent years by grandson Lynn Haines, who kept a room dedicated to the history of the garage and the Lincoln Highway; he even had a Rickenbacker there. But in 2003, Haines annnounced that he was ready to retire to his cattle farm. His dad, Harry, had worked there fifty-three years, and after forty-seven years himself, Lynn was still working seventy-five hours a week. Finally, in May 2004, Haines closed the place, so that Turkey Hill could replace it with a convenience store. Some locals had pushed for renovating the building, but the convenience store chain felt that it was making adequate concessions by incorporating murals and Lincoln Highway signage, and offering to trim the roofline of the market and pump canopy in a stair-step pattern reminiscent of the original station's roofline.

As in Lancaster, the route through **York** is complicated by one-way streets. Westbound

drivers on Market Street must follow signs for PA Route 462 and go north to East Philadelphia Street. Then at George Street, the central square is one block south on Market Street.

When Frederic Van de Water came through in the 1920s, he got tangled in the maze of directional lines and was sure an approaching officer was going to chew him out. But instead, "'Swing out into this track here, brother, and you'll be all right,' the policeman directed. 'Where you heading for? Gettysburg? Halfway around the square and turn right. Good luck!'"

Highlights in York are the circa 1920 Yorketowne Hotel, at 48 East Market Street, and the restored 1740s Golden Plough Tavern, at 157 West Market Street. Nearby attractions include the Harley Davidson Final Assembly Plant and the York Barbell Weightlifting Hall of Fame and Museum.

Just past the intersection of Philadelphia Street and George Street is the 1888 Central Market House, the traditional gathering spot for merchants and farmers to sell their crops and Pennsylvania Dutch and German foods. At the west end of town, near the county fairgrounds, PA Route 462 jogs back down to Market Street.

In the 2600 block is Lincolnway Bowling Alley, with a tall neon sign. The Lincolnway Fire Company and Lincolnway School are nearby.

The U.S. Route 30 bypass ends west of York. The merge point was long a congested spot, so the road west was recently widened, easing traffic but further erasing the old roadscape.

Lee's Diner, a red-and-blue-trimmed 1952 Mountain View to the south, was enlarged in the 1990s by swinging the stainless steel left side to the front when a dining room was added. The diner retains its classic style inside, too. Behind the diner is Lincolnway Pool, and across from it is Smith's Motel, originally Myers.

A small airstrip marks what was once the site of the York U.S. 30 Dragway. It was the widest drag-racing facility in the country—the only one to host four lanes of drag racing at one time. No wonder: Even then, it was on an operating airport that closed on Saturday nights for the races. Sometimes the races would be delayed when an airplane had to take off or land. Locals lament its passing and now have an annual Musclecar Madness event to honor it.

East of **Thomasville**, Aspen Transport Village marks the former site of the Lincoln Drive-In Theater, closed about 1990. Ahead and on the right is O'Brien's Restaurant; behind are the remains of the Lincoln View Motel. A mile later to the left is the 81 Diner, and just west of it is the second Road of Remembrance marker.

Except for the addition of a minimart, the center square of **Abbottstown** at the junction of PA Route 194 has changed little. Many eighteenth- and early-nineteenth-century Pennsylvania towns were laid out on the "Philadelphia Plan," with a wide market square at the intersection of the two main streets. The proper term for this is a "diamond," though today it is used in only a few towns, such as Ligonier in western Pennsylvania. The square at Abbottstown, like most, has evolved into a traffic circle. On the southwest corner is the Altland House, a 1790 inn that received its present facade in 1911 and continues to serve travelers.

The junction of PA Route 94 was known as **Cross Keys**, and postcards show a Cross Keys Diner here, but today the corner has Cross Keys Family Restaurant. The **New Oxford** "diamond" was also converted to a traffic circle; on the lawn is a 1928 concrete Lincoln Highway marker. Signs mark the road as Lincoln Way.

The eastern approach to Gettysburg was lined with cabin camps and tourist courts. *America's Fascinating Highways* (1941) mentions Herrick's four miles east, with twelve cottages from $2 to $3. It was better known as Sunken Gardens, built in 1936 by the Herrick brothers. The nineteen-cottage motel offered shuffleboard, horseshoes, a swimming pool, croquet court, and a Hammond organ concert every night. Across from it was a faux-log structure opened in 1947 as the Lincoln Logs Restaurant.

York Road continues toward Gettysburg. Just before the U.S. Route 15 interchange, a 1928 concrete marker sits on the right. Like

Flags line the route in York.

LINCOLN HIGHWAY, MARKET STREET, YORK, PA.

Lancaster, the 1990s saw a burst of commercial growth east of town, and chain stores now line the road. As the road enters **Gettysburg**, it bends right. On the corner at Stratton Street is a former garage with a corner canopy carved into its first level. Just east of the square was the Globe Hotel, renamed the Lincoln Way Hotel when the highway came through and later to become Hoffman's, one of several on the Lincoln Highway.

The traffic circles around Lincoln Square. (It was likewise called a diamond long ago.) On the northeast corner is the 1797 Gettysburg Hotel, which closed in 1964 after a venerated history, then served as apartments until a 1983 fire nearly destroyed it. It was refurbished and two stories were added in 1991.

On the southeast corner is the Wills House, where Abraham Lincoln finished the Gettysburg Address in November 1863. A statue depicts Lincoln directing a tourist; it's possibly the most accurate statue of Lincoln, as its sculptor modeled the face and hands after lifetime casts, based the shoes on an outline made by a Pennsylvania bootmaker, and copied the outfit from Lincoln's own clothing.

Gettysburg rose to infamy in July 1863 as the locus of a three-day Civil War battle here. The convergence of roads drew the armies to battle here. To get to the Gettysburg National Military Park's visitor center, go south from the square on U.S. Route 15 Business. Across

As the Lincoln Highway headed west from Gettysburg, most tourists could not resist snapping a photo at the monuments to Union generals John Buford and John Reynolds, seen here in 1922. The equestrian statues are coded: Four hooves planted means the rider survived the battle; one raised shows that he was injured; two raised indicates that he was killed in action.

from the center is the National Cemetery, scene of Lincoln's Gettysburg Address.

Tackling the Allegheny Mountains

West of the square on Chambersburg Street is the restored Blue Parrot Bistro and the small James Gettys Hotel. A large concrete and terra-cotta building on the southwest corner of Washington Street was built as a theater in 1916 by Frank Eberhart, proprietor of the Eagle Hotel, which sat across the street. It never became a theater, but instead Eberhart's Garage, then about 1925, Epley's Garage. Since 1960, it has held numerous businessess.

From here west for 140 miles, the road is now part of the Lincoln Highway Heritage Corridor. In 2004, the corridor was erecting fifty-eight interpretive signs to point out places of interest. Also going up were twenty-two fiberglass gasoline pump replicas and four "Picture Yourself" exhibits featuring life-size images for photo opportunities. Local artist Wayne Fettro was adding three more

Lincoln Highway–themed murals to the five he'd already painted along the corridor.

West of Gettysburg, the road passes the seminary that played a role in the first day's battle. Across the street, behind the small building known as Lee's Headquarters, is a Quality Inn that evolved from a pair of tourist camps. They eventually merged and became Larson's, one of the first in the Quality Courts chain. Rooms were also available in the family home. It may have been in one of these that Frederic Van de Water stayed in 1927:

> At the Gettysburg auto camp, we found a broad field stretching away from a white farmhouse in which to pitch our tent. There were ovens for those who wished to use them, a special building with shower baths and an immense barrel of ice water on the porch, blazoned with a sign: "Help yourself." The cost per car per night was fifty cents.

Just before leaving town, you come to the Buford and Reynolds monuments, a popular

SPECIAL COLLECTIONS LIBRARY, UNIVERSITY OF MICHIGAN

photo stop for motorists then and now. To the west, the small Willoughby Run Bridge, built in 1919, was replaced in 2003, because of the heavy volume of traffic. Two miles to the west and then south is the Land of Little Horses, featuring shows and petting opportunities with miniature Falabella horses.

The original road angles off through **McKnightstown** and **Cashtown**. Travelers have a choice of accommodations. In McKnightstown is the Country Escape B&B, operated by LHA state secretary and newsletter editor Merry Bush. A couple miles west, the 1797 Cashtown Inn served as the headquarters for Confederate general A. P. Hill in 1863 as Southern troops approached Gettysburg.

The old road climbs and dips. As the hill crests, the Lincoln crosses U.S. Route 30 and winds behind Mr. Ed's Elephant Museum. Ed Gotwalt has been collecting elephants since the 1960s, when he got one for a wedding present. In 1973, he started Mr. Ed's General Store just east on Route 30, then moved to this location in 1984. You'll find candy, souvenirs, and a small museum full of every imaginable elephant-related object, some five thousand pieces. Outside is Miss Ellie Phunt, a ten-foot-tall fiberglass pachyderm who talks and blinks her eyes.

The old and new roads again rejoin on a downhill slope. The wooded area is part of the eighty-two-thousand-acre Michaux State Forest. Then, at the Adams–Franklin County line, begins Caledonia State Park, named for the charcoal iron furnace that Thaddeus Stevens erected here in 1837. The congressman and abolitionist lived at times in Gettysburg and Lancaster. His antislavery stance led Confederate soldiers to burn the furnace on

ON THE LINCOLN HIGHWAY, 8 MILES WEST OF GETTYSBURG

CASHTOWN GARAGE
DANIEL S. MICKLEY, Prop.
"A BETTER SERVICE"

PHONE - GETTYSBURG 564-R-31   CASHTOWN, PA.

Daniel S. Mickley owned the Cashtown Hotel and the Cashtown Garage along the Lincoln Highway, so the U.S. Route 30 bypass had a huge impact on the family. His daughter Suzanne remembers his prescient prediction: "Cashtown will become a ghost town."

their way to Gettysburg in June 1863. A mile later, just after PA Route 233, are a museum and reconstructed furnace at the Thaddeus Stevens Blacksmith Shop. The Appalachian Trail, which runs along the backbone of the Appalachian Mountains, crosses the road just west of here. More than two thousand miles long, it's the longest continuous marked foot trail in the world.

The original road branches to the right through Fayetteville. A former cottage-style Gulf station sits along Main Street. On the U.S. Route 30 bypass (also marked Lincoln Way West) is the Rite Spot Motel. Lincoln Lanes Bowling is just past where U.S. Route 30/Lincoln Way rejoins the old road. Dodie's is a 1960s-style drive-in restaurant.

Miss Ellie greets a visitor at Mr. Ed's Elephant Museum.

Lincoln Way becomes congested east of **Chambersburg**, then makes its way into the small city. At the center is Memorial Square, around which westbound traffic snakes on

1927. Bingham's Fruit Market still sells fruit plus cider, jams, and baskets. Bingham divided his orchard among nieces and nephews; the others became Shatzer's and Appleway. Shatzer's Orchards was started in 1933. Their ninety acres still produce cherries, peaches, plums, pears, and apples, as well as pumpkins, gourds, corn, and Indian corn. The market carries fruit, gift boxes, and Pennsylvania Dutch cookbooks.

Three circa 1818 tollhouses survive from the Chambersburg and Bedford Turnpike. Numbers 2 and 3 are west of St. Thomas; number 4 is east of Fort Loudon.

Old Lincoln Highway branches right and heads into **Fort Loudon**. A 1928 concrete Lincoln Highway post points the way right at a bend in the tiny town. In the fork, an old granite marker with a tablet remains to commemorate Fort Loudoun, a 1756 fort (with a different spelling) to defend against Indians.

Old and new routes rejoin and then give Lincoln Highway drivers their first real climb since the coast. Cove Mountain is part of the Buchanan State Forest, named for President James Buchanan, who was born in the area. The road levels briefly, then climbs Tuscarora Mountain. Atop the summit sits the Mountain House Bar and Grill, in the former Doc Seylar's. This was one of the state's well-known mountaintop stops and appears in hundreds of postcards.

both sides. In the middle, a bronze Civil War soldier stands next to Memorial Fountain, which was a prize-winning exhibit at the 1876 Centennial Exposition in Philadelphia.

For years, a memorial arch at the square's entrance noted the Confederate route through here to Gettysburg. Henry Joy wrote to the town's motor club and suggested a sign be added noting the Lincoln Highway. The letter made the front page of the newspaper on October 8, 1913, and the sign was hung soon after.

In 2004, the Chambersburg Heritage Center opened in the former Valley National Bank building. Initiated as a museum and interpretive center for the Lincoln Highway Heritage Corridor, it highlights five themes, including transportation.

The Oak Forest Family Restaurant in **St. Thomas** is an old road stop; a string of cabins remains in back. This town was among the first to officially change its main street name to Lincoln Highway.

The road passes through orchards, particularly apples. Many of them can be traced to Billy Bingham, who opened a fruit stand in

"Doc" Seylar produced hundreds of different postcards of his Tuscarora Summit Inn, between Fort Loudon and McConnellsburg.

An often-photographed view looking west to Sideling Hill.

JUN 21, 1926
Tuscarora Summit on Lincoln Highway, looking towards McConnellsburg, Pa.

Passing through here at 11 AM. So steep had to let motor cool on top.

Robert

Within seconds, the road changes to a descent, curving its way downhill. Where it becomes four lanes, the original road branched left, though today that seems impossible, as the road is high above the treeline. A bit further, a left turn toward **McConnellsburg** joins that road—both had "horseshoe curves"—and descends into town. At the forks on the east end of town, the Mercersburg Turnpike joined the Lincoln, the former Chambersburg and Bedford Turnpike.

Before 1940, the road at left was the route to Baltimore and Washington for eastbound traffic following the Lincoln Highway; this junction is now located at Breezewood, where the Pennsylvania Turnpike meets I-70.

Two important hotels in town were the Mellot and the Harris, but better known is the Fulton House, a 1793 inn at 112 Lincoln Way East. It now houses the Fulton County Historical Society and has a 1928 concrete marker out front pulled from Tuscarora Summit for fear of more surreptitious removal.

West of town is another former tollhouse, then the road climbs Scrub Ridge. At the summit, it passes the Scrub Ridge Inn, a bar and restaurant here since the mid-1920s.

The Lincoln goes down, then up, then at PA Route 655, it goes through tiny **Harrisonville**, named for President William Henry Harrison. The Hollingshead Grocery Store remains, along with a couple other buildings. Just past it to the right, a home has a 1928 concrete marker in its small front yard.

As the road again rises, a battered building on the right is the former Green Hill Toll House. It was built in 1838 as a tollhouse on the Chambersburg and Bedford Turnpike and was used until the road was made free in 1913.

Suddenly, you top the hill, and the view ahead to Sideling Hill is little changed from period views taken by the LHA (see above). In the valley, a number of roadside businesses were once found in the village of **Saluvia**; today the main one attracting motorists is the Eagles Club, likely the Johnson Hotel found

in old tourist guides. On the right are a few double cabins remaining from DeShong's Oil and Gas.

Now the road begins climbing Sideling Hill, tops it, and then winds like a ribbon upon the twisting terrain. The former Shorty's Place, with at least three single cabins and one double remaining, has featured exotic dancers for the past decade.

As the road rises to Ray's Hill, with the Pennsylvania Turnpike becoming visible to the right, a dilapidated wooden building is the former McIlvaine's Inn or Old Mountain Home. This circa 1780 inn was along the Forbes Road, but the traces of that road were mostly destroyed by the turnpike.

At the summit of Ray's Hill, you can pause and check out some short abandoned bits of road. Until the hill was cut away for the Pennsylvania Turnpike, Bill's Place sat

William Wakefield started Bill's Place as a small refreshment stand.

"BILL'S PLACE," LINCOLN HIGHWAY, ELEVEN MILES EAST OF EVERETT, PA

"Greetings from Bill's Place, Penna."

When the recipient of this card opened it, the rubber band–powered butterfly inside was said to fly out thirty-five feet in the air.

Often misidentified as the road east of Grand View, this view actually looks east through Breezewood, with Bill's Place at the gap in the distant left.

here. William Wakefield started his place on June 10, 1923, selling snacks and souvenirs and gewgaws. He built a tower across the road and had some gags, too, including a sign advertising, "See the Oregon Red Bats"; a traveler would climb the steps to find a barrel with a couple bricks in it (a bat, or brickbat, is a brick fragment, often used as a weapon). He also claimed to have the smallest postal town in the United States, but a 1954 consolidation drive canceled his contract. Bill sold his place and it closed in the late 1960s, when the turnpike took the land to bypass its own tunnel. Bill's was bulldozed, and U.S. Route 30 was realigned to a new bridge across the turnpike.

Long before it was known as the Town of Motels, **Breezewood** was a hamlet on the Lincoln Highway. With the arrival of a turnpike interchange in 1940, service businesses

Visitors to Bill's Place were enticed to "See the Oregon Red Bats," but all they found was bricks, as in "brickbats."

blossomed, accelerated by the coming in the 1960s of I-70, which hits a traffic light and has to take the Lincoln Highway for one commercialized block. A few circa 1960

motels remain, as does Crawford's Museum and Gift Shop.

As the road climbs from town, just to the west are an 1815 inn and 1935 garage. U.S. Route 30 curves through road cuts, the original Lincoln lost to the left. The road crosses the Raystown Branch of the Juniata River on a concrete bridge. It replaced a covered bridge in 1935, and just in time; the old one was swept away in the notorious St. Patrick's Day Flood of 1936. The original bridge had been built in 1818 as a two-lane covered bridge for the new Chambersburg and Bedford Turnpike. When a flood swept away half of the bridge, the rebuilt part was made only one-lane, as traffic had declined over the years. When the Lincoln Highway came through in 1913, drivers reached a point in the middle of the covered bridge where it went from two lanes to one—no wonder it was replaced.

Today the Juniata Crossings Hotel remains between the old and new roads, trading as the Juniata Crossings Country Mercantile and selling Americana gifts. Traces of the old piers can be seen at the riverbank.

The road continues alongside the river, which can be seen to the left. At the Travelers Rest motel and restaurant, the original Lincoln Highway runs between the office and the motel rooms.

Ahead, U.S. Route 30 bypasses **Everett**. Exit to go through town on the original road, and you'll find a pleasant town. Check out the Everett Theater's Deco facade and the corner sign on Carolyn Court Motel.

The road west of town rejoins U.S. Route 30. The road was widened to four lanes in 2004, erasing some of the charm of the drive. As you climb a hill, you can see the just-bypassed road to the right, along with the original Lincoln Highway. The descent on the other side is near unrecognizable to those who have traveled it in years past; the four-lane highway now dominates the hill. At the bottom, the area called Mile Level is also being widened, spelling the end to more of the old roadscape east of Bedford.

As U.S. Route 30 passes beneath the turnpike, here the original Lincoln bent right and crossed the Raystown Branch of the Juniata River on an iron bridge and met a tollgate on the west end. The old bridge is long gone, and the Lincoln now crosses the Narrows Bridge, a curved, concrete-arch span built in 1934. This gap in the mountains, the Bedford Narrows, has drawn overland travelers for three centuries.

U.S. Route 30 bypasses **Bedford**, but the Lincoln Highway enters town on Pitt Street.

Some hotels serving early motorists were the Fort Bedford Inn, the Pennsylvania, and the Washington, but most famous was the Hoffman Hotel.

In the 1915 guide, LHA consul and hotelier Lee Hoffman proclaimed his Hoffman House and Garage "the best known garage in U.S." Later ads called it the most unusual hotel and garage in the world.

In *At Ease*, future president Dwight Eisenhower recalled that on July 9, 1919, the First Transcontinental Army Truck Convoy pulled into Bedford to an enthusiastic crowd of two thousand people. They had a band concert, street dancing, and the usual speeches. Eisenhower noted that since leaving Washington, D.C., the convoy had gone 165 miles in 29 hours on the road, for an average speed of 5²/₃ miles an hour. "Before we were through, however, there were times when the pace of our first three days would seem headlong and the four speeches at Bedford only a slight taste of the hot air ahead."

Bedford is a town of many fine old buildings. A few hotels remain that early Lincoln Highway travelers would recognize, even if

Juniata Crossing, west of Breezewood, was a nineteenth-century inn on the Chambersburg-to-Bedford Turnpike that became the Lincoln Highway.

today they serve different uses. At a bend on Pitt Street is Dunkle's Gulf, a beautiful Art Deco gas station, its walls different creamy hues of terra-cotta. Jack Dunkle still runs the station, which his father, Dick, opened in 1933.

On the west end, the Coffee Pot is a restoration success story. Opened in the 1920s as a café, it deteriorated over the decades and was moved in the winter of 2003–04 across the road

While J. R. Manning was filling up his 1929 Ford Model A, named Sonja, at Dunkle's Gulf in Bedford, a local woman pulled up in her Model A replica.

The Coffee Pot on the west edge of Bedford advertised Pittsburgh-based Alcoa's new "Wear-Ever" line of cookware. Lightweight, rust-resistant aluminum pots and pans would have appealed to tin-can tourists.

to the county fairgrounds. Under the guidance of the Lincoln Highway Heritage Corridor, the building is back to its original glory and is set to serve as a visitors center.

The U.S. Route 30 bypass rejoins the route, the old Lincoln Highway running through **Wolfsburg**. Ahead, two Indian paths once met at "the forks," the site of an Indian village. The old Glade Road/PA Route 31 branches left, the Lincoln Highway to the right. The 1762 Jean Bonnet Tavern sits in the fork.

At the top of Tull's Hill is Lincoln Motor Court, built in 1944, and the former Lincoln Hotel, built in 1926 on the foundation of an 1870 boardinghouse. The U-shaped motel is one of the few remaining cabin courts still serving travelers. Debbie and Bob Altizer have fixed up the place over the past two decades, and it's sought out by roadside fans. The old road can be seen to the east, and it's

The cabins are arranged in a U shape at Lincoln Motor Court, one of the few surviving tourist courts.

rumored that it even cut through what is now the court.

The road passes Shawnee Sleepy Hollow campground and Sleepy Hollow Tavern, built in 1775 along Forbes Road. Ahead in the woods are two parallel generations of Lincoln Highway, each with a small bridge; to see them, turn right at T496 and look left. As U.S. Route 30 descends into **Schellsburg**, the Lincoln Highway splits left and comes out behind the Shawnee Inn. You can walk back there and even discover a 1917 state-built bridge, but the road becomes a private driveway. Across the street from the tavern is the Shawnee Motel, 1950s accommodations that people rave about. It advertises "fresh mountain-air-dried bed linens."

Schellsburg, spread along the former turnpike road, is called a "stringtown." An 1818 marker is right past the motel, and two more are in the vicinity. Two 1920s garages also survive, Colvin's and May Brothers. West of town, a giant Pied Piper marks the entrance of the long-closed Storyland kiddie park. On the left, the Lincoln branches off and runs through a cemetery, built around the 1806 Union Church.

The Pied Piper is a remnant of Storyland, a fairy-tale park on the west edge of Schellsburg.

As you head downhill, the view to the distant ridge is stunning. On the right is the Lincoln Highway Farm, its name painted on a barn since 1918. Across the road is a string of tourist cabins.

Starting uphill again, don't be surprised if you see some buffalo. The Bison Corral features a gift shop full of Native American ephemera and bison meat.

The road becomes shaded, turns a tight bend, and climbs to an overlook. This was the site of the Lincoln Highway's best-known

The stand at Grand View had grown to a castle-themed hotel by the late 1920s.

attraction, but in October 2001, the S.S. Grand View Ship Hotel burned down.

The Ship Hotel was the brainchild of Herbert Paulson, a Dutch immigrant who left Holland in the 1910s. After various jobs, he built a stand just above Grand View Lookout in about 1923, calling it Grand View Park. A year later, he bought a small stand here at Grand View Lookout. He enlarged it, then built it into a four-story, castle-themed hotel hanging off the mountain. But he wasn't finished. "Captain" Paulson, nicknamed for his love of the sea, then enlarged the hotel into a steamship. Paulson's son said it took 63.5 tons of steel. A fifth floor on top added "first-class" rooms, and the roof was topped by smokestacks.

The grand opening of the S.S. Grand View Point Hotel (later Ship Hotel) was at noon on May 29, 1932, with music by a German band and flowers dropped on the deck from an airplane. Paulson lived there with his wife and three children. His granddaughter Clara Gardner has the distinction of being the only person ever born there—early in 1931, as the Ship Hotel was being completed. She recalled

that the budget-priced rooms on lower floors were called "second-class," while employees and some family on the next floor down joked that they lived in steerage.

The Ship Hotel kept a log of visitors. It was filled with celebrities of the day, among

them Clara Bow, Joan Crawford, Thomas Edison, Henry Ford, Greta Garbo, and Tom Mix. The ninth log, which ran from September 1936 to June 1938, had more than 102,000 names, including tourists from every state and seventy-two foreign countries.

It became an icon of the road, but only eight years later, the opening of the Pennsylvania Turnpike started its slow decline. Herbert died in a fall there in 1973, and five years later, the family sold the Ship Hotel to a couple who tried retheming it as Noah's Ark. That failed, as did other attempts, and it sat empty in recent years until a late night fire destroyed the entire building. Luckily, perhaps, the contents had been sold over the

MAIN DINING ROOM S.S. GRAND VIEW POINT HOTEL

The Ship Hotel's dining room comes alive in this detailed shot. Owner-builder Herbert Paulson faces the waitress at the leftmost table.

A rare Ship Hotel souvenir ashtray.

My cousins, from left, Edward, Joan, David, and Janice Butko visited the Ship Hotel in 1963.

years, leaving a Ship Hotel plate or anchor-backed chair to occasionally turn up at local antique shops.

In 2002, Clara Gardner visited the three houses her grandfather had built in Sittard, Holland. "I was so surprised to learn that my grandfather originally wanted to build the Ship Hotel in Holland but the government refused it. The people who told me this have lived in one of the 'Famous American Houses' ever since my grandfather sold them. They were so nice to me and invited me to come back. The houses are protected by the government and just so beautiful."

The Ship Hotel was not so lucky. Cars still regularly stop at the turn, many visitors recalling their visits to the steamboat in the mountains and its famous claim that one could "See 3 States and 7 Counties."

Bald Knob Summit tops out at 2,906 feet. From this point west is the Seven Mile Stretch, where you can see from one ridge to the next. Repeated measurings by me and many others, however, come up a bit short of seven miles.

Beatrice Massey wrote in *It Might Have Been Worse* (1920), that the road west of Bedford was "the best part of the Lincoln Highway," particularly this section:

> This was a stretch of seven and a half miles of tarvia [*sic*] road on the top ridge of the Allegheny Mountains, as smooth as marble, as straight as the bee flies, looking like a strip of satin ribbon as far as the eye could

This ledger page from August 7, 1936, has signatures from Canada and fourteen states: Maryland, Pennsylvania, New Jersey, Michigan, California, Connecticut, Missouri, Florida, Wisconsin, Ohio, Kentucky, New York, Indiana, and Illinois.

see. On both sides were deep ravines, well wooded, and green valley with abundant crops . . . as one of us remarked, "We may see more grand and rugged scenery later on, but we shall not see anything more beautiful than this"—and it proved true.

In the middle of the stretch is **Reels Corners** at PA Route 160, and farther on, **Buckstown**. Duppstadt's Country Store is a throwback to the general store, selling a little of everything, even locally made maple syrup. The old road bears left at Castagna's Restaurant (formerly Emerald Park); parts of this long stretch have closed in recent years as a result of strip mining. Signs at Lambertsville Road direct drivers off the route south to the Flight 93 Temporary Memorial, a reclaimed strip mine that was the site of the hijacked airplane crash on September 11, 2001. Locals interpret the site while visitors continue to leave flags, notes, and other mementos, which are regularly collected and preserved. Heading back, just before U.S. Route 30, Lambertsville Road crosses the original Lincoln Highway. You can drive west on the old road, past a long-shuttered nut farm on the right, with only a few walnut and chestnut trees remaining. The next rise was once home to Blue Bell Camp, so named because campers called the morning glory flowers here "blue bells." The old road eventually meets U.S. Route 30 at an auto wrecker.

The Lincoln Highway continues across U.S. 30 and winds down toward **Kantner**, but the bridge is gone, so the road ends at Stony Creek. You can backtrack to U.S. Route 30 and make the next right onto PA Route 403 North to rejoin the old road at Kantner. It continues west uphill into **Stoystown**. The Hite House, a popular stop for early motorists, has been renovated into apartments for seniors and added to the National Register of Historic Places. At the hilltop, where old and new roads rejoin, is the Kings and Queens, an old roadhouse decorated to look like a castle.

Just past the new U.S. Route 219 is a giant praying mantis at Second Time Around resell shop. A couple businesses at PA Route 601 make up **Ferrellton**. At PA Route 985, the crossroads of **Jennerstown**, "Our" Coal Miners' Café is named in honor of the Quecreek and other local miners who risk their lives every day. Across from it is the Tudor-style White Star Hotel, built in 1934 on the site of an earlier White Star. It recently was a bed and breakfast, but is again up for sale. Half a mile north is Green Gables restaurant and the adjacent Mountain Playhouse, which offers performances in a restored 1805 gristmill.

The town was named for Edward Jenner, originator of the vaccination process for smallpox. A settler lost two daughters to the infection around 1820, but the vaccine arrived in time to save his third daughter; in a show of gratitude, he named his landholdings for Jenner.

Past the intersection is a large neon sign at Turillo's Steak House. The town's best-known roadside oddity was the Zeppelin, a café with adjoining tourist camp built in 1926 next to what is now Jennerstown Auto Body. John Schmucker, born in 1910, recalled the Zep:

Travelers still recall the Zeppelin Tourist Camp, even though it left Jennerstown half a century ago; blimp-shaped buildings have that effect.

There was a counter with stools inside the Zeppelin, and a good meal cost 35 to 50 cents. . . . Six bus lines all stopped here, and every other person in town kept tourists because the Lincoln Highway was the number one road in the area, and the 219 crossroads [now PA Route 985] was an important New York–to–Maryland road. My brother Robert had Schmucker's Cabins. He had these chickens in coops, and he asked me if I could wash 'em up—clean 'em and fix 'em. So I hosed them out, and then we boarded up between them and put bathrooms in there, and we stone-cased most of it in. This was about 1934, and that became his motel cabins.

Schmucker said the turnpike's opening in 1940 strangled businesses, including the Zeppelin. About 1945, it was moved to Ohio, but it reportedly was demolished a few years ago.

Two stone pillars on the right have plaques announcing "Jenner Pines" and "Camping Park." Three tourist cabins and an office

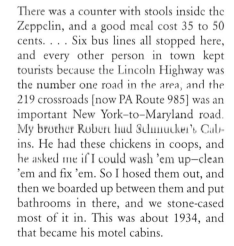

The Ship Hotel the day after it burned in October 2001.

FLAG ROCK. WASHINGTON PARK ON LINCOLN HIGHWAY ON LIGONIER MTS.

Flag Rock meant you were halfway up—or down—Laurel Mountain.

remain. The name reveals that this site dates from the early 1920s, when towns and individuals opened places for roadside campers. It was a short-lived era between when tourists camped by the roadside and when cabin camps were built.

At the hilltop past Jennerstown, U.S. Route 30 dips and stretches into the distance, but the Lincoln branches right. If taken, it makes one sharp turn—be careful, as loose gravel makes it slippery. A historical marker where the roads rejoin indicates where automaker Frederick Dusenberg was fatally injured in a 1932 accident.

At the top of Laurel Mountain, signs warn of the steep descent. It was here, Dwight Eisenhower later wrote, that the only truck was lost during the two-month, thirty-three-hundred-mile trip made by the First Transcontinental Army Truck Convoy. As Pete Davies described it in *American Road* (2002), a bolt of lightning struck behind a GM cargo truck, startling the driver and causing the truck to slide off the road. The crew all jumped to

safety, but "stunned and shaken, they watched their truck tumble down the hill."

In *Roaming American Highways* (1931), John T. Faris wrote of the two centuries of difficulties in traversing the final fold of the Allegheny Mountains: "The skill of drivers—now and then—is tested on the last of the great heights, Chestnut Ridge and Laurel Ridge."

Harriet White Fisher noted this ridge in *A Woman's World Tour in a Motor* (1911). Before heading across the globe, she ran a trial trip in spring 1909 that looped from Trenton through Washington, D.C., Pittsburgh, Cleveland, and the Catskills. She crossed the Allegheny Mountains, following what would become the Lincoln Highway, disappointed that the forests she'd hoped to see had fallen to sawmills, but glad that at least water remained: "We were able to find now and then on the mountain-side a bubbling spring, where we could rest and make our tea."

On the hill are the remains of Flag Rock, an early landmark topped with an American flag; it was blasted into smaller pieces when the road was widened.

As the descent bottoms out, the road passes through **Laughlintown**, another stringtown along the highway. A remnant from its past is the Compass Inn, a 1799 stagecoach stop.

Just a mile past Laughlintown, the original road branches right while U.S. Route 30 passes Ligonier Beach. Bathers at its 1926 opening parked on the old road, which is above the new one here, and descended a wooden stairway to the pool and nightclub.

The original road continues into **Ligonier**, where it is lined with old homes and businesses. The town square, with bandstand, is

known as a "diamond." The Breniser and Fort Ligonier hotels served early motorists. The latter, three times larger, had rates to match.

Just before Main Street merges with U.S. Route 30, a street marked Old Lincoln Highway continues parallel. There are three generations of Lincoln Highway here. The original is the northernmost of the three; a lone cabin from Shirey's Lake View Motel survives on it. In 1928, the two-way road was moved south to what now serves as U.S. Route 30's westbound lanes. Finally, a railbed was converted to U.S. Route 30 eastbound.

Farther on, the road runs between an old Sunoco and the former Ridgeway Inn. This is set to become the headquarters and visitors center for the Lincoln Highway Heritage Corridor. In the future, the site will include tourist cabins and the former Serro's Diner, as well as an archives and exhibits.

Idlewild Park began as a picnic park for the Ligonier Valley Railroad in 1878; it's considered to be the nation's third oldest amusement park. Thanks to the Lincoln Highway Heritage Corridor, it features a Lincoln Highway–themed antique auto ride.

The lanes head downhill into the Loyalhanna Gorge, where the east- and westbound lanes split to opposite sides of Loyalhanna Creek. The eastbound lanes, which were the original roadbed, still cross Long Bridge here, but the bridge is not the concrete Art Deco one that appears in postcards. Even earlier, an iron bridge crossed much closer to the water level. The westbound lanes were laid on the Ligonier Valley Railroad railbed when the line closed in 1952 and are much more level. About midpoint, there's a crossover to Sleepy Hollow, a 1940 roadhouse.

The gorge ends and the lanes rejoin, then the road heads uphill past the Hi Way Drive-In Theater. The original Lincoln Highway runs south of here through **Youngstown**; to reach the old road, turn left at PA Route 981, then left on Arnold Palmer Drive.

Back westbound, the Arnold Palmer Regional Airport is on the left (Palmer was born nearby). The airfield is built atop the old road.

The Lincoln again splits to the north. Sitting between old and new is Mountain View Inn. The original part of the hotel opened in 1924; it's been in the Booher family since 1940.

U.S. Route 30 bypasses **Greensburg**, founded in 1785 and named for Revolutionary War general Nathanael Greene, but the Lincoln Highway goes into town. In the 1924 LHA guide, the town's control point was the Lincoln Highway Drug Store.

In 1997, LHA members Margie and Wib Albright bought and planted a replica 1928 concrete Lincoln Highway marker at 505 East Pittsburgh Street. The road splits into east- and westbound lanes; the original route followed Pittsburgh Street. In 1937, it was made one-way eastbound and Otterman Street one-way westbound. The Lincoln then rejoins U.S. Route 30 and heads into congestion.

At **Adamsburg**, the original road branches right and continues into **Irwin**, where it becomes Pennsylvania Avenue. The business district lies to the north along perpendicular streets. Few midcentury businesses remain on U.S. Route 30; one of the best is the Penn-Irwin motel, with a neon sign above the office.

Pennsylvania Avenue climbs and rejoins U.S. Route 30, heading west. In the Blue Dell area, the cabins at Park's Motel are the main remnant of a thriving midcentury tourist bonanza in this area, which included a diner, two drive-in theaters, a swimming pool, and other tourist courts. In fact, the road through **East McKeesport** was lined with tourist homes. Today a road named Lincoln Way, which banks to the left, is a reminder of the repeated attempts of the city of McKeesport to route the highway through town. In January 1926, the LHA announced that it was even planning a bypass of Pittsburgh via McKeesport, Dravosburg, Castle Shannon, and Mount Lebanon.

The Lincoln Highway crosses PA Route 148, and near a hilltop, it branches right on Greensburg Pike and descends into **Turtle Creek**. It crosses a 1925 iron bridge, then winds around the former Westinghouse Electric plants in **East Pittsburgh**. By the 1920s, the works employed some twenty thousand people to produce everything from radio tubes to locomotives.

Sleepy Hollow Tavern, nestled in the Loyalhanna Gorge, has been remodeled, but is still serving travelers.

The Lincoln Highway in East McKeesport was lined with tourist homes such as the Rock Garden. Note the attempt to retouch the photo at left with white paint.

Mrs. Anna Kliment with a new 1929 Hupmobile at the family's garage on Ardmore Boulevard.

In *A Frenchwoman's Impressions of America* (1920), Comtesse Madeleine de Bryas wrote of visiting the plants in 1918 to raise awareness of World War I battles in Europe: "I spoke three consecutive mornings at the Westinghouse factories, encouraging the men to work harder if possible, and endeavoring to make them realize that their war work was as important as if they were fighting in the trenches."

The route was bypassed in 1932 with the opening of the George Westinghouse Bridge across the Turtle Creek Valley. It was then the world's largest reinforced concrete-arch bridge.

At Yost Boulevard in **Forest Hills** is a 1928 concrete Lincoln Highway marker, the last to be seen until Chester, West Virginia. Until a

Driving east across the Westinghouse Bridge.

few years ago, Kliment Bros. Garage was perhaps the longest-running Studebaker dealership. Even though the make had ceased in 1966, the garage carried on, servicing cars it had sold. It even still had a Studebaker for sale in the window—a cream-colored 1951 coupe bought new there and traded in. Pete Kliment had immigrated from Austria-Hungary and opened Kliment Garage in 1913, repairing horse-drawn wagons and a growing number of cars. He also sold gas and became a seller of Chalmers cars. But the brands he sold kept going out of business. Chalmers was taken over by Walter Chrysler, who shut it down but then launched his own cars. Kliment switched to Cleveland cars, but that brand was absorbed by Chandler. He then switched to Chandler, but that brand was absorbed by Hupmobile. So he switched again, but Hupmobile folded. About 1940, Kliment took on

Studebaker. His sons took over the garage in 1954 and ran it until late 2001.

As U.S. Route 30 splits away to follow the Parkway around Pittsburgh, the original route goes straight into **Wilkinsburg**; a wall on the right marks where the old cross-state William Penn Highway came in from that side. The triangle of land formed by the two is home to a copper and bronze statue of Abraham Lincoln, paid for in 1916 by schoolchildren who donated their dimes toward the $800 cost. The statue and six others were designed by Alfonso Pelzer and made by the W. H. Mullins Company of Salem, Ohio. Two were placed and remain along the Lincoln Highway—in Fremont, Nebraska, and Wooster, Ohio (see the Ohio chapter for more information).

Twice in recent years, Wilkinsburg's statue was broken off at the feet. The first time, a couple confessed ten months later that they'd stolen and buried it (they got "carried away after drinking beer," a newspaper reported). The thieves paid $10,000 to repair it in exchange for the charges being dropped. In 1992, strong winds blew it over, and it then waited for repairs at the municipal building until 2001, when it was restored at a cost of $23,000 and remounted, this time protected by a fence.

The Lincoln Highway merges with the William Penn Highway and follows Penn Avenue through Wilkinsburg, past the once glorious Penn Lincoln Hotel. The hotel that once offered lavish accommodations, and rented rooms to blacks when few other hotels would, is now a tattered apartment house. Boy Scout Bernard Queneau slept here July 9, 1928: "We travelled till midnight but lost our way in the suburbs of Pittsburgh. In Wilkinsburg we stopped after running out of gas there." The next day, "after a delicious night at the Penn-Lincoln hotel, we were escorted into Pittsburgh with a great band [and] ate at a banquet provided by the Portland Cement Co. who are on a safety plan."

Ahead, a diner for sale at 7619½ Penn Avenue was Scotty's, a stainless-steel National-brand diner built in 1939. There are very few such diners, as National became Fodero after only a few years. Charles Huwalt managed it for twenty-three years, then bought it in 1993. He and his wife revitalized the diner as Charlie's, but health reasons forced an early retirement, and one recent operator failed at trying to introduce a menu with organic foods.

Penn Avenue now becomes more residential. A century ago, this was "millionaire's row" for Pittsburgh's industrialists. Most notable today is Clayton, the home of Henry Clay Frick, operator of the coal mines and coke ovens that fed Andrew Carnegie's steel mills. The site includes an art museum plus a car and carriage museum that highlights locally used and made autos.

Starting in 1920, an alternate route was offered to the Lincoln Highway through East Liberty. This southern route turned left on Dallas Avenue, then took Wilkins Avenue, Beeler Street, and Forbes Avenue to Oakland, the cultural center of Pittsburgh and home to the University of Pittsburgh and Carnegie Institute of Technology (now Carnegie Mellon University). It then jogged onto the Boulevard of the Allies; its construction in 1922 offered a less-congested, high speed entry into Pittsburgh, inspiring this routing.

The original route continues on Penn Avenue past a marker shaped like a tree stump commemorating the 1758 Forbes Road. The route enters **East Liberty**, now dominated by Penn Circle, a 1960s attempt at urban renewal. The Lincoln turns left on Highland Avenue, then right onto Baum Boulevard. On the left is Motor Square Garden, opened in 1900 as the East Liberty Market House and now home to AAA.

On Baum, a historical marker for the first drive-in filling station notes where Gulf Oil opened a station on December 1, 1913. (There were earlier gas stations, but this was the first to be designed by an architect.) Baum Boulevard is lined with vestiges of "automobile row," when this was the early nexus of auto garages and dealers. In 1913, if not yet quite that, the area was already sprouting sales and service businesses. A 1910 atlas shows about half a dozen car-related busi-

nesses, including the auto club just a couple blocks east. Soon to follow was an Autocar sales, service, and truck assembly plant on the northwest corner of Liberty Avenue and Baum Boulevard; Pierpoint Motor Company on the northweast corner of Melwood Street; a Studebaker showroom at the southeast corner of Enfield Street; and Packard sales and service at the northwest corner of Enfield.

Most notable, and perhaps the business that clinched this as auto row, was a Ford assembly plant that opened in March 1915 on the corner of Baum and Morewood Avenue. It was one of two dozen assembly plants where Ford sent, via the Pennsylvania Railroad in the ravine, knocked-down Model Ts to be assembled and distributed regionally—up to one hundred cars a day. The plant also had a garage and showroom. The ghost of the "Ford Motor Company" script can still be seen along the roofline. Down the block is a garage with a wheel in relief above the door. One other attraction on Baum for roadside fans is Ritter's Diner, a 1976 Mediterranean-style Fodero-brand diner that replaced the original 1951 Ritter's across the street.

As Baum curves right onto Craig Street, amusement park enthusiasts will recognize the bend as the former main entrance to Pittsburgh's Luna Park. The park was out of business by 1909, though portions remained. By the 1920s, it had been replaced by auto sales and service ventures.

A block later, Craig Street merges into Bigelow Boulevard, built in 1900 as Grant Boulevard, an extension of Grant Street in Pittsburgh, to carry commuters to the eastern suburbs (though, as planner Frederick Law Olmsted noted in 1910, its sliding hillsides

BIGELOW BOULEVARD, LOOKING EAST, PITTSBURGH, PA.

Grant Boulevard (now Bigelow Boulevard) overlooks the Allegheny River and the Strip District, a long, flat strip of land that was filled with steel mills and factories when the Lincoln Highway came through. The famous description of Pittsburgh as "Hell with the lid off" was written by someone looking down on the Strip District.

and lack of proper width and overlooks made it a boulevard in name only). About 1920, it was renamed for the city's public works director who conceived it, Edward Bigelow. It was widened to four lanes in 1939.

Bigelow Boulevard overlooks the Allegheny River as it descends into **Pittsburgh**. Grant/Bigelow entered downtown and turned right onto Oliver Avenue; that intersection no longer exists, lost to a tangle of ramps. Drivers can exit onto 6th Avenue and proceed to Liberty Avenue (Oliver Avenue is parallel, but no longer meets Liberty). The major hotels for early motorists included the Hotel Fort Pitt, the Pittsburgher, the Roosevelt, and the William Penn, built by Henry Clay Frick to be the finest hotel in the country; it still operates, as the Omni William Penn, on Grant Street between 6th Avenue and Oliver Avenue.

If you are following the later Boulevard of the Allies route, its westbound entry into town is also blocked; curve right onto Crosstown Boulevard, then immediately exit onto 7th Avenue, and three blocks later turn left on Liberty Avenue.

By 1913, Pittsburgh's rivers were lined for miles with steel mills and related industries, making the region one of the world's leading workshops. In *A Frenchwoman's Impressions of America*, Comtesse Madeleine de Bryas described the town during her 1918 visit:

> We had gathered the curious impression from what some Americans had told us about Pittsburgh that it was an ugly city, very black and fearfully smoky. . . .
>
> One of the great attractions of Pittsburgh is to drive in the evening on the hill that dominates the city and get a view of "Hell with the lid off," as that place has been called. It certainly is one of the most remarkable impressions I have experienced, to see those many blast-furnaces belching forth flashes of fire that illuminate the whole city. . . .
>
> In the day time the town does not present the same artistic attraction, but it is splendid in its ugliness, it is, if I may use the word, the most colossal sight I have ever seen.

The Lincoln Highway followed Liberty Avenue a few blocks to Pittsburgh's Point, a triangle of land between the Allegheny and Monongahela Rivers where they meet to form the Ohio River. The Point has been the site of forts, an industrial and commercial area, and the locations of bridges heading west for Lincoln Highway travelers. The original route crossed the Manchester Bridge over the Allegheny River to Pittsburgh's North Side, or as the city now wants to call it, the North Shore. That bridge was replaced decades ago by the much larger Fort Duquesne Bridge.

The 1927 routing through West Virginia turned from the Boulevard of the Allies to cross the Point Bridge over the Monongahela River. That bridge is also gone; the wide, double-deck Fort Pitt Bridge has taken its place.

Pittsburgh to Ohio via Rochester, 1913

The route from Pittsburgh to Rochester followed the Ohio River for fourteen years, but the streets were congested, one town running into another. Their traffic laws changed without warning at each border, and ticketing was excessive. The 1924 LHA guide noted that a new route (now U.S. Route 30 through West Virginia) was being considered, but it was not yet improved. It had been marked by the Auto Club of Chester, West Virginia, but was not passable in wet weather, nor was it a state highway eligible for funding.

West of Rochester, a road continued along the Ohio River to Midland, but it was susceptible to flooding and was often muddy and so a ridgetop road was chosen; it was likewise dirt, but at least it dried faster. The 1915 guide predicted that it would soon be a beautiful drive, but improvements never came.

By 1924, the LHA could no longer abide by these bad roads and recommended that drivers use the eastern shore of the Ohio River via McKees Rocks to Rochester, and from there detour north through East Palestine and Salem to Canton, Ohio. That stretch was all brick and concrete, and it's surprising that the Lincoln Highway wasn't just changed to this route, but it never was.

In 1919, Beatrice Massey headed toward Youngstown, likely on this road, but as she wrote in her memoir, it was little better: "The roads were poor and the many detours were almost impassable—over high hills, on narrow sandy roads, winding like a letter S through the woods."

When the first Lincoln Highway drivers headed west from Pittsburgh, the Manchester Bridge was just being constructed. The earliest drivers may have crossed the Union Bridge, turning from Liberty onto Federal (now 6th) Street, crossed the Allegheny River, then turned left on Stockton to Western Avenue and met the official route a few blocks later. After the Manchester Bridge opened, it carried drivers over the river to Galveston Avenue; an old abutment remains by the river's edge. Galveston Avenue would have cut straight through Heinz Field, the new home of the Pittsburgh Steelers. On the far side of the stadium, traces of Galveston can be found climbing the hill into the campus of Community College, where it cuts through a parking lot.

Drivers now take the Fort Duquesne Bridge and exit to the stadium; a left at the bottom goes to the riverside abutment, a right goes to Ridge Avenue. Turn right on Ridge and meet Galveston a couple blocks later. The college parking lot is to the right. Turn left on Galveston to get back on the Lincoln Highway. Two blocks later, turn left on Western Avenue, and a few blocks later, with the West End Bridge straight ahead, turn right on Chateau Street. Exit at California Avenue; the original route is lost here, but follow the looping ramp to get on California and the Lincoln Highway. If you don't exit, you'll wind up on Ohio River Boulevard/PA Route 65, a 1930s bypass of the dense river towns.

California Avenue runs through various neighborhoods. It crosses Jack's Run Bridge over the Pittsburgh city line into **Bellevue**.

The 1925 span has pylons decorated with lions and topped with eagles, as well as a plaque dedicating it to the men and women of World War I. The road becomes Lincoln Avenue, though the name was in place before the Lincoln Highway came through. As you pass through numerous stops and lights, it becomes apparent why this section was deemed too congested by LHA officials.

Within a dozen blocks is **Avalon**, and the road becomes California Avenue again. On a downgrade where the road makes a wide curve to the right, the Lincoln Highway goes straight onto Brighton Road and into **Ben Avon**. The intersection has some yellow bricks, then the road descends into a small hollow. At the bottom curve, a tiny 1896 bridge with stone rails crosses over Spruce Run. In a 1910 study of Pittsburgh streets, noted planner Frederick Law Olmsted recommended that this little bridge be bypassed by a long viaduct, just as it later was. Ohio River Boulevard to the left now crosses the chasm. Brighton Road winds uphill to a stop sign at Ohio River Boulevard and Dickson Avenue. The route merged onto what is now Ohio River Boulevard, but the merge is now forbidden; drivers have to make a loop through residential streets to get back to it.

A few blocks later, the Lincoln Highway angles right on Brighton Road again. Upon entering **Emsworth**, the road changes to Beaver Avenue, then rejoins Ohio River Boulevard. Concrete pylons on each side of the road mark the boulevard; bas-relief scenes tell of earlier local transportation wonders.

The road drops down parallel to railroad tracks and the river at left. The Lincoln Highway originally crossed the tracks. Go straight

toward I-79. Follow signs for the small neighborhood of **Glenfield** and turn left across a tiny viaduct over the tracks; this curves down to the yellow-brick Dawson Avenue. It can be driven a bit each way; it's likely the longest stretch of yellow brick on the Lincoln Highway.

Back on Ohio River Boulevard, **Haysville** is to the left with part of the old road, then the route turns right and heads uphill into **Osborne** on Beaver Road. The name was changed to Lincoln Highway through the forthcoming boroughs, but here it was changed back. The road enters **Sewickley**, an early suburban retreat for Pittsburgh's elite, where many large Victorian homes remain. You pass through a small business district, then enter **Edgeworth**, where the road curves around a park on the left. Here the First Transcontinental Army Truck Convoy camped on July 11, 1919. The road was closed overnight while the trucks parked on it.

A small stone bridge over Little Sewickley Creek, dating to 1841, was widened in 1918 to handle the increased traffic. Into **Leetsdale**,

Looking southeast from an overpass to the yellow brick Lincoln Highway through Glenfield.

the road becomes Beaver Street. After a sharp, sloping S-curve, the road starts uphill over Big Sewickley Creek; until a few years ago, the road was brick and then crossed a masonry-stone bridge like the last one. This bridge dates to 1827, and was widened in 1919. Recent improvements include road paving and a chain-link fence atop the rails. This fate has befallen most local bridges, even small historic ones like this.

Beaver Road enters **Ambridge**, named for Andrew Carnegie's American Bridge Company, long closed but once the world's largest steel-fabricating plant. It passes through the business district and turns right on 14th Street, at the edge of Old Economy Village, the last home of the Harmony Society, a Christian community in which all members shared property equally. The group practiced adult baptism, pacifism, and celibacy. After founding two towns called Harmony, one to the north and the other in Indiana, the group settled here in 1824, establishing themselves as a manufacturing community noted particularly for their textiles. The group went in decline toward the end of the nineteenth century, and as the last of the celibates died off, the society was dissolved in 1905. Since 1921, the state has administered fourteen of the original structures as a historic site.

A few blocks later, the route turns left on Duss Avenue/PA Route 989 and passes through an area of light industry. A bronze tablet on a large rock marks the site of Logstown, one of the largest Indian settlements on the Ohio River in the eighteenth century. At **Legionville** are four markers commemorating the training camp of Gen. "Mad" Anthony Wayne on his expedition against Northwest Indians, which resulted in the Treaty of Greenville. About twenty-five hundred men in five hundred structures waited out the winter of 1792–93, and seventeen are buried here. Still, the site is eyed by developers.

The road becomes State Street as it enters **Baden**. It briefly merges onto Ohio River Boulevard, then branches past a field with the telltale layout of an "ozoner": For thirty-five years it was the ABC Drive-In Theater. Just past Northern Lights Shopping Center is **Conway**. The road again rejoins Ohio River Boulevard. On the left spreads the Norfolk Southern Conway Terminal, where train cars are sorted and trains assembled over almost four miles. Opened in 1880, it was rebuilt and automated in the 1950s. Today it is reportedly the country's largest push-button yard. Look for the hump that helps cars roll to the correct track.

The Lincoln branches off at **Freedom**, past the circa 1830 cut-stone Vicary house, built by sea captain William Vicary when the view to the river was not obstructed by concrete and rails. It follows 3rd Avenue for a few blocks, then merges back onto Ohio River Boulevard/PA Route 65. The original road jogged southwest, crossing a bridge over the railroad, and turned on Railroad Street (called Sycamore Street in the 1914 *Blue Book*, and indeed, a little piece of Sycamore survives). It runs between the railroad and the river through **East Rochester** to the **Rochester** borough line.

The Lincoln Highway turned right on New York Avenue at the Pennsylvania Depot and Speyerer Hotel (now Beaver Valley Bowl). The at-grade crossing is gone; a viaduct now takes traffic across the tracks. The Lincoln turns left on Brighton Avenue. If you're driving Ohio River Boulevard, this is accessed by taking the exit for Monaca/Zelienople and PA Route 18/PA Route 68. The road climbs through **Rochester**, which grew as a canal and railroad hub, then turns west over the Beaver River into the small town of **Bridgewater**. Riverside Park overlooks the Beaver River, just before it meets the Ohio. Bridge Street dead-ends, so follow signs for PA Route 68 West and enter the **Beaver** business district on 3rd Street. A marker notes the site of Fort Macintosh, the first U.S. military post north of the Ohio River, in 1778.

In 1913, a road headed due west from here, but because its location was so close to the river and its tributaries, LHA officials instead chose Tuscarawas Road, along a ridge to the north. This road had been part of the Great Path Indian trail that went to Tuscarawas (now Bolivar), Ohio. The Lincoln therefore turns right on Buffalo Street, then left on 4th to reach Tuscarawas. The road climbs the ridge and passes through **Esther** and **Ohioville**. A branch named Lisbon Road leads to that Ohio town, but LHA planners wanted to pass through East Liverpool first; it was the medium-size kind of town they often aimed for, one that offered amenities to early drivers.

From Tuscarawas Road, the Lincoln turned left at Smith's Ferry Road to descend toward the Ohio River. The circa 1895, stone-arch Upper Dry Run Bridge was recently reinforced. At the bottom of the hill, about fifteen miles from Beaver, you arrive at PA Route 68/Midland Road. The original route bears left and passes under the highway and railroad tracks, then turns right on Liberty Avenue and through **Glasgow**, formerly **Smith's Ferry**.

After a few blocks, a right turn and another underpass lead back to PA Route 68 (coming from the north is the other end of today's Tuscarawas Road, which is not the Lincoln Highway). Turn left on PA Route 68 and head west toward Ohio, where Midland Road becomes OH Route 39.

Three markers at the state line commemorate the "Point of Beginning" of the survey of the Western Lands as required under the Land Ordinance of 1785. This platting of lands to the north and east led to the rectangular section line boundaries of the Midwest; the Lincoln Highway was often forced to follow these by making numerous left and right turns.

Pittsburgh to Ohio via West Virginia, 1927

After fourteen years of turmoil and planning, the LHA changed the route west of Pittsburgh in December 1927. No longer would it traverse the business districts and industrial areas of the Ohio River towns. A rarely used road through Chester, West Virginia, became the official route.

The new Lincoln Highway left Pittsburgh by crossing the Point Bridge and heading through the city's West End neighborhood, where today you'll find Laverne's Diner on Main Street. This 1955 Silk City was originally the Blue Dell Diner on the Lincoln Highway east of Pittsburgh. The road follows PA Route 60 as it winds its way through **Crafton**. It then picks up Steuben Street and merges onto Steubenville Pike, still PA Route 60, where a number of older businesses can be found.

The road passes over the Penn-Lincoln Parkway West, which carries the U.S. Route 30

Looking east in Glasgow, a forgotten remnant of the Lincoln Highway near the Ohio line.

bypass around Pittsburgh. U.S. Route 22 and U.S. Route 30 leave the parkway to head west, but then the original Lincoln branches off at Steubenville Pike. Along this parallel road, the 1950s Fort Pitt Motel offers "Pocono Touch Rooms" with heart-shaped whirlpool baths as a way to compete with chain motels. Next door, the Fort Pitt Inn was built in the 1930s to resemble Pittsburgh's 1764 British fort.

The Lincoln Highway now turns northwest, rejoining U.S. Route 30. (U.S. Route 22 continues west toward Weirton, West Virginia.) A mile later, a small business district along the road marks **Imperial**, including a nice neon "Chuck's Liquor's" sign. Half a mile past that is a large canopy station, now closed but one of the few obvious roadside remnants along this route. There are also

some old motels, but these are harder to spot. Right across from the canopy station looks to be one. Up the road another half a mile, Davis Oil Sales once had a string of cabins; one remains in back, while up front you can still gas up.

Late in 2003, ground was broken on the Southern Beltway, yet another new toll road from the Pennsylvania Turnpike Commission. The first six-mile section, called the Findlay Connector, heads southwest from the Greater Pittsburgh Airport on PA Route 60 to U.S. Route 22 in Washington County. An interchange is being built where the road crosses U.S. Route 30. In 2004, trucks were rumbling and dust was flying just south of **Clinton**.

The Lincoln leaves Pennsylvania with only a few miles left to Chester, West Virginia.

Greetings from West Virginia

West Virginia can be called the "last Lincoln Highway state." It was added to the route at the close of 1927, when the highway west of Pittsburgh was moved to a more southerly route. The few miles through the state pass through Chester, which grew up in the shadow of East Liverpool, Ohio, across the Ohio River. Like that larger town, Chester's growth was fueled by the ceramics industry, but it also had a trolley park that drew visitors from afar. Still, most in-town shops had only served locals; come spring 1928, they were suddenly on the premier transcontinental route.

U.S. Route 30 now speeds through the northern tip of the state but bypasses downtown Chester. Lincoln Highway explorers can

	WEST VIRGINIA	U.S.
Population in 1910	1,221,119	92,228,496
Population in 2000	1,808,344	281,421,906
Persons per square mile in 2000	75.1	79.6
Approximate miles of Lincoln Highway	5	3,389

exit to see the town, the original bridge crossing, three 1928 concrete markers, and the famous giant Teapot.

The Short Road through Chester

The Lincoln Highway enters West Virginia on U.S. Route 30. After a couple small hills, WV Route 8 is to the left; roadside fans may want to detour on it to the Hilltop Drive-In Theater. The one-screener opened in 1950 and was closed from 1984 to 1989. The former projectionist along with his wife and daughter have operated it since. The Hilltop offers FM radio sound but still has some speakers in its five-hundred-car lot.

Back on U.S. Route 30, a fuzzy black-and-white postcard advertised the Snake Farm but left its location vague. According to Joe Ciccarelli, it was at the top of the hill just east of the former Terrace Lanes Bowling Alley, the site now occupied by a small frame ranch-style house:

> The Snake Farm was owned by A. G. Floyd, who also operated a dry cleaners on Carolina Avenue, just west of my grandparents' store. My father worked at the Snake Farm

in the 1930s. This was an early version of a tourist trap, featuring various reptiles and a pet bear. My father had a close call once when a box of rattlesnakes upset near him. He was rescued when A. G. corralled the snakes with a snake hook.

U.S. Route 30 descends toward **Chester**. The area was first called South Liverpool, or just South Side, reflecting its growth as an extension of the city across the river. The town reportedly was named by settler William Pusey for Chester County in eastern Pennsylvania, where he was from.

To follow the Lincoln Highway, exit U.S. Route 30 at Johnsonville Road, which curves right, then left. The descent into town was notorious for the danger here at Newell's Bend. As Roy Cashdollar wrote in *A History of Chester* (1985):

> Trucks would start down from the hilltop area and think they were down the worst part of the grade just before they got to the bend so would speed up a little. . . . After so many accidents the state hauled dirt and formed a banked curve. After this the trucks would either ride the bank out or go over it into the creek, of which many did.

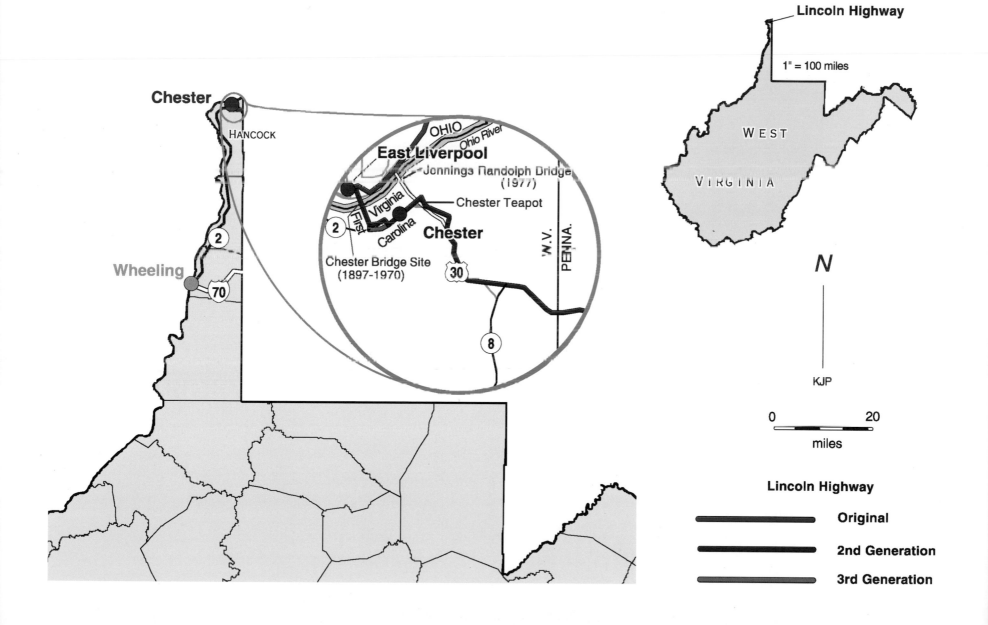

Chester

HANCOCK

OHIO

East Liverpool

Ohio River

Jennings Randolph Bridge
(1977)

Chester Teapot

Virginia

First

Carolina

Chester

2

Chester Bridge Site
(1897-1970)

W.V.

PENNA.

30

8

Wheeling

2

70

Lincoln Highway

1" = 100 miles

WEST

VIRGINIA

N

KJP

0   20

miles

Lincoln Highway

Original

2nd Generation

3rd Generation

Looking east to Pennsylvania at the West Virginia state line, 1926.

SPECIAL COLLECTIONS LIBRARY, UNIVERSITY OF MICHIGAN

RUSSELL REIN

Wright's Motor Court was one of many motels that lined the few short miles of the Lincoln Highway through West Virginia.

The approaches for the U.S. Route 30 bridge have since eliminated this final fatal hill, though some of the curves can still be found along the original road into town.

At a stop sign on the old road is the restored Teapot. The fourteen-foot-tall stand was built as a root beer barrel in Oakdale, Pennsylvania. In 1938, Wilford "Babe" Devon

brought it here and remade it as a teapot as a nod to the local ceramics industry. He put it at the other end of town near the corner of Carolina and First Street, right where traffic had to turn on the town's just-changed U.S. Route 30 alignment. The Teapot was one of more than two dozen pottery stands that lined the road to draw in tourists.

Hungry drivers could buy ice cream and other refreshments from the red-and-white teapot; behind it, Devon sold pottery and souvenirs. The Teapot itself was sold in 1947 and changed hands a few times afterward, slowly slipping into disrepair. In 1984, the local phone company bought the property and gave the Teapot to the city. It sat abandoned not far from today's location, then locals restored it and rededicated it in 1990. Unfortunately, it's no longer accessible except for photos taken over a fence. Chaney's Sunoco straight ahead sells Teapot postcards.

The Hill Top cabins, bar, picnic area, and restaurant were on a hilltop near the Pennsylvania–West Virginia state line.

BERNIE HEISEY

By E.E. Bandy, Trafford, Pa.

Close Cover Before Striking

HILL TOP INN   2 Mi. East of CHESTER, W.Va.   Route 30-2

East Liverpool lies north of Chester and the former Rock Springs Park, across the Ohio River.

The Teapot has been restored and moved to the U.S. Route 30 cloverleaf, where it overlooks both the Lincoln Highway and its replacement. The Jennings Randolph Bridge, behind the Teapot, carries Route 30 across the Ohio River.

Looking east on Carolina Avenue, with the Rock Springs Park coaster at upper right.

Turning left on Carolina Avenue, the Lincoln Highway passes under the ramps to the Jennings Randolph Bridge, which carries U.S. Route 30 across the river. The bridge is named for the senator who advocated national toll superhighways in the 1930s and later authored the Twenty-Sixth Amendment, setting the voting age at eighteen. On the left is a historical marker for Rock Springs Park, a popular amusement park that stood at the site from 1897 until the new bridge came through in the 1970s.

George Washington camped in this area on October 21, 1770, looking at lands along the Ohio River. Deeds reportedly show that he claimed and was granted the land that would become Rock Springs Park. Named for its natural springs, the land was developed in 1897 as a trolley park; the East Liverpool–Chester Bridge formally opened opened on May 26, 1897, providing trolley access from Ohio to the park. It was no coincidence that the bridge principals also owned the park, which had the usual assortment of rides and amusements such as a swimming pool, baseball diamond, and scenic railway.

The park was bought in 1900 by Charles Smith, who likewise became involved in the bridge company, the park, traction lines, and just about everything else in town. He owned the first car in town, a Stanley Steamer, and is said to have driven across the Ohio River when the water was low. Smith made Ripley's Believe It or Not in 1935 when his East Liverpool–Chester bridge was rebuilt without stopping traffic.

Looking west on Carolina Avenue in Chester.

Carolina Avenue Business Section
Chester, West Virginia

The Cyclone coaster was sold at auction for just $1. The park was cleared to make way for the approach ramps for the new bridge, and today the springs are under the southbound lanes of the four-lane bypass.

On Carolina Avenue at Third Street is a remodeled cottage-style gas station. The Lincoln Highway originally turned right here and crossed a bridge over a railroad cut, which has since been filled in. Near the corner of Third Street and Virginia Avenue is a concrete 1928 Lincoln Highway marker. Follow its arrow left on Virginia, and find another concrete marker at Second Street. The Lincoln Highway then turned right on First Street. The Standard Oil station at Virginia and First (now a repair shop) was said to have led the state in gasoline sales, and one year led the entire Sohio system.

Joe Ciccarelli grew up on Virginia Avenue, and his parents still live there in a house located between the two Lincoln Highway markers. "You knew you were a 'big kid' when you were tall enough and strong enough to vault yourself up and perch on top of one."

His grandfather had come to Chester to work in the American Sheet and Tin Plate Mill. "My grandparents owned a grocery store on Carolina Avenue from the teens through the early 1960s, and my father navigated the Lincoln Highway to Pittsburgh daily from the time he was fifteen to pick up wholesale items at the Strip on old Penn Avenue. That was before the Fort Pitt tunnel, of course; that forty-mile trip must have been something." Joe bought firecrackers at Babe Devon's Teapot and hung out a few blocks east of it at his grandparents' house, situated among the numerous tourist homes near the present

Rock Springs Park drew crowds by street-car from as far as Beaver, Pennsylvania, and Pittsburgh companies held picnics for their employees, who arrived via boat or rail. The dance pavilion, built in 1906, had a Japanese teahouse, six bowling alleys, a shooting gallery, a barbershop, and dancing on the second floor. Rules published in 1914 forbade wiggling the shoulders, shaking the hips, flouncing the elbows, or even hopping. An early park entrance was right into the dance hall from Carolina Avenue.

Attendance started falling after World War II and the park closed after Labor Day 1970.

One of three markers in Chester, this one on Third Street.

bridge. "I spent many hours across many summers with my cousins on the front porch swing watching the world pass by on Route 30."

The highway took Virginia Avenue for two blocks until 1938, when a small bridge was built to connect First Street to Carolina Avenue, taking the traffic off Virginia. The C&P Telephone building on Carolina just east of First was the original site of the Teapot.

From either Carolina Avenue or Virginia Avenue, turn right on First Street; at California Avenue is a third concrete marker beneath a green "Pughtown" sign, the former home of the town's famed physician Dr. David S. Pugh. First Street continues to the ramp of the East Liverpool–Chester Bridge, built in 1897 across the Ohio River. In 1938, the state acquired the bridge from Charles Smith; he

took in $360,000 in tolls during his last year of ownership. Ohio charged tolls until June 1951, when it was made free. The bridge closed in spring 1969 because of safety concerns. It has been removed, but the short approach ramp is now an overlook of the Ohio River valley, dedicated in Pugh's name.

Until the Jennings Randolph Bridge opened in November 1977, Lincoln Highway/U.S. Route 30 traffic had to continue west from Chester on WV Route 2 a couple miles and cross the Newell Bridge. Travelers today still may want to do so. Homer Laughlin China built the bridge in 1907 to carry workers from East Liverpool to its new West Virginia plant. The open-grate steel bridge remains and is fun—and rumbly—to cross. You can find Homer Laughlin China by con-

Looking across the Ohio River from Chester.

tinuing one mile west on WV Route 2. Most famous for its Art Deco Fiesta line, it's the country's largest pottery, having produced more than twenty-five thousand china patterns. A retail outlet is open daily, and the factory offers two tours each weekday. Farther south on WV Route 2 is the Mountaineer Racetrack and Gaming Resort.

If you cross the Ohio River on the Newell Bridge, you pay a toll at the north end. The road then bends onto 5th Street. It skips downtown East Liverpool, but you can easily pick up the Lincoln Highway on the west end of town by turning left on Jefferson Street.

Purists wishing to continue west on the Lincoln Highway through East Liverpool must backtrack to U.S. Route 30 and the Jennings Randolph Bridge. You'll pass the Teapot on the access ramp, but it's just barely visible to through traffic, even less so when the trees grow in.

Joe Ciccarelli's father (cowboy) and uncle (Indian) in about 1925, behind their parents' grocery on Carolina Avenue. It was located across from the site of the present-day McDonald's.

Greetings from
Ohio

After the hills and river routes of western Pennsylvania, the straight roads of Ohio were a welcome change to motorists. In his 1927 memoir, *The Family Flivvers to Frisco*, Frederic Van de Water wrote that after following detours through and west of Pittsburgh, "the broad, paved, clearly identified roads of Ohio were like the awakening from a bad dream. We found no better anywhere."

Not all the roads were flat, but they were far less mountainous and generally straighter. The bulk of the route followed a corridor across the state blazed decades earlier by the Pittsburgh, Fort Wayne, and Chicago Railroad. Its route was just what LHA planners wanted: a direct way to reach Chicago, the Midwest's

	OHIO	U.S.
Population in 1910	4,767,121	92,228,496
Population in 2000	11,353,140	281,421,906
Persons per square mile in 2000	277.3	79.6
Approximate miles of Lincoln Highway	239	3,389

leading metropolis. Towns had sprung up along the railroad, as did radiating roads. Some of these roads were linked together across Ohio as Main Market Route Number Three, connecting Lisbon, Canton, Mansfield, Marion, Lima, and Van Wert. Thus Lincoln Highway planners had a general path laid out for them across the state.

On September 29, 1913, just three weeks after the Proclamation Route was declared, a "correction" was announced for the seventy miles between Galion and Lima: Marion and Kenton were removed in favor of a path through Bucyrus and Upper Sandusky. The bypassed towns, still reveling in the glow of being chosen for the Lincoln Highway, were infuriated. The LHA hoped the new route would be upgraded to a more direct road, but for the time being, its five rail crossings and twenty-nine turns actually added three miles. State senator (and future president) Warren G. Harding pleaded the case for his hometown of Marion but then conceded the LHA's case.

The correction route was straightened in June 1919 in anticipation of the First Transcontinental Army Truck Convoy. The zigzag

course through Dunkirk and Lima was bypassed by a straighter route through Williamstown, Beaverdam, and Cairo. Although it certainly had fewer turns, it was still in poor shape; five years later, the 1924 LHA guide warned that part of it was the worst section between New York and Chicago. The same guide had a twelve-page advertising section sponsored by Lima in an effort to lure back traffic. Two more realignments were made on each side of Bucyrus. One removed Galion in favor of Crestline and Leesville; the other bypassed Nevada in favor of Oceola.

The removal of Galion, late in 1920, inspired the town's boosters to found the Harding Highway along the spurned road in honor of the senator. The headquarters was eventually moved to Marion. In March 1921, Harding became the first president to ride to his inauguration in an automobile, but he would die suddenly in San Francisco two years later during a cross-country tour. Later the two roads were designated U.S. Route 30 North and U.S. Route 30 South. In 1973, the northern route became U.S. Route 30, and the original southern route became OH Route 309.

Clay deposits in eastern Ohio account for the many brick-paved sections and brick Lincoln Highway pillars, both restored and new. The Ohio Lincoln Highway Heritage Corridor was established several years ago, and in December 2003, it was designated a state scenic byway. Led by president Larry Webb, the renamed Lincoln Highway Historic Byway is now eligible for mapping, promotion, signage, and beautification. Best of all, this lends credibility to the preservation of old alignments and roadside attractions.

Those wanting to follow every segment and learn the reasons behind the many route changes will want Michael Buettner's amazingly detailed *A History and Road Guide of the Lincoln Highway in Ohio*. It includes narrative, maps, and odometer charts. There have been five hard-copy editions, the last now available online for free.

Through the Pottery City

The Lincoln Highway originally entered the state from Pennsylvania along the Ohio River. After passing the Point of Beginning markers, the old road is OH Route 39. It enters the village of East End on Harvey Street, then turns right on Elizabeth Street around Hall China Company. Founded in 1903, Hall is the largest maker of specialty chinaware, best known for a glazing process that protects against chipping and crazing. The Hall Closet retail store sells seconds and one-of-a-kind food-service products at a discount. The company is one of the few survivors of the region's once-thriving ceramics industry, which produced everything from bricks to pottery to porcelain insulators.

The route turns west on Pennsylvania Avenue and heads to **East Liverpool**. OH

Laying brick four miles west of the Pennsylvania state line, near East Liverpool.

Route 39 bypasses downtown. The Jennings Randolph Bridge to the left brings U.S. Route 30 across the river from Chester, West Virginia. If you are on U.S. Route 30, exit onto Broad. At 5th Street, you rejoin the Lincoln Highway. At this intersection is a relocated 1928 concrete marker in front of the old post office, now the Museum of Ceramics, which documents the area's history. The rich deposits of clay spawned more than two hundred potteries; East Liverpool was originally named for the English pottery-producing city, the East being added later.

At Riverview Cemetery, north on St. Clair Avenue, is the grave of LHA field secretary Henry Ostermann, killed in an accident while driving the Lincoln Highway west of Tama, Iowa. This was his wife's hometown.

Looking east above Hall China toward Pennsylvania. Westbound Lincoln Highway travelers come toward the foreground of this photo, then turn north (a right turn for the driver but toward the viewer's left) around the factory.

On July 12, 1928, Boy Scout Bernard Queneau wrote of East Liverpool, "We made a demonstration there, then another at the Aramic theater and another at the American. Here we went into West Virginia and saw the largest pottery in the world."

The Lincoln Highway took Fifth Street west a few blocks, then turned north on Jefferson. The road bends left and descends, passing connected garages that appear in Drake

These markers at the state border commemorate the Point of Beginning, from which land surveys west of here began.

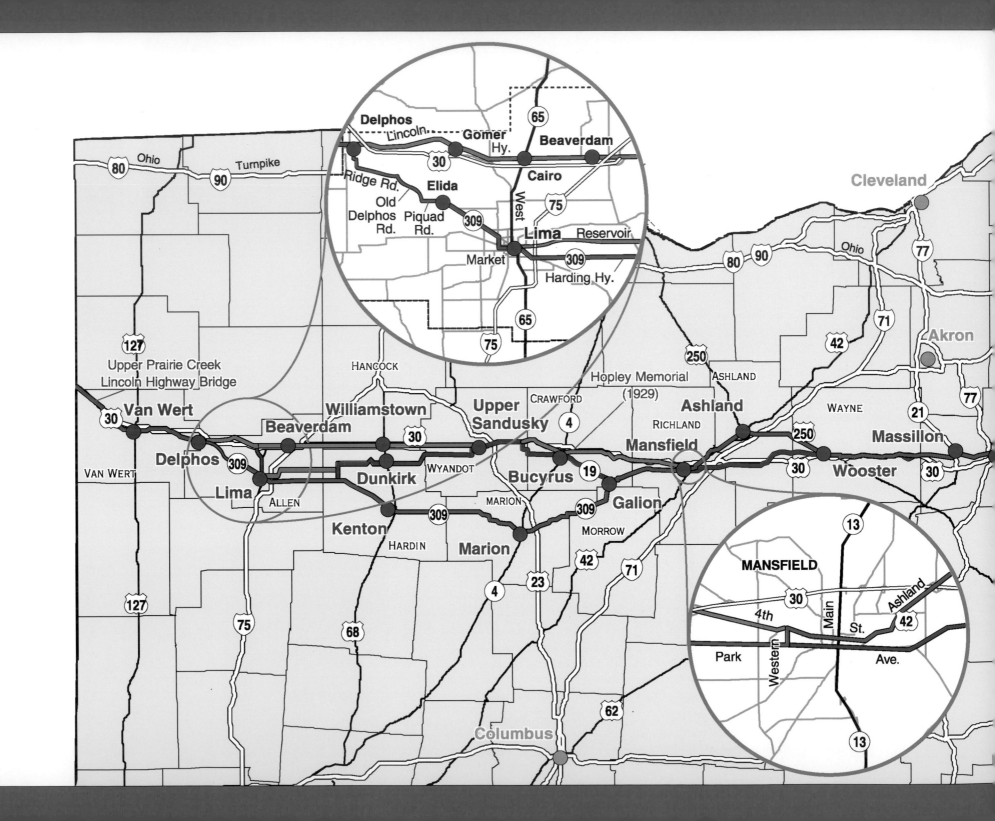

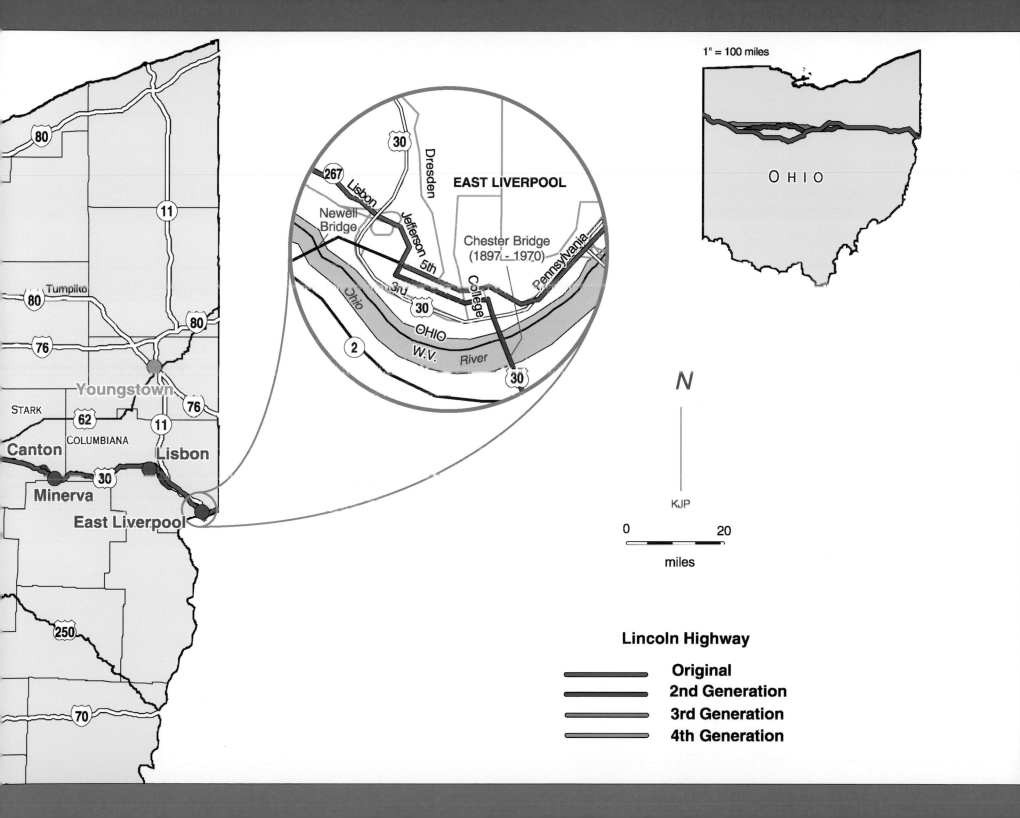

1" = 100 miles

OHIO

80

11

80

Tumpike

80

80

76

76

STARK

62

11

COLUMBIANA

Canton

Lisbon

Minerva

East Liverpool

250

70

EAST LIVERPOOL

30

267

Lisbon

Dresden

Newell
Bridge

Jefferson

5th

Chester Bridge
(1897 - 1970)

College

Pennsylvania

3rd

30

OHIO

2

W.V.

River

OHIO

30

N

KJP

0   20

miles

Lincoln Highway

Original
2nd Generation
3rd Generation
4th Generation

Looking east from Lisbon's square, past a new brick monument. The Steel Trolley Diner is two blocks in the distance.

Hokanson's Lincoln Highway book, to merge onto 8th Street. This passes under U.S. Route 30 and turns right to climb out of town on Lisbon Street/OH Route 267.

After 1927, the new route through West Virginia crossed the river onto College Street, then turned left on 3rd Street and continued to Jefferson to rejoin the original route.

Note: If you take the toll Newell Bridge across the Ohio River, it exits onto 5th Street; turn left on Jefferson Street to pick up the Lincoln Highway.

While the Lincoln climbs Lisbon Street, named for its destination sixteen miles away, U.S. Route 30 heads north through Califor-

In this ad from the LHA *Road Guide*, 3rd ed. (1918), the Standard Garage in East Liverpool made sure ladies were welcome.

nia Hollow, the original two-lane road now itself bypassed by a four-lane. A couple favorite stops on the old road were Hoge's restaurant, still going strong, and the Pine Breeze, a small restaurant that sold only ice cream, apple pie, and chicken. The chickens were raised on-site.

The original route passes through **Glenmoor**; the later route then dipped south under today's U.S. Route 30 and proceeded to **West Point**. The original alignment kept north of U.S. Route 30, though it can't be entirely followed, as a bridge is out. The Lincoln then followed Rollercoaster Road, aptly named for the heartstopping up-and-down terrain. The route was soon moved to Stookesberry Road; Lincoln Highway researchers have determined that one of Ohio's two Seedling Miles was along this three-mile segment. (The state's other is two hundred miles west near the Indiana border.)

Like East Liverpool, **Lisbon** had enough clay deposits to make it a ceramics producer early in the twentieth century. Today Lincoln Way leads through a charming town, perhaps

the only one with a vintage factory-built diner at each end. To the east, Earl and Jacki's Steel Trolley Diner is a 1956 O'Mahony, one of the last made by that company. It spent its first years in nearby Salem but was moved here in 1979. On the west end of town, the mid-1930s Crosser Diner, made by Sterling, is even more rare. At the center of Lisbon is a town square where a new Lincoln Highway pillar was erected in 2003.

A worthwhile side trip is thirty-five miles north, to the National Packard Museum in Warren, Ohio. One of the company's first cars, a 1903 Model F nicknamed "Old Pacific," was caught up in the "race" that year to be the first to cross the country. It is on display at the museum, along with Henry Joy's 1916 Twin Six touring car.

The highway west of Lisbon makes a sudden climb, then levels into a pleasing, rural landscape. Barns advertise Mail Pouch and Kentucky Club Pipe Tobacco.

At **Hanoverton**, a block north of the Lincoln Highway on Plymouth Street is the restored Spread Eagle Tavern, offering both food and lodging. The shaded street looks unchanged since the tavern was built in 1837.

A block later, at First Street/OH Route 9, another brick Lincoln Highway pillar was erected in 2000, a replica of the kind that still dot the route through Ohio. Along with the ceramic Lincoln Highway logo, it has a plaque for the Mansion House Hotel, on this site from 1844 until it burned in 1918. Before the current U.S. Route 30 was built, the Lincoln turned south here, then west; look for the short segments to the left.

The opening of the Sandy and Beaver Creek Canal in 1848 brought activity to town, at least until it closed four years later. It included the country's longest canal tunnel. West of town, the canal can be seen running along the north side of the Lincoln Highway.

The road dips southwest, then makes a ninety-degree right turn at **Kensington**. Just east of **Minerva** was the Star Motel, still there but now renting apartments. In the vicinity was Old Homestead, which offered rooms and log-timbered cabins along with meals. A few cabins also remain from the Green Gables Tourist Court on East Lincoln Way.

Minerva, named for a niece of the town's founder, was another canal town. Just east of the main intersection is a concrete Lincoln Highway marker, recently located and replanted. On the other corner of Market Street is a small canopy gas station that served as the LHA Control Point. It's been converted to the Coffee Station. Restored pumps and signs decorate the outside walls.

Main Market Route Number Three diverted north from town (via Market Street) on its way to East Canton, so it was not followed by the LHA, which wanted a more direct

route. The highway heads west following U.S. Route 30. Just west, Mezzaluna's Italian Grill, in a turn-of-the-century home, advertises, "The best food on the Lincoln Highway!"

West of town are a number of brick segments, more in one area than anywhere else along the highway today. Starting three miles west of town, Baywood Street to Robertsville is a 2.4-mile stretch of brick, the longest on the highway. It was built in the 1920s and bypassed about a decade later. Originally sixteen feet wide, it was extended two more feet by pulling the bricks apart and filling the gaps with pebble sand. This stretch tops a rise at 1,290 feet and also retains some of its concrete post-and-cable guardrails.

At **Robertsville**, the Grange hall has a stage backdrop with a vintage mural depicting the Lincoln Highway through town. West of town are three bypassed segments marked Cindell Street, one of them brick.

East Canton was originally Osnaburg, which is how it appears in four of the five LHA guides. The Lincoln turns right, then left onto West Nassau Street, rejoining Main Market Route Number Three. A 1928 concrete marker greets you on the south side, and a building to the north sports a new LHA Control Station sign. At 800 U.S. Route 30/West Nassau, Nicole's is fashioned after a 1950s restaurant, with chrome stools, booths, and a wide selection of ice cream. It also sells various Lincoln Highway souvenirs.

Just before Belden Avenue is the Top-O-The-Mark, the only motel incorporating Lustron-brand enameled steel panels. Lustron was a postwar manufacturer of prefab houses made entirely of steel. The original owner of the motel got materials at the Lustron foreclo-

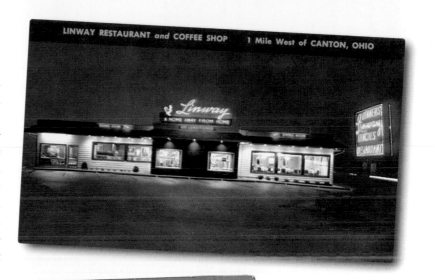

The Linway—a great contraction of "Lincoln Way"—specialized in pastries.

Lincoln Way Garage calendar, Minerva.

The Coffee Station in a converted service station in Minerva.

sure auction in 1950. If you wish to bypass Canton and Massillon, you can turn left at Belden to take the U.S. Route 30 bypass.

Canton was once a major processor of steel, but is perhaps best known as home to the Pro Football Hall of Fame: The NFL was founded here in 1920. On the east edge of downtown is the Landmark Inn, the town's oldest structure and once a thriving hotel and restaurant. It went from stagecoach stop in 1883 to Lutheran seminary to bank during Lincoln Highway days, then to a brothel and finally a boxing arena. It was abandoned in the 1980s, but stabilization and renovation started in 2004, which included removing the stucco exterior. Across on the south side of the road is a new public transit hub.

A few blocks south on Market Avenue is the Canton Classic Car Museum, housed in a former car dealership. In the 1920s, its repair shop stayed open twenty-four hours a day, seven days a week.

To follow the LHA's 1923–27 detour to Pittsburgh, which avoided Tuscarawas Road between East Liverpool and Rochester, turn north on McKinley Avenue, right on 12th

This brick stretch of Baywood Street lies between Minerva and Robertsville, just east of Canton.

Street Northeast, then head out Mahoning Road toward Alliance. The 1927 opening of the Lincoln Highway/U.S. Route 30 through Chester, West Virginia, made the detour unnecessary.

Also to the north in Akron is Stan Hywet, the sixty-five-room home of Frank Seiberling, president and cofounder of Goodyear Tire and Rubber. The Tudor Revival manor is surrounded by seventy acres of lawns, gardens, and a private stream. Seiberling also served as president of the Lincoln Highway Association; he made the first big contribution at Carl Fisher's September 1912 meeting, pledging more than $300,000 to the project. Akron was once the world's rubber-manufacturing capital and was also home to B. F. Goodrich and Firestone.

At 4164 West Tuscarawas Street is a 1958 Kullman-brand diner that has gone through a number of owners in recent years. In 2004, it reopened as the Cité Diner. Next door is the Towne Manor Motel, dating to the same era. Just past and across the street is the yellow-frame Canton–Lincoln Highway Station, for an excursion train that runs to Akron.

The Lincoln Highway between Canton and Massillon is congested; these were and still are the first- and third-largest cities along the Ohio route. Tuscarawas Street becomes Lincoln Way, and a number of Lincoln-named businesses remain amid the growing sprawl. Unfortunately, a recent victim was the Lincoln Motel, 4012 Lincoln Way East. The main house survives—for now—but the knotty pine-paneled, 1940s-style motel rooms to each side were destroyed to accommodate a car dealership. Just past it, you'll find the Lincoln Way Barber Shop and the Chase Motel, easy to miss along the strip, but its brick cottages look much like they did in old postcards. Two Twistee Treat stands are each shaped like a giant ice cream cone.

Milton Stoddard recalls that his father owned the Sunset Motel on Lincoln Way East in about 1960. "It was yellow and white, with a big white house in front and with the motel in the back. Across the street was a Howard Johnson." That's all he remembers, and he is searching for more information.

In **Massillon**, the Lincoln Theater dazzles on the north side of Lincoln Way East/OH

This 1958 diner has gone through numerous owners in recent years but hangs on next to a motel from the same era.

Route 172. Across from it (facing First Street) is the equally impressive Massillon Museum. The 1931 Art Deco beauty was built as Gensemer Brothers Dry Goods Store, later Stark Dry Goods and also known as the Giltz Building. Since 1996, it's housed a museum of art and history, with more than fifty thousand photographs and fifty thousand artifacts. A concrete Lincoln Highway marker has been relocated to the street corner, just outside the museum's Lincoln Highway Café.

As the road heads west from downtown, the Four Chaplains Memorial Viaduct carries traffic uphill across OH Route 21, railroad tracks, and the Tuscarawas River. The Lincoln Highway rolls westward through more fields and farms. You'll find four 1928 concrete markers: one in **Dalton**, one in a yard west of town, another west of Kidron Road in **McQuaid**, and yet another in a rock garden at **Riceland**. According to Buettner's Ohio guidebook, in the early 1950s, Dalton was the state's first town to receive a U.S. Route 30 bypass. And just south in Kidron is Lehman's hardware and kitchen appliances store, known to restorationists and history buffs for carrying thousands of products more in common use a century ago.

At 3421 Lincoln Way East is the Lost in the '50s Drive-in Restaurant. Approaching **Wooster**, U.S. Route 30 breaks off to bypass town; the Lincoln Highway continues downtown on Pittsburgh Avenue. The road crosses the 1920s Apple Creek Bridge; the original crossing would have connected to Sylvan Drive. A left turn takes you to a remnant of ten-foot-wide brick road with concrete curbs that ends at the creek.

The highway follows Pittsburgh to Liberty Street and into the pleasant downtown. Wooster was named for Revolutionary War general David Wooster and is known today for the College of Wooster. One of the famed Mullins-company statues of Lincoln can be found on the west porch of the Andrews Library at the college. It was made by the W. H. Mullins Company of Salem, Ohio, and was a gift from Wooster alumnus James Mullins. The statue is one of six based on a plaster sculpture by John Segesman, the Mullins Company chief sculptor, and was patterned after an earlier statue of Lincoln created by Alfonso Pelzer

for the Mullins Company in 1896. Six Segesman models were made between 1915 and 1921. Three of them were placed along the Lincoln Highway in Wilkinsburg, Pennsylvania; Fremont, Nebraska; and Wooster. Of the others, two went to Detroit (Packard and Lincoln/Mercury headquarters) and one was sent to the Old Soldiers' Home in Boise, Idaho. The Wooster statue, installed in 1915, was moved a number of times until pranksters severely damaged it. Its pieces were stored beneath the school's stadium in 1986. In the late 1990s, the college asked 1970 graduate J Stewart Simonds, a blacksmith, to restore it, and in June 1999, Lincoln was rededicated.

The marquee has been restored at the Lincoln Theater in Massillon.

It looks like the owner of the Parkette went into business by building a string of cabins next to the family home.

The town's Gerstenslager company made five different models of the Oscar Meyer Weinermobile in the early 1950s, using a Dodge chassis. A 1952 model is displayed at the Henry Ford Museum in Dearborn, Michigan. The carriage maker settled here in 1907, switched to van bodies and special truck bodies such as bookmobiles, expanded to vehicle parts, and remains the county's leading employer after Rubbermaid.

Boyd's Drug Store on the square is an old-fashioned pharmacy. Heading west, the road follows OH Route 302/Liberty Street. Follow OH Route 302 onto Old Lincoln Way. Two miles west, you leave OH Route 302 but stay on Lincoln Way. Carefully cross four-lane U.S. Route 250. After two more miles, at **Jefferson** is an intersection with Jefferson Road. The motel on the northwest corner is the site of the old Log Cabin Tourist Camp, whose cabins were named for U.S. presidents. Here the original Lincoln Highway turned right; the 1928 route continued straight.

Both a 1928 concrete post, tilting badly, and a pole sign marked the route in Dalton.

Turning north on Jefferson, the Lincoln Highway meets U.S. Route 250 and generally follows that to **New Pittsburg** and **Rowsburg**. West of town is a monument marking the site of the Studebaker family residence between their moves from Pennsylvania to South Bend, Indiana, where they founded the automobile firm by their name. Entering **Ashland**, the route follows Main Street/OH Route 96. New for 1915 was the Lincoln Inn, offering thirty rooms from 50¢ to $1.25.

Once in Ashland, turn left on U.S. Route 42/Claremont Avenue. The 1918 LHA guide offered an alternate route from Ashland to Mansfield via Olivesburg while the original dirt Lincoln Highway was improved. This road, now OH Route 96 west, was taken by the First Transcontinental Army Truck Convoy in 1919.

U.S. Route 42 continues south through **Five Points**. Just to the south, the old road breaks away to the right and includes a couple brick sections. Back on U.S. Route 42, it passes below U.S. Route 30 and heads into Mansfield on Ashland Road, then Park Avenue.

The Ashland route was bypassed early in 1928, half a year before the Lincoln Highway was marked with concrete posts. At Jefferson, the 1928 alignment continues straight west to **Reedsburg** on Old Lincoln Way/CR 30-A, passes through **Jeromesville**, then crosses U.S. Route 30 and heads to **Hayesville**. On the southeast corner of the main intersection is an 1886 opera house; its interior is mostly original, and it still operates as a theater. At **Mifflin**, a 1928 concrete marker greets Lincoln Highway followers.

The route becomes OH Route 430; after crossing over I-71, it also becomes Park Avenue. At 1182 Park Avenue East, a 1950s Stewart's Root Beer Stand is one of a chain

that began in Mansfield in 1924. The town also is the founding home of Isaly's dairy, creators of the Klondike ice cream bar.

The road heads into **Mansfield** and rejoins the original route at Ashland Road/U.S. Route 42. Park Avenue goes through Central Park, the town's square, which has a fountain, a memorial to President Lincoln, and a reproduced 1928 concrete post.

Two blocks north of the park is the Carousel District, which includes not only an amazing merry-go-round, but also Coney Island Hot Dogs, Main Street Books, and other thriving businesses. At its center, at the corner of 4th Street and Main Street, Richland Carrousel Park opened in 1991 with the first new, hand-carved carousel to be built and operated in the United States since the 1930s. Fifty-two animals and two chariots were carved and painted in the style of the revered Dentzel Company by the town's Carrousel Works. Its scenery panels depict the town's past and present attractions.

The Proclamation Route of the Lincoln Highway routed the road west from Mansfield through Galion, Marion (once famed as the world's steam shovel capital and home of twenty-ninth president, Warren G. Harding), and Kenton to Lima. A "correction" three weeks later bypassed Marion and Kenton in favor of Bucyrus and Upper Sandusky. Buettner's Ohio guide has an advertisement published by Marion interests, which reads, "Especially is the Lincoln Highway, between Lima and Galion, regarded as a huge joke among tourists, who prefer the shorter boulevard way, the Marion Way, to a crooked lane thru swampland." Today the three-week Marion routing is usually disregarded, but it *was*

The Log Cabin Tourist Camp, west of Wooster, featured accommodations named for U.S. presidents. A motel replaced the cabins, but the main building, a gas station, survives as a nightclub.

part of the Lincoln Highway, if briefly; it is mapped here but not followed in the text.

Mansfield to Delphos

From 1913 to 1920, the Lincoln Highway west of Mansfield followed today's OH Route 309/Park Avenue southwest. Just west of **Ontario** at 4018 Park Avenue West/OH Route 309, on the northwest corner, is the Sunset Drive-In Theater, which opened during World War II. It shows double features nightly in summer, weekends in spring and fall, with room for six hundred cars—about half still with working speakers.

OH Route 309/Harding Way enters **Galion**, a small city that grew on railroad repair shops, then telephone and road-building equipment. A Lincoln Way Garage west of the square was the LHA control point. The J. C. Penney Building was renovated by Craig Harmon into the Lincoln Highway National Museum and Archives, but it closed after a few years. In 2004, a replica 1928 concrete

post was dedicated across the street, although this route was bypassed in 1920.

The Lincoln heads west on OH Route 19/Harding Way to **Bucyrus** (Bu-SI-rus). It

Past the barbershop at the crossroads town of Hayesville is an old hardware store and the Hayesville Opera House. This day it was showing a silent Charlie Chaplin film for free.

Park Lanes on Park Avenue West in Mansfield.

A 1960 Chevy at the Galion Theater.

joins Hopley Street, which merges onto South Walnut for half a block; the gas station at this corner was the site of the home of state consul John Hopley. His addess was 1 Lincoln Way, renamed Hopley Avenue when the route changed in 1920. At 119 South Walnut is the D. Picking Company, the last hand-hammered copper kettle factory in the United States. The town was a center of kettlemaking; this business has been in the same building since 1874 and is now considered a working museum. Bucyrus also calls itself the Bratwurst Capital of America and holds an annual bratwurst festival every August.

Follow Walnut for half a block, turn left on Charles Street, then enter town from the south on Sandusky Avenue. Three blocks later you reach Washington Square.

The Sunset Drive-In Theater on OH Route 309 at OH Route 314, just west of Ontario.

Back at Mansfield, in 1920, the new road to Bucyrus left town via Fourth Street, then followed U.S. Route 30. *America's Fascinating Highways* (1941), listed Mancrest Park Lodge (named for the two closest towns) five miles west on U.S. Route 30, with twelve cabins at $1.50 each.

Crestline was a railroad town named for its location near the state's watershed. On Main Street, a pair of brick monuments flanking Clink Boulevard honor LHA local consul J. F. McMahon and LHA secretary and vice president Austin Bement. Housing developer C. A. Stephen built them independent of the other local markers, but they look similar. Dedicated in 1922, both were restored in 1993 by the Mid-Ohio Lincoln Highway League.

The old highway branches south to **Leesville**. Check out J&M Trading Post, built in 1829. It was the town's first general store and is now an antique shop listed in the National Register of Historic Places.

Crawford and Wyandot Counties built a number of brick pillars along the Lincoln Highway to mark the route and honor local

efforts. Each had a ceramic Lincoln Highway logo embedded. Of perhaps twenty, only two remain (plus two contemporary look-alikes). The first is two and a half miles east of Bucyrus at Stewart Cemetery and was dedicated to LHA county consul E. J. Songer. It was originally set in 1918 along the Galion alignment,

This brick pillar honoring LHA director Austin Bement is on the southwest corner of Main Street at Clink Boulevard, half a mile west from the center of Crestline.

ceramic Lincoln Highway logos were embedded in the abutments.

Mansfield Street continues to the county courthouse and Washington Square. The *Great American Crossroads* mural, painted by Eric Grohe in 1999, depicts Bucyrus Square in 1917 and includes two Lincoln Highway logos.

The Lincoln Highway left town via Mansfield Street from 1913 to 1928. A few blocks west is a tune-up shop in a cottage-style gas station. The route west of Bucyrus, pieced together from news clipping by researchers like Mike Buettner, went through **Nevada** (nuh-VAY-duh). It's not obvious today—there's no straight line from Bucyrus through Nevada—but the route made a number of ninety-degree turns. In 1921, this was bypassed by a direct road through **Oceola**, named for the Seminole Indian chief. The road is called Lincoln Highway and becomes concurrent with U.S. Route 30 west of Bucyrus. In 2001, a replica marker was erected at the town's main intersection. A van had destroyed the original in 1993; a plaque was added to the new one honoring onetime LHA president Frank Seiberling. A mile east of Oceola is Ohio's other original brick pillar, though this one does not have a dedication plaque; instead, it honored the bricking of this road and even included a celebratory brick saying so.

Two of the missing pillars between Bucyrus and Upper Sandusky flanked the driveway of L. A. Kuenzli. He was an advocate of making the highway a memorial to the president, so when brick pillars were being erected, he asked

This 1929 memorial on the east end of Bucyrus honors John Hopley, who, with his brother Frank, served as Ohio state consul. They were largely responsible for Ohio's many brick Lincoln Highway monuments.

that two be located as entrance posts to his driveway. They can be seen in the University of Michigan photo collection, Ohio 271.

The route, marked Lincoln Highway, continues to **Upper Sandusky**. East of town, the Lincoln Highway Farm still operates. On the eastern edge is a sixteen-foot-wide brick remnant that led to the first bridge over the Sandusky River; this iron "Red Bridge" collapsed in 1931. A classic concrete arch span, the George Washington Bridge, replaced it and

now OH Route 19, and was moved two years later when that route was bypassed.

U.S. Route 30 now bypasses Bucyrus, but the 1920 Lincoln enters town on Mansfield Street. On the east end is a memorial dedicated in 1929 to John Hopley, state consul from the LHA's founding until his death in 1927. It was built in 1929 of stones collected from places associated with Hopley's life, plus one from Lincoln's birthplace. It has a pair of ceramic Lincoln Highway signs, a memorial tablet, and a bronze bust of Hopley. Upon Hopley's death, his brother Frank succeeded him as Ohio consul.

A little to the west, a round stone pillar marking the Lincoln Highway was likely made from leftover stones from the Hopley memorial. And beneath some railroad viaducts, two

Huffman's farm near Upper Sandusky.

The P-K was at the crossroads of the Lincoln and Dixie Highways.

lasted until 1998, when the newest crossing was built. In 2001, a state historical marker honoring the Lincoln Highway was dedicated here.

The Lincoln went through town on Wyandot Street, named for the last Indian tribe to live in Ohio until being removed to the West in 1842. Their reservation became the town.

The road west of town originally zigzagged through **Forest**, **Patterson**, **Dunkirk, Dola,** and **Ada** via OH Route 53 and OH Route 81, then took OH Routes 235 and 309 to **Lima**, once an oil town and later a producer of locomotives, car bodies, appliance motors, and neon signs. A 1920 Blue Book ad shows a Lincoln Highway Garage in Lima at 120 East Market Street. By the time Boy Scout Bernard Queneau made it to Lima on July 13, 1928, the trip was already wearing on him, as evidenced by his assessment of the state: "Ohio is full of pigs, cattle, bad roads, and rain."

From Lima, the 1913 Lincoln Highway went west through **Elida** and **Scott's Crossing** and entered **Delphos** on Main Street. In 1915, that was changed from Lima north to a turn at Ord's Corner, then west to **Gomer** and along a prehistoric beach ridge into Delphos. The complex routings are detailed in Michael Buettner's *A History and Road Guide of the Lincoln Highway in Ohio*.

The twisty route from Upper Sandusky was bypassed in June 1919 by a much straighter road. It is the first obvious use of the section lines resulting from the land surveys that extend from the Point of Beginning at the Pennsylvania border. U.S. Route 30 also uses this road until Beaverdam, where a four-lane bypass continues almost to the Indiana border.

In **Williamstown**, the Lincoln would have been on CR 332 through town, crossing a concrete bridge over railroad tracks and U.S. Route 68. In the 1950s, a four-lane bypass opened around the small town. The original route was closed about 1990 because of safety concerns about the bridge. The crumbling structure was pictured in Drake Hokanson's book; the span's walls have since been removed and its Lincoln Highway logos are missing.

Beaverdam called itself a crossroads of the nation, as the Dixie Highway crossed through town from the northeast to the southwest. (Actually, when it got to town, it squared up and overlapped the Lincoln for a few blocks.)

Old postcards show that the Dixie-Lincoln Restaurant was a popular truck stop. A replica brick pillar was erected at the intersection in 1999 on the concrete pad of the original there. The first one had no dedication plaque, but the new one honors Carl Fisher, who conceived both highways. Before the 1919 rerouting, the Dixie would have crossed the Lincoln in Lima.

The still-straight road proceeds through **Cairo** (West Cairo until 1922). At 640 West Main Street, the original part of the Lincoln Log Cabin restaurant dates to the 1850s. Two and a half miles west of town, the road meets the earlier route from Lima at a right-hand bend called Ord's Corner and follows it through Gomer into Delphos.

There are a number of 1920s bridges on the final route, including one across Pike Run east of Gomer and a refurbished triple-arch bridge over the Auglaize River east of Delphos. A triple-arch concrete span across the Ottawa River west of Gomer was recently replaced. U.S. Route 30 also crosses the Lincoln east of town.

Delphos to Indiana

Delphos grew with the north-south Miami and Erie Canal, long abandoned but partly preserved half a block west of Main Street. Where the Lincoln Highway/5th Street crosses it is a historical marker detailing its history. A replica concrete LHA post sits across the street.

As in Galion, a Lincoln Way Garage carried an LHA control sign; K & M Tire at 502 North Main Street now occupies the vintage station. Collectors also snap up bottles from the Lincoln Highway Dairy, located west of Delphos from 1915 to the 1970s.

Balyeat's is a popular stop on East Main Street in Van Wert.

Craig Harmon acquired this photo of a Lincoln Highway monument in Cairo, Ohio, from the daughter of David R. Lane, whom his research uncovered was the author of *The Lincoln Highway: The Story of a Crusade that Made Transportation History*. The picture shows Gael Hoag around the end of May 1933, on a trip Lane and Hoag made with their wives from California to visit Frank Seiberling in Akron to pitch the book. The monument had been dedicated in 1929 across from today's post office, but is long gone and forgotten in the small town. Cairo is between Beaverdam and Delphos, just north of Lima.

The Lincoln Highway leaves Delphos on 5th Street. A few miles west, the road rejoins the beach ridge formed by a prehistoric glacial lake, the predecessor to Lake Erie.

The route is well marked through Van Wert County. The county historical society also has posted four sets of Burma Shave rhymes. East of Van Wert is the Van-Del Drive-In Theater, run by Jim and Joyce Boyd. Can you figure out the name? Near the junction of the old Lincoln Highway and U.S. Route 30 is Conrad's Truck Stop, dating from the 1950s.

Entering **Van Wert**, the road is lined with walnut trees. The town still has a number of historic buildings, including the castlelike Brumback Library, but is best known to roadies for Balyeat's Coffee Shop, just east of the courthouse. Open since 1924, it was described in the 1941 *America's Fascinating Highways* as "one of the choice restaurants in this part of the country." The neon sign advertising "young fried chicken" is a definite photo stop.

Across Main Street, the Marsh Hotel was the LHA control point, one of five hotels listed in the 1924 guide. The hotel no longer rents rooms but has been partially restored and serves as a community center.

Leaving town on West Main, the road heads northwest through gently rolling land. You'll see the BK Root Beer stand from the 1950s, and at 10721 West Ridge Road/Lincoln Highway is the Lincoln Drive-In Theater, opened in 1950. It was called the Ridgeway for years, but in 2002, the Boyd family (owners of the Van-Del) switched back to its original name. Sadly, a tornado later that year with winds up to 260 miles per hour killed four local people and wrecked the drive-in, an indoor theater, and the Boyds' home. The indoor screens reopened for Christmas 2004, but the drive-in is likely beyond repair.

Seven miles west, on the left, is a residence that was once part of Webb's Hi-Speed Service Station and Cabins. Only the main building and garage remain from this one-stop that opened in 1946. Larry Webb, who grew up there, is now president of the Lincoln Highway Historic Byway.

Immediately to the west, the road forks right at Dixon-Cavett Road, and the Lincoln Highway rejoins U.S. Route 30, but a short bypassed segment bears right, marked "road closed." Take it to cross Upper Prairie Creek on a circa 1930 concrete bridge. A 1995 refurbishing revealed ceramic Lincoln Highway emblems embedded in the ends of its parapet

WEBB'S HI-SPEED SERVICE STATION AND TOURIST CABINS   C-241

Webb's satisfied travelers' needs between Van Wert and Fort Wayne.

walls. The road continues but dead-ends at U.S. Route 30; a little backtracking puts you back on the four-lane U.S. Route 30, which has obliterated the original route. One of the losses was an LHA Seedling Mile, a concrete slab meant to inspire further improvement after locals experienced the contrast between driving on the old and new surfaces.

Some six miles farther west, the Lincoln Highway enters Indiana.

Greetings from
Indiana

Though the landscape differs little from Ohio, Indiana seems to follow a slower pace, perhaps a result of southern migration in the early nineteenth century or the continuing influx of Amish into Elkhart and Goshen Counties. As drivers headed west in 1913, the increasingly rural landscape also meant fewer hard-surfaced roads. There was speculation that Carl Fisher wanted the Lincoln Highway to go through his hometown of Indianapolis and then cut through Kansas and Colorado, but LHA directors aimed for suburban Chicago and South Pass in Wyoming.

Because the Lincoln Highway followed, more or less, the Pennsylvania Railroad's

	INDIANA	U.S.
Population in 1910	2,700,876	92,228,496
Population in 2000	6,080,485	281,421,906
Persons per square mile in 2000	169.5	79.6
Approximate miles of Lincoln Highway	163	3,389

Pittsburgh, Fort Wayne, and Chicago line across Ohio, one would think it would do likewise along the railroad's straight shot across Indiana. That would have suited the LHA fine, but roads along the route were unimproved and disconnected—poor enough that a northerly course was taken instead.

Lincoln Highway planners chose an emigrant trail northwest from Fort Wayne. At Ligonier, it met the road some early motorists were taking from New York City via Cleveland. It also picked up the course of the Lake Shore/New York Central Railroad through Elkhart, South Bend, and LaPorte. Just before LaPorte, it joined the Chicago or Sauk Trail running west. At Valparaiso, it rejoined the course of the Pittsburgh, Fort Wayne, and Chicago line. Combining these made for a good, if not straight, road across the state.

Effie Gladding drove it in 1914. She wrote in *Across the Continent by the Lincoln Highway* that the state's roads "are in excellent condition and take us through a lovely rolling country of oaks and beech forests, and of fields of grain breathing pastoral peace and prosperity."

Once Yellowstone Trail boosters had broad-

ened their aspirations to a coast-to-coast road, they chose the Pittsburgh, Fort Wayne, and Chicago route across Indiana, an odd choice in that they were connecting Toledo to Chicago. In *The Family Flivvers to Frisco* (1927), Frederic Van de Water wrote that his family was advised to follow the Yellowstone Trail in Indiana. The Lincoln Highway, others said, "was torn up, it was filled with detours, it was deep in dust. Beware the Lincoln Highway! We discovered later it was the custom of almost all tourists to decry this route though it is, to-day, undoubtedly the best of the transcontinental roads. Why it is decried we never discovered. Probably because it is the best."

But before he knew the truth, Van de Water took the Yellowstone, which turned out to be a loosely graveled road: "We sneezed and coughed in its billowing dust clouds and thought, poor gullible innocents that we were, how much more those who traveled on the Lincoln Highway must be suffering. Our acquaintance with road liars had just begun."

In 1928, the Lincoln Highway would be rerouted to follow that cross-state Pittsburgh, Fort Wayne, and Chicago alignment through

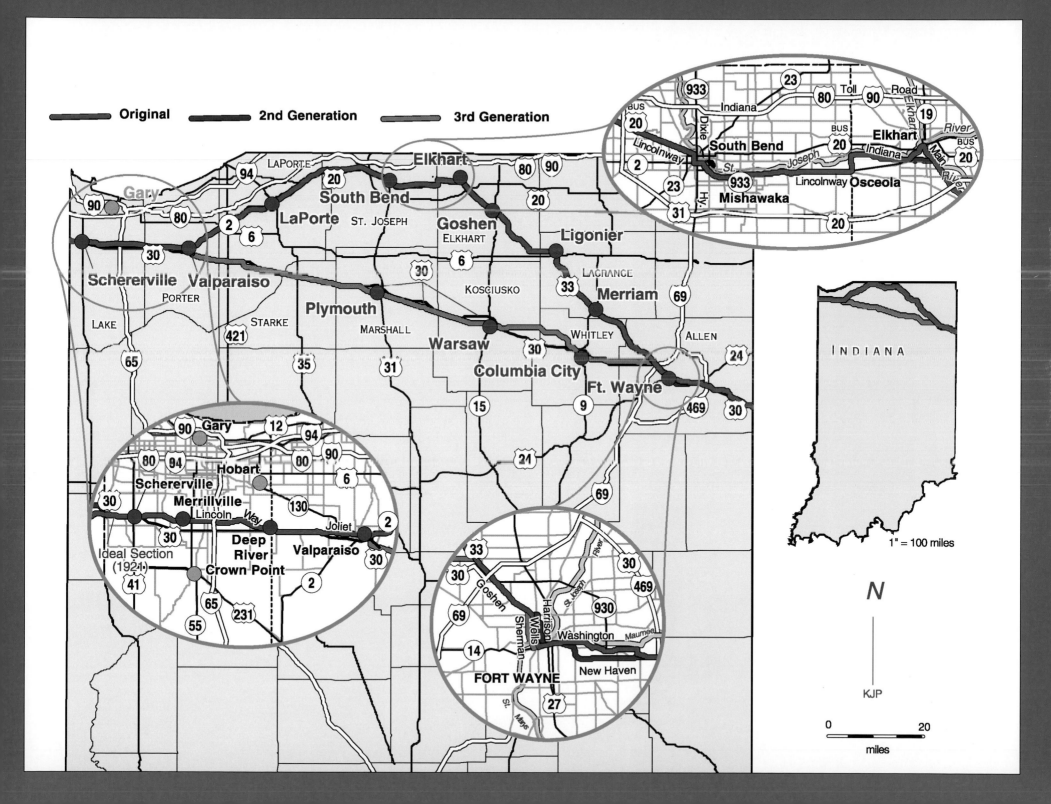

Original   2nd Generation   3rd Generation

LAPORTE
Gary
Elkhart
South Bend
LaPorte   ST. JOSEPH   Goshen   Ligonier
Schererville   Valparaiso   ELKHART   LAGRANGE   Merriam
PORTER   Plymouth   KOSCIUSKO   Columbia City   Ft. Wayne
LAKE   STARKE   MARSHALL   Warsaw   WHITLEY   ALLEN

933   23   80   Toll   Road   90
BUS   Indiana   19
20   Lincolnway   South Bend   BUS   Elkhart   River
2   23   933   20   Indiana   BUS
31   Mishawaka   Lincolnway   Osceola   20

INDIANA

1" = 100 miles

90   Gary   12
80   94   94   90
Schererville   Hobart
Merrillville   Lincoln   Way   130
30   Deep   Joliet   2
River   Valparaiso   30
Ideal Section   Crown Point   2
(1921)   65   231
41
55

33   River   30
30   Goshen   469
69   Sherman   930
14   Washington   Maumee
FORT WAYNE   New Haven
27   St. Mays

N

KJP

0   20
miles

The cast-iron state line marker at the Ohio-Indiana border was a good photo stop.

Warsaw and Plymouth, rejoining the original route at Valparaiso.

Starting in 1923, drivers could enjoy one more Lincoln Highway innovation at the west end of the state: the Ideal Section, the ultimate Seedling Mile.

Toward Fort Wayne

A quarter mile after entering Indiana on U.S. Route 30, turn right and get back on a road marked Lincoln Highway East. The old road, which is also IN Route 930, is rural, passing

This arch spanned the brick road entering Fort Wayne.

33. LINCOLN HIGHWAY, ENTRANCE TO FORT WAYNE, IND.

FORT WAYNE POP. 80,000

through the little settlements of **Townley** and **Zulu**, where one building serves as gas station, general store, and post office. Tiny **Besancon**, centered around the white-stone St. Louis Church, with a tall, cross-topped steeple, was settled by French immigrants. It's named for a town in France that bills itself as "the city of art and history." A small brick schoolhouse dates to 1892. Here, about eight miles from the border, can be seen three parallel roads: the Lincoln Highway, a later routing to the north, and U.S. Route 30 to the south.

The old road meets U.S. Route 30 and becomes a series of frontage roads called Old Lincoln Highway. U.S. Route 30 goes north to bypass Fort Wayne. IN Route 930 continues into **New Haven** past a few cabin camps and turns right on Green Street and then left on Dawkins Road/Lincoln Highway.

IN Route 930 becomes Washington Boulevard and heads into **Fort Wayne** but then IN Route 930 turns right to follow the original U.S. Route 30 bypass north of town. The Lincoln continues west; the original route was via Maumee Road/Maumee Avenue, but some of it is lost in today's sprawl. The main part of Maumee remaining is one-way eastbound. About where it meets Jefferson, a grand arch welcomed early motorists. The post-1928 route took New Haven Avenue and jogged up to Maumee.

Maumee intersects Washington, which westbound drivers are already following. The Lincoln Highway turns north at Harrison Street. At 830 South Harrison Street is the bustling Cindy's Diner, with white porcelain enamel and a red neon tube around the roof. It moved a couple times before John and Cindy Scheele bought it at

auction and moved it to its current site on the corner of Wayne Street. They opened Cindy's Diner on October 1, 1990, and still operate it daily.

The diner was manufactured in 1954 by the Valentine company of Wichita, Kansas. The company produced prefab buildings from 1938 to 1974. These are prevalent in the Midwest and West, where diners by traditional East Coast manufacturers are sparse because of the difficulty, and hence cost, of transporting them over the Appalachian Mountains. Valentines also looked different, resembling small boxes more than railcars, which also made them easier to transport across the great western distances. Cindy's was one of the larger units the company produced. Another Valentine sat just west on Wayne Street, remodeled and most recently called Tiny Tim's Diner; it was demolished in 2004.

A block north on Harrison, then two blocks east on Berry Street, is the Lincoln Museum, which details the president's life through more than eighteen thousand artifacts courtesy of Lincoln National Life Insurance, which has its headquarters in the city. A related attraction is a Lincoln log cabin in Foster Park.

Fort Wayne is located where the St. Mary's and St. Joseph Rivers meet to form the Maumee River. The confluence led to an Indian outpost, followed by French Fort Miami, a fur-trading village, and then a manufacturing center. The Landing Historic District along Harrison is one of few remaining concentrations of historic nineteenth- and early-twentieth-century commercial buildings in the city. Fort Wayne dedicated its section of the Lincoln Highway on June 21, 1915, with a huge parade to New Haven and back. U.S. vice president Thomas Marshall attended, likely because he was from nearby Columbia City.

From Harrison, the Lincoln veered left on Wells Street and originally crossed the St. Mary's River on the 1884 Wells Street iron bridge, distinctive in its plank flooring and Gothic details. About ten blocks later, the route turned left into Goshen Road to leave town.

Late in 1915, the Lincoln was rerouted across the new concrete-arch Lincoln Way/Harrison Street Bridge. Traffic took that north to Putnam, then over to Wells, where it rejoined the original route. This bridge was

Beyond this restored train station, the iron Wells Street Bridge carried the Lincoln Highway before its concrete replacement was built just to the east on Harrison Avenue.

rebuilt in similar but modern style in the 1980s and features restored mile markers at the ends noting the distance to the coasts. The Wells Street span is open only to pedestrians.

A worthy side trip north of Fort Wayne is the Auburn Cord Duesenberg Museum in Auburn. The company's restored 1930 headquarters houses more than one hundred cars of this make, along with other displays, such as regionally made cars. Adjacent is the less formal National Automotive & Truck Museum of the United States, housed in former Auburn and Cord service and production buildings.

Fort Wayne to Valparaiso, 1913

Goshen Road becomes U.S. Route 33. North of town, the route enters rolling farmland and passes through small towns little changed from Lincoln Highway days.

Just after crossing U.S. Route 30 is Washington Center Road. This is the route of the Lincoln Highway after 1928 and will be followed near the end of this chapter. U.S. Route 30 originally followed this, too, but was later upgraded to a four-lane highway.

On the way northwest, a number of section-line, right-angle corners have been bypassed. Most still have the original 1920s concrete surface, though one south of Ligonier is actually brick. Another remnant on the right halfway to Churubusco has an iron bridge.

About fifteen miles from downtown Fort Wayne is **Churubusco**, named for the site of a U.S. victory in the Mexican War. The 1918 LHA guide carried an ad for a Lincoln Highway Garage that was the control point as well. It was advertised as being opposite the hotel; the town's listing noted only one hotel, so it's

By 1926, this new bridge seven miles west of Churubusco was almost ready for traffic.

unlikely motorists needed even that much info to find it.

The claim to fame of the small town of **Merriam** is that America's Uncle Sam is said to be buried here. Samuel Wilson, a meat packer in Troy, New York, stamped supplies with "U.S.," meaning "Uncle Sam," his nickname, and soldiers began using the term Uncle Sam to mean any delivery from the government. It should be noted that Troy, New York, also claims to be Sam's burial place.

The road continues west through tiny **Wolf Lake** and **Kimmell**. West on U.S. Route 33 are a few Lincoln Highway remnants, including one at Stone's Tavern before a slight rise. The tavern, built in 1839, served travelers and locals as a gathering place, jury room, dance hall, and post office. The climb over Stone's Hill was quite a challenge to early drivers, but it was smoothed out long ago.

At **Ligonier**, U.S. Route 33 turns left, but the Lincoln continues into town. On Lincolnway at Union Street, a renovated gas station houses the Indiana Historic Radio Museum, featuring more than four hundred radios of all ages. The adjacent Triangle Park includes a fountain and street clock.

Ligonier was traditionally the distribution point for surrounding onion farms. A Lin-

The Anthony Hotel—Fort Wayne's leading hostelry—is the only fireproof hotel in Fort Wayne, on the Highway.

—Ad, The Complete Official Road Guide of the Lincoln Highway, *1915*

A bypassed brick section south of Ligonier.

coln Highway Garage here placed an ad in the 1915 LHA guide.

The Lincoln Highway turns right at the center of town and follows CR 50/Lincolnway West. On the west edge of town, a small park was the town's tourist camp. At U.S. Route 33, the route turns right.

Half a mile east of **Benton** are remnants of Benton's Log Cabin Camp, seen in old postcards. Just off U.S. Route 33 is a curved segment of brick pavement that can still be driven. U.S. Route 33/Lincolnway East heads into **Goshen**. The town traces its history to the Amish and Mennonites, who settled here in 1834; their descendants still populate the area and can be seen driving their horses and

buggies. Early motorists found a Lincoln Way West Garage at 510 Lincoln Way West.

The highway stair-stepped through Goshen; the map in the 1924 LHA guide shows ten turns. Follow Madison Street, Main Street, and Pike Street to Chicago Avenue, which heads west from town. On Main Street, at the southeast corner of the courthouse square, the town erected a bulletproof police lookout in 1939 to protect against gangsters who might use the highway. The WPA-built, limestone booth has streamline Art Deco styling and gun portholes.

At 1122 South Main, the South Side Diner was built to resemble a 1930s diner.

Heading west from town, at 1100 Chicago Avenue is the Old Bag Factory, a consortium of shops in a former manufactory of bags and paper products ranging from burlap sacks to the tiny paper strips used in Hershey's Kisses. The scientific nature of the work led to the term "bagology," and this factory was even referred to by that term. Changing economics closed the plant in 1982. It was bought a couple years later by Larion and Nancy Swartzendruber when they had to find a new home for

This bridge, shown in 1923, welcomed motorists to Goshen.

their custom furniture company. It was far larger than they needed, so the extra space became a shopping area, today home to nineteen artisans and craftspeople plus a café, all of it attracting more than one hundred thousand visitors annually. The Swartzendrubers continue to make custom furniture, notably in the Arts & Crafts and Prairie styles.

Chicago bears right onto Elkhart/U.S. Route 33 west. West of Goshen, the original Lincoln Highway crossed railroad tracks several times, but the alignment has been lost to

The people of Goshen celebrated the highway's one-year anniversary in 1914.

Lincoln Highway travelers also got a big welcome at Chicago Avenue on the west end of Goshen in 1914. In the car here are Dow Gorham and son. At left rear is the Goshen Bagology, popularly known as "the bag factory."

Lincoln Highway Day in Elkhart brought a crowd and even a motion picture camera. The Bucklen Hotel was owned for a time by Herbert Bucklen, who made his fortune from a salve medication. He invested it in real estate and the Elkhart and Western Railroad, locally called the Pleasant Valley Line. He aquired the hotel after a fire. During restoration and enlargement, he put a gazebo cupola on top with a telescope to keep an eye on his workers in the adjacent rail yards.

development. Follow U.S. Route 33 toward Elkhart. U.S. Route 20 comes in from the east and bypasses the town plus Osceola, Mishawaka, and South Bend. The old highway continues into **Elkhart** on Main Street. Two Lincoln Highway routes ran through town: one into the business section, and one cutting due west on Indiana Avenue. The Bucklen Hotel took out half-page ads in the LHA guides. It was also the town's LHA control point; the guide's listing unfortunately spelled the hotel's name wrong.

Elkhart is at the confluence of the Elkhart and St. Joseph Rivers. Some sources say a small island where the rivers join was described by Indians as resembling an elk's heart, hence the settlement's name. But there was also a Shawnee chief Elkhart. And his daughter was said to be Mishawaka, for whom a town just to the west is named.

Elkhart has long been the center of the trailer and camper universe, with most recreational vehicles being built here. Today the RV/MH Heritage Foundation archives contains all information on recreational vehicles and motor homes back to the 1930s. Exhibits include more than twenty restored vehicles circled around campfires where two-dimensional families enjoy the scenery. You can tour many of the trailers, including a 1940 New Moon just like Lucy and Desi's in *The Long, Long Trailer*. It's south of downtown and the railroad tracks at 801 Benham Avenue/IN Route 19. The town was also a leader in band instruments and still makes most of the U.S. output.

The Lincoln heads west through **Osceola**. As the anonymous author of *Two Thousand Miles on an Automobile* neared Osceola in 1902, he found a bridge out:

> The stream was quite wide and swift but not very deep. From the broken bridge the bottom seemed to be sand and gravel, and the approaches on each side were not too steep. There was nothing to do but go through or lose many miles in going around. Putting on all power we went through with no difficulty whatsoever, the water at the deepest being about eighteen to twenty inches, somewhat over the hubs.

Pritchett's was at the intersection of U.S. Route 20 and IN Route 112 in Elkhart.

Mishawaka in the early 1910s.

Also west of South Bend, Howell's put tepees atop its buildings to attract customers.

There was no doubt which road ran past the Lincoln Highway Inn, which served dinner—with music —until midnight.

Lincolnway/IN Route 933 west of town is parallel but south of the St. Joseph River. On the edge of **Mishawaka** is the former Lincoln Highway Inn. Another theory about the town's name is that it comes from a Potawatomi word for "dead trees place," since the settlers had to clear trees to start the town. A cottage-style gas station remains on the east end. Then Lincoln Way West leaves town, with the St. Joseph River still to the north.

South Bend was named for its location at a bend in the St. Joseph River. Like Fort Wayne, it grew from fur trading to manufacturing, but it is perhaps most familiar for the University of Notre Dame and its football team. The Studebaker National Museum and Archives, a few blocks south of downtown at 525 South Main Street/U.S. Route 31, tracks the carmaker's history from making wagons and buggies through its last model in 1966. The museum includes the carriage that Lincoln rode in to Ford's Theater.

Turn-of-the-century homes along the St. Joseph River are now part of the East Lincolnway Historic District. The First Shot marker at 615 East Lincolnway commemorates a local son who commanded the battery in France that fired the first American shot in World War I in 1917.

Lincoln Way enters downtown, but development and one-way streets make navigating the old route difficult. Heading north on Main Street at West Washington Street, a Holiday Inn sits where the Hotel Oliver once hosted early motorists. Two blocks later, the route turned left on LaSalle, then bore right back onto Lincolnway West. West of town, it rejoins the U.S. Route 20 bypass, which had circled south of Elkhart, Osceola, Mishawaka, and South Bend.

The South Bend Regional Airport has plans to expand, affecting U.S. Route 20/Lincolnway West, but it is discussing its plans with the LHA Indiana Chapter.

The author of *Two Thousand Miles on an Automobile* wrote that during his 1902 trip, the one-hundred-some-mile leg from South Bend to Chicago took eight hours, an average of about twelve and a half miles per hour, "including all stops, and stops count in automobiling; they pull the average down by jumps." Even with stops deducted, he still averaged only eighteen miles per hour that day.

New Carlisle has the world's largest living sign: the Studebaker name spelled out by trees on the former automaker's proving grounds. South of our route, on the south side of Western Avenue/IN Route 2 are 8,259 white pines arranged into letters, each up to two hundred feet long. Planted in 1938, they've grown quite high, and the former test track today is Bendix Woods County Park. The ad for the defunct car company is not visible to people in cars, but only to those flying overhead.

The Lincoln Highway/U.S. Route 20 heads west from New Carlisle. On the way to Rolling Prairie, the road bends left; Blue Books called this the "boot jack corner" for its odd shape

The Big Wheel restaurant on Lincolnway, Valparaiso, has been in the same family since 1963.

where the Chicago or Sauk Trail forked toward Niles, Michigan. Guidebooks warned drivers that it was confusing, but U.S. Route 20 makes a smooth pass through it today.

The Lincoln Highway turns right on Oak Knoll Road and quickly reaches a confusing area anchored by the former Bob's Bar-B-Q, famous for its hospitality and landscaped lawn. Now L&L's Restaurant, it can be identified by its curvy roofline edges.

When Oak Knoll arrives at the intersection, U.S. Route 20 comes in from the left and crosses to the right. Oak Knoll goes straight but dead-ends just ahead, so jog left on CR 450, then right on IN Route 2.

At **LaPorte** is the Door Prairie Auto Museum. Leaving town, the route followed Eggebrecht Road (now one-way eastbound), named for a landowner who also ran a tourist camp. IN Route 2 passes through **Westville**; west of town are three bypassed remnants of the Lincoln Highway.

As you approach **Valparaiso**, a giant mug of "Frostop" Root Beer towers over Hannon's restaurant. In town, on Lincolnway at the southeast corner of Roosevelt Road is the Big Wheel Restaurant, with a huge, wheel-shaped neon sign. The restaurant has been in the same family since opening on July 18, 1963.

In 1910, Harriet White Fisher passed through, heading east. She wrote, "We struck an awful washout, and again broke a leaf in the right spring, but we managed to go on slowly until we reached LaPorte."

The Wheeler-Elam Company operated a Lincoln Highway Garage in Valparaiso, first

Decorative gardens, cabins, and a twenty-four-hour restaurant awaited patrons at Bob's at the junction of IN Route 2 and U.S. Route 20, Rolling Prairie, seen here in 1937.

This Bob's Bar-B-Q menu from July 12, 1940, offered a pot of chicken chow mein for 50¢, a Bar-B-Q sandwich (beef or pork) for 15¢, and an extra-large T-bone steak (sizzling in butter) with potatoes, salad, bread with butter, and a drink for $1.

at 301 East Lincoln Way; an ad in the 1915 LHA guide shows its bunting-bedecked facade. By the 1918 guide, it had moved to a newer building at 212–16 East Main Street. It was the town's LHA control point, too.

You might figure that by 1918, most people had likely ridden in a car, but one account reveals that wasn't the case. Stoyan Christowe wrote about visiting the university here in his 1938 book *This Is My Country*, as quoted in *Travel Accounts of Indiana*:

BARBOUL'S, Jct. 30-49, Valparaiso, Ind.

Barboul's Waitresses

The wait staff poses at Barboul's.

The town of Valparaiso stood picturesquely on an elevation above the tracks, the courthouse tower and some church steeples showing above the treetops. There was no trolley going from the station to the campus, so I had no choice but to take a taxi, thus treating myself to my first automobile ride, which I only half enjoyed, considering it an unnecessary but inevitable luxury. The taxi struggled up the hill for a short distance and presently came upon a broad street with autos and carriages parked against the curbs.

Lincolnway through town becomes Joliet Road to the west and soon merges with U.S. Route 30.

Fort Wayne to Valparaiso, 1928

A major rerouting in 1928 bypassed most of the original route across the state in favor of a straighter alignment that paralleled the Pennsylvania Railroad's Pittsburgh, Fort Wayne, and Chicago line. It was also designated U.S.

Horn's Sunnymede Restaurant, "where Hoosier land people come to relax and play," was east of Warsaw at 2229 East Center Street.

Route 30. The state's WPA guide from 1941 states, "U.S. 30 is one of the most heavily traveled routes across northern Indiana; it is also, for 20 miles, a part of the transcontinental Lincoln Highway." Just after World War II, even that was bypassed by the four-lane U.S. Route 30.

Washington Center Road heads west from Fort Wayne, with U.S. Route 30 parallel to the south.

America's Fascinating Highways, also from 1941, mentioned three cabin camps west of Fort Wayne on Route 30: Chapman's Camp (twelve cabins) and Dixie Tourist Cabins (six cabins) two miles west, and Black and White Cabins (fifteen cabins) three miles west, all starting at $1.50.

Columbia City is a crossroads town, the former home of Thomas Marshall before he became governor of Indiana and then vice president to Woodrow Wilson. He's best remembered for his comment "What this country really needs is a good five-cent cigar."

The old road enters on East Chicago Street (also East Lincolnway and Business Route 30), turns right on South Main, left on West Van Buren, and heads out on North (soon West) Lincolnway, crossing U.S. 30. Passing through farmland, the road becomes Old U.S. 30, then approaches **Warsaw**. A factory-built diner at 1901 East Old Route 30 is a 1995 Starlite, built to look like a diner from the 1940s. First called the Boston Grille, around 2003 it became Schoop's, a local chain. Just as Old Route 30 is about to meet U.S. Route 30, it briefly takes East Kosciusko Drive, then crosses Route 30 to follow Center Street.

On the east end of Warsaw, south of U.S. Route 30 in Kmart plaza on Lake City Highway, is the Hallmark Ornament Museum in the back of The Party Shop. It has a complete

The Plaza 30 serves truckers and other travelers on U.S. Route 30 between Plymouth and Wanatah.

Mrs. Bennett's Railside Inn, west of Grovertown, grew from a small brick building selling chicken to a full restaurant with gift shop. A matchbook advertised its chicken: on toast 35¢, southern fried 50¢, pan fried 75¢.

collection of every Hallmark ornament from 1973 to present, more than three thousand in all, from special editions to test ornaments.

Warsaw is the county seat of Kosciusko County. The county was named for the Polish hero and aide to George Washington during the American Revolution, and the town was named for the capital of Poland. From Center Street, the highway turns right on Lake Street and curves westward. A 1928 concrete marker is in Funk Park; locals beautified the area and rededicated it in 1995. It was thought to be the state's last marker in an original location, but one has been found east of Warsaw and another in a yard west of Marshall County.

The Lincoln meets Old Road 30 and passes the Warsaw Drive-In Theater. The road crosses the Tippecanoe River and passes through the small towns of **Atwood**, **Etna Green**, **Bourbon**, and **Inwood**, with the railroad immediately to the south. Before the 1928 route opened, the old paths could be seen as section roads between the towns.

Lincolnway heads into **Plymouth**, where the restored, century-old Italianate Marshall County Courthouse, with bell and clock tower, can be found. The old road bends onto

Jefferson and heads out on the Lincoln Highway. On the west edge, at 800 Lincoln Highway, is Hemminger Travel Lodge, a 1937 Colonial Revival hotel listed in the state's Register of Historic Places. West of town, U.S. Route 30 is concurrent with much of the old route except for a couple short segments. East of **Wanatah**, the Plaza 30 is a truck stop and minimart along the four-lane. The state's WPA guide had a memorable description of this town, saying it was "named for Wa-na-tah (keep knee deep in mud), an Indian chief who is said to have been noted for his laziness."

U.S. Route 30 heads into Valparaiso, turns right on Sturdy Road, then left onto IN Route 130/Lincolnway.

Valparaiso to the Illinois Line

U.S. Route 30/Joliet Road leaves Valparaiso and heads to **Deep River**. U.S. Route 30 goes south of town, but the Lincoln Highway takes CR 330 to **Ainsworth**, then it becomes 73rd Avenue into **Merrillville**.

These towns were along the Sauk Trail, originally used by the Sauk Indians traveling east to Detroit to collect payment from the British for their aid in the War of 1812. The trail's name reappears just west of the Illinois line. In fact, sixteen other Indian trails are said to have once converged upon the Sauk Trail at present-day Merrillville. In the 1918 LHA guide, the town was listed as having one hotel and one garage. That garage was run by the Walter brothers, who also served as the local LHA consuls and offered their business as the control point. Besides specializing in Buick and Dodge cars, they advertised, "Special attention to Lincoln Highway tourists."

CR 330/73rd Avenue continues west, then becomes Joliet Street. Before rejoining U.S. 30, the road crosses a new wide bridge over Turkey Creek with "Old Lincoln Highway" in its concrete sidewalls. According to the 1918 LHA guide, **Schererville** had no accommodations, just "gas oil, and meals procurable if needed."

A noted attraction to generations of travelers has been Teibel's Restaurant and Tourist Court at U.S. Route 41, another "Crossroads of the Nation" intersection. The restaurant has been located here since 1929. It has been greatly expanded, though the court is gone. A dazzling red, blue, and orange neon sign from

At the time of the late-1930s postcard, top, Teibel's also offered thirty steam-heated cabins. By the 1950s, bottom, a snazzy neon sign attracted motorists.

Chester's Camp in Lake County specialized in "Dixie barbecue."

1958 was knocked down accidentally a few years ago and replaced by a modern version.

Between Schererville and **Dyer** was the "Ideal Section," a road segment built from 1921 to 1923 to showcase the best in pavement, lighting, safety, and landscaping. In March 1920, LHA secretary Austin Bement convinced U.S. Rubber to fund a two-mile experimental stretch of highway. Meanwhile, LHA field secretary Henry Ostermann began driving through the Midwest looking for a location. By the time of his death that June, four locations were being considered: west of Pittsburgh; near Findlay, Ohio; near Dyer, Indiana; and central Nebraska. The Pennsylvania choice was rejected, because it would require moving the Lincoln Highway, and Nebraska was deemed too far away for proper publicity.

Sauzer's in Schererville dropped the "Little" from its name when it expanded to a twenty-four-hour restaurant. The family also operated Kiddieland one block west; it featured an old merry-go-round with hand-carved animals, including thirty galloping horses and three big chariots.

In spring 1921, the Dyer location was chosen—close to the major media outlet of Chicago but still able to show a contrast between surrounding dirt roads, crowded city streets, and the new wide and straight section. Landscape architect Jens Jensen oversaw the beautification.

U.S. Rubber eventually contributed $130,000. Company vice president J. Newton Gunn became LHA president in December 1921, perhaps to make sure his investment was used wisely. The same month, Bement assembled seventeen highway engineers and economists in New York City; the result was nineteen resolutions for the Ideal Section, many of which became the first standards for roadbuilding in the United States.

A farmer with adjacent land held out for more money, and the section had to be revised. The reluctant farmer finally sold them seventeen acres along the south side for an "ideal campsite": campgrounds, a council fire, a store, and a filling station were to be run by Standard Oil. Sketches were prepared by John Van Bergen, but lack of funds and the trend away from motor camping left those plans unrealized. There were other troubles, too. The contractor for the bridge reportedly committed suicide using dynamite. The local electric company stopped paying for the lighting, so it was turned off. By the late 1920s, locals had carried off landscape shrubbery.

It's often labeled as 1.3 miles, but Ideal Section authority Art Schweitzer says that doesn't include where the road tapered from four lanes to two. This began one mile from the state border and went for 871 feet more to the west. The wide part alone measured 1.3569318 miles—Art is very precise—with the tapered bit making it a total of 1.5218939

Proposed for the Ideal Section but never built were this campsite and rustic service station, drawn by John S. Van Bergen in 1925.

miles long. Art was there when it was rebuilt in 1998; the loss of the original road at least allowed him perform archaeological research and measurements otherwise impossible.

The Ideal Section widening also obliterated the original scenic intent. At least a new bridge received Lincoln Highway markings. Art helped with that, too, and got Walgreens to mount a historical plaque on its building and place some old macadam in its sidewalk.

Looking west at the Gary crossroad, about five miles from the Illinois line. The road is typical of the conditions at what would become the Ideal Section, just to the west. An arrow at right points to Chicago, thirty-four miles away. The white pole at center holds a curved Lincoln Highway marker.

Drivers in Schererville today will find this decorative bridge rail on the widened Ideal Section.

Also surviving are a stone bench memorial to Ostermann and, in front of it, an Ideal Section monument. The four-lane arrangement, however, makes them dangerous to visit.

One of three feeder routes into Chicago branched north at Dyer, marked with red-white-red signs. It went through Hammond, then to Jackson Park, Washington Park, and east on Michigan Avenue, some thirty-four miles. The preferred eastern access route, though, was the Dixie Highway north from Chicago Heights.

Today drivers cross into Illinois less than a mile from the Ideal Section, never knowing they just drove what was once the country's most important piece of pavement.

Greetings from
Illinois

Though in the northeast corner of Illinois, Chicago dominates the state. Three-fourths of the state's population lives within commuting distance, leaving the rest of the state predominantly rural. These farms make Illinois the country's third-largest agricultural producer.

The Lincoln Highway never enters Chicago, but circles halfway around the great metropolis. The 1935 LHA history noted that its founders intentionally routed the road around the city "because they realized, even so early, that it was desirable to keep through traffic out of the congestion of cities." Instead, three feeder routes were marked into town for those wishing to visit the city, as many no doubt did.

The surrounding towns naturally were bustling, too. On her 1909 trip across the country, Alice Ramsey encountered the endless tracks around Chicago that made the city such an important rail center: "For miles and miles we crossed tracks—singly, in pairs, and in groups; back and forth we wound around and over them until we almost got dizzy. Bump! Bump! Up and down, again and again."

The arc around Chicago hit its northernmost point at Geneva. The route west from there was determined not so much by the rest of Illinois, but by a low pass in the northern Rockies eleven hundred miles to the west.

When Carl Fisher first outlined his plan for a coast-to-coast highway in 1912, he proposed raising $10 million before choosing a route. Less than a year later, with the reality of raising such an amount looking futile, he had a new idea: choose a route and present it to the Conference of Governors at Colorado Springs in August 1913. This would garner support and funding, and perhaps stem the growing tide of suggested routings. One of those consulted about potential routes was Col. Sidney Waldon. As general manager of Packard in 1902, it was Waldon who had proposed the transcontinental trip of "Old Pacific," one of three autos to cross the United States the following summer. Lessons learned from that and yearly trips to follow, plus his own experiences crossing the Rockies, led him to advise a route for the Lincoln Highway via Omaha, Cheyenne, Salt Lake City, and Reno.

Colorado, meanwhile, campaigned for a route via Denver and across Berthoud Pass. Carl Fisher took this route on his Hoosier Tour of July 1913. Colorado rebuilt 60 miles of road across the pass in anticipation of the tour, but when crossing it, the caravan made only 105 miles in fourteen hours. Some cars even had to turn around on the steep grades lest their engines die from the carburetors being higher than the gas tanks.

What has this to do with Illinois? Had Berthoud Pass been chosen, the Lincoln Highway might have gone southwest from Chicago, perhaps even through Kansas, but Berthoud and other crossings were rejected in favor of Wyoming's gentler South Pass.

	ILLINOIS	U.S.
Population in 1910	5,638,591	92,228,496
Population in 2000	12,419,293	281,421,906
Persons per square mile in 2000	223.4	79.6
Approximate miles of Lincoln Highway	179	3,389

LHA planners determined that a highway using this pass would have better weather and road conditions along its entire length for a greater portion of each year.

With South Pass as a goal, the highway's routing was backtracked across Nebraska and central Iowa. That meant the road from Chicago needed to go fairly straight west. The Lincoln Highway adopted the old Overland Trail at Geneva, which was likewise along the route of the Chicago and Northwestern Railroad (bought by the Union Pacific in the 1990s). It followed the tracks across the state.

Early motorists noticed that the land west of Chicago was changing, that there were hints of the mucky gumbo to come in Iowa. As Alice Ramsey wrote of her 1909 trip, "The dark clay soil here could sop up huge quantities of water, gradually becoming a thick viscous mass, sticky as glue, and deep as your wheels could descend—at times, even deeper!"

In her 1916 book, *By Motor to the Golden Gate*, Emily Post wrote that when they rejoined the Lincoln Highway thirty-six miles west of Chicago, they were disappointed:

> As the most important, advertised and lauded road in our country, its first appearance was not engaging. If it were called the cross-continent *trail* you would expect little, and be philosophical about less, but the very word "highway" suggests macadam at the least. And with such titles as "Transcontinental" and "Lincoln" put before it, you dream of a wide straight road . . . and you wake rather unhappily to the actuality of a meandering dirt road that becomes mud half a foot deep after a day or two of rain!

The "meandering" Lincoln was bypassed in 1937 when a major U.S. Route 30 bypass was built straight west from Aurora, choosing directness over the old practice of connecting towns. The original route was designated a National Scenic Byway in 2000; directional signs give Illinois one of the best-marked stretches of the Lincoln Highway in the country.

Skirting Chicago

Just after leaving the Ideal Section in Indiana, the Lincoln Highway enters Illinois on U.S. Route 30. In **Lynwood**, while busy U.S. Route 30 angles right, the Lincoln Highway follows the Sauk Trail to the left through a more suburban environment. It goes through Sauk Village; formerly Strassburg it was renamed in 1957. The original road crosses IL Route 394/Calumet Expressway, then meets IL Route 1/Chicago Road. The Sauk Trail continues westward through Richton Park to Frankfort. In 1913, this was a dirt road, but it was the one that had to be taken. Research by LHA member Larry McClellan has revealed

that this was the intended route for the Lincoln Highway, but boosters from Chicago Heights and Matteson had different plans.

They suggested bringing the highway north to Chicago Heights on a partially paved road, then west over a full mile of pavement toward Matteson. This would also bring traffic two miles closer to Chicago, which gained support from businesses along the feeder routes. Those along the proposed route even promised to improve the entire road to Matteson, so by the end of November 1913, the Lincoln was rerouted from the Sauk Trail north on Chicago Road then west on 14th Street.

A couple years later, Chicago Road became the route of the Dixie Highway, and for almost two miles, the two routes pioneered by Carl Fisher ran concurrently. The Lincoln-Dixie Theater hinted that drivers were following the famous pair. In 1931, the rest of Sauk Trail was

Long's declared, "We specialize in fine food and modern restful tourist court accommodations."

The Arche Memorial Fountain, at the crossroads of the Lincoln and Dixie Highways (now U.S. Route 30 and IL Route 1), was erected in 1916 as a place of rest for long-distance travelers.

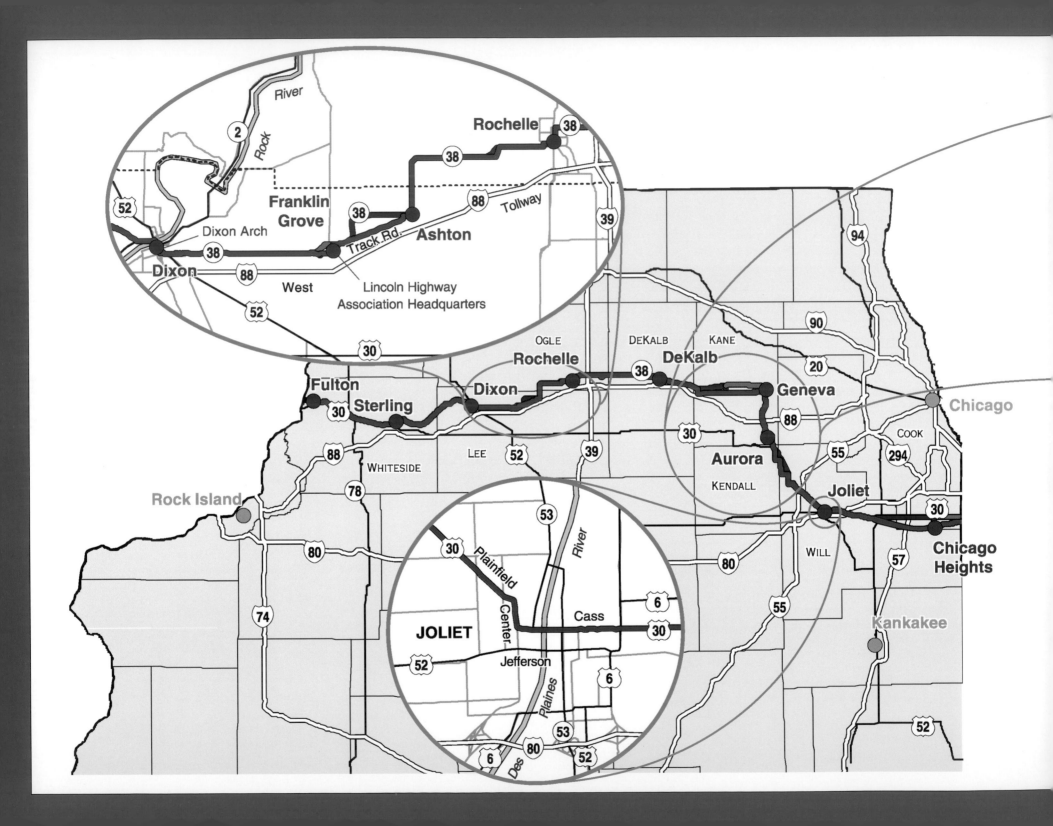

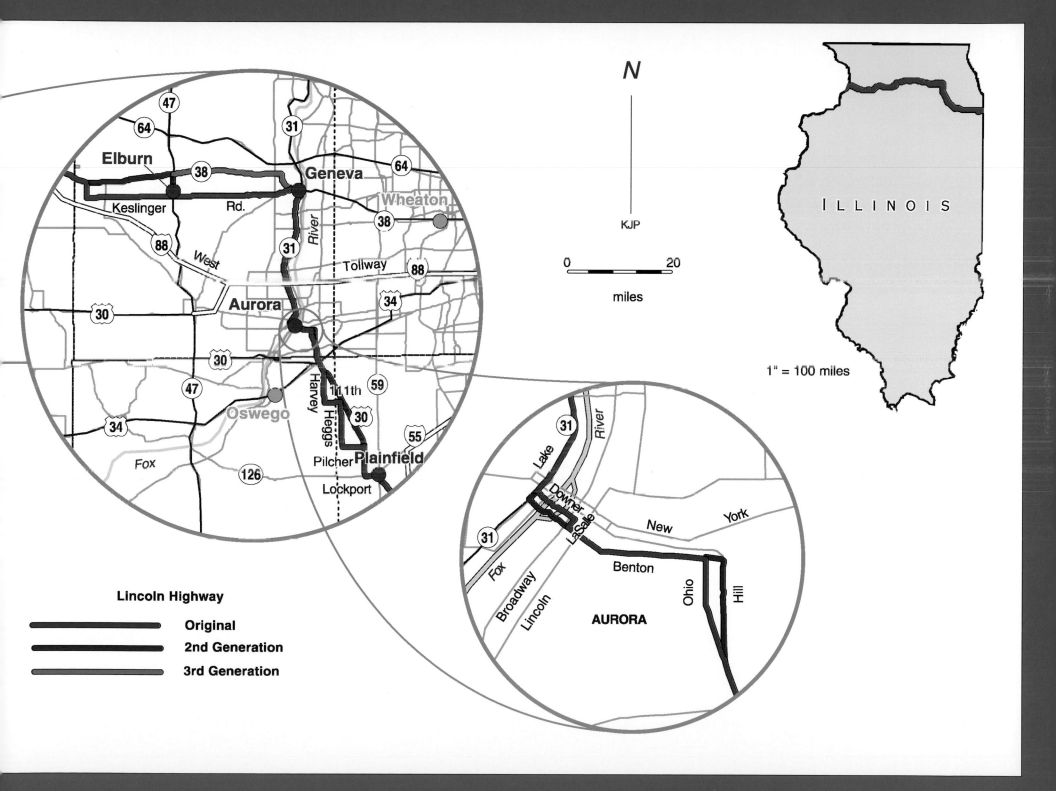

N

KJP

0   20

miles

ILLINOIS

1" = 100 miles

47
64
Elburn
38
Geneva
64
Keslinger   Rd.
Wheaton
38
River
31
88
West
Tollway
88
Aurora
34
30
30
47
Harvey
111th
59
Oswego
Heggs
30
34
55
Fox
Pilcher   Plainfield
126
Lockport

31
Lake
River
Downer
31
Fox
LaSalle
New
York
Broadway
Benton
Lincoln
Ohio
Hill
AURORA

Lincoln Highway

Original

2nd Generation

3rd Generation

This bridge west of Chicago Heights sported a permanent Lincoln Highway logo.

bypassed with a straight road—today's U.S. Route 30 from the state line through Ford Heights to Chicago Heights.

At **Chicago Heights**, the intersection of the two great routes is commemorated at Arche Park by the Arche Memorial Fountain, built in 1916 by the Conservation Committee of the Arche Foundation. The park was intended as a place of rest for cross-country travelers. The fountain—with what appears to be a large Lincoln penny—is pleasant, but with traffic rushing by, it's hard to imagine ever being able to pull over here for a rest.

The second of three feeder routes to Chicago continued north here through Homewood, Blue Island, Morgan Park, and Garfield Boulevard, then headed east to Michigan Avenue. The LHA guide recommended this route as being less congested than the feeder from Dyer, Indiana.

Those who do head north to Chicago will find not only a major city, but also twenty-nine miles of shorefront with more than thirty public beaches. Gentle lake breezes earned Chicago the nickname "Windy City" as early as 1885, contrary to a popular myth that it was bestowed by a New York City writer who thought town boosters were windbags for sug-

gesting they could compete with New York to host the 1893 Columbian Exposition.

Those searching out remnants of the Lincoln Highway era will find a number of classic hotels, theaters, auto showrooms, neon signs, and of course, Wrigley Field. Dearborn Station, an 1880s Romanesque railroad depot on West Polk Street downtown, has been converted to shopping. In Des Plaines, northwest of downtown, the McDonald's Museum is on the site of Ray Kroc's first red-and-white striper with arches. The 1955 original at 400 North Lee Street was torn down, but the reproduction has mannequins serving food at the repro counter, and a museum in the basement. Two blocks south, have your food delivered on a model train at the Choo Choo Restaurant.

The Lincoln Highway goes west from the Arche Park intersection, once again with U.S. Route 30. Road guides noted a Lincoln Way Garage here, which also served as the LHA control point.

In *The Long, Long Trailer*, Clinton Twiss recalled that his wife, Merle, had a dream about the Lincoln Highway, which she insisted meant that they were to immediately change course and take the Lincoln. They did, and Twiss wrote: "[We] rolled along snappily until we encountered Chicago Heights. From Chicago Heights to Aurora, Illinois the highway was a shambles—a well-marked strip of rubble. . . . Apparently not a lick of work had been done on it since Lincoln finished it." It's all the more amazing that he was writing not in 1913 but in 1951.

Today the road is at times six-lane and busy through **Olympia Fields** and **Matteson**, where you'll find a Lincoln Mall to the left (south). Cross over I-57 and pass Lincoln

Estates. West of Matteson, at the county line (where IL Route 43 goes right), the road reverts from four-lane back to two-lane.

While the Sauk Trail led to **Frankfort**, the early realignment of the Lincoln Highway passes half a mile north of downtown. West of town, the Lincoln Highway rejoins the Sauk Trail to Joliet and is again a busy road.

At 10841 West Lincoln Highway, the Abe Lincoln Motel is one of the few survivors from an earlier era. Tom and Mary Lou Lockard stayed here in the summer of 2004 as they toured the highway and described it for me:

It was built in 1958 and is still operated by the original owners. Today, though, it is a seven-acre island surrounded by a sea of new condos and upscale housing. A For Sale sign is in the yard, and the owner told me that she is being taxed out of existence. The $50 a night we paid could be $250 a night with the "12 deluxe air-conditioned units" filled every night and she still couldn't satisfy the taxman.

Lots of places here use the Lincoln Way name, and there is also a wonderful stretch of bypassed pavement. Where the current road bends left, about one hundred yards of 1920s concrete lies to the right, since converted to a walking-biking path.

The route is noted by Lincoln-Way Central High School and a 1928 concrete Lincoln Highway post from Joliet that was saved and moved by a local history class in 1996. Lincoln-Way East High School was built in 2001 in Frankfort, but is off the Lincoln Highway. The original route branches left from U.S. Route 30/Lincoln Highway along East Haven Avenue to **New Lenox**. It then turns right on Cedar Road, then left to rejoin U.S. Route 30.

The Lincoln Highway enters **Joliet** on U.S. Route 30/Cass Street. Effie Gladding wrote, "Joliet is a smoky city, full of factories and busy with the world's work." The town is also known as the "city of spires" for its more than 120 churches. Joliet grew as a stop along the ninety-seven-mile Illinois and Michigan Canal, which connected the Great Lakes to the Illinois River and hence the Mississippi River. A state heritage corridor follows the canal's entire towpath and interprets its history.

Cass Street is one-way westbound; the eastbound route follows Jefferson Street. Between the two, on Chicago Street, is the Rialto Square Theater, a stunning vaudeville showcase from 1926. Route 66 was originally routed through Joliet via Chicago Street. The famous highway began in downtown Chicago and headed southwest through Joliet and on through St. Louis. In 1940, Route 66 was diverted west around Joliet, roughly following today's I-55. The four-lane bypass—the first in

Austin Bement and Henry Joy prepare for the mud ahead near Joliet, 1915.

SPECIAL COLLECTIONS LIBRARY, UNIVERSITY OF MICHIGAN

This Mexican restaurant with pagoda-style roof was originally Wadham's, a 1920s service station on Hill Avenue across from Phillips Park, site of a camping pavilion.

Illinois—was built to accommodate area munitions production needs.

The Des Plaines River flows through the west end of Joliet. Cass Street crosses it on a circa 1920 rolling-lift drawbridge.

The revised Route 66 went through the next town west on the Lincoln Highway, **Plainfield**. U.S. Route 30/Lincoln Highway follows Plainfield Road (then Joliet Road) between the towns. In Plainfield, the Lincoln angles right (north) on IL Route 59/Division Street for three blocks. It was for these three blocks that the Lincoln Highway and Route 66 shared the same road. The downtown is precious; all but one building in the business district dates to the 1910s or earlier. Banners along the route celebrate both famous highways.

After three blocks on Division, the Lincoln Highway turns left on U.S. Route 30/Lockport Road, passing Larry's Restaurant. The Lincoln then follows U.S. Route 30 north. Soon Route 30 bears left and aims for Aurora; old bits of Lincoln Highway keep branching off to the left as section line roads. U.S. Route 30 departs from the Lincoln by turning left on U.S. Route 34/Ogden Avenue. It then bears right and heads straight west almost to the state border.

The Lincoln Highway continues straight on what has become Hill Avenue. At the intersection of Montgomery Road is Hi-Lite 30 Drive-In Theater, in a classic roadside arrangement with a bowling alley and skating rink. The "30" in the 1947 theater's name indicates that U.S. 30 probably came north here originally to turn left.

The Lincoln Highway continues north on Hill Avenue. A pagoda-style gas station–turned–Mexican restaurant is on the right, then on the left is a remnant of the Lincoln Highway bordering the century-old Phillips Park. A brick shelter there survives from the autocamping era. The shelter was mentioned in the LHA's 1924 guide, and efforts are under way to preserve it. Mastodon Lake at the park was dug from a peat bog as a federal works project; among the entombed finds were several three-foot-long mastodon skulls, now at the Aurora Historical Society.

Also on the left is Swony's Drive Inn restaurant, with spaces under an awning for twenty cars. A great round sign sports a frosty mug and a racing-bulb arrow.

The Lincoln turns left onto Benton Street, which is one-way eastbound into **Aurora**; westbound traffic now has to go a block north

Swony's drive-in restaurant was for sale in 2003.

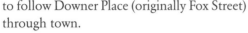

Aurora, celebrating its place on the Lincoln, also always noted its distinction of being a pioneer in streetlighting.

to follow Downer Place (originally Fox Street) through town.

At LaSalle Street, the Lincoln Highway went north from Benton Street to Fox Street/ Downer Place until the Benton Street Bridge was built in the mid-1920s. Because of LaSalle's many historic buildings, it has been listed on the National Register of Historic Places. A century ago, Aurora proudly hailed itself as the "city of lights"; starting in 1908, Fox Street had triglobe streetlamps. The city also had tall Lincoln Highway streetlights that reportedly were adopted by other towns. Downtown, the Paramount Theater has an impressive brick facade with terra-cotta embellishments and a vertical incandescent-bulb sign. Across the street is a corner dining room with neon signs advertising steaks and cocktails.

Both roads cross the Fox River at an island, so both eastbound and westbound drivers cross the water twice; a few old buildings remain on the island. The Lincoln Highway then turns north on IL Route 31/Lake Street and enters **North Aurora**, where it becomes Lincolnway, as noted by banners.

The campground at North Aurora, 1922.

North of that town is **Mooseheart**, named for Mooseheart Child City and School. The fraternal organization played an important role in Lincoln Highway history. The twelve-hundred-acre community was dedicated on July 27, 1913, and included new offices and a home for children of deceased Moose members (extended in 1994 to any family in need). When the Lincoln Highway was established to run right past the lodge's new door, the Moose made a deal with the state: The lodge would pay for paving a stretch of the Lincoln if the state provided the equipment. The lodge held Good Roads Day on April 15, 1914, when fifteen hundred members from across the country, led by the governor, turned out to pave two miles in front of the lodge.

Everyone who worked for fifteen minutes received a check for 1¢, which was more a souvenir than payment. The segment, which cost $12,000, became the first paved road in rural Illinois. The highway still passes the entrance, but it is much changed and the pavement was long ago redone; only a ten-foot widening done by the state as a nod to the original Moose efforts can still be spotted.

IL Route 31 heads north through **Batavia** and into **Geneva**. On the right is Fabyan Villa, once home to George Fabyan, a charter member of the LHA. It was remodeled by Frank Lloyd Wright.

The Lincoln Highway enters downtown Geneva on 1st Street. (The last few blocks of 1st Street were bypassed by the Lincoln Highway via 3rd Street in the 1920s.) At State Street, the Lincoln Highway turns left, leaving IL Route 31 and picking up IL Route 38. A right turn allows you to follow the third feeder into Chicago by taking Roosevelt Road to Wheaton, then connecting with Jackson Boulevard.

Geneva was founded along the Fox River in 1833 as a trading post for westbound travelers. In *The Family Flivvers to Frisco*, Frederic Van

On April 15, 1914, the Moose Lodge headquarters celebrated Good Roads Day by inviting members from across the country to help pave a two-mile stretch in front of its headquarters.

de Water noted how much his family enjoyed tourist camps in Plymouth, Indiana; Marshalltown, Iowa; Omaha; and Cheyenne. But he wrote of Geneva that it had "the worst we had encountered and in the three thousand odd miles remaining of our journey we never saw its equal. . . . The sanitary arrangements were unspeakable. There were no garbage cans and we were told when we asked how to dispose

The front window of this B. F. Goodrich store on State Street in Geneva is filled with kiddie wagons and tricycles.

of the litter remaining when we broke camp the following morning: 'Just throw it out into the field.'"

This was just the kind of thing chambers of commerce feared. As Van de Water noted, "The motor tourist may be blind to the natural and civic beauties of a town but he will remember the camp he stayed in and forever after refer to the place that harbored it accordingly."

On State Street at 2nd Street, the storefront of the B. F. Goodrich Car Care Center is filled with red wagons, rocking horses, and other memorabilia. On State Street at 5th Street is a mid-1920s cottage-style Pure Oil Station, now a repair business, but still amazingly intact and painted its original blue and white. Even a garage extension matches, right down to a cottage-style peaked roof on the far end.

After a few more blocks on State Street/IL Route 38, the original route bent left on Kaneville Road; in 1922, the highway was extended out State Street to 14th Street, then north to Prairie Street and rejoining IL Route 38. Both meet up in a few miles. Either way,

early motorists felt victorious. They had conquered Chicago's suburbs and were once again pointing westward.

West from Chicago

Most people associate U.S. Route 30 with the Lincoln Highway from Pennsylvania to Wyoming; they are indeed parallel, and U.S. Route 30 is often the old road's replacement, but the original Lincoln Highway is rarely a modern highway. West of Geneva, it took Kaneville Road, which becomes Keslinger Road. At Schrader Road, the Lincoln turned right and traveled north. A bit farther, it turned west again onto today's IL Route 38. (A 1921 shortcut connected Keslinger Road to IL Route 38 via Main Street through the town of Elburn.) The highway continues west, skirting tiny **Cortland** and passing close to I-88, which is south.

DeKalb was once known as "Barb City" in honor of the invention and commercial production of barbed wire there and the wealth it brought. On North 1st Street, you can tour the massive Victorian home of barbed-wire pioneer Isaac Ellwood. He and his partner Joseph Glidden used Glidden's patent to revolutionize livestock fencing.

In *Across the Continent by the Lincoln Highway*, Effie Gladding recalled staying at DeKalb's Glidden Hotel, "built, they tell us, by Mr. Glidden, the 'barbed wire king.'" She thought it a "funny old hotel," for its ceilings were twenty feet high, making the rooms feel like deserted banquet halls. The Joseph F. Glidden Homestead, at 921 West Lincoln Highway, documents the life of the farmer-turned-inventor.

Agriculture brought equal riches to De-Kalb, evident in the buildings and DeKalb Genetics's well-known logo of winged corn. The town celebrates Corn Fest every August, serving more than seventy tons of corn. The Soldiers and Sailors Memorial Clock has watched over the corner of the Lincoln Highway and 1st Street since 1921. Behind it, a mural depicts local heritage, from Glidden's niece Annie—an award-winning farmer—to an original ghost sign for the *Daily Chronicle*. The mural is on a building constructed by Glidden for the newspaper in 1889; it's the town's oldest three-story structure.

The city was among the first to rename its main street Lincoln Highway. Businesses embraced the name, too. One spread in the 1915 LHA guide advertised two garages, a restaurant, and a camping spot all named for the roadway at their door. Local garageman A. F. Johnson even changed the name of his repair shop from his own name to Lincoln Highway Official Garage.

The LHA car stops at DeKalb.

Where the West Begins

Many an easterner felt that the West had finally begun once they passed Chicago. The change in landscape remains subtle but apparent: Instead of towns surrounded by suburbia, or at least scattered homes and businesses, the land east of Geneva opens up. Farms line the road for much of the visible drive. Roadside services between towns are rare.

Drake Hokanson recognized it in *The Lincoln Highway: Main Street across America*, his insightful 1988 look at the road:

> Chicago lay at a strategic point of intermission between the first and second acts of a three-act play of American travel experience. For travelers from the East coast headed to . . . San Francisco, this first third of the coast-to-coast trip was a shakedown cruise, an easy trial run to test equipment and skills. From here the going would be tougher, the towns farther apart, the countryside much less like home.

After her 1909 trip, Alice Ramsey sensed that the change came a bit farther west:

> We felt the great Father of Waters was the logical division between the conservative, conventional East, with the busy hum of of industries, and the wide-open spaces of the little-known West. In a matter of distance, we were still far from half-way, but there is a discernible difference in land and people once the Mississippi has been crossed.

In *A Long Way from Boston*, Beth O'Shea referred to Arthur Chapman's popular poem:

The gift shops all the way from Boston to California used to display among the sentimental framed verses a little gem called "Out Where the West Begins." According to the poet, you knew you had reached the West when you began to notice that the sun was shining more strongly and that hearts were beating with a correspondingly greater warmth.

She became more specific when recalling her own trip with her friend Kit: "The West did not actually begin for us until we bobbed our hair and shed our inhibitions along with the nets and hairpins." Short hair was just coming into vogue in 1922, "in spite of resistance from parents, clergy and conservative employers." It also symbolized that they were ready for the rigors that lay ahead, so after a night at the Blacktone Hotel in Chicago, the pair had their hair shorn by its barber the next morning.

In *The Family Flivvers to Frisco*, Frederic Van de Water wrote that the West didn't begin until even farther west, after they'd crossed the Missouri River:

> In Nebraska, you encounter your first prairie dog village with its inhabitants sitting like hitching posts beside their burrows and little prairie owls forever bowing jerkily at each other. In Nebraska, the first magpie flops heavily across the road. Here also you scare up your first jack rabbit, a moth-eaten, ungainly hare who hobbles out of the way with a stiff, rheumatic gait. The jack rabbit is a creature with no discretion whatever. The roads of the West are dotted with his tire-flattened corpses.

The vintage Egyptian Theater graces DeKalb.

In *Fill 'er Up!* Bellamy Partridge recalled getting a hand-drawn map from Robert Carson, an acquaintance of AAA pathfinder A. L. Westgard: "I had often heard of the 'place where the West begins,' but Carson was the only person I ever met who had the spot marked. It was, he said, at the white line in the middle of the bridge across the Missouri River between Council Bluffs and Omaha."

The impression of the Wild West was often influenced by books, movies, and childhood attendance at one of Buffalo Bill's traveling shows. Emily Post wrote, "Where, Oh, where is the West that Easterners dream of. . . . Are the scenes no longer to be found except in the pages of a book, or on a cinematograph screen? We have gone half the distance across the continent and all this while we might be anywhere at home."

In her 1920 book, *A Frenchwoman's Impressions of America*, Comtesse Madeleine de Bryas similarly wrote of her 1918 trip: "Nothing can depict our keen disappointment on discovering that what we had imagined America was going to be, a country thickly peopled with Indians and cowboys, was almost a pure invention of the famous American films that have overrun Europe for several years."

Still, that image was hard to shake. In his book about the 1908 New York–to–Paris race, George Schuster recalled

a conversation at Cheyenne with the Thomas Motor Company sales manager:

> "Have you got a gun?" Morse asked me. "It will be wide-open country from here on." I showed him a small .32 that I was carrying.
> "Get a real gun and carry it in a holster," he ordered. I went to a hardware store and spent part of $500 that he gave me for expenses on a .38 Colt with a six-inch barrel.

In the 1934 *Sweet Land*, Lewis Gannett was a bit more whimsical: "The West begins where the garage men greet you with a warmer smile, refuse to take a tip for cleaning your windshield, and send you off with a winning invitation to 'Come see us again soon.'" He also paraphrased Anne Peck and Enid Johnson in their *Roundabout America*, who claimed it was "where the hot-dog stands give way to the barbecue-sandwich signs."

Gannett noted that the West was filled with Model Ts, although production had ended in 1927: "All through the West the college boys and high school girls buy them to ride home in, and the farm lads piece them together to hunt work and prosperity. . . . They mark, it is not too far-fetched to suggest, the decent democracy of the West."

More fittingly, he concluded: "The West, wherever it may begin, is never quite what an Easterner expects it to be."

The Lincoln Highway, marked as IL Route 38, courses through town. At 2nd Street, a right turn finds the Egyptian Theater, opened in 1929. Its design was inspired by the tomb of Ramses II, and the ceiling also features stars and a cloud generator. It was set to be bulldozed in 1976, but local volunteers bought and renovated the theater. It now hosts plays, concerts, and occasional movies. Also in the international theme, you'll find Thai Pavilion restaurant at 131 East Lincoln Highway; this and other ethnic restaurants are likely an outgrowth of Northern Illinois State University, with a large campus on the west end of town serving twenty-five thousand students.

During her 1909 trip, Alice Ramsey noted that DeKalb's streets were lined with elms. The land west of town also made an impression: "Now we saw plenty of pigs, for a change: big pigs, little pigs, all sizes and all different colors, and all over the roads as well as the fields."

Looking west on IL Route 38 to the first Lincoln Highway Seedling Mile, west of Malta.

About a mile west of **Malta**, small signs note the location of the very first LHA Seedling Mile. A short detour to Kishwaukee Community College finds a historical marker that details its story. Started in September 1914, the Lincoln Highway's first Seedling Mile was paved and dedicated in November of that year. The idea was to inspire further improvements by putting a slab of flat, smooth, hard concrete in the middle of a bad stretch of road. Additional Seedling Miles were paved in Morrison and Chicago Heights the following year.

Emily Post indeed found the roads west of DeKalb even worse than the roads she'd been bemoaning since Chicago: "The only 'highway' attributes left were the painted red, white and blue signs decorating the telegraph poles along the way. The highway itself disappeared into a wallow of mud!" Once in Rochelle, Post, her son, and a friend walked to the end of the brick street to see the muddy Lincoln Highway heading west. The next day, they pressed on to Sterling, where

they turned off the Lincoln onto another road. This one was not muddy, prompting Post to note its condition in comparison to the Lincoln Highway: "The ordinary, unadvertised River to River road that we had dreaded was splendid."

The Lincoln is fairly flat and straight, lined with fields of corn growing tall. Today IL Route 38 flies past **Creston**, but as with so many towns on the original route a century ago, the road led into the little settlement. Creston had grown a few blocks south along the railroad. Drivers on the Lincoln had to turn left and jog through its streets. There they encountered a Lincoln Highway fountain. These were donated in about 1914 by California businessman Carl Parker to towns along the Lincoln Highway in Illinois. The gifts were in memory of his mother, born in the state, though some murmured that it was all a publicity stunt. DeKalb likewise had one in front of its post office, removed when the intersection was widened in the 1980s.

IL Route 38 enters **Rochelle**, where you can stop for a bite at the Rochelle Beacon restaurant, which has a lighthouse-shaped sign. The Lincoln Highway leaves IL Route 38 for a few blocks, turning left as Lincoln Highway and proceeding through the small downtown; look for the 1930s Hub Theater. The next right turn, on Lincoln Avenue, is easy to find: On the southeast corner is a restored 1918 Standard Oil Station with vintage gas pumps. A welcome center now fills the canopy station. Heading west on Lincoln, a quick jaunt across the tracks to the south

LHA consuls Martin Kennedy and J. W. Comings at the Lincoln Highway fountain in tiny Creston, Illinois.

takes you to Railroad Park, where the tracks of the Union Pacific and Burlington Northern/Santa Fe railroads cross. It's unique to have two major lines of the west crossing, especially in a diamond-shape. A pavilion overlooks the spot where more than one hundred trains pass daily.

IL Route 38 rejoins the Lincoln Highway on the west end of town. Together, they cross railroad tracks and head west again. IL Route 38 stairsteps southwest to **Ashton**. West of town, the Lincoln follows Track Road straight along the railroad, while IL Route 38 again takes to section lines. The path along the rails is gravel; the second-generation road has an amazing four 1928 concrete posts within a mile. Three are easy to spot along the fence line; the other, the westernmost, is in tall grass between U.S. Route 38 and Track Road. I-88 runs a couple miles to the south.

The Lincoln Highway again leaves IL Route 38 to enter **Franklin Grove** on Elm Street. The former Harry Isaac Lincoln building at Elm Street and Whitney Street is now

This Standard Station at a bend in downtown Rochelle has been restored and serves as a visitors center.

home to the National Headquarters of the Lincoln Highway Association. Harry, a distant cousin of the president, built it as a dry-goods store before the Civil War. The 1860 building was completely renovated in the 1990s, and visitors can now browse displays, books, and souvenirs. Across the street, eat lunch at the Lincoln Highway Café.

West of town are more abandoned pieces of road, including two crossings of Franklin

Creek. Only the abutments remain from the original, but the 1920 bridge still exists and can be seen from the current, third-generation bridge on IL Route 38.

The highway continues west to **Dixon**. IL Route 38 ends at Galena Avenue/U.S. Route 52. A couple blocks to the left, at 816 South Hennepin Avenue, is Ronald Reagan's boyhood home. He was born in nearby Tampico but moved to Dixon at age nine and lived here

from 1920 to 1923. None of the furnishings are original, as the family moved around so much.

The Lincoln Highway turns right (north) and follows Galena Avenue under the Victory Memorial Arch, built to honor the county's returning World War I veterans. In the 1919 dedication parade, fourteen Civil War veterans marched and occasionally fired their old rifles. The memorial was made permanent in 1920. A second arch was installed in 1949, a third arch was needed in 1966 when Galena Avenue was widened, and this one, the fourth, was dedicated in 1985 and made of fiberglass to slow its aging. It had to be located 145 feet to the south because of plans calling for a turning lane to IL Route 2.

The Beacon bar and restaurant still serves tasty food on Jones Road, east of downtown Rochelle.

BERNIE HEISEY

Crushing rocks into gravel for the Lincoln Highway at Ashton.

RUSSELL REIN

The Collier Inn was a welcome respite in central Illinois for early motorists.

Track Road, the original Lincoln Highway between Ashton and Franklin Grove.

A recent repaving of Galena Avenue—the Lincoln Highway—in Dixon.

The restored Harry Lincoln Building on Elm Street houses the LHA headquarters in Franklin Grove.

It now sits adjacent to the former Nachusa House hotel, built in 1837 and redone in 1853. The hotel is named for town founder John Dixon's Native American name.

The Lincoln Memorial Bridge over Rock River was built in 1939 and rebuilt recently. Across the bridge over the river, in Statue Park on the left, is a rendering of Lincoln as he was in 1832, when stationed here at Fort Dixon during the Black Hawk War. The nineteen-foot-tall bronze statue, depicting him as a twenty-three-year-old captain, was dedicated in 1930. It's believed to be the only statue of Lincoln in uniform.

At the north end of the bridge, the Lincoln Highway turns left on Everett Street and heads west. It briefly follows IL Route 2 but then branches right on Palmyra Road. It passes through **Prairieville** and rejoins IL Route 2 toward **Sterling**.

4th Street is one-way westbound, and 3rd Street is one-way eastbound. The 1924 LHA guide carried an ad for the Lincoln Tavern: "Sterling's new, modern hotel, a beautiful home for commercial men and tourists." The town is proud of its seven recently painted murals. On the west end, IL Route 2 bears left, while the Lincoln Highway goes right on Emerson Road. Bricking the highway west of Sterling in 1917 cost $19,500 per mile.

The Lincoln Highway passes through the tiny town of **Emerson** and continues on Emerson Road. U.S. Route 30 rejoins our route after making its straight shot west from Aurora. Some of the adjacent farm lanes have pieces of bypassed Lincoln Highway concrete across them. New signs near Lincoln Road and Yager Road point out the location of a 1915 Seedling Mile.

U.S. Route 30 heads to **Morrison**, which features Lincoln Highway lightpole banners and a mural just past Cherry Street showing a 1928 concrete post and garage scene. The Hillendale Bed and Breakfast is a large Tudor home with twenty-nine rooms and seventeen baths. It was run by Lincoln Highway fans Barbara and Mike Winandy, but they put it up for sale at the end of 2004. Mike also painted the town's mural. The restored 1891 home was once owned by the LHA county consul. It's at Olive Street; look for a replica concrete marker at the road. Also west of

The Hillendale B&B in Morrison is in an 1891 Tudor home. Former owners Mike and Barb Winandy planted this reproduction concrete post.

Lincoln Highway Tires featured the road's name in the sidewall.

town but east of Rock Creek are a couple log cabins remaining from an old tourist camp.

Just before **Fulton**, U.S. Route 30 branches left and crosses the Mississippi River about a mile south of the original span. The Lincoln

At Fulton, this new windmill overlooks the spot where the Lincoln once crossed the Mississippi. Friendly workers keep the machinery spinning and explain the process of grinding the grain.

Highway enters Fulton on IL Route 136. The town celebrates its Dutch heritage in many ways, such as Dutch Days every May. A few years ago, a full-size windmill was built in the Netherlands, then taken apart and shipped here for reassembly at the river's edge. It was dedicated as "De Immigrant" in May 2000. Grain is ground using windmill power, and a small counter at ground level serves as an information center.

IL Route 136 enters town on 16th Avenue, but the Lincoln Highway jogs up to 15th Avenue, then turns right on 4th Street, left on 10th Avenue, and right on 1st Street. The windmill now overlooks this intersection.

A block north on 1st Street, the Lincoln Highway curved left onto the Fulton and Lyons Bridge, a long, rickety span. Alice Ramsey described it well: "The floor of the bridge was of wood planking and just wide enough for passing. Altogether its width in proportion to its length looked pretty formidable, high above the wide water. . . . It was rather scary to contemplate as we approached."

Four decades later, Clinton Twiss wrote in *The Long, Long Trailer* that it "must be the world's narrowest bridge." He was not alone in his opinion:

> In the middle of the Mississippi, we encountered a woman driver aiming at us from the opposite direction. She zigzagged her way to within twenty feet of the trailer, stopped the car in the middle of the bridge, got out and thrust the key at me.
>
> If there was any passing to be done, she informed me, I would have to do it. . . .
>
> If these arrangements weren't suitable, she implied that the next twenty-four hour period was completely free and she would just as soon spend it in the middle of the Mississippi as anywhere else. . . .
>
> I admired her and envied her a little as I parked her car as close to the bridge rail as possible and squeezed The Monster past. The clearance would have torn tissue paper to shreds.

The Fulton and Lyons Bridge is gone now, only a bit of the approach road remaining north of the windmill. Today's drivers take IL Route 136 onto a wide span, to the relief of those who fear narrow bridges.

Greetings from
Iowa

As the Lincoln Highway in Ohio is known for brick pillars, in Iowa it is rich in concrete bridges. West of Jefferson is the five-span Eureka Bridge, west of Ogden is a "rainbow" arch bridge, east of Grand Junction is a small bridge with a Lincoln Highway "L" at each end, a bridge in Chelsea has lightposts on each corner, and most famous is a bridge at Tama with "Lincoln Highway" carved into each of its concrete railings.

The Tall Corn State is not nearly as flat as easterners might imagine, but it certainly fulfills its nickname, cornstalks sometimes stretching to the horizon left and right, forward and back. With all of this farmland, one-mile-square section lines become conspicuous; for early motorists, that meant straight roads and high speeds—when those roads were dry. As transcontinental regular Lester Whitman sped across Iowa in 1906, the Marshalltown paper reported that since leaving Carroll, he and his relay drivers sometimes reached sixty miles an hour, though in the process killing more than twenty chickens and wounding a pig. In *Across the Continent by the Lincoln Highway*, Effie Gladding likewise recalled that "one could cross Iowa on a trail marked by dead fowls. I had never before seen so many chickens killed by motor cars."

Many parts of Iowa's Lincoln Highway were bypassed decades ago, if not by shortcuts, then by U.S. Route 30, and then in 1966, by I-80. That leaves much of the original route the way it was when driven by the early motorists—an estimated 85 percent of the original highway is still drivable. The Lincoln makes random ninety-degree turns at section line corners on dirt and gravel roads with names like E53 or R38 or U Avenue or 219th Street. Sometimes there is no apparent name at all, making Gregory Franzwa's book or the state LHA's map pack necessary to trace the route. Lincoln Highway fans have painted the red, white, and blue logo on phone poles, but as late LHA director Doug Pappas wrote in his online diary, "Those poles are much more readable at a Model T's speed than at the pace of modern traffic."

The Lincoln Highway adopted a collection of paths across Iowa called the Transcontinental Route, connecting the Mississippi and Missouri Rivers via Clinton, Cedar Rapids, Ames, and Denison. Early speculation was that the Lincoln might follow the more southerly River-to-River Road through Des Moines, the state capital, but the Transcontinental Route was much flatter and had two river valleys (the Iowa and Boyer) to follow, plus it paralleled the Chicago and Northwestern Railroad just as the Lincoln Highway had done since Chicago.

The Lincoln didn't follow every turn of the Transcontinental Route, but that didn't stop the AAA from simply substituting the word "Lincoln" for "Transcontinental" in its *Automobile Blue Books*, confounding travelers for years. In *The Good of It All*, Thornton Round wrote that during their 1914 trip, his family noticed

	IOWA	U.S.
Population in 1910	2,224,771	92,228,496
Population in 2000	2,926,324	281,421,906
Persons per square mile in 2000	52.4	79.6
Approximate miles of Lincoln Highway	360	3,389

a difference between the two: "The Transcontinental Route is marked much better than the Lincoln—we find oftentimes by following the Lincoln we are led into towns quite unnecessarily, thereby losing a mile, possibly two miles, whereas the Transcontinental goes oftentimes straight through." The LHA didn't hesitate to bypass downtowns, but roads leading in and out of a town may have been a bit better tended. That may not have been such a concern in the East, but Iowa was notorious for its "gumbo" mud, a result of the land between the Mississippi and Missouri Rivers once having been submerged. The soil is superb for crops, but not so good for cars to cross when wet.

Making things worse was that Iowa's road building was determined and performed at the county level, and local voters preferred to have a little improvement done to all roads instead of lots of work on their portion of one long-distance route. LHA president Henry Joy even wrote a scathing article for *Collier's* in 1916, taking the state legislature to task for not fixing the situation: "Not a wheel turns outside the paved streets of her cities during or for sometime after the frequent heavy rains. . . . Millions of dollars worth of wheeled vehicles become, for the time being, worthless."

By 1920, with more than 430,000 registered vehicles, the state still had only *twenty-five miles* of paved roads outside of cities. The 1924 LHA guide warned, "It is folly to try to drive on Iowa dirt roads, during or immediately after a heavy rain."

Early motorists writing about their cross-country journeys had little to say east of the Mississippi; once on Iowa's dirt roads, they couldn't stop. Wrote Emily Post:

Illinois mud is slippery and slyly eager to push unstable tourists into the ditch, but in Iowa it lurks in unfathomable treachery, loath to let anything ever get out again that once ventures into it. Our progress through it became hideously like that of a fly crawling through yellow flypaper.

She *did* call the state much prettier than Illinois, but neither was she done complaining:

Twenty-five minutes of drizzle turned the smooth, hard surface of the road into the consistency of gruel. Not only that, but as though it were made in layers, and the top layer slid off the under layers and the under layers slipped out between, or the reverse. Our wheels, even with chains on, had no more hold than revolving cakes of soap might have on slanting wet marble.

It took Alice Ramsey thirteen days to cross the state's 360 miles. She wrote, "The accumulated rains of the past several days had already soaked deep enough below the surface of the roads to render them bottomless." Her radiator kept boiling over from having to plow along in low gear, and the flying mud filled the fenders until the wheels could no longer turn.

In *Fill 'er Up!* Bellamy Partridge wrote that when he crossed the country in 1912, the road was delightfully hard and smooth—until rain made it "the most treacherous, slippery, and dangerous highway on the face of the earth."

Fifteen years later, Frederic Van de Water found the state little changed. When his family crossed into Iowa and stopped at a camp in Lyons, they were greeted by the manager, Little Ella: "'Drive right in, folks,' she chanted; 'you're welcome. You're in Iowa now, the best state in the Union—with the worst roads.' We were to learn on the morrow that there was no exaggeration in the final portion of her state-

ment at least." Van de Water later concluded, "Iowans labor over their farms and let the roads take care of themselves."

When the mud dried, wagon wheels cut it into hard chunks that banged at fenders, and hard-edged ruts tore up tire sidewalls. The roads could be so rough that Van de Water, driving with his wife and six-year-old son, whom he nicknamed Supercargo, joked, "We seriously considered putting a leash on the Supercargo to guard against his being bounced entirely out of the machine."

Dry spells also brought horrible clouds of dust. While crossing the United States in 1928, Boy Scout Bernard Queneau wrote in his journal, "During the night there was a cloudburst, but it only helped to keep the dust down."

But it was the gumbo that was forever remembered. George Schuster said it best in his recollection of Ogden, Iowa, during the 1908 New York–to–Paris race: "It rained all day, the mud is nearly hub deep. We slid from one side of the road to the other. We covered more miles sidewise than ahead."

Into Iowa

The spindly Lyons and Fulton Bridge, named for the towns it connected, carried the Lincoln Highway across the Mississippi River. At the western shore, the bridge made a sharp right turn, not dangerous for horse traffic when built in 1891, but a hazard once automobiles began using it. A ramp then descended two blocks to street level in **Lyons**. The highway turned left from the ramp onto Main Street/24th Avenue (some sources say 25th Avenue), then a few blocks later, left onto 6th Street. Inside this turn was Little Ella's campground

A popular tactic of local boosters was to produce a map or guide like this 1928 foldout with ads for businesses on—and off—the route.

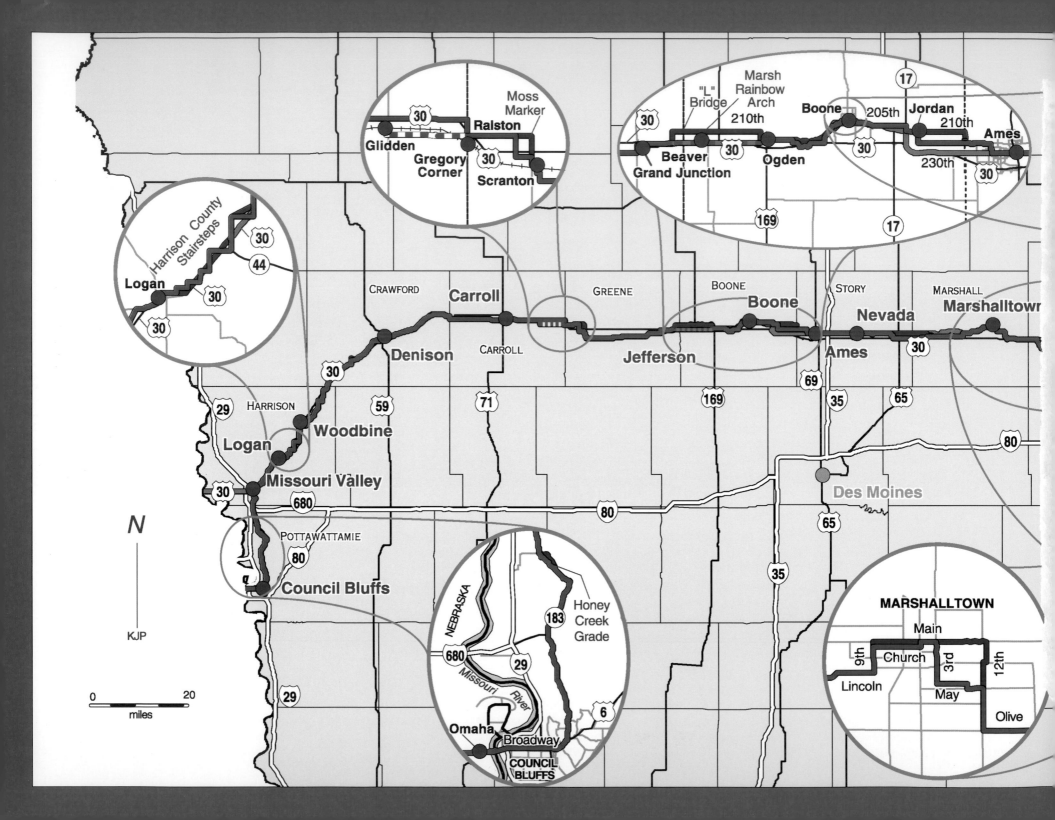

N

KJP

0   20
miles

Moss Marker
30
Glidden
Ralston
Gregory Corner
30
Scranton

"L" Bridge
Marsh Rainbow Arch
210th
30
Boone   205th
Jordan   210th
17
30
Beaver
Grand Junction
Ogden
30
169
17
Ames
230th
30

Harrison County Stairsteps
30
44
Logan
30

CRAWFORD
Carroll
GREENE
BOONE
STORY
MARSHALL
Marshalltown

Denison
CARROLL
Jefferson
Boone
Nevada
30

HARRISON
59
71
169
Ames
69
35
65
80

Logan
Woodbine

Missouri Valley
680
80
65

29
Des Moines

POTTAWATTAMIE
80
65

29
Council Bluffs
35

NEBRASKA
Honey Creek Grade
183
680
29
6
Missouri River
Omaha
Broadway
COUNCIL BLUFFS

29

MARSHALLTOWN
Main
9th
Church
3rd
12th
Lincoln
May
Olive

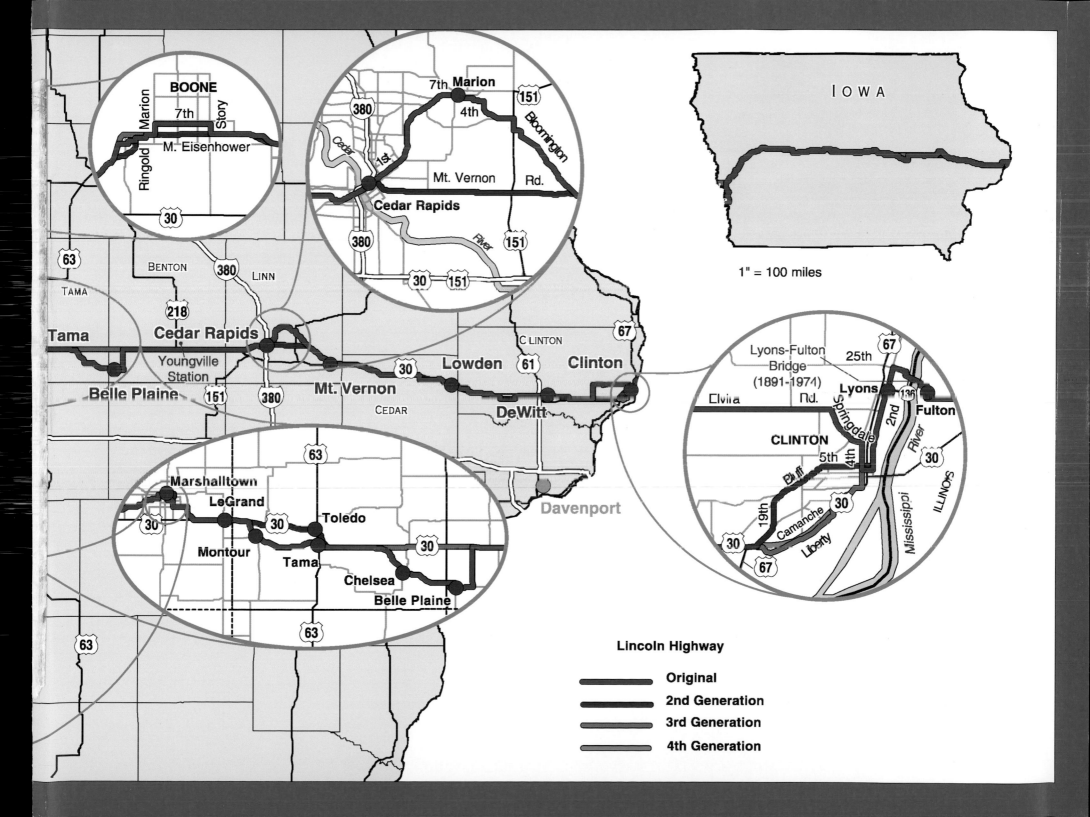

BOONE

Ringold Marion 7th Story

M. Eisenhower

30

7th **Marion**
4th
151
Bloomington

380

Cedar 1st

Mt. Vernon Rd.

Cedar Rapids

380 151

River

30 151

IOWA

1" = 100 miles

63

BENTON 380 LINN

TAMA

218

Tama **Cedar Rapids**

Youngville Station

Belle Plaine 151 380 **Mt. Vernon**

CEDAR

30 **Lowden** 61 **Clinton**

C LINTON

67

DeWitt

Lyons-Fulton Bridge (1891-1974)

Elvira Rd.

Lyons 25th 67

136 **Fulton**

Springdale 2nd

River

CLINTON

5th 4th 30

Bluff 19th

30

Camanche

Liberty

67

Mississippi River

ILLINOIS

63

Marshalltown

LeGrand

30 30 **Toledo**

Montour **Tama** 30

Chelsea

Belle Plaine

63

Davenport

Lincoln Highway

Original
2nd Generation
3rd Generation
4th Generation

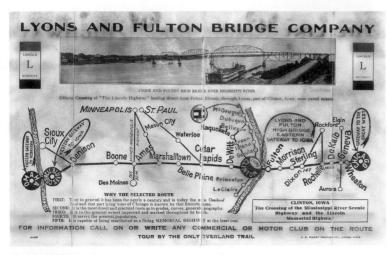

The rivalry for traffic across the Mississippi led this bridge company to establish its own information bureau to supply materials, such as this map, to tourists.

mentioned by Frederic Van de Water. Friendly, colorful Ella Sullivan didn't charge overnight guests, but made her living by hawking snacks and souvenirs.

The 1916 LHA guide noted that another route via a bridge to the south was also marked as the Lincoln Highway. By the next guide, the Lyons-to-Fulton crossing was the

only one mentioned, and by 1924, the Lyons and Fulton Bridge Company was running an ad calling itself the official crossing. However, the Clinton-Illinois Bridge Company likewise took out a full-page ad, claiming that its route was shorter and quicker. Additionally, "No speed cops patrol this stretch as is the case with the other routes and you also have a splendid view of the C. & N.W. Ry. Bridge over the Mississippi River, which is a sight worth seeing." This "Clinton High Bridge" spanned three islands and crossed over the railroad bridge, then dropped travelers onto 2nd Street at 6th Avenue.

The Lyons and Fulton Bridge was demolished in 1974; a replacement three blocks south now carries IA Route 136. Two miles south, the High Bridge is gone too, succeeded by a wide span carrying U.S. Route 30 onto 8th Avenue South.

Where 6th Street crossed from Lyons into **Clinton**, the road name changed to North 2nd Street. Clinton eventually incorporated the smaller town, and 6th Street was even renamed 2nd Street. The shell of the Lyons High School building remains, as do other old buildings along 2nd Street. It also carries U.S. Route 67 through town.

The Clinton chamber of commerce took out a full page ad in the LHA's 1924 road guide for "The Crossing City," as it called itself. The chamber invited motorists to visit for up-to-date road and weather conditions,

La Fayette Hotel, Clinton, Iowa.
On the Lincoln Highway.
Horton & Warden.
R. M. Fawcett, Mgr.

First Trans-Continental Sign erected on the Lincoln Highway.

BERNIE HEISEY

The signs above the Lincoln Highway logo announce "Transcontinental, New York–San Francisco" and "Clinton." The sender of this card wrote in 1919, "We spent the night here right on the banks of the Mississippi. Have stayed in a different state each night so far."

and it also maintained a comfort station at 4th Avenue and a free tourist camp at the western edge of town.

In *A Long Way from Boston*, Beth O'Shea wrote that she and her friend Kit decided to make their first attempt at camping here, so they drove along the Mississippi until they came upon "a large field where an old flivver touring car was parked in a grove of cotton-woods, and a man and a woman were sitting in camp chairs before a fire. . . . 'Is this a tourist camp?' I asked, looking around with interest. We had heard about them, but had expected something more elaborate."

The Lincoln Highway originally turned left from 2nd Street onto 6th Avenue—the intersection where the Clinton High Bridge rejoined the route. The LHA Control Point, from which guidebook distances were measured, was here at the Lafayette Hotel, now apartments. The original route went west two blocks on 6th Avenue, then back north along 4th Street and Springdale to head west toward **Elvira**. The route was soon changed to turn west from 2nd Street onto 5th Avenue. On the northwest corner is the Van Allen Department Store building, by noted architect Louis Sullivan. From 5th Avenue, two variations headed west, one via Bluff Boulevard and the other turning south on 4th Street, then curving west on Camanche Avenue (with a short bit on Liberty Avenue). This passes the Clinton stockyards and becomes Lincoln Way. Roadside researcher Russell Rein is a big fan of the Timber Motel, at 2225 Lincoln Way, which he calls "cheap, clean, and quiet."

The middle route from town took Bluff to 19th Street, then angled right on Old 30. It intersects Camanche Avenue from the

On August 2, 1925, a monument was unveiled in Clinton to honor Iowa's first state consul and LHA honorary vice president W. F. Coan.

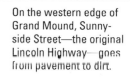

north, just as Liberty Avenue rejoins from the south.

Just past that, where U.S. Route 67 (the old Mississippi River Scenic Highway) turns left (south), is a block pillar dedicated in 1925 to Iowa's first state consul, W. F. Coan, for "promoting and establishing the Lincoln Highway." Coan had been made an honorary vice president of the LHA in 1914.

After five more miles, just outside the city limits, the Elvira route rejoins too; the Lincoln Highway heads west.

Early motorists found that the bad roads started as soon as they left Clinton. Frederic Van de Water wrote in 1927, "Before us lay a long cow-lane of caked mud, into which the tires of earlier cars had driven canyonlike ruts." After consulting guidebook, map, and terrain, there was no doubt: "This nightmare distortion of a road was a portion of the Lincoln Highway in the rich state of Iowa."

At **Malone**, U.S. Route 30 breaks south while the Lincoln Highway goes northwest and skirts the north edge of **DeWitt**. The Cross Roads Tourist Court, just east of town, was advertised in many travelers' guides of the 1930s and 1940s. Today the town has a cottage gas station on 11th Street at 4th Avenue. After **Grand Mound**, another cottage station can be found in **Calamus** on Clinton Street/U.S. Route 30 at 2nd Street.

On its way to **Wheatland**, the Lincoln Highway bears right, but a circa 1920 pony truss iron bridge across Calamus Creek has been closed for years. On its other side, the road crosses the Wapsipinicon River and traverses its wooded floodplain. The route

On the western edge of Grand Mound, Sunnyside Street—the original Lincoln Highway—goes from pavement to dirt.

A couple old businesses grace the Lincoln Highway at 11th Street in DeWitt.

The restored Lincoln Hotel in Lowden.

features pavement from the 1920s and three more vintage bridges. A local group hopes to turn the bypassed road into a hiking trail.

From Wheatland, the original route stair-steps its way to **Lowden**, once the main station for the railroad between Clinton and Cedar Rapids; the town's historical society is in the relocated depot. A third cottage station is on the east end. The highway enters town on Main Street and turns right on Washington Avenue. At the corner is the 1915 Lincoln Hotel, restored in 1995 and now offering two hotel rooms and five apartments. Washington Avenue also serves the Herbert Hoover Highway, designated in 1923 as a tribute to the food relief programs administered by President Herbert Hoover, which had fed an estimated 318 million victims of war and drought in Europe and the Soviet Union since 1914. Hoover was born southwest of here, near Iowa City.

Along the Cedar Rapids–Mount Vernon Cutoff, 1922.

A mile west of town, while U.S. Route 30 makes a straight line to the northwest, an abandoned section of the original Lincoln runs along the north side of the tracks. Weeds are overtaking it, as are stray trees to each side. It's on private land and is blocked, but soon rejoins U.S. Route 30. In **Clarence**, a refurbished cottage station and a mural of the town in earlier days are on the west end of U.S. Route 30.

George Schuster stayed here during the 1908 New York–to–Paris race. He wrote that once they entered Iowa, the sun was melting the frozen roads:

> We now had a battle with mud, heavy and black, the tires of our car throwing it in big gobs onto fenders and running boards. . . . Covered with mud, we stopped that night in Clarence, Iowa. "Take your car over to the fire station," somebody told us. "That's the only place you can get that mud washed off." . . . This was so effective that we visited fire stations at several later stops.

More vintage filling stations can be found in **Stanwood** and, after passing through **Mech-** anicsville, in **Lisbon** on East Main Street, U.S. Route 30 passes south of Lisbon and Mount Vernon and completely bypasses Marion and downtown Cedar Rapids.

On the west end of **Mount Vernon** is a short but striking brick section on 10th Avenue leading to a pony truss viaduct. The bridge, an early grade separation over the Chicago and North Western Railroad, was closed in the 1980s and scheduled for removal, but local Dick Thomas led a crusade to save it. Permission was arranged with the railroad (now the Union Pacific), grants were secured, and the bridge was beautifully restored with new wooden floor planks and rededicated in 1999. The arched span is again open, but only to foot traffic.

About four miles west of Mount Vernon lies Iowa's Seedling Mile. These were an LHA brainstorm: Find the worst stretch of dirt road and pave a mile with wide, hard concrete, in hopes that locals will be so impressed that they press for more good roads. The best part was that it cost the LHA nothing; cement

SPECIAL COLLECTIONS LIBRARY, UNIVERSITY OF MICHIGAN

The Twin Towers in Cedar Rapids about 1939.

companies donated the materials, and locals did the work. Small signs mark the stretch, and recent efforts by LHA members Van and Bev Becker resulted in score marks indicating the mile of roadway, as well as a marker being erected on the west end.

This Seedling Mile caused unforeseen complications; once it was complete, there was a proposal to pave from its end straight west to Cedar Rapids, bypassing Marion. The county courthouse was moved to Cedar Rapids at about the same time, adding insult to injury. The "shortcut" is now Mount Vernon Road; it indeed bends left at the end of the Seedling Mile and continues about seven miles to Cedar Rapids, passing the old Light House restaurant. Meanwhile, the original gravel Lincoln Highway continues straight, stair-stepping through the edge of Squaw Creek County Park to **Marion**.

There, the Lincoln heads west on U.S. Route 151/7th Avenue. A Maid-Rite restaurant, famed for its "loose meat" sandwiches, is at the corner of 10th Street. The Maid-Rite Corporation traces its origins to 1926, when Muscatine, Iowa, butcher Fred Angell was experimenting with spices in a loose grind of beef. A customer reportedly told Fred the sandwich was "made right," inspiring the name, which was changed to "maid" to capitalize on the trend at the time for cleanliness and purity. The sandwich is somewhat like a Sloppy Joe, but without the sauce, and is served with a spoon. Amazingly, the first four franchises are still in business, one of them on the Lincoln Highway in Marshalltown.

U.S. Route 151 bends southwest to **Cedar Rapids**. A 1940 travelers' Motor Court Service guide pictures Lincoln Way camp "east of the business district," with seventeen cottages from $1.50 to $3. The road into town becomes 1st Avenue, and at 10th Street, the "shortcut" rejoins the route. Ten blocks later, the Lincoln Highway crosses the Cedar River, then leaves town via Johnson Avenue. The Twin Towers café, an old one-stop, has been

rehabbed as apartments, though its famed towers are still discernible.

In her 1916 book, *By Motor to the Golden Gate*, Emily Post said she had a dreadful time reaching here, the roads and weather tainting her view of her hotel and Cedar Rapids itself: "It was all drenched in rain, and the little we saw of it looked ugly and brown, and finally our rooms were completely sapping to joyfulness of spirit. . . . Dingy bottle-green paper, a stained carpet, a bathroom in which the plumbing wouldn't work, a depressing view of a torn-up street!" When she wrote about her trip for *Collier's*, the local paper took her, one of the "dyspeptic authoresses in the East," to task. She conceded that "it is a very distorted judgment that appraises a town by a few rooms in a hotel" but that hotel rooms inevitably color tourists' impressions.

Johnson Avenue meets 16th Avenue, and both have 1928 concrete posts on them. The U.S. Route 30 bypass rejoins the Lincoln Highway/16th Avenue. Together they head west for an amazing twenty-four-mile straightaway.

It's no coincidence that right in the middle of this stretch is a rural roadhouse. There isn't really a town of Youngville, but the regulars at Youngville Station don't mind. Built by Joseph Young in 1931, the Tudor-style station also had a café and cabins—a "one-stop" to serve all a traveler's needs. By the 1990s, it was closed and in terrible shape, but many volunteers have helped restore it (though three renovated cabins were burned in 2004). The volunteers have built historical displays and offer a limited lunch menu—stop for a piece of pie. It's at

A lot of work went into restoring Youngville Station.

The Lincoln Cafe still serves locals and travelers in Belle Plaine.

the intersection where U.S. Route 218 turns north. A little east, the Ced-Rel Motel and Supper Club added another roadside rest to the long stretch just after World War II.

South of the route are the seven villages comprising the Amana Colonies, founded in 1855 by a traditional Protestant religious sect. Communalism was discontinued in 1932; two years later, Amana Refrigeration was founded in the group's woolen mill. Tourists now shop here for handmade furniture and crafts, plus German-themed food and gifts.

At IA Route 131, U.S. Route 30 continues west across nine ridges—the Bohemian Hills—but the Lincoln avoided them by turning south and following section lines through Belle Plaine. Perhaps LHA planners also realized the prudence of adding a town on this sparse stretch; it would have been another sixteen miles to Tama. Sounds short today, but not over hilly, muddy terrain. It wasn't until 1937 that U.S. Route 30 bypassed Belle Plaine and Chelsea.

The Lincoln turns south on IA Route 131, then west on E66; Wayfarer's Camp on this corner is seen in old postcards.

The highway enters **Belle Plaine** on 13th Street. Thornton Round wrote that when his family came through in 1914, "This town claimed a great distinction. It had a paved street! But we were not permitted to ride on that street. The police were routing traffic onto another detour, as the street was being repaired."

Sankot's Garage, east of 8th Avenue, has changed little since the family opened it in 1914. The Lincoln originally turned north at 8th Avenue; later it continued straight on 13th Street. West of 8th Avenue are two more landmarks: the Lincoln Café to the left, and the former Herring Hotel on the right, which also served as the LHA Control Station (used to determine mileages for LHA guidebooks). The hotel is now an apartment house, but in 1909, Alice Ramsey gushed about having breakfast there. Two decades later, Dallas Lore Sharp wrote in *The Better Country* of staying overnight at what was advertised as "the swellest little hotel in Iowa." He and his wife, Daphne, found the owner eager to please:

> "You're in the home of the literati," said mine host. . . . "I've entertained other great men, you see."
>
> I braced up visibly, and asked about something to eat.
>
> "We don't serve meals," he replied with fervor, "but I have the best radio set in this town, if not in the entire State. Be my guests at the concert to-night, I beg you."

After dinner at a café, perhaps the Lincoln across the street, they returned to the parlor "to attend the concert upon the air." Except the hotel "was too full of 'bones,' the static spoiling everything over Belle Plaine that night except the Bedtime Story." The awful interference along with the gentle tale of two baby woodchucks lost in the woods put Sharp to sleep.

Continuing west on 13th Street takes you to the town's best-known landmark, George Preston's filling station on the corner of 4th Avenue. The station was originally at 7th Avenue and 19th Street, on the original routing of the Lincoln through town, but it was moved with the route in 1921. George started working there in 1925, at age thirteen, and later bought the business. He covered the walls of the station and storage shed with tin and porcelain enamel signs advertising oil, tires, gasoline, batteries, and heaps of other auto accessories. He was even more renowned for the endless stories he could tell about the road. In December 1989, the station long closed, Preston launched George's Story Line, a 900 telephone number that offered prerecorded tales from his repertoire of thousands. That landed him on Johnny

George Preston's famously decorated gas station and storage shed on the western end of Belle Plaine.

Chelsea enters the auto age.

The King Tower complex, a 1930s one-stop, still had its adjacent gas station in this view from the late 1950s.

Carson's "Tonight Show" in March 1990. I met him one year later, still spinning his tales and pulling out road history relics from every cranny of his station. George passed away in 1993, but the station remains a shrine to early motor travel—so much so that new traffic signs warn, No Stopping.

After their night at the Herring Hotel, Dallas and Daphne Sharp headed west, wary that "two abysmal ditches . . . one on each side of the road, ran like a Nemesis under and along with us." The sky turned dark, "the wet side of a sagging Western sky," and a lone snowflake wafted down. "Then everything began to spit. And simultaneously everything began to slide. . . . Here was something new—a new form of motion."

There was nothing for the car to get hold of, "nothing even gritty geological, the very order of the universe without firmness or fiber! The car seemed about to dissolve, its reins no longer a frame of fabricated steel, but spilled and quaking jelly. And when it

stopped going round, it lay sprawling in the elemental ooze of that Iowa road."

They were lucky that they came to rest across the crown of the road and not off it like so many others, but as Sharp noted to Daphne, "The only gears in this car that I know about go forward or reverse. In either of those directions lies a ditch." Still, they needed to move, so by a combination of chains, spread-out newspapers, flying mud, and a bucking car, they managed to turn westward.

The road continues to **Chelsea**, which still has an early brick garage with a DX gasoline sign. The route, now Irish Street, crosses Otter Creek, turns north (marked by a 1928 concrete post) and crosses Otter Creek again on a concrete bridge featuring vintage lights at its corners. The old road rejoins U.S. Route 30 and heads west to **Tama**. Grab a bite at the two-story King Tower Café. The adjacent streamlined-tower gas station is gone, but a cabin remains in back. A stunning Indian-head neon sign also survives.

Immediately west of the café, U.S. Route 30 bends right (north), but the original Lincoln Highway went straight west on 5th Street; that's obvious by one of the road's best-known landmarks, the one-of-a-kind Lincoln Highway Bridge. It was built in 1915 with "Lincoln Highway" formed into its railings and small lightpoles atop each corner. The town was bypassed in 1926, but the bridge was added to

Perhaps the most photographed bridge on the Lincoln Highway is on the east end of Tama, despite a nearby sign warning drivers not to stop.

the National Register of Historic Places in 1976 and restored in 1987. Just north of it are a couple parking spots and a sign with a history of the bridge and a request that fans examine it from their cars because of safety concerns.

The Lincoln Highway jogged through Tama, then went west following E49. U.S. Route 30 passes north through Tama's sister city, Toledo. You'll find a fading neon sign for the Twin Town Motel and a Maid-Rite restaurant diagonal to a corner; a colorful 1959 postcard called it Scudder's Maid-Rite Cafe.

An ad in the 1915 LHA guide promotes Tama's Lincoln Garage, "strictly modern" and open till midnight. At the west end of town, a pair of pillars were built in 1915 to welcome travelers. West of Tama is the Mesquakie (or Meskwaki) Settlement, founded as a reservation for Sac and Fox Indians. The tribes now own and operate the Meskwaki Bingo, Casino, and Hotel.

The Lincoln Highway crosses the Iowa River two miles west of Tama. Until the grade was raised with fill, the road through the river bottoms was among the stickiest in the state.

Two and a half miles west of the Iowa River, halfway uphill, is the site where LHA field secretary Henry Ostermann died on June 8, 1920. Driving the LHA's 1918 Packard Twin Six, he tried to pass another car but lost control on wet grass along the shoulder. The car flipped twice, landing on its wheels, but Ostermann's head had been crushed.

The route jogs through **Montour** and rejoins U.S. Route 30, which zips through **Le Grand**.

Three miles east of **Marshalltown**, the Lincoln Highway turns north on Shady Oaks Road. A sign advertises, "Historic Shady Oaks RV Campground and Big Tree House." The tent sites and RV hookups are still shaded by oaks from the mid-nineteenth century. A restored office/residence from 1925 remains, as do a dayroom and one of five cabins. The cabin served as a garage for forty years, but a two-year restoration has brought back its orig-

inal charm, with modern amenities. Overlooking the site is the treehouse, the hobby of Mick Jurgensen, who has lived here since age three. Since he first started adding to the giant maple in 1983, it's grown to twelve levels, fifty-five feet high, and five thousand square feet of floor space, and it is outfitted with a phone, a microwave, a grill, music, running water, a spiral staircase, fourteen porch swings, and a small museum. You can tour it if weather permits and a guide is available, but reservations are necessary. Mick also re-created a 1918 Marsh rainbow-arch bridge that was once located west of the camp. The last such concrete-arch bridge remains on the Lincoln sixty miles farther west.

The 1916 LHA guide carried ads for Marshalltown's Pilgrim Hotel and the Rude Auto Company—perhaps not the best name to attract travelers.

In *The Family Flivvers to Frisco*, Frederic Van de Water wrote of the town's "lovely and spacious tourist park. Great trees lay down wide rugs of shade and the sward on which these rest is thick and comforting." The camp, half a mile north of town, had showers and a swimming pool, but it was shade and grass—meaning that there would not be mud and dirt—that meant the most to tired travelers.

The original way through Marshalltown took travelers over to 3rd Avenue, where they drove north past Stone's Restaurant, founded just before the turn of the twentieth century. Stone's is famed for lemon chiffon pie. A modern viaduct towers over the restaurant, though a bit of old road remains to keep it company, while a rooftop sign advertises to those crossing the viaduct.

To eliminate a railroad crossing east of Marshalltown in 1923, a bridge across the tracks was constructed above the road, then earthen ramps were built up to meet it.

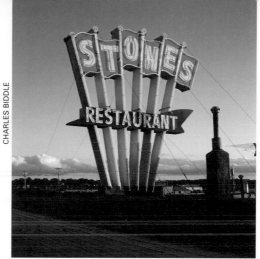

Stone's sign can be seen from the 3rd Street viaduct, but the business still fronts the original path of the Lincoln below.

enty-five-year-old "cooker" where customers can see it. The menu also includes fish, pizza, salads, malts, and other sandwiches with the "-rite" name: Cheese-Rite, Bacon Cheese-Rite, Chili-Rite, Mega-Rite. Souvenirs include a small beverage glass for $2.

At Marshalltown's main intersection, turn left (west) from 3rd Avenue onto Main Street, where an eight-story apartment house was once the prestigious Tall Corn Hotel.

The route turns down 9th Street, then right on West Lincoln Way, where a giant pin oversees a bowling alley. Two miles west of Marshalltown drivers met a notorious descent called Four Mile Hill. A sharp curve at the bottom was the undoing of many whose brakes had overheated on the way down or who slid down on rainy days. The climb for westbound drivers was equally challenging. In 1914, the county began leveling the slope; Effie Gladding was impressed by the newfangled steam shovel which she dubbed "a dirt-eating machine."

The route passes the south edge of **Lamoille**; two generations of the road split, the older to the south going through **State Center**, "the rose capital of Iowa," the newer to the north just skirting the town.

Just ahead is another famous food stop, Taylor's Maid-Rite. It's run by Don Taylor Short, great-grandson of founder Clifford Taylor, who purchased the second Maid-Rite franchise in 1928 for $300. The family baked pies at home and sliced whole pickles from a nearby vinegar works. The current restaurant was built in 1958; you can still sit on a stool around the U-shaped counter. They butcher the meat downstairs, then bring it up to a sev-

Loose meat sandwiches are the staple at Taylor's Maid-Rite in Marshalltown.

As Jacob Murdock crossed the country in 1908, he came to a water hazard four miles west of State Center. As reprinted in McConnell's *Coast to Coast by Automobile*, he described it as "a swamp called 'Duck Pond' credited with having the worst bit of mud road in the United States. This stretch of road is about two miles long, it being graded up about two feet, with the water of the Duck Pond on both sides. It is undermined in so many places by beavers and muskrats."

The original Lincoln Highway is believed to have rejoined present U.S. Route 30, the later Lincoln still to the north, both heading west into Story County. If so, the original stepped north through **Colo**, the later Lincoln eventually crossing a concrete span at the intersection of the Jefferson Highway. The original Jefferson came from the north and shared the road with the Lincoln from here to Nevada, Iowa. U.S. Route 65 was later routed through this intersection; the crossroads was remade in 1938 into a grade separation with

Chippewa Lanes, on the west end of Marshalltown.

ramps, making a partial cloverleaf. Adjacent landowner Charles Reed fought against a full cloverleaf.

The Jefferson Highway was organized in November 1915 at New Orleans (though the idea was actually conceived at Des Moines). The route extended from New Orleans north to Winnipeg, Manitoba, Canada, in honor of Thomas Jefferson and his role in the Louisiana Purchase. A concrete marker for the Jefferson is in a yard adjacent to the curve running north of that highway.

Just beyond the bridge Charles Reed built a "one-stop," a place that offered gas, food, and lodging for early travelers. He opened the L&J Service Station (named for the highways) in 1923, then built a new station three years later. At the same time, the Niland's, his nephew's family, moved a building adjacent and opened a café. They also built some cabins. The busy crossroads was prosperous, but the station closed in 1967. U.S. Route 30 had

been rerouted to the south five years earlier, plus Reed had died and I-80 was completed across the state the year before. The café closed in 1991 but the building remained, as did the station, motel rooms, and washhouse.

The city of Colo bought the buildings in the late 1990s with hopes of reviving the complex. LHA member Lyell Henry worked for more than five years on the restoration of Reed's service station, Niland's Café, and the Colo Motel. The café reopened in late 2003. Inside are vintage road signs, a cool jukebox, and an exhibit about road travel set in a 1940s-style display. The front half of a 1939 Cadillac juts out of a corner. The interior of Reed's station looks like the 1930s have stood still.

About two miles west, four cabins that marked the site of Shady Point Cabin Camp were recently demolished. Another couple miles farther is an underpass beneath the rails of the C&NW, and just past that, the Lincoln crossed a lesser railroad.

The main dining room in the restored Niland's Café.

Nevada (nuh-VAY-duh) is most famous for starting (and continuing) the first Lincoln Highway Days celebration in 1984. The annual event, held the fourth weekend in August, features dances, a rodeo, car show, big parade, and the crowning of a king, queen, prince, and princess. A stone welcome monument greets visitors: "You are traveling on the original Lincoln Highway." The town has three 1928 concrete markers, one to the east, two to the west.

Approaching **Ames**, the now-closed Colonial Motel on East Lincoln Way opened as the Conoco in 1938, very early for a motel building. The Ames Motor Lodge, opened in 1926, was likewise a very early tourist court. A food treat is Hickory Park Restaurant, 1404 South Duff Avenue, between Lincoln Way and U.S. Route 30. Its website recounts that the business started in 1970 when a closed barbecue at 604 East Lincoln Way was bought and reopened as Hickory Park, with a mir-

rored ice cream fountain added and church pews brought in to provide more seating. A decade later, having outgrown its space, Hickory Park moved to Southeast 16th Street, but even triple the room wasn't enough, so in 1997, the business resettled on Duff Avenue. The pews remain, as does the ice cream fountain. There's a huge selection of banana splits, sundaes, and parfaits, and you can add a flavor to beverages for 15¢. On the wall is a tin Lincoln Highway cigar sign.

The route follows Lincoln Way through town but eventually jogs north and heads west on gravel roads. Effie Gladding noted that this was the land of wheat and oats and, of course, corn. Indeed, west into Nebraska, cornfields still stretch impossibly ahead to the horizon.

As you come into **Boone**, a short stone marker cut with the words "Lincoln Highway" and "County Road" marks the corner of Snedden Drive and Mamie Eisenhower Avenue. The former first lady was born in 1896 on Carroll Street at 7th Street, the Lincoln Highway. The small Victorian home has been restored and features two of her cars. The town also once had an iron-frame welcome arch.

Thornton Round wrote in *The Good of It All* that his family camped near Boone during their 1914 trip as they were returning eastward. When they asked a farmer whether they might camp near his house, he replied, "You sure can. We get a little lonesome at times, and I think it would be nice to talk to you about the western country you just came from."

The road heads southwest from Boone, descending a scenic curve—said to be the state's last portion of the Lincoln Highway to

Reed's Standard Service Station was adjacent to the café and cabin camp.

Looking west to the restored complex.

Looking southwest to the Des Moines River Valley, west of Boone.

Located on U.S. Highways Nos. 65 and 30 At the East edge of town

AMES TOURIST COURT
J. W. OGLE, Prop. ~ AMES, IOWA

Furnished Cabins
Room for car inside

Some buildings remain at the once prosperous Ames Tourist Court, captured on a postcard in 1930.

be paved—and across the Des Moines River. A circa 1930 postcard shows the Riverside Tourist Camp snuggled next to a 1924 iron bridge. Another bridge peeking from the trees beyond is likely the Rose Ferry Bridge, which served the route first; only bits of its piers remain. The original route went south, then turned west where U.S. Route 30 is today. Along the western riverbank was Nic-O-Let amusement park; as with the bridge, only foundations remain.

U.S. Route 30 passes south of Boone and **Ogden**, but the Lincoln Highway enters on Walnut Street, where original pavement has been saved. At the corner of 6th Street is a streamlined, cream-colored and porcelain-enamel-paneled Standard service station. A more humorous sight is footprints crossing the road here, embedded since someone walked across the wet concrete in 1929.

The Lincoln Highway west of Ogden was bypassed in 1919. The original route headed west from town along the path of today's

U.S. Route 30. It jogged north of the railroad and through **Beaver**, where the cinder-block Sparks Garage is an early roadside remnant. Beaver had the distinction of being the first town bypassed by the Lincoln Highway in Iowa; within the first year, the route was moved a mile north to eliminate several rail crossings. That route, along gravel 210th Street, leads to the 1915 Marsh rainbow arch bridge, five miles west of Ogden and just north of Beaver. The Marsh Engineering Company designed, patented, and built these graceful spans. Two miles past that is the "L" bridge, so named for the letters cut into its end walls. The Lincoln was rerouted again back south in 1919, near but not through Beaver, leaving the bridges among the fields.

East of **Grand Junction**, the Lions Club Tree Park will some day include a Lincoln Highway interpretive site for the four bridges

over West Beaver Creek: a C&NW Railroad bridge, a U.S. Route 30 bridge, and a pair of Lincoln Highway–era bridges. One, abandoned and north of the railroad embankment, is difficult to access. When the bridge was in danger of being destroyed, LHA cofounders Bob and Joyce Ausberger bought the land around it.

Grand Junction gets its name from its 1869 founding at the intersection of two railroads. Greene County, like much of the state, was settled for farming in the mid-nineteenth century. The railroad followed soon after, spurring settlement. Leaving town, the Lincoln passes canopy gas stations, remnants of Camp Cozy Tourist Camp at 8th Street and E53, and the abandoned Star Motel. Another concrete span, now gone, crossed Buttrick Creek. The Head Memorial Bridge was opened in October 1914, a year after the Lincoln Highway was established. The road just west of it is abandoned.

U.S. Route 30 stays north of **Jefferson**, but the Lincoln enters the center of the small town. Jefferson was laid out in 1854 as New Jefferson, named for President Thomas Jefferson. A Lincoln statue was dedicated on September 22, 1918, on the lawn of the Greene County Courthouse. The Mahanay Memorial Carillon Tower, on the southwest corner of the courtyard, was given to the people of Jefferson and Greene County in accordance with the wills of Mr. and Mrs. Floyd Mahanay. The tower, dedicated on October 16, 1966, tops 168 feet and has fourteen bells cast in Holland. These chime on the hour, quarter, and half hour. The electronic bells may be played automatically or manually from the same keyboard. Every June, the town sponsors a Bell Tower Festival that's packed with events.

West of the square, the old Five Spot Café, like the White Towers and White Castles of its day, was famous for nickel hamburgers, or a bag of twenty-four for a dollar. It is now the headquarters of the Greene County LHA.

The entire Lincoln Highway in Greene County is a multiple-property listing on the National Register of Historic Places. Besides the Lincoln statue, other highlights are the many stretches of dirt road and original pavement, Lincoln Highway markers, canopy gas stations, and five historic bridges.

Leaving Jefferson on E53, the route crosses Raccoon Creek on the graceful five-span concrete Eureka Bridge. The road then climbs what was once "Danger Hill," made worse by a sharp turn at the bottom that prevented getting up to speed quickly. Alice Ramsey wrote

that during her 1909 trip, her Maxwell, with chains on, pulled a stuck car over the hill. The danger was recognized and reduced by 1914 with a road cut at the top, but until then, motorists often climbed it in reverse, so that the carb would not rise above the gas tank and because the gearing made for better traction.

The original road jogs north through **Scranton**, making eight turns through town. A later routing headed straight north on IA Route 25, then turned left (west) onto today's E39. A pair of concrete monuments near that corner, facing each road, were built in 1924 by landowner James Edward Moss, a Civil War veteran and fan of President Lincoln. Moss

Three wonderful concrete bridges can be found on the old Lincoln between Ogden and Grand Junction, including the Marsh rainbow bridge (built in a rainbow-arch shape by Marsh Engineering Company) north of Beaver.

SPECIAL COLLECTIONS LIBRARY, UNIVERSITY OF MICHIGAN

LHA's Western Iowa consul E. B. Wilson inspects a road cut in Greene County in 1918.

In his eighties, Civil War veteran J. E. Moss erected two matching monuments to Lincoln on a curving corner of his farm, where the highway turned, near Scranton. Mr. and Mrs. Moss, here flanking the monument, gathered with others for the dedication in 1926.

George Gregory erected this marker at the corner of his farm northwest of Ralston, Iowa, where the Lincoln Highway turned north for a mile before heading west again toward Glidden. The concrete monument is thirteen feet long and a foot thick. Other Gregory corner markers remain in the vicinity.

erected them two years after the Lincoln Highway was paved in 1924; Greene County was first in the state to gravel, then pave, its portion. The monuments were vandalized in the 1950s, but one of the heads was found in 1993 and was used to create new ones. Twenty-three Moss descendants attended the unveiling in July 2001, including two grandchildren.

The road passes the north edge of **Ralston**. At the county line is "Gregory Corner," named for a concrete marker placed on the northwest corner in 1902 to mark a farm boundary. The routing west to **Glidden** is questionable; Gregory Franzwa told the intriguing tale in his Iowa book. He concluded that the official LHA route turned north at Gregory Corner, thereby skipping two rail crossings and downtown Glidden, factors that surely would have swayed the LHA. But Franzwa, personally familiar with the town, also concluded that Glidden's townspeople marked the route going straight at Gregory Corner, directing traffic through their tiny business district, and that's the way everyone came to know it.

Go straight on 210th Street so that five miles later, you too can turn right on Idaho Street, Glidden's main street. A few blocks later, turn west again, rejoining U.S. Route 30.

With such strong town boosters, it's not surprising to see this fawning text in Huebinger's 1912 Iowa road atlas:

> Glidden, by reason of its most favorable location on the Iowa official transcontinental Route, is a real resting place for tourists. Plenty of shade, excellent drinking water, refreshment parlors, cafes and a hotel whose home cooking, chicken dinners, rich cream, fresh butter and eggs have made it famous all over the west. . . .

It wants more factories, more business houses, more citizens and will meet half way any prospect or proposition having such an end in view.

Half a mile west of town on U.S. Route 30 is a granite monument to Merle Hay, one of the first three U.S. soldiers—the first from Iowa—killed in World War I. In July 1919, the First Transcontinental Army Truck Convoy made a point of visiting Hay's parents in Glidden.

It's seven miles to **Carroll**, where the Lincoln enters on 6th Street. After a few blocks, the Lincoln Highway turns left onto Carroll Street while U.S. Route 30 continues straight. Road enthusiast Russell Rein recommends the Motel 71-30, where U.S. Route 30 intersects U.S. Route 71, which has its own miniature golf course.

Overlooking the 6th Street and Carroll Street is Wittrock Motor Company, a Chrysler dealership that retains its 1931 double-canopy station and a small early showroom, with a couple muscle cars among the new offerings. The business goes back to 1913, when it was Swaney Auto Company. Each corner of the intersection had a station, but Swaney was the only one to run an ad in the LHA's 1916 guide. It also became the LHA control point for Carroll. A showroom was built adjacent, as was the double-canopy, mission tile–roof station. The business changed hands a number of times. Then, in the 1960s, it was purchased by Mike Wittrock Sr. In the mid-1990s, Wittrock and his son, Mike Jr., restored the station and showroom, which has a tin ceiling and polished oak floor. The station was converted to offices.

Nearby, Tony's restaurant was founded by the late Anthony Vorsten in the 1950s. He

Mike Wittrock in front of his Carroll car dealership, which retains this rare double-canopy station.

was the last president of the Iowa Route 30 Association, a promotional entity that disbanded with the formation of the current LHA. Vorsten saw to it that the remaining association funds went to the LHA. His family still operates the restaurant.

In 1914, Effie Gladding liked Carroll, which she called "a pleasant little town, with fine street lamps, and with a green park around its Courthouse. We were surprised to find so good a hotel as Burke's Hotel in a small town." Eating supper at a nearby restaurant, she was intrigued by a party of four young people: "The two young gentlemen, by a liberal use of twenty-five cent pieces, kept the mechanical piano pounding out music all through their meal. They were both guiltless of coats and waistcoats." The custom

of men wearing shirts and trousers sans coats was just one of many they found peculiar in the West.

The Lincoln Highway heads west from town on 3rd Street, with U.S. Route 30 parallel a mile to the north. Passing south of **Arcadia**, the route stair-steps through **Westside** and turns to the southwest. It heads this general direction all the way to Nebraska.

The Lincoln rejoins U.S. Route 30. After the town of **Vail**, the road enters **Denison** on 4th Avenue. U.S. Route 30 stays on 4th Avenue, but the Lincoln turns left on Main, then right on 4th Avenue, only to dead-end at U.S. Route 59. Back on 5th Avenue are the Ho Hum Motel (900 block) and Trees Motel (1400 block), but most notable is the Park Motel at 803 Highway 30, which is listed on

the National Register of Historic Places. The two-story, Spanish Colonial Revival structure was built in 1940 by Ted Port. He had opened a gas station across the road in 1926 on the newly christened U.S. Route 30, and added a café in 1929, all in the same style. Port sold the café to L. J. Cronk in the 1930s, but once the motel was built, it and the café continued to be advertised together. The motel offers single rooms in the main building, many with original furniture. Two detached wings were

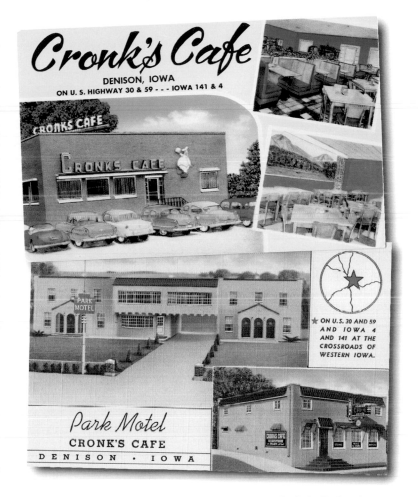

Both the Park and Cronk's remain, a bit remodeled but serving folks driving the old highways.

added in 1965. Themed rooms range from Fisherman's Delight and Leopard Jacuzzi to the Donna Reed Suite.

Every June, the town throws a weeklong Donna Reed Festival and Workshops for the Performing Arts. Reed, who was born in Denison in 1921, was known for her roles in the classic films *It's A Wonderful Life* and *From Here to Eternity* and the TV series "The Donna Reed Show."

Leaving town, the road continues its southwest course; a gravel remnant on the right was built up to keep above the floods of the Boyer River. The road stair-steps through the little town of **Arion**. Southwest of town, two culverts in a field mark the original course of the Lincoln. The route then enters the slightly larger **Dow City**. Paralleling U.S. Route 30, it continues through **Dunlap**, and then briefly follows a stagecoach route from the 1850s. The zigzag road once entered **Woodbine** on an iron bridge over the Boyer River, but the bridge was destroyed by high waters in 1998, severing the route into town.

Woodbine is famous among Lincoln Highway fans for its brick roads and sidewalks. In 2003, an estimated 322,156 bricks were reset along six blocks of Lincoln Way, and streetlights were added. The town takes a lot of pride in the road, which also has three canopy gas stations and homes that are little changed from when the street was originally bricked in 1921. The bricked section of the road is on the National Register of Historic Places.

As you drive west from Woodbine on U.S. Route 30, roads that angle away are remnants of the Lincoln Highway as it stair-stepped southwest to **Logan**, where the city park still

has a band shell. Five culverts hidden in the fields mark an abandoned second-generation road. An old bridge continues to be used by trucks to a rock quarry. To the west, a permanent Lincoln Highway exhibit is featured at the Iowa Welcome Center east of **Missouri Valley**. Writer Margaret Soboslay, whose daughter lives here, says it's a great little town of twenty-eight hundred where folks can walk to work, though she jokes, "According to my seventeen-year-old granddaughter, it's a great place to live if you write stories, because there is no nightlife."

The route enters town on East Lincoln Highway, which bends right onto Erie Street. The Lincoln Highway takes two paths west from Missouri Valley. The original route turns south on 6th Street (now IA Route 183). A streamline Deco gas station is at the corner. This routing heads south to Council Bluffs and Omaha, but it was bypassed in 1928 by a bridge crossing to Blair, Nebraska. The new route follows U.S. Route 30. Though the rerouting technically took place after the dissolution of the LHA, it was still considered official. Reportedly, the Lincoln Highway signs were quietly moved one night. The people of Council Bluffs and Omaha were outraged, but both routes have LHA concrete markers. The U.S. 30 routing continues west on West Erie Street. At 420 West Erie, the Dairy Den drive-in has been famous for its malts and "secret recipe" loose meat sandwiches since July 1954. Back then, it was at the western end for Erie Street cruisers—turning around was to "scoop the loop." Local resident and former police chief Darrel Cates and his wife, Daryl, have run the drive-in since 1990.

The original Lincoln Highway drops straight south from Missouri Valley, roughly following IA Route 183; the C&NW tracks likewise turn south and run parallel a mile to the west. The Lincoln crosses the Boyer River, and at Findley, it meets the Illinois Central Railroad. Near **Loveland**, wedged in the floodplain between the Missouri River and the bluffs of the loess hills, the Boyer River, the Lincoln Highway, IA Route 83, two railroads (whose tracks actually cross), and I-29 all converge. Loess is an unstratified loamy deposit brought by the wind. The hills were created when glacial deposits from the Missouri River valley blew the material here. The hills have become a famed natural attraction.

About four miles later, the Lincoln entered the town of **Honey Creek**, then bent southeast to climb Honey Creek Hill, reaching a staggering 15 percent grade near its crest. The 1915 LHA guide alerted the driver that the hill "is liable to cause him more trouble than at any point across the entire State of Iowa. In bad weather, due to the location of the road, much trouble is liable to be encountered." It was soon realigned, but even the new road had a 6 percent grade up a sheer-sided cut through the loess, the idea being that the thirty-foot-high perpendicular walls would deter erosion. Today shrubs and overhanging trees are growing on the rock walls.

The old cut reverted to private land, and for years it was off-limits, with one farmer enforcing this rather sternly. It also filled with discarded appliances and other junk. But good news for road fans: The Pottawattamie County Conservation Board bought the property from the farmer's heirs, cleaned it up, and made a campground on twenty-two of its acres, with an on-site ranger and three cabins renting for $40 a night, bedding not included. Best of all, an observation deck was built overlooking Honey Creek Grade. The grade itself still needs to be cleared, and plans are to someday make it a walking trail.

The road south meanders through the wooded hills some ten miles. Some of the original remnants are unreachable. One abandoned section of Lincoln Highway offers a scenic view of the river valley. Effie Gladding wrote that on her 1914 jaunt, these twenty miles east of Omaha were extremely poor and dusty. Today, along the modern road is the Aeroplane Inn still serves dusty travelers.

The road winds through **Crescent**, named for the shape of the loess hills that hover over it. Mount Crescent Ski Area to the north draws many tourists. The short main street has four restaurants. From here south, the Lincoln was cut into the hillside just high enough to keep it above the floodplain. Today this "shelf road" is barely discernible at times, running through fields and forest, and even used as driveways. IA Route 183 is often parallel.

Seven miles beyond Crescent, the road comes into **Council Bluffs**, still following IA Route 183. The route becomes Broadway, then joins U.S. Route 6, bending westward and crossing the Missouri River. The highway originally crossed the (almost) mile-long Douglas Street Bridge; an ad in the 1924 LHA guide bragged that the toll bridge was 49 feet wide and 5,152 feet long. Tolls were listed as 15¢ per car and 5¢ per passenger. Demolished in 1968, this bridge has been replaced by one a block to the north, which is signed I-480 and connects to Dodge Street in Omaha.

Frederic Van de Water wrote in *The Family Flivvers to Frisco* that as his family approached Council Bluffs from the west, he wondered why traffic was suddenly acting frantic. His wife spied the reason across the Missouri Valley: "A thunderstorm was brewing and motorists who understood the quagmire consistency of Iowa roads when moistened by even a heavy dew were streaking for cover like frightened chickens."

Council Bluffs is home to both the Western Historical Trails Center and the Railswest Railroad Museum and HO Model Railroad. In addition, and most relative to the Lincoln Highway, the Union Pacific Museum is in a restored Carnegie Library on Pearl Street. Its archives contains some 590,000 images (1,200 lo-resolution versions are online). The rail company grew from the establishment of the first transcontinental railroad, whose inspiration, as with the Lincoln Highway, was motivated as much by profit as by necessity. Surveys began in the 1850s, and Congress considered various bills, but it always bogged down along North-South lines; each side knew that a cross-country rail line would open new lands, and therefore congressional seats. The eventual secession of the South made the route choice simpler: The Pacific Railroad, as it was called, would cross the Great Plains, the Laramie Mountains (then called the Black Hills) of Wyoming, the high plains of the Wyoming Basin, the Wasatch Mountains, the Great Salt Desert, the ranges across Utah and Nevada, and the tall Sierra Nevada.

In 1862, President Abraham Lincoln signed the Pacific Railroad Act, authorizing the creation of the Union Pacific Railroad.

The eastern terminus was set at the Iowa side of the Missouri River, making "transcontinental" a relative term. As no eastern railroads reached Council Bluffs until 1867 (and no rails yet crossed the river), all supplies, rolling stock, and locomotives had to be sent to St. Joseph, Missouri, then floated north 175 miles and sent west from Omaha. Even wooden ties—of which twenty-five hundred were needed per mile—were sent west until the line reached Sherman Summit in Wyoming, where pine and other hardwoods became available.

In fact, the Union Pacific had no interest in bridging the river to start in Iowa; the great cost would have returned little added revenue, and the same was true for eastern lines that later ended at Council Bluffs. So the Union Pacific initially interpreted the western Iowa border as the riverbank at Omaha. When the railroad finally relented, it took from 1868 until 1872 to complete a bridge. The width of the river itself—about 750 feet wide at that point—was not so much of a problem as the four-mile-wide floodplain, which could become covered with water. A two-mile trestle (later made earthen) rose above the flat lands on the eastern end, then a 2,750-foot-long bridge connected to the bluffs on the Nebraska side. Even then, the Union Pacific ran a shuttle train between the banks, forcing through passengers to switch trains on each side, plus pay a toll for the crossing.

The Union Pacific has grown to be one of the largest railroads in the world, with more than seven thousand locomotives and one hundred thousand freight cars. The Lincoln Highway follows much of its route for the next two thousand miles.

Greetings from Nebraska

Travelers have long thought of Nebraska as just an empty expanse to be endured on the way west. "Often as far as the eye can see, there is not even a shack in the dimmest distance, and the only settlers to be seen are prairie dogs," wrote Emily Post. "That whole vast distance from Omaha to Cheyenne was one to be crossed with as little stop-over as possible."

Eight decades later, humorist Bill Bryson declared in *The Lost Continent*, "Nebraska must be the most unexciting of all the states."

The river valley that the Lincoln Highway follows indeed appears flat; the highway settles into a repeating pattern of small towns with grain elevators, but the state is filled with

	NEBRASKA	U.S.
Population in 1910	1,192,214	92,228,496
Population in 2000	1,711,263	281,421,906
Persons per square mile in 2000	22.3	79.6
Approximate miles of Lincoln Highway	463	3,389

well-kept homes and farms, interesting roadside business, and remnants of an absorbing, sometimes violent, past. Perhaps it's just the length of Nebraska that makes it seem to travelers as if they'll never get across it.

Emily Post did admit that were it not for the speed limits and few accommodations, "the interminable distance was in itself an unforgettably wonderful experience." Once through the plains, "you forget the wearying journey and feel keenly the beauty of their endlessness."

Explorers and pioneers crossing the Great Plains wrote always of the sea of grasses. Corn has been the dominant crop since the nineteenth century, earning Nebraska the nickname of "Cornhusker State," and the eastern half resembles Illinois and Iowa in landscape and economy. Moving west, the landscape subtly changes: Grasses go from tall to short, corn is supplanted by wheat, flat fields evolve into sand hills, and there are fewer people but more cows.

Much of this is a result of the subtle but significant rise in elevation of four thousand feet across the state (and another one thou-

sand by Cheyenne, Wyoming). As Frederic Van de Water wrote in his 1927 book, *The Family Flivvers to Frisco*, "Beyond the Missouri, it starts uphill so slowly that you know you are climbing only by the altitude figures beneath the eaves of the Union Pacific stations while the green fades into brown and the air becomes clear and diamond bright."

The roads in the eastern part of the state weren't much different from Iowa's gumbo. Alice Ramsey wrote that shortly after crossing into Nebraska, her Maxwell needed to be pulled from a hole twice within a mile: "The farmer's son caught one of their horses in pasture and pulled us out—for a fee—then walked on to the next hole, repeated his towing but doubled his fee!"

Bellamy Partridge wrote in *Fill 'er Up* that the state's rich, loamy soil turned to dust in dry weather and "a brown liquid resembling bean soup" when wet.

The 1924 LHA guide reported that eighty-four miles of the Lincoln Highway were still dirt and warned, "When it rains in Iowa or Nebraska, the tourist should stop if he wishes to save his car, his time, his tires and his temper." When dry, as Frederic Van de Water wrote: "A hundred yards ahead, the Nebraska highway always looked reasonably good. . . . [but] it is corrugated as though it had contracted into ridges. Over these, a car as light as ours shudders all day long."

With Wyoming's South Pass as the goal, LHA planners had an obvious choice across central Nebraska: a braid of paths that followed the Platte River drainage system. The river valley had been a transportation corridor for buffalo, Indians, fur trappers, traders, and immigrants on the California and Oregon and Mormon Trails. Parts were used as the Overland Trail once stagecoach service started in 1859 and by the Pony Express during its short life in 1860–61, put out of business by the transcontinental telegraph, which likewise followed this corridor.

Then came the transcontinental railroad. If a flat, straight line is not an option, the next best thing for a railroad is a river valley, leveled over time by the drainage of water. In July 1865, the Union Pacific began laying rails west from Omaha toward the Platte River. A year later, passengers could make the 190-mile trip to Kearney, and by May 1868, they could ride all the way to Cheyenne, Wyoming. In western Nebraska, the rails followed Lodgepole Creek, a Platte tributary, but had to leave it where adjacent land became too steep, instead following a mountain ridge to Cheyenne and Sherman Summit. (Likewise, the Central Pacific, building eastward through the Sierra Nevadas to meet the Union Pacific, could not follow the rivers, which descend into canyons, and also had to follow a ridge.)

The Union Pacific made a broad S-curve across the state, but the dozens of towns along

This welcome sign was painted on a Grand Island railroad overpass.

the railroad were otherwise constrained to section lines. Wagons and cars had to make their way by a series of interminable left and right turns. Some drivers stuck to the Union Pacific, either beside the tracks or maneuvering onto them. George Wyman followed the railroad in 1903 as he crossed the country, recalled in "Across America on a Motor Bicycle," his five-part article in *The Motor Cycle* magazine:

> If you take a map of the Union Pacific Railroad you will see the line of it studded with names as closely as they can be printed, and if you have not crossed the continent you will very naturally be deluded into thinking of them as villages at least. These are the "places" through which I passed, or, rather, past which I rode, for I was riding right on the tracks most of the way. They are localities arbitrarily created by the railroad. Many of them are nothing more than names given by the railroad officials to designate a sidetracking junction, and when you reach it all you see is the sidetrack and a signpost put there by the railroad. Other places bearing names are mere telegraph stations.

The divisions are places where the freight and passenger trains change engines. Quite often they are something of places, with from 200 to 5,000 population. There two or three hotels will be found, several saloons and a couple of stores. The stranger marvels to find a community even of this size in such a God-forsaken country. He wonders why anyone lives there, but if he is wise he does not ask any such question, for even though the wildest days have passed, it is a hot-blooded country still, where fingers are heavy and guns have hair triggers.

A decade later, this was still the landscape that the Lincoln Highway motorist encountered. That same year, 1913, also saw the publication of *O Pioneers*, Willa Cather's novel of the intertwined relations of the Nebraska land and its people. The Lincoln Highway followed the stair-stepping section lines between towns. This forced dozens of rail crossings, which led to deadly accidents, not to mention costly delays for the railroad. The Union Pacific gladly granted some of its 4.8 million acres in Nebraska so that the Lincoln High-

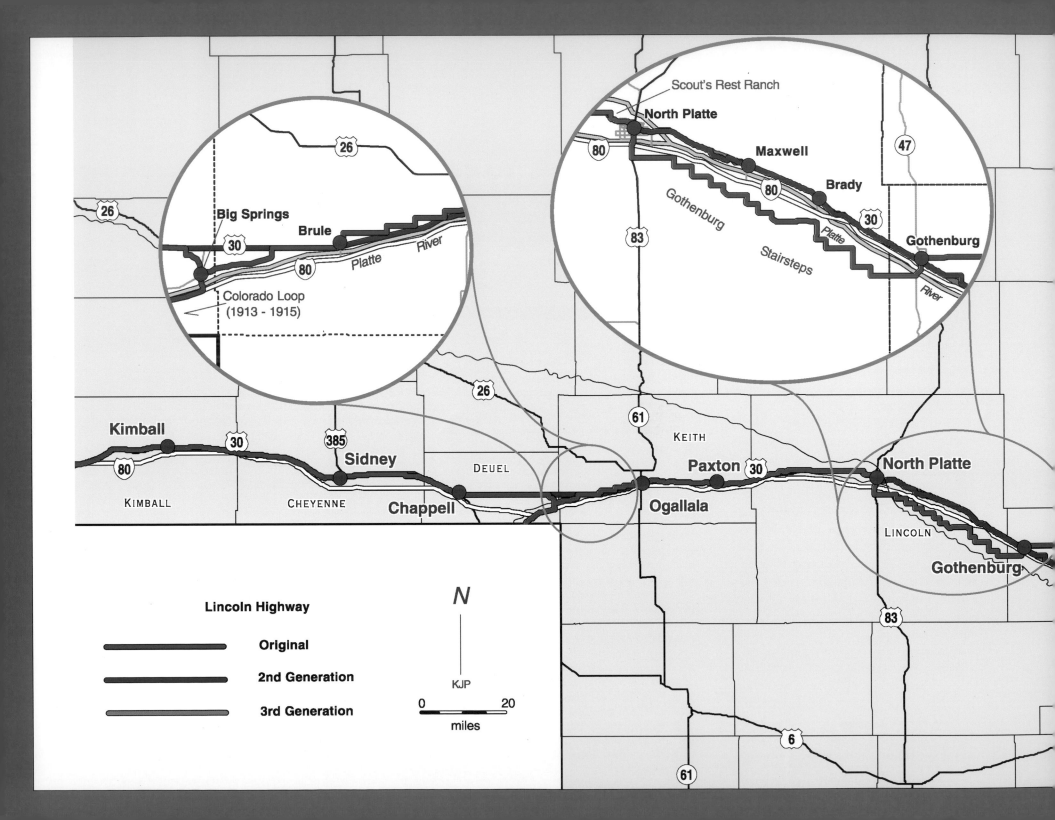

Scout's Rest Ranch

North Platte

Maxwell

Brady

Gothenburg

Gothenburg

Stairsteps

Platte

River

Big Springs

Brule

Platte   River

Colorado Loop
(1913 - 1915)

Kimball

Sidney

KIMBALL

CHEYENNE

Chappell

DEUEL

KEITH

Paxton

Ogallala

North Platte

LINCOLN

Gothenburg

Lincoln Highway

Original

2nd Generation

3rd Generation

N

KJP

0   20
miles

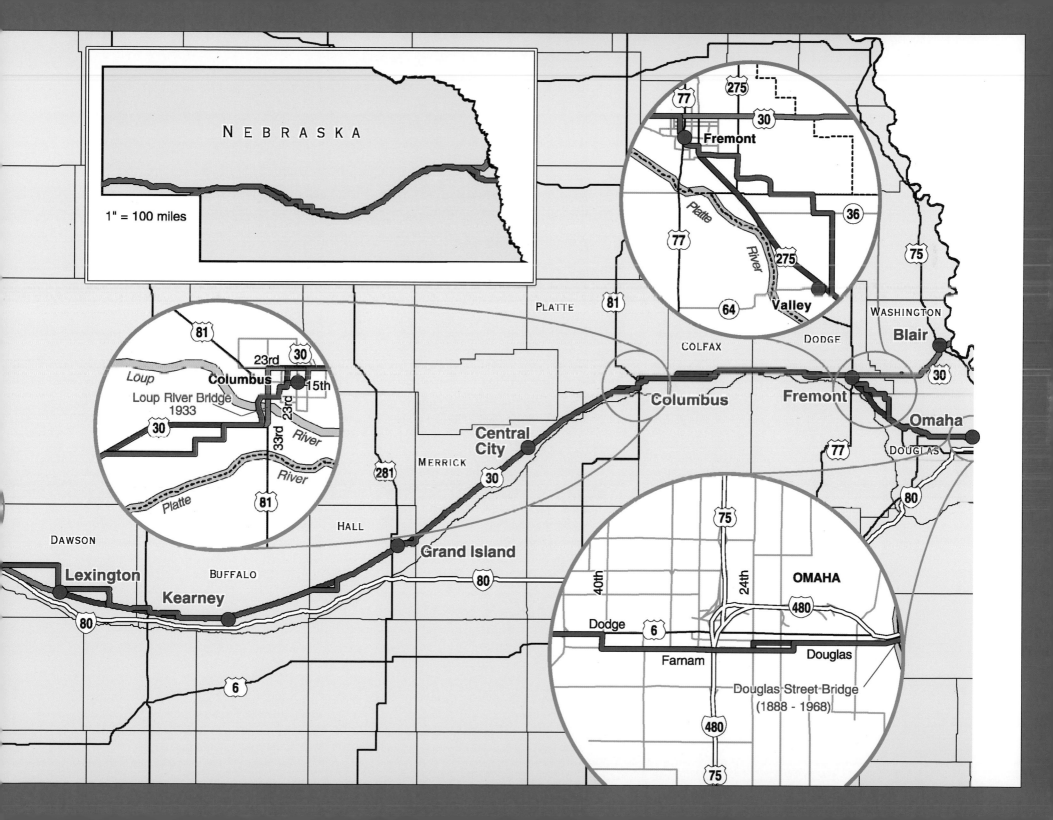

way could be rerouted parallel to the tracks, eliminating as many crossings as possible.

The biggest change to the route was the bypassing of Omaha in 1930. The Lincoln Highway and U.S. Route 30 moved twenty-four miles northwest to take advantage of the new toll-free Abraham Lincoln Memorial Bridge across the Missouri River. Locals were angered not only by the rerouting but also by the way the LHA went about doing it; signs were moved to the new route in the middle of the night without telling Omaha or Council Bluffs officials. After Omaha's newspaper complained, LHA field secretary Gael Hoag responded that the markers were private property, so permission was not needed to move them.

The last section of the entire Lincoln Highway to be paved was purportedly finished in 1935 west of North Platte, but the bypassed sections remain dirt and gravel to this day. Cross-state drivers still are accompanied by countless long trains and pass numer-ous towns dominated by co-op elevators. Van de Water's words of eight decades ago still hold true: "From grain elevator to grain elevator, we laid our course through Nebraska, traveling over a terrain that grew continually stranger to eastern eyes and a heat that amazed and almost frightened even New Yorkers who have spent summers in town."

Crossing Nebraska

The Lincoln Highway crossed the Missouri River into Nebraska via the Douglas Street toll bridge, built in 1889 and widened in 1924. It stood a block south of today's I-480 bridge, which replaced it in 1968. The new bridge exits to Dodge Street, which you must take if you're westbound, as Douglas Street is one-way eastbound.

The land that became **Omaha** was occupied by the Omaha Indians when whites came. Once a treaty was signed in 1854 opening Nebraska to settlement, the company running a ferry at the site had the land surveyed and named it for the just-displaced Indians, not unlike today's housing developments named for trees and farms. The town grew quickly after it became the eastern terminus of the Union Pacific Railroad in 1863. (The terminus was to be the western border of Iowa, but the railroad interpreted that as the eastern bank of the river.) Omaha grew to serve both agricultural interests and industry, starting with supplies for farmers and westbound travelers. Stockyards and then packing houses developed in the 1880s, bringing thousands of mostly southern European immigrants.

The Knights of Ak-Sar-Ben formed in the 1890s to promote patriotism; the name (spell it backward) is used for an airport, recreation field, and at one time, the bridge over the Missouri. The civic group had also purchased the Douglas Street Bridge in 1938 to remove the tolls, which it did in 1947.

On the northwest corner of Douglas Street and 18th Street was the Hotel Fontanelle, named for an early white explorer, and serving as the LHA control point.

Emily Post praised the town and her accommodations in 1914: "Omaha is a big up-to-date and perfectly Eastern city, and the Fontanelle is a brand-new hotel where we are going to . . . luxuriate in our rooms." But she couldn't partake of the tony hotel's tempting luncheon—its café served only men.

The Lincoln followed 18th Street south for a block, then continued west on Farnam Street. (Later it stayed on Douglas to 24th Street, then dropped to Farnam.) The grand lighted arch pictured on page 149 (and reproduced in the new Archway Monument at Kearney) spanned Farnam at 18th Street.

The Lincoln took Farnam to 40th Street; car dealerships and garages between 30th and 40th made this the city's Automobile Row. On Farnam at 36th Street, the Blackstone Hotel, one of Omaha's leading accommodations for Lincoln Highway travelers, survives as an office building. Across the street and west in an old gas station is McFoster's Natural Kind Café, a vegetarian restaurant. For meat eaters, the state is known for the runza, a German-Russian specialty of spicy ground beef in a bread pocket.

On July 22, 1928, Bernard Queneau and three other Boy Scouts crossing the country spent a Sunday in Omaha, which included a visit to an atmospheric theater:

In 1938, the Douglas Street Bridge became the Ak-Sar-Ben Bridge—Nebraska spelled backwards. It was demolished in 1968.

For once, the first time in fact, we slept till 9 o'clock. Then after a little breakfast we went to the Lutheran church where we enjoyed a wonderful sermon. In the afternoon we went to the Riviera Theater. A very fine theatre indeed and we enjoyed the program a lot. The ceiling was the blue night sky, with twinkling stars and moving clouds.

His caravan was joined by the Omaha Automobile Club, which accompanied them the next day to Cheyenne. "Their purpose," he wrote, "is to try to get the people to understand that they would be benefited by having an increase in traffic and to accomplish that the Lincoln Highway must be paved." A local newspaper noted that the boosters wore cardboard banners around their hats saying, "The Lincoln Highway—Main Street of the U.S.A."

A worthwhile stop is the Art Deco Union Station on 10th Street, recently converted to the Durham Western Heritage Museum, with exhibits on the history and culture of the Great Plains. A fun lodging option a few blocks south of the Lincoln Highway is the Satellite Motel, with a great Sputnik sign. The round 1966 building resembles a spaceship and has triangular rooms. It's on U.S. Route 275/L Street at South 60th Street, close to I-80.

At 40th Street, the Lincoln jogs north to Dodge Street; west of town, that becomes Dodge Road and is now a high-speed corridor also marked U.S. Route 6. A few blocks to the south, Leavenworth Street served as an alternate route west. It retains a number of classic neon signs, including LaCasa, an Italian restaurant founded in 1953 at 45th Street, and Bronco Burger drive-in, a block west.

On Dodge at 78th Street was Tower Tourist Village; postcards show strips of brick rooms and a service station topped by an Art Deco tower. In later years, it had a tiki bar too, but it was leveled for a strip mall. It was near Peony Park, a favorite local swimming and dancing hangout, which was also demolished.

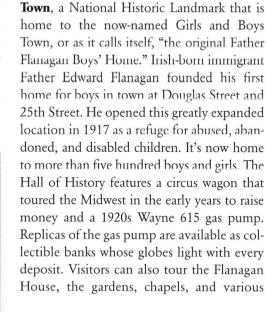

Omaha's arch gave a memorable welcome to the city.

Ten miles from downtown, between 132nd Street and 144th Street, is the village of **Boys Town**, a National Historic Landmark that is home to the now-named Girls and Boys Town, or as it calls itself, "the original Father Flanagan Boys' Home." Irish-born immigrant Father Edward Flanagan founded his first home for boys in town at Douglas Street and 25th Street. He opened this greatly expanded location in 1917 as a refuge for abused, abandoned, and disabled children. It's now home to more than five hundred boys and girls. The Hall of History features a circus wagon that toured the Midwest in the early years to raise money and a 1920s Wayne 615 gas pump. Replicas of the gas pump are available as collectible banks whose globes light with every deposit. Visitors can also tour the Flanagan House, the gardens, chapels, and various

McFoster's Natural Kind Café occupies an ornate 1931 service station across from the Colonial Hotel (now apartments) on Farnam Street at 38th Street in Omaha.

In 1923, the Omaha Automobile Club snapped this view of its municipal tourist camp's community kitchen.

Omaha, Nebraska, Tourist Camp

This camp is on the Lincoln Highway and is one of the most complete in the United States.

High and sightly location, well fenced. Fine Rest Rooms—Kitchen, Laundry and Baths—Well Policed and Courteous Attendants.

A small charge of 50 cents per car per 24 hours is charged to eliminate the undesirables.

—A Complete Official Road Guide of the Lincoln Highway, 5th ed., 1924

memorials and statues, including one of a boy carrying another, embodying the motto, "He ain't heavy, he's my brother."

About two and a half miles west of Boys Town, exit right at 174th Street, following a Lincoln Highway sign. A little interpretive display explains that just ahead is a near-pristine section of brick roadway laid down in 1920. The highway also joins the Union Pacific here, and both head northwest. A left turn puts you on the bricks for almost four miles, perhaps the country's best stretch of rural brick pavement. One mile of it is listed on the National Register of Historic Places and includes a reconstructed truss bridge

The restored brick road between Omaha and Elkhorn was listed on the National Register of Historic Places in 1988 and includes this interpretive site.

over West Papillion Creek. The display was installed in 1988, along with eight replica concrete markers.

In the summer of 2004, a contractor was replacing thousands of the bricks between 174th Street and 204th Street in place of asphalt patches. The bricks had been removed in the 1980s, when concrete was placed at 192nd Street. Nearby Blondo Street was to be extended from 192nd Street to 204th Street to give motorists an alternative route, and signs were posted to discourage driving on the brick road in an effort to lengthen its lifespan.

From **Elkhorn**, the Lincoln Highway generally follows NE Route 64 west to **Waterloo** and then NE Route 64/U.S. Route 275 northwest past **Valley**. The original then turns north and zigzags its way west, part of it still dirt. The highway was later rerouted along U.S. Route 275. The original and later routes rejoin

at the southern edge of **Fremont** and enter town on Bell Street amid rail yards.

The route jogs its way northwest through town via 1st Street, Main Street, 6th Street, Broad Street (U.S. Route 77), 10th Street, and Nye Avenue. On the southeast corner of 6th and Broad was the famed Pathfinder Hotel, the town's LHA control point. It took its name from the nickname of the famed western explorer John C. Fremont. It shows up in old postcards, but the building burned in 1976. The 1918 LHA guide carried an ad that touted all sixty rooms as having "toilets, telephone, hot and cold water, and circulating ice water." It also said, "Slogan: Traveling Men First" and "Notice Tourists: We are watching for your arrival."

At 605 North Broad Street, the Fremont Historic Visitors Center, in a restored 1893 post office, has a Lincoln Highway display.

Two blocks north on Broad is John C. Fremont Park, with one of seven Abraham Lincoln statues made by the Mullins Company, this one dedicated in 1921. (Others are along the Lincoln Highway in Wilkinsburg, Pennsylvania, and Wooster, Ohio.) A brick stretch of road can be found on 10th Street between Broad Street and Nye Avenue.

The Lincoln turned left from Nye Avenue onto 22nd Street. That street has been erased so today you must go another block north and turn left on 23rd Street. This also is old U.S. Route 30, and the route from **Blair** rejoins here. When the Abraham Lincoln Memorial Bridge opened from Missouri Valley, Iowa, to Blair in July 1930, U.S. Route 30 was rerouted to bypass the highway through Honey Creek, Iowa, and Omaha. The more direct route trimmed almost twenty-five miles. It was considered a rerouting of the Lincoln Highway, too, though the citizens of Omaha would beg to differ. Advertising for the bridge touted its assets: "Saves Time, Saves Miles, No City Traffic, Lincoln Hiway." The old Lincoln Highway through Omaha became 30-Alt. or 30-S.

From Blair, U.S. Route 30 goes through **Kennard** and **Arlington**. The state's WPA guide noted an intriguing free attraction in Arlington: The W. E. Antrim Garden had "a maze of canals with wind- and water-powered mechanical contrivances, built by the owner 'to pass the time,'" and "a model of a feudal castle with moat and drawbridge and a collection of unusual bottles."

U.S. Route 30 passed through Fremont on 23rd Street; today a bypass loops north of town. Old postcards advertised the Red Arrow Cabin Camp, just north of the intersection of old U.S. Route 30 and U.S. Route 77, man-

The Erin Swiss Motel in Fremont was one of a chain owned by Pat Murphy, which included three others along U.S. Route 30: the Erin Rancho Motel in Grand Island, the Erin Hotel and Motel in Cozad, and the Erin Welsh Court in Ogallala.

The Blair Bridge opened the way for the Lincoln to bypass Omaha between Missouri Valley, Iowa, and Fremont, Nebraska.

In Omaha and elsewhere throughout the West, residents consider the local auto camp as a zoo of sorts. A favorite evening pastime is to walk out to the tourist park and observe whatever strange specimens have been added to its population during the last twenty-four hours.

—Frederic Van de Water,
The Family Flivvers
to Frisco, *1927*

MAY 31, 1944
**Pathfinder Hotel,
Fremont, Neb.**

*Dear Mary—
I have a very nice room here. Tonight I have a radio and it seems so good. Wish I owned one. . . . The sky is lovely pink now. It's 9 P.M. and I have my washing to do—Darn it all.*

Lots of love—Nancy

aged by the same folks who ran a General John C. Fremont Court.

Also at this junction was the Cedar Motor Court. The fifty brick units, advertised as deluxe cabins, had a somewhat chateau style. It was soon renamed Erin Swiss Motel Court, one of four motels run by L. S. "Pat" Murphy. He next opened the Erin Welsh Court and Hotel, three hundred miles west in Ogallala, then also acquired the Erin Cozad Motel in Cozad and the Erin Rancho Motel in Grand Island. These were some of the few motels serving African American travelers.

West from Fremont

As U.S. Route 30/23rd Street heads west from Nye Avenue, the original road (22nd Street) is actually a few feet to the south but has been consumed by Fremont's airport. A mile west of Nye Avenue was one of the LHA's Seedling Miles, a strip of concrete meant to impress locals with the advantages of a hard-surfaced road. This was begun in 1914, but with the war intervening, it took five years to complete. The upside was that by then, the one improved mile grew to six. The downside is the concrete has been covered with asphalt.

The road continues to **Ames**, where the original route turns left on County Road 13, crosses tracks, then turns right onto a gravel road, which it follows for three miles. It rejoins U.S. Route 30 through **North Bend** and **Rogers** to **Schuyler**, named for Schuyler Colfax, U.S. vice president in 1869, when the town was platted. Northeast of town is an abandoned drive-in theater, where the original Lincoln Highway branches off from a 1925 rerouting, now U.S. Route 30.

The highway jogs through town, eventually going south on B Street and turning right on 11th Street. At the next corner, the Kopac Brothers garage was the LHA Control Point; it survives, today housing the town's Department of Utilities. The route then turns left on A Street, two blocks later turning right on 9th Street, then left on Road 10, and then finally right (west) on Road D to depart town. For seven miles, U.S. Route 30 (Road E) is a mile north, then it drops down to rejoin the Lincoln Highway at **Richland**.

Another seven miles west is **Columbus**. The Rosebud Motel, east of town, has a nice original neon sign. U.S. Route 30 is 23rd Street as it enters town. In 1881, Columbus was the site of the first performance of the Buffalo Bill Wild West Show. A WPA-built concrete arch later greeted travelers on the east end. It pictured an Indian man in headdress and woman carrying a papoose, a horse-mounted buffalo hunter, and an ox-drawn covered wagon. Across the top, it declared Columbus the "city of power and progress," and an arrow directed drivers to turn left to the city.

From U.S. Route 30/23rd Street, the original route turned left (south) on 12th Avenue and jogged over to 27th Avenue. Later routings turned south on 23rd Avenue, and another directly onto 27th Avenue. Franzwa's Nebraska guide is helpful if you want to hit all the LHA-designated streets.

The earliest route took 13th Street to reach 27th Avenue. A 1920s Chevrolet-Buick Garage remains on 13th at 23rd Avenue, and the Art Moderne style Columbus Theater is between 24th Avenue and 25th Avenue. At the corner of 13th Street and 27th Avenue was the Evans

Hotel, built in 1913, now the Park Plaza. A block west on 13th, off the official LHA route, is a large, two-story auto dealer turned restaurant. Max Gottberg built his Gottberg Auto Company in 1920 and operated as a Ford dealer until 1944. Today, Gottberg Brew Pub and Dusters Restaurant draw old cars to where they were once sold and repaired. Near the roofline are original terra-cotta renderings of the front ends of old autos.

The Lincoln Highway continues south on 27th Avenue, then turns west on 8th Street.

U.S. Route 30 turns south through town on 33rd Avenue. This also serves U.S. Route 81 and the old Meridian Highway, or Mexican Road, which ran from Canada to the Gulf of Mexico. Keen Korner was a well-known cabin court here.

South of town, 33rd Avenue crosses 8th Street. The Lincoln Highway then crosses the Loup River. The original wiry Lincoln Highway bridge was replaced in the 1920s, so travelers must follow U.S Route 30. After the bridge, U.S. 30 curves west, while U.S. Route 81 continues straight south. Immediately west of this turn, the Lincoln rejoins. A piece of road in the woods on the north side is believed to be an LHA Seedling Mile dating to perhaps 1921.

U.S. Route 30 continues southwest to **Duncan**; the original route crossed the tracks to the north to enter town. At midtown, two rows of hackberry trees run for a block to the south; these mark the original Lincoln Highway. Former National Hobo King and LHA member Karl Teller says he camps and sleeps under the trees when he's passing through. Trees closely lining a street would have posed no hazard to early motorists; the 1916 guide lists the speed limit in Duncan and the next two towns as eight miles per hour.

Nine miles on is **Silver Creek**; a mile to the west, LHA guides noted, the Lincoln passed through Wooster's Lover's Lane, an almost mile-long canopy of trees. Trees remain in the vicinity, but according to Franzwa, the row on the south side was removed in 1926 for road widening and that on the north side a decade later because of safety concerns. They had been planted on either side of the private grade crossing to the Charles Wooster farm.

West of town was the Dutch Windmill Cabin Court, with a windmill atop the service station. The name was later tweaked to Dutch Mill Motel, Café, and Sinclair Service.

In the middle of a twenty-two-mile stretch from Silver Creek to Central City is **Clarks**. Again, as U.S. Route 30 speeds past on the south side of the tracks, the original route crosses to pass through town on East Millard Street. Part of it in town is still brick just east of Green Street. At that intersection, a Lincoln Highway mural was painted by high school students.

Central City holds an interesting distinction in Lincoln Highway history: The first, and perhaps only, meeting to ratify the LHA Proclamation was held here in early October 1913. Piecing together the story, it likely was inspired by news leaked out of the Lincoln Highway Congress in Detroit on October 2 that Nebraska's Platte Valley route had been chosen for the Lincoln over a routing through Denver. Local booster Dr. H. E. Glatfelter brought $5 membership certificates back from the meeting, and LHA vice president and secretary Arthur Pardington called the meeting in Central City to reassure

The Dutch Mill Motel, Café, and Sinclair Service west of Silver Creek.

Nebraskans of the routing and to sign up members.

Ironically, by the time of the 1916 guide, the town was the scene of a dispute. A "Special Warning" in the margin cautioned, "Local antagonistic influence has removed the official markers from the direct efficient route, which goes directly west from Central City, paralleling the Union Pacific on the south side to Chapman and on to Grand Island." A look at a map leads one to guess that someone wanted to bend the Lincoln south to Aurora.

Some ten miles southwest, U.S. Route 30 passes **Chapman**; as at Clarks, the original route crosses the tracks to the north to pass through town.

East of Grand Island, Alice Ramsey noticed that the roads were changing as she drove west in 1909, now having "a very noticeable gravelly content, allowing us to run along more smoothly and make much better speed." A fierce storm, however, forced them to pull against a farmhouse. They were invited inside, only to discover that the Danish farm family spoke no English.

George Schuster, writing about his 1908 New York–to–Paris trip, likewise noted that the gumbo was disappearing between Columbus and Lexington. "The soil was now sandy. The highway consisted of wagon tracks paralleling the miles of barbed wire which kept the cattle from ranging over the road. It followed the old emigrant trail along the Platte River and for long stretches ran close to the Union Pacific tracks."

Two miles east of **Grand Island** on U.S. Route 30 is Shady Bend, once the site of a tourist camp famed for having a buffalo herd on each side of the road; a tunnel connected the north and south sides. The tourist home

*Dear Mother:
Didn't find anyone to go
with me from C.C. but the
Lord solved that problem
when I got to Boone. I
picked up a fellow that was
going to Oregon so I have
company. He also helps
drive some.*

Bye for now, Ralph

At this Grand Island
Camp, signs directed
guests to pay at the
gate, but the larger sign
at center let travelers
know they could enter
free for dinner.

opened in 1929, and thirty-three cottages were soon added, along with tennis courts. The December 10, 1932, *Grand Island Independent* reported that Shady Bend Tourist Homes had purchased "a 3-year-old [buffalo] bull with a magnificent head and weighing 1,260 pounds . . . and, with two heifers, will become the inhabitants of a zoo located just east of the homes." A canopy gas station remains, converted into a bar.

The original road turns left at Shady Bend, onto what is now Shady Bend Road, then turns right half a mile later onto Seedling Mile Road. This was the site of a 1915 concrete Seedling Mile. A mile later, it crosses U.S. Route 30. (Of course, U.S. Route 30 wasn't there in 1915, and now, traffic is blocked from crossing the highway.) On the north side of U.S. 30 is Kensinger's Service and Supply; a remnant of the Seedling Mile can be seen branching behind the small, square station built in 1933. This short stretch is the only original Seedling Mile concrete remaining

A Lincoln Highway Seedling Mile runs behind Kensinger's, a compact Deco station in Grand Island.

along the entire highway. Nebraska had two more Seedling Miles at Elkhorn and Kearney, plus a late one at Fremont and a possible one south of Columbus.

The Lincoln travels the two dozen blocks through Grand Island on 2nd Street. This town still resembles an eastern agricultural community, whereas the towns to come have a more western feel in layout and architecture. On 2nd Street at South Locust Street is the ten-story Hotel Yancey. Construction began in 1917, but the hotel didn't open until 1923. Though named for owner William L. Yancey, it was part of a chain operated by the North American Hotel Company; the idea was to coordinate hotels in Nebraska, Iowa, and Kansas towns, accessible to the railroad depots and business districts, with cost savings realized by bulk purchasing and standardization. As travelers increasingly chose motels, it was renamed the Yancey Motor Hotel, but tourists knew better and it closed in 1982. It has since been rehabbed as apartments.

Dozens of motels, cafés, gas stations, and repair shops began lining 2nd Street. The busiest section ran from South Locust Street—the Yancey corner and the main road southwest to Eddy Street, likely because this stretch of 2nd was also U.S. Route 281 as it cut north-south through the city.

Pioneer Park, on 2nd in the center of the city, was the site of the original courthouse and is the city's oldest park, dating to 1868. A display in the northwest corner features different Lincoln Highway markers, from a painted post to concrete posts to a Route 30 shield, all surrounding a state historical marker about the road.

Grand Island's central location makes it a popular convention spot. It's the birthplace of Henry Fonda, and the 1939 WPA guide also revealed that it was home to world champion gum chewer Jake Eaton, "capable of chewing 300 sticks at a time." Yet another claim to fame is that Grand Island was the first U.S. town to install mercury vapor streetlights, in 1936.

*GRAND ISLAND MODERN TOURIST CAMP
GRAND ISLAND - NEBR.*

BERNIE HEISEY

At the west end of town, a viaduct carries the Lincoln Highway over the railroad. The Lincoln branches south while U.S. Route 30 continues straight. They rejoin a mile and a half west. In between, they each cross U.S. Route 281; a side trip south on that highway at the intersection with U.S. Route 34, is the Stuhr Museum of the Prairie Pioneer. The museum depicts pioneer life and features a Pawnee earth lodge, tepees, century-old shops, homes, a complete 1893 farmstead, and an 1860s log cabin settlement.

Three miles west of town, Jerome's Tepee once attracted tourists. Various vintage post-cards show it starting as a large, perhaps tin-covered tepee souvenir stand, selling everything from window decals and film to ice cream and cherry cider. An addition purportedly made it the state's largest gift shop. Today no traces remain.

A couple miles farther, the Lincoln Highway passed through **Alda** and continued about nine more miles to **Wood River**. Where the highway bears right into town at 11th Street, Gloe Brothers built a service station in 1933; closed long ago, it is listed on the National Register of Historic Places and has been rehabbed as a drive-through bank.

It's another nine miles to **Shelton** (the original highway followed section lines between towns). Shelton has really embraced the famous road, calling itself the Lincoln Highway Capital of Nebraska. The Wood River Valley Historical Society has celebrated this moniker since 1998 with an annual Lincoln Highway Festival and Car Show. Locals have restored part of a bank building at the corner of U.S. Route 30 and C Street, transforming it into the Lincoln Highway Visitors Center. It

includes five eighty-year-old Lincoln Highway porcelain enamel mileage signs from western Nebraska, one with a bullet still embedded. Across the road in Railroad Park, a concrete post was reset in 1998.

The 1924 LHA guide carried an ad for Lincoln Highway Garage on Main Street. On the east end of town, Ryan's garage and used-car sales occupies a 1920s mission-style garage built onto a cottage-style station.

It's about six miles to **Gibbon** and then another twelve miles southwest to **Kearney**. East of town, at 3600 U.S. Route 30 East, is Cabela's, one of a chain of retail showrooms inspired by a hugely successful mail-order company. The place is filled with outdoor gear and wildlife exhibits, plus horse and dog kennels. Dick Cabela started the business at his home in Chappell in 1961 with a tiny newspaper ad: "2 hand-tied flies for $1." His brother, Jim, joined him in 1963, and a Sidney warehouse opened in 1969. It has grown to a huge company offering two master catalogs (topping five hundred pages) and more than forty specialty catalogs annually. It employs more than seven thousand people but is still family-run. The Lincoln Highway and U.S. Route 30 bend right at the eastern edge onto 25th Street. The LHA Control Station was the Midway Hotel on 25th Street at Midway Avenue (now Central Avenue), which was home to the main business district to the south. It proclaimed its presence on the Lincoln Highway with a glowing "L" in its corner tower.

The town is said to be named for Fort Kearny, which itself was named for Gen.

The Plane View Drive-In and Café took some artistic license in filling the sky, though Kearney *was* home to the 8th Air Force during World War II.

Jerome's Tepee, west of Grand Island, claimed to be the state's largest souvenir and gift shop.

BERNIE HEISEY

The Lincoln Highway display inside the Kearney arch.

the village in 1953. The place has stayed stuck in earlier decades but now comprises twenty-eight buildings on twenty acres with fifty thousand items, including lots of antique cars, grouped and then arranged in chronological order.

The other is the privately owned Great Platte River Road Arch, a massive arch that opened in July 2000 and spans I-80. A museum here recounts emigration through the area, from pioneer travels up to a 1950s diner. Visitors wear headsets that change narration through various sections. A Lincoln Highway exhibit features a 1914 Model T Ford, a 1927 Oldsmobile, and a scale reproduction of Omaha's Lincoln Highway welcome arch. It's an inspiration to some historians, a tourist trap to others, but a godsend to long-distance motoring parents. Dis-

couraging visitors is that there's no direct I-80 exit, meaning that drivers have to exit farther west and drive back a couple extra miles; not terrible, but a deterrent to spontaneous visits.

The Lincoln Highway had to turn left at 9th Avenue; blocking the way was the Nebraska State Teachers College and Normal School (now a branch of the University of Nebraska). A block later, the highway heads west again on Watson Boulevard. Trees arching over the road were once so thick that it was like driving through a tunnel. They were planted by H. D. Watson, the "father of alfalfa." They also shaded a Seedling Mile, opened on November 6, 1915. A postcard showing its paving noted that the concrete was fifteen feet wide and eight inches thick, requiring sixty-nine cars of gravel, twenty-four cars of sand, and sixteen cars of cement.

Stephen Kearny (the correct spelling). Fort Kearny State Park, site of the army post, is just south of the Platte River and I-80. It was the first government fort along the Oregon Trail for protecting settlers.

Two of the best-known area attractions aren't along the Lincoln Highway. The older and larger of the two is about twenty miles to the south, near Minden on U.S. Route 6. Pioneer Village holds a spot alongside Wall Drug and South of the Border as one of the places that wear you down with endless billboards about their can't-miss attractions. Plastics pioneer Harold Warp had returned from Chicago in the 1940s and purchased his old school. Soon he added a church, post office, and train depot, filled them with exhibits, and opened

On one of his cross-country trips in the early teens, Henry Joy paused for a photo at the 1733 Ranch. Packard chief engineer Russell Huff and general superintendent B. F. Roberts were testing a new Packard Six.

The Covered Wagon, four miles west of Kearney, and adjacent to the 1733 Ranch, was a must-stop for decades, but today it is closed and deteriorating.

Just past it are the remains of a pair of concrete oxen and a covered wagon. They stood out front of the Covered Wagon. Owners Mr. and Mrs. Boyd McClara advertised that it was "a 'must' for tourists, where they can relax, and obtain worthwhile souvenirs at reasonable prices." Ceramic cows, pigs, horses, and deer were among the geegaws sold. It also traded on its being 1733 miles to each coast.

It is about here that the Platte River, and hence the railroad and the highway, change direction from a southwesterly course and begin heading northwest.

The original road stair-steps to **Odessa** and **Elm Creek**. The Red Top Cabin camp, with service station, café, "apartments," and hotel, advertised on a 1936 postcard that it was "on U.S. Highway 30, paved from coast to coast." A couple miles past Elm Creek, Alice Ramsey recalled getting stuck "in a slimy mud hole" and having to walk back to a railroad team shack for help.

A mile west of downtown was St. John's Motor Court, named for the last proprietor. The units included connected, lockable garages. Also west of town was White Eagle Camp, which had cabins and a trailer park.

Three miles west of town was the 1733 Ranch, home of H. D. Watson. This was a regular photo op for tourists, with its two-way-pointing sign of "1733 miles to San Francisco, 1733 miles to Boston." It was mentioned in memoirs such as Harriet White Fisher's *A Woman's World Tour in a Motor* and by Jacob Murdock, who called it one of the most notable landmarks during his 1908 cross-country drive. Effie Gladding noted that she'd seen it on the cover of the Lincoln Highway guide issued by Packard in late 1913. The ranch later had a campground and large swimming pool. The 1939 WPA guide noted that the eight-thousand-acre ranch had been divided into smaller farms after Watson's death but the house remained. In the 1990s, it finally made way for a housing development, the only clue remaining to its existence a pair of signs for "1733 Estates."

This tiny bridge east of Overton marks the location of the original Lincoln Highway between the tracks and U.S. Route 30.

Just before entering **Overton**, the Lincoln ran between U.S. Route 30 and the Union Pacific tracks. On the left are the remains of a concrete bridge, from perhaps 1920, with almost no road visible on either side.

Again, the original route follows section lines west to **Lexington**, where many of the north-south streets are named for presidents. The Lincoln Highway enters town on 13th Street, turns right on Washington, then left on 17th Street and departs town via Adams Street. Later it stayed with the railroad, much as today's U.S. Route 30 does, but it entered from the south side of the tracks on Washington.

Settlement around here began south of the river, as a trading post and Pony Express station on the Oregon Trail called Plum Creek. When the railroad was built, the town was moved and renamed in honor of the Battle of Lexington.

The stream of white settlers and the building of the Union Pacific led to two Indian attacks in this area, most notably the Plum Creek Massacre east of town, a Cheyenne attack against a wagon train in 1864. Eleven men were killed or scalped, two women taken prisoner, and nearby cabins burned, driving settlers back to Columbus. Turning south on NE Route 21 will start you on your way to the site and monument. On the west side of town, a stone monument marks the site of the Turkey Leg Raid, named for the Cheyenne chief who in 1867 used telegraph lines to derail a Union Pacific freight train, then scalped the crew and looted the cars.

Lexington took a half-page ad in the 1924 LHA guide. PR was different in those days—the ad is dominated by a picture of a cattle feed lot. The Cornland Hotel was also a regular advertiser.

A couple 1928 concrete markers are displayed at the Dawson County Museum on Taft Street. At 6th Street and North Harrison Street is a late-1920s Spanish Mission-style motel.

The original route again takes section lines: north on Adams for five miles, then west on Road 761. U.S. Route 30 meanwhile makes a direct line for **Cozad**. The old road enters on Main Street (the equivalent of 8th). The 100th Meridian Museum here is named for the line of longitude that is just west of town. It was one more indicator to early travelers that they were reaching the West. An arch touting the 100th Meridian is out on U.S. Route 30. The town is also known for its alfalfa mills and feed plants; the 1924 LHA guide carries the claim that this was the leading shipping point for alfalfa, but today the land is increasingly used for grazing.

A decaying motor court on U.S. Route 30 still has its neon "Cabins" sign. The Lincoln Highway again follows section lines north and west, while U.S. Route 30 speeds directly northwest through **Willow Island** to **Gothenburg**, founded in 1882 by a native of Sweden who worked for the Union Pacific. He named the town for Göteborg, Sweden. The town also calls itself the Pony Express capital of Nebraska, but neither of its two stations may truly be Pony Express stations, according to overland trails expert Gregory Franzwa. One in town at Ehmen Park was relocated from the Machette's/Upper 96 Ranch southwest of town in 1931. It was but one of many buildings at the ranch that served the Western Stage Company. It'a a popular draw for tourists,

Gothenburg Camp served as an LHA Control Station.

who also visit the surrounding park. The other station, on its original location at the (private property) Lower 96 Ranch four miles south of Gothenburg, was likewise an outpost of the Western Stage; it is sometimes called the Midway station, but the true Midway was five miles east and burned in 1864.

Gothenburg is also home to the Sod House Museum, established in 1988. In areas where timber was sparse, sod houses were built with walls of stacked layers of cut turf. There's also a bison made of four and a half miles of barbed wire. Take NE Route 47 south from U.S. Route 30; it's just north of the I-80 exit.

The 1918 LHA guide listed the town's Lincoln Highway Garage as having the LHA Control Sign.

Beginning in 1913, for at least a few years, the original route headed south across the Platte River on a long wooden bridge, then zigzagged its way northwest along section line roads on the south side of the river, making about twenty-eight turns. It can still be accessed by taking NE Route 47 south across I-80 and turning right a mile later, then staying with paved roads.

The "Gothenburg Stairstep" travels the same path as the Oregon-California Trail and the Pony Express, passing the sites of forts, stagecoach stations, and a rumored Sioux lookout, marked by a heavily vandalized statue of a Sioux overlooking the area. It was also the path of the Overland Stage. A more direct path may have existed north of the river but it was not as improved as the well-traveled stair-step.

A 1915 B. F. Goodrich guide from Kearney to Cheyenne detailed the route, beginning with the turn south across the railroad and crossing what it called an iron bridge, then making twenty-three turns, three jogs, and two "bears" before crossing a long wooden bridge over the river into North Platte about forty-six miles later.

The town of North Platte campaigned for a better road to its east, and the Union Pacific eventually donated the right-of-way. The 1916 guide announced that a $50,000 bridge at North Platte would soon trim eighteen miles from the route and allow motorists to head directly northwest from Gothenburg through **Brady** and **Maxwell**. (Today U.S. Route 30 makes an S-curve over the railroad west of Maxwell.) So confident was it that the guidebook listed those towns, but the road was still incomplete when the 1918 guide was published. At least the bridge was completed, but motorists were advised to inquire about the road—"quite sandy" to Brady, "quite rough" the rest of the way—and if it was in bad shape, to take the stair-step route.

West of the town of **North Platte**, the Platte River splits into north and south branches. The highway stays between the two, separating from the emigrant trails. The Mormons continued along the north fork. The Oregon Trail, already south of the river, kept to the south fork. Until the first bridging, wagons lined up to cross the cold, swift current, usually paying a fee for a primitive ferry while their animals swam.

Eventually the wooden bridge was built south to the stair-step route, just east of the current U.S. Route 83 bridge. It was pretty shaky by the time motorists began arriving. Alice Ramsey described it in 1909: "We crossed the river on a long wooden bridge, on

the sides of which we could read the name of the store where we might purchase good 'men's suits' in town! Just what four women wanted!" In *The Good of It All*, Thornton Round wrote that when they drove through in 1914, it was "a rickety old bridge which we surely thought would shake apart when the Winton went across." When the Lincoln Highway was rerouted to bypass the stair-step, it entered the east end of North Platte via the new 1917 bridge; today U.S. Route 30 crosses on a modern span.

North Platte started as a Union Pacific construction camp in late 1866. When the camp was moved to Julesburg, Colorado, half a year later, most of the town—people and buildings—went with it, but North Platte was made a division point, a place where trains changed engines, which brought railroad machine shops. The town also served as a link between New York and San Francisco for transcontinental airmail service.

Emily Post found the town to be picked on to the point monotony; she was repeat-

A nice match: coast-to-coast air service and a Lincoln Highway concrete marker.

edly told, "You have had fine hotels and good roads so far, but wait until you come to North Platte!" She thought this the most unfounded of all the negative tales about the road, instead finding the town "a serious railroad thoroughfare, self-respecting and above reproach."

This, to me, is where the West begins, if such a place can be said to exist. The landscape is changing, cowboy hats begin appearing, and the home of Buffalo Bill and spin-off businesses herald the start of western archetypes. Heading west, the landscape becomes predominantly grazing lands, extending into Wyoming and northern Colorado. Bellamy Partridge wrote about the area on his 1912 trip, "Farms were further and further apart. There was less plowland and more grass. And the time came when we discovered that there were no more farms—all cattle ranches."

Early motorists crossing the long wooden bridge to the south entered town on Locust Street (now Jeffers Street), traveling two dozen blocks north before turning west again. The later route (generally U.S. Route 30) over the new bridge enters on 4th Street and intersects Jeffers Street at midtown. A block east was the LHA Control Station, the McCabe Hotel, still at the corner of Dewey Street. A good stop for traveling families is the children's museum in the former Carnegie Library at 314 North Jeffers Street.

Jeffers crosses the Union Pacific railyards on a viaduct; to the west is Bailey Yard, the world's largest railroad classification yard. It handles more than 130 trains—10,000 railcars—daily, making it a leading employer. The Lincoln Highway then turns left on 12th Street. (If you continue straight on Jeffers, you'll find Cody Park, bordering the North Platte River.)

North Platte spawned a number of motels on both ends of the city. On the east end, Black and White cabin camp opened in the mid-1930s; each cabin had its own heat, toilet, and shower. On the west end is the nicely kept Cedar Lodge (originally Campbell's Motor Court), with Spanish styling and shaded central courtyard. The Western Motel was once connected to the building next door, when it was the Western Café and Bar-B-Q. Both motels still sport stunning neon signs. The 1939 WPA guide noted that the town had six hotels and six principal tourist camps, along with rooming houses and smaller camps. It also said there weren't yet any traffic lights.

Overlooking the I-80 exit is Fort Cody Trading Post, a great roadside attraction that traces its roots to the Lincoln Highway. The business was started by Royce Henline in 1950 as the Buffalo Bill Trading Post on the west end of North Platte on U.S. Route 30; it was sold in 1954. In 1952, Henline had opened the Sioux Trading Post in Ogallala, also on U.S. 30. He tried the highway west of North Platte again in 1963 with Fort Cody Trading Post, built to resemble a stockade. In 1967, the current post was built at the I-80 exit. The original closed the following year (remodeled into offices, but its log walls still visible), as did the Ogalalla location in 1969. The Whitecalfs, a Sioux family from South Dakota, began performing Native American dances at the Ogallala location, then moved to Fort Cody, where they stayed until 1977. Mr. Henline would drive them back to South Dakota after every season.

The current trading post is still in the family. The main building is a huge gift shop filled with shirts, postcards, and plastic tomahawks. A miniature Buffalo Bill Wild West Show has twenty thousand hand-carved figures, from cowboys to circus acts, many animated during a show every half hour.

Lincoln Highway researcher Carol Ahlgren spoke to Chuck Henline in 2001 about the post and the famous Muffler Man Indian in back. Henline said that it had been at a filling station across the street as a Muffler Man, a fiberglass giant originally made to hold and advertise a muffler. His dad was at a bar one night and the owner of the giant said something like "give me $100 and its yours," and the next morning, they owned a Muffler Man. They made it into an Indian by adding rope for braids.

Henline told Ahlgren that he had just conducted a visitor survey to determine why people stopped. Half were repeat visitors. "They would say things like, 'I used to come in here, now I'm bringing my son,' or 'It's just the way we remembered.' And I always think—is that good or bad?" Many of us think it's just right.

Henline also told her of one of their publicity ploys: His dad would drive the Whitecalf family around to local motels, beating on a drum to literally drum up business for the evening dances.

U.S. Route 30 continues west on 12th Street; at Buffalo Bill Avenue, it becomes Rodeo Drive and passes the decaying Pawnee Drive-In Theater. The Lincoln Highway, however, turns north on Buffalo Bill Avenue, passing the Lincoln County Museum on the right and the Wild West Arena on the left,

The Buffalo Bill Trading Post, at Scout's Rest Ranch in the early 1960s.

home of Nebraskaland Days every June. Straight ahead, where the road bends west, is Scout's Rest Ranch, onetime home to Buffalo Bill Cody and one of the town's main tourist draws through the years.

Probably no one did more to mythologize the West than Cody. He first gained fame providing buffalo meat in 1867–68 for the Kansas Pacific Railroad and is said to have killed 4,280 buffalo in eight months. He organized the Old Glory Blowout here on July 4, 1882, which is credited as the birth of rodeo. It became the formula for his Wild West shows that toured the country and the world starting

The 1886 home of William Cody and large barn at his Scout's Rest Ranch is now part of the Buffalo Bill Ranch State Historical Park in North Platte.

in 1883. As his shows prospered, Cody built Scout's Rest, which includes a modest-size but elaborate eighteen-room house, in 1886. After his 1911 tour, with his finances low, Cody sold Scout's Rest to his show partner, Pawnee

Bill, for $100,000 and then moved his family to Cody, Wyoming, which he had founded in 1896. In 1965, the four-thousand-acre Scout's Rest ranch became the sixteen-acre Buffalo Bill Ranch State Historical Park. In addition to his restored home, it includes a great barn, now filled with Cody memorabilia. The barn has regular showings of a short documentary on Cody's life, with numerous early clips of the Wild West show, some filmed by the Edison company.

The Henline family owned a number of western-themed businesses, including Fort Cody, on U.S. Route 30 at the west end of North Platte, from 1963 until 1969. The building is still standing, but the "guard towers" were removed. Today the Henlines' Fort Cody is at the North Platte interchange of I-80.

YOUR FAMILY WILL ENJOY A DRIVE-IN MOVIE TONITE

Ask at Court Office For FREE GUEST TICKET

MOVIES UNDER THE STARS

PAWNEE DRIVE-IN Theatre

3 MILES WEST ON HIGHWAY 30

IN THE PRIVACY OF YOUR CAR

NORTH PLATTE, NEBRASKA

FREE 8 - Horse Merry-Go-Round

ADULTS, 60c CHILDREN FREE

Delicious Snack Bar Refreshments

FREE Kiddies Playground

THIS IS A SERVICE OF THIS MOTEL TO OUR GUESTS

The Pawnee Drive-In smartly handed these out to tourist court operators.

The Cider Mill at Paxton was known for Marvin's Delicious cherry or raspberry juice blends.

The old road and U.S. Route 30 rejoin a mile west of Scout's Rest. The next six-mile stretch was proclaimed the last section on the entire Lincoln Highway to be hard-surfaced. A ribbon cutting on November 5, 1935, was accompanied by a parade and a telegram from President Franklin Roosevelt.

Ahead is **Hershey**, just thirteen miles west but a hundred feet higher in elevation. The Lincoln passes through **Sutherland** a few blocks north of U.S. Route 30. The Lincoln and U.S. 30, as well as adjacent Union Pacific tracks, stay close together for the twelve miles to **Paxton**; the original route once may have followed section lines, but no traces remain. The town had a Lincoln Highway Garage.

On the corner of U.S. Route 30/2nd Street/Main Street and North Oak Street is Swede's Lounge, with a couple tiny neon signs saying Swede's Bar. Connected to the immediate south is Ole's Big Game Steakhouse and Lounge, a well-known rest stop filled with mounted trophies bagged by Rosser "Ole" Herstedt. When Prohibition ended at the close of August 8, 1933, it was no coincidence that Ole opened his watering hole at 12:01 A.M. on August 9. A deer he bagged in 1938 was mounted and displayed in the bar, starting the tradition; the bar now has more than two hundred big-game trophies from Ole's thirty-five years of adventures around the globe. When he retired in 1988, it was sold to Paxton native Tim Holzfaster, who had been visiting since a boy and who runs it with his wife, Deb. The facade was recently remodeled with wooden planks but retains a hint of its stucco, cool oval windows, and repainted neon sign (though a larger neon "scene" is now gone). Billiard tournaments and keno are popular, and the menu features local beef and buffalo. South of town at Exit 145 of I-80 is Ole's Lodge, a full-service travelers' oasis.

The Lincoln Highway, which has been running between the branches of the Platte River since the town of North Platte, now veers much closer to the South Platte River. The river's wide swath comes right up to the southern edge of the railroad; I-80 can be seen across the river, about a mile to the south.

The condition of the early roads and the vagaries of driving them were vividly described by George Wyman as he drove a motor bicycle east across the continent in 1903:

At Ogallala, Nebraska, I was told that there had been nothing but rain there for the last two weeks. The roads were in terrible condition, I know, when I left there at 6:45 o'clock, on the morning of June 8. After 10 miles of heavy going through the mud, I struck sand, and then took to the railroad track once more. After going six miles over the ties it began to rain so hard that I had to get off and walk three miles to the station at Paxton. There I waited for three hours until it stopped raining, and set out again at 12:30 o'clock.

It's about twelve miles to the little settlement of **Roscoe**, then another seven to **Ogallala**. Halfway to Ogallala, the original road breaks off to the right. It's assumed that the Lincoln passed through town about three blocks north of today's U.S. Route 30, but no map has been found to show the exact routing.

Ogallala was named for a Sioux tribe. A mile west of town were the terminus and stockyards of cattle drives in the 1870s and 1880s along a branch of the Chisholm Trail. Five blocks west of Main Street, on a road between 10th Street and 11th Street, is Boot Hill Cemetery, so-named because cowboys were usually buried with their boots on. Cowboy tombstones from the great cattle drives remain, though the bodies were removed long ago. All this has led Ogallala to declare itself the state's Cowboy Capital and inspired the building of Front Street (on East 1st Street), a 1960s re-creation of what once might have lined the street in the 1880s, including a steakhouse, saloon,

The Whitecalf family poses at the Henlines' trading post in Ogallala, about 1960.

like Ogallala, it was named for a Sioux tribe, whose name actually derived from a French word for "burned."

The Lincoln Highway follows U.S. Route 30 west from Brule. Four and a half miles west is a historical marker for California Hill on the right. Overland emigrants felt they had reached a milestone, having crossed the South Platte and begun the first big climb. Optimists dubbed it California Hill. The land, now owned by the Oregon-California Trails Association, has traces of the thousands of wagons that climbed the rise between 1841 and 1860 while heading west on one path of the California and Oregon Trails. You can walk up the hill and see the ruts; turn right at the sign, and follow the dirt road half a mile to a pull-off on the left.

Gregory Franzwa described the trials of the trails in *The Oregon Trail Revisited*:

> The emigration headed up the hill, their wagon wheels still tight from the swelling induced by the waters of the South Platte. They moved to the northwest, onto the broad, level plateau stetching between, and high above, the forks of the Platte. . . .

JULY 16, 1929
Harmon's Tourist Camp, Ogallala, Neb.

Dear Mom
Arrived here O.K. and a perfect score 549 M from home It's shure hot—riding could of made Cheyenne easily but the kids were hungry so we turned in early.
WRW

western museum, jail, undertaker, and windmill. It features a nightly shootout and revue.

In 1914, Effie Gladding stayed overnight here at the Hollingworth, a "very comfortable lodging house . . . built over a garage."

Today in town, the rounded office building of the former Erin Welsh (later Plaza) Court stands across from Hokes Café and the Oregon Trail Motel, which has a cottage-style station and Spanish-style motel strip. The Erin was one of four motels that were owned by "Pat" Murphy and served African American travelers. It also employed a Spanish-style motif. Now just called the Plaza Inn, it advertises a hot tub and heated pool; a single room cost about $35 in the summer of 2004. All three show up on old postcards, and it's nice to see the trio surviving at the same intersection. Hokes serves all meals, including Mexican food nightly.

The Ogallala Main Street Organization recently restored a vintage gas station for its headquarters at 220 North Spruce Street, a

couple blocks north of U.S. Route 30. The former Standard Oil Red Crown Station was built in 1922, and a garage was added in 1937 with an open-air hydraulic lift.

The original Lincoln Highway again followed a stair-step west of Ogallala; as late as the 1924 LHA guide, the route from here to Wyoming was noted to be gravel. A later rerouting, now U.S. Route 30, went straight southwest along the railroad tracks to **Brule**;

The Old West is re-created at Front Street, an attraction on East 1st Street in Ogallala.

Now the waters of the South Platte left the wagon wheels and the dry air took its toll. Tires rolled off, dry axles shrieked. Spokes pulled out of the hubs and brittle wagon tongues snapped.

There was little wood now—there would be some at Ash Hollow but no more for weeks after that. The emigration had still another reason to bless the American bison. Fuel from here on, for the most part, would be the *bois de vache* used by the mountain men.

U.S. Route 30 continues west; to follow the original route through Big Springs—the location of a controversial Lincoln Highway intersection—turn left (south) on the gravel road at the marker. After half a mile, as the road curves, stop and look south. Ahead is the part of the South Platte called the Lower California Crossing, where those heading west on the Oregon Trail forded the water before ascending California Hill. Accounts of the crossing are fascinating, most calling the river something like "a mile wide and a foot

Ogallala's new Spruce Street Visitor Center in a restored gas station.

deep." There were no trees at the time; they had been burned off by prairie fires. (Another branch of the Oregon Trail, via Upper California Crossing, was thirty-five miles to the west near Julesburg, Colorado.)

There's also a new road into town another four and a half miles west: U.S. Route 138 goes two miles south to **Big Springs**, named for natural springs that were used to cool locomotives from the town's founding in

1884 until 1950. The springs also drew tourists to camp there; a private camp charged 25¢ per car.

The original Lincoln Highway entered town on Railroad Street, then turned right on Third Street. Railroad Street now ends before that, so bear right on Fourth Street and go a block left (south) to reach Third. The little town's main intersection was at Third Street and Chestnut Street; here the Big Springs

Oregon Trail Motel has served travelers for more than half a century.

BERNIE HEISEY

Looking west on U.S. Route 30, with California Hill to the right. The Lincoln Highway turns left here, out of frame.

Dueling signs at the west end of 3rd Street in Big Springs, 1925, competed for motorists to follow either the one-time Lincoln Highway loop through Colorado or the main route into Wyoming.

Café and Garage caught travelers no matter which way they went. "One Stop Service" is still visible on the side of the garage. The buildings remain but no longer serve travelers.

A block later, on 3rd Street at Pine Street (erroneously marked Vine in the 1924 LHA guide), the Lincoln Highway turns right (north). The road to the left also was part of the route for a short while, when pressure from Colorado led to an official Lincoln Highway loop south through Denver in 1913. After the LHA quietly dropped that loop by early 1915, Colorado boosters erected a billboard to point motorists their way; Lincoln Highway advocates responded with their own signs, and LHA guides gave numerous warnings not to be duped into following the road south.

If you turn south on the road to Denver, you'll immediately pass the Phelps Hotel (a.k.a. House of Three Chimneys), built in 1885. It has been restored as a bed and breakfast, coffee shop, and gift shop and is listed on the National Register of Historic Places. The four wire-mesh buffalo beside it make it easy to spot. A block later, the road bends right on its way to Colorado.

Travelers often took the road into Colorado for just a few miles to Julesburg, then turned back northwest and followed Lodgepole Creek and the Union Pacific Railroad to Chappell, Nebraska. The Pony Express and a branch of the Oregon Trail also crossed the river at Julesburg and took a northwestly course. Julesburg residents naturally favored motorists taking this route whether they were continuing to Denver or turning toward Chappell. And the road through Julesburg was relatively better than the direct route from Big Springs to Chappell.

"Relative" is the key word. George Wyman took this slightly longer way in 1903, after having lunch (what he called dinner) at Chappell. From there, he headed southeast on his motor bicycle "and quickly found that the good road was at an end. It became so bad, in fact, that I took to the railroad and rode the ties most of the way into Ogallala."

Still, the 1915 Goodrich guide from Kearney to Cheyenne directed drivers southwest from Big Springs to Julesburg and then back north, some nineteen miles off the Lincoln Highway, which curiously is not even mentioned other than perhaps as "stripes on poles."

Emily Post was stopped from taking the Colorado Loop: "In May, 1915, the road by way of Sterling to Denver was impassable; all automobiles were bogged between Big Spring and Julesburg, so on the advice of car owners that we met, we went by way of Chappell to Cheyenne."

The main route of the Lincoln continues north on Pine Street/U.S. Route 138; half a mile later, it bears left (west) on North Fork Road. This road, the one the LHA billboard touted as the main route west, remains gravel. Bellamy Partridge remarked in *Fill 'er Up* about the solitude of the place in 1912:

> Without realizing what I was doing I stopped the car and shut off the engine. . . . You couldn't see a tree or a house, not anywhere. . . . I listened intently for the music of the spheres, the whispering of the stars passing overhead in the daytime, the swishing of the planets through the immeasurable nothingness—but I couldn't hear a thing.

Eight decades later, Gregory Franzwa did the same:

> Just for the fun of it, stop here, turn off the engine and get out of the car. Look around. There is a windmill in the distance. Fields of grain all around. Don't talk to anyone, even yourself. Absolute, utter silence. Can there be a place on this earth more beautiful and more serene than the prairies of the American west?

It is indeed a quiet, haunting area, on the cusp of landscape change. From here on, cattle pens predominate and sagebrush appears.

The Lincoln rejoins U.S. Route 30 and makes a twenty-mile straight shot to **Chappell**.

Dude's and the Brandin' Iron grace the west end of Sidney.

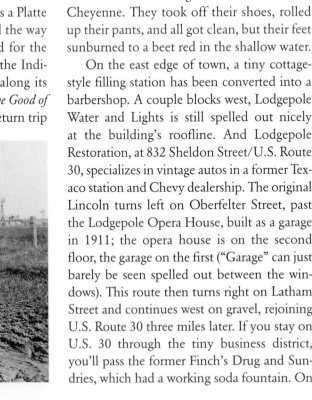

At the east edge, where U.S. Route 30 enters town on 2nd Street, the Lincoln continues straight on 1st Street for a few blocks. On the east end is a small, red and white-trimmed Sno-King Drive Inn. The Lincoln jogs north a block at Babcock, then continues west on 2nd Street. Back east a couple blocks on 2nd Street at Cutler Avenue is Sweden Creme dairy stand in a 1950s service station. An abandoned Mission-style motor court sits on the northwest intersection of Ochs Avenue.

Bumping against the Union Pacific tracks, the Lincoln Highway curves right and again heads northwest, parallel with the railroad the nine miles to **Lodgepole**. It also joins a Platte River tributary, Lodgepole Creek, all the way to Cheyenne. The town was named for the creek, which derives its name from the Indians who cut poles for their tepees along its banks. Thornton Round wrote in *The Good of It All* that during his family's 1914 return trip

Austin Bement and Henry Joy struggle west of Lodgepole during their 1915 trip.

eastward, the gravel-bottomed creek was a convenient place to wash their cars—and themselves—after being caked in mud west of Cheyenne. They took off their shoes, rolled up their pants, and all got clean, but their feet sunburned to a beet red in the shallow water.

On the east edge of town, a tiny cottage-style filling station has been converted into a barbershop. A couple blocks west, Lodgepole Water and Lights is still spelled out nicely at the building's roofline. And Lodgepole Restoration, at 832 Sheldon Street/U.S. Route 30, specializes in vintage autos in a former Texaco station and Chevy dealership. The original Lincoln turns left on Oberfelter Street, past the Lodgepole Opera House, built as a garage in 1911; the opera house is on the second floor, the garage on the first ("Garage" can just barely be seen spelled out between the windows). This route then turns right on Latham Street and continues west on gravel, rejoining U.S. Route 30 three miles later. If you stay on U.S. 30 through the tiny business district, you'll pass the former Finch's Drug and Sundries, which had a working soda fountain. On

the left is a nice park platted by the railroad at the center of town; it was mentioned in LHA guides as always available for tourists. The west end of town has an old court with "Cabins" fading above a corner doorway.

Six miles west, little remains or ever existed of **Sunol**, then it's another fairly straight ten miles to **Sidney**. This town was another Union Pacific division point where trains changed engines. At 6th Street and Jackson Street are the Fort Sidney Museum and Post Commander's House. Fort Sidney was built to protect workers from Indians. It became an outfitting post for those heading to the Black Hills during the gold rush of 1876–77. Daily shipments of gold arrived from the Black Hills, and the town grew rowdy. One block was renowned for having twenty-three saloons. Shootings here were commonplace, as demonstrated in one story in the state's WPA guide. During a dance, someone was shot and killed. The body was propped in the corner so the fun could continue. The same was done for victim number two. "It was not until a third corpse was added to the group that the party came to an end."

East of town, the former Mayfair Service Station retains its brickwork from 1947. The Lincoln enters Sidney on Illinois Street. The Fox Theater at 1120 Illinois Street retains its 1951 feel, even though it has been divided into two screens. At 1026 Illinois Street, a false front hides the 1916 Brewer's Garage, a popular stop for Lincoln Highway travelers. The Lincoln went north on 13th Avenue for one block (no longer a through road), then west out of town on a still-dirt road and rejoined U.S. Route 30. If you stay on Illinois Street, now the main way west, within one block on the west end are Dude's Steak House, the Brandin' Iron bar, and the U-shaped El Palomino Motel, with glass-block windows and neon sign.

Just off I-80 is Cabela's Sidney store, which the outdoor gear company claims is the state's leading tourist attraction. Cabela's also has a gun library, gift shop, restaurant, eight-thousand-gallon aquarium with game fish native to the state, meeting facilities, boat service center, RV and truck parking, and campground.

Boy Scout Bernard Queneau wrote about his travel through Sidney on July 25, 1928: "In the morning we ran over a couple large rats. In the afternoon we ran over some kind of snake, and at night we saw some prairie dogs for the first time. We are staying in a tourist camp in Sidney, just a morning's ride from Cheyenne."

It was near here that Thornton Round encountered a fierce hailstorm, with golf ball–size chunks of ice shredding the side isinglass curtains of his automobile. I also was caught in hail here, fifteen minutes of fearsome pounding, and then, as usual, the sky cleared to blue.

Thirteen miles west, the highway skirts Point of Rocks, a bluff to the north. Bluffs on both sides of the river contain fossilized bones from the time when this was a swamp.

A couple miles later, the Lincoln crossed the tracks to the north and entered **Potter**, which grew from a Union Pacific station house built in 1870. The station house also served as the town's land office, post office, and schoolhouse. The Lincoln proceeds west on dirt for three miles, then rejoins U.S. Route 30, veering quite close here to I-80. Six miles farther is **Dix**; again, the original road bears right from town on dirt. Five miles later, it bends south to rejoin U.S. Route 30, and three miles after that, it enters **Kimball** on 3rd Street.

After following 3rd Street for about ten blocks, the Lincoln turned north on Chestnut, then west on 1st Street. A block east of the exact route, but once a major stopover, was the Wheat Grower's Hotel at 1st Street and Oak Street. It is easily spotted by its name spelled out in buff brick near its second-story roofline, but this place that once embodied the region's agriculture is closed. West on dirt-surfaced 1st Street is the City Artificial Ice Plant/City Light and Power Plant, bricks similarly spelling the names along the roofline.

Frederic Van de Water stayed at the town's municipal camp. As he recalled in his 1927 *The Family Flivvers to Frisco,* "The parking place was without manager or attendant. . . . toward bedtime a booted town marshall, with black slouch hat and a large tin star entered shyly, collected a quarter as camp fee from each party and vanished."

The dirt road rejoins U.S. Route 30 just west of town. A drive-in theater sits abandoned to the south. A mile and a half later, an underpass to the north is the original route of the Lincoln Highway. Stay on U.S. 30 south of the tracks. During the next nine miles to **Bushnell**, a number of concrete culverts (one with spikes) that mark the old road can be seen to the north beyond the Union Pacific tracks. On the west side of Bushnell, a pair of tubes carry the original highway south beneath the railroad.

About eight miles farther west is the Wyoming border, marked by the State Line Station. The complex once had a tall tower announcing its name, but that collapsed in the winter of 1995, and the rest of the place is deteriorating. Among the debris is a small building with a line painted on it denoting the state border. A quarter mile to the south I-80 traffic races by.

Looking north from U.S. Route 30 to the Lincoln Highway underpass, a couple miles west of Kimball. It was originally an S-curve that went right in the foreground, not left. Both road and rails cross Lodgepole Creek here.

Greetings from Colorado

Credit for naming the Lincoln Highway often goes to Henry Joy, a fan of the sixteenth president, but a Colorado woman had the idea first. Frances McEwen Belford met Abraham Lincoln in 1860, when she was twenty-one, and never forgot the man whom she called the "greatest American." In September 1911, Belford proposed a coast-to-coast highway named for Lincoln, one year before Carl Fisher suggested his idea. In August 1912—still a month before Fisher's first meeting—she had a bill introduced in Congress "establishing the Lincoln memorial highway from Boston, Mass., to San Francisco, Cal." The bill died, but Belford did not give up, nor

	COLORADO	U.S.
Population in 1910	799,024	92,228,496
Population in 2000	4,301,261	281,421,906
Persons per square mile in 2000	41.5	79.6
Approximate miles of Lincoln Highway	351	3,389

did she forget; years later, she wrote Henry Joy, reminding him of who had thought of the name first. He admitted that she was first, but that "it takes more than sentiment to build a highway."

Though the Lincoln Highway name was conceived in Colorado, the LHA originally bypassed the state. The route actually did go through for a while, but the Lincoln Highway's "Colorado Loop" quickly became the organization's biggest regret. After having carefully chosen a route, LHA directors bent in a weak moment, added Colorado, and forever after fretted that critics would say, "Here you were swayed; at this point you deviated from your announced principle." They had, but not without reason. It's a long story, much of it unearthed by LHA member Mark Wolfe, while the routing was pieced together mostly by former LHA president Jim Ranniger.

In 1913, as LHA directors considered where their highway would go, three potential routes crossed Colorado:

1. What is now known as the Santa Fe Trail, through the southwest corner of the state and into New Mexico.

2. The Golden Belt Route from Kansas through Limon and Colorado Springs, then over Ute Pass to Leadville and Grand Junction.

3. The Midland Trail to Colorado Springs, then north to Denver and west over lofty Berthoud Pass. The National Midland Trail Association was established further west in November 1912 in Grand Junction.

Boosters for all three, and variations thereof, were eager to be on the Lincoln Highway. In May 1913, Fisher proposed a tour to the West Coast for the Indiana Automobile Manufacturers' Association and the Hoosier Motor Club. It would mostly follow the Midland Trail but was not to be associated with choosing the Lincoln Highway route—so of course, it was. On July 1, at the same hour that Henry Joy and others were in Detroit formally establishing the LHA, seventeen cars and two trucks departed Indianapolis.

Towns along the tour route began improving their roads in hopes of gaining favor. Fisher and company were feted from Indiana to eastern Colorado. They stayed over at Colorado Springs, despite the advice of famed pathfinder A. L. Westgard that the highway

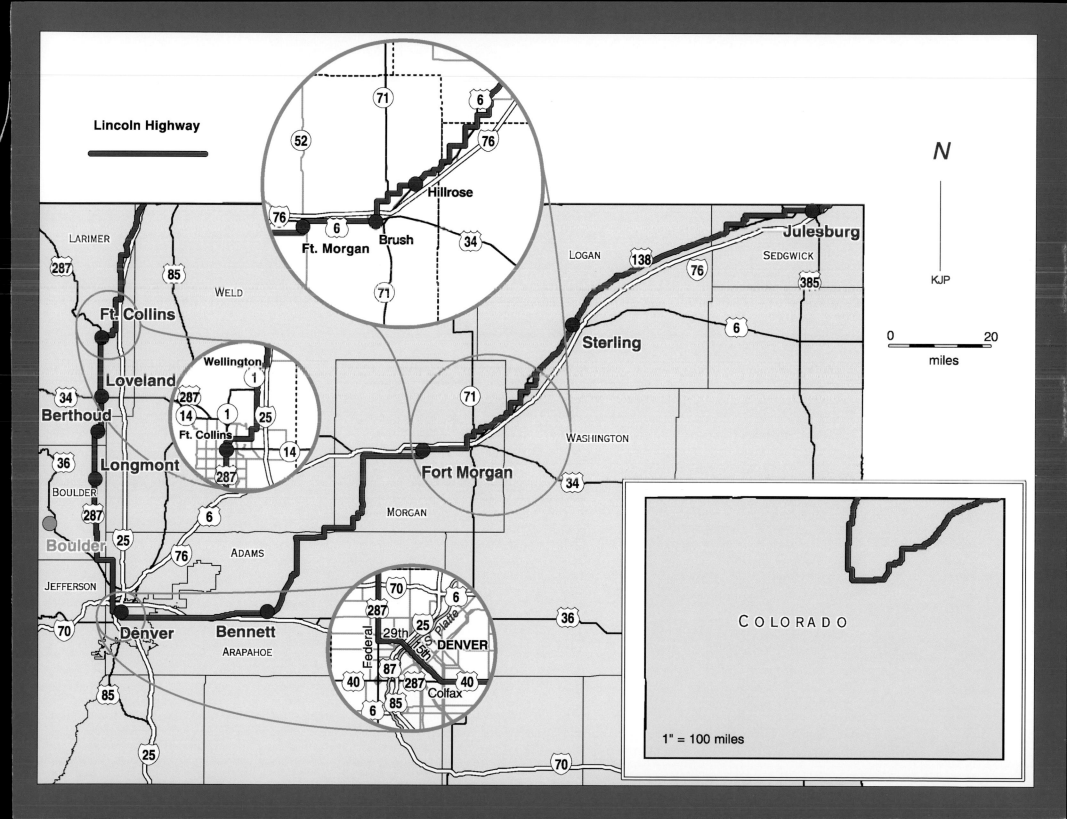

should bypass that city and go from Limon directly to Denver. When the caravan arrived in Denver, it was welcomed by Colorado governor Elias Ammons and stayed at the renowned Brown Palace Hotel. The governor favored the Midland Trail. He led the Indiana cars over Berthoud Pass—snowy even in July—reaching Grand Junction a couple days later. Governor Ammons left them at the Utah border and returned triumphant, unaware that the drivers had bogged down and were seething at their Colorado friends for not being forthright about how poor the trail was in Utah. The combination of steep climbs, bad roads, and perceived deception undid any goodwill resulting from Colorado's paving and glad-handing.

It had been almost a year since Fisher had announced his plan to raise $10 million to build the Lincoln Highway, but with fund-raising stuck, he knew he'd better find another way to build his road. Fisher came back from the thirty-four-day Hoosier Tour with a plan: Western governors had been so receptive, why not choose a route now and announce it to the annual Conference of Governors, to be held a few weeks later in Colorado Springs? LHA leaders could gain their endorsement and perhaps reap some financial pledges. The meeting was scheduled for August 26, 1913.

Joy, Fisher, and Secretary Arthur Pardington made the trip by train, carrying a map with a red line across it. In the meeting, they went to great lengths to explain how the route was chosen: They had compiled data on roads, climate, and topography. They had used logic to pick one route alone, the most practical possible, and said they would not be swayed. They were sure, they said, that this would meet with approval.

When the route was finally announced, the governors of Kansas and Colorado—having rolled out the red carpet for the Hoosier Tour but both left off the Lincoln—were "bitterly disappointed." Ammons especially pleaded the case for Denver, which still smarted from being snubbed by the transcontinental railroad half a century earlier.

Colorado had been left off the route for good reason: LHA directors, particularly Henry Joy, wanted the route as straight and level as possible. Wyoming offered a relatively easy grade that reached 8,835 feet, whereas the climb over Berthoud Pass reached 11,314 feet. Not only were its steep hills slippery and dangerous, but early cars could only tilt so far before the gas tank was below the carburetor. With gravity making it impossible for fuel to reach the engine, cars had to drive up such hills backward.

Nevertheless, the three LHA directors relented, perhaps ashamed at announcing the route in a state that had been left off it. They added a dogleg to Denver and asked Ammons to sign an agreement verifying the route and pledging that the state would pay for improvements. The road would branch south from Big Springs, Nebraska, to Denver (about 227 miles), and then head back north to rejoin the Lincoln at Cheyenne (another 114 miles). *Proclamation of Route of the Lincoln Highway* announced to the public on September 14, included the towns of Julesburg, Sterling, Fort Morgan, Denver, Longmont, Loveland, and Fort Collins.

As recalled in the 1935 LHA history, no other single act caused "so much regret, difficulty and trouble." Seemingly every town and everyone now wanted a diversion for it too, all the way up to President Woodrow Wilson, who campaigned for Washington, D.C. (After an initial rejection, directors relented and that city got Lincoln Highway feeders.)

Towns on the Midland Trail ignored the news, or perhaps didn't believe it. Postcards were printed of the "Lincoln Trans-Continental Highway" through Ute Pass. And the official announcement of the Colorado Loop only intensified competition. Greeley wanted the loop bent to it. The Northeastern Colorado Lincoln Memorial and State Highway Association co-opted LHA letterhead and listed towns between Julesburg and Greeley. The Lincoln Highway Association of Colorado (no relation to the LHA) still advocated for the Midland Trail.

All this was too much for the LHA, frustrated about having included Colorado in the first place and now having to fend off every town left off the loop. Late in 1914, Colorado boosters decided to put a billboard at Big Springs, Nebraska, to remind motorists of the loop, but with winter coming, they delayed. By then it was too late; when the first LHA guidebook was published in the spring of 1915, Colorado had been dropped from the Lincoln Highway. The boosters still erected a billboard, but in revenge, it showed only Colorado roads. The photo on page 165 shows that the route through Fort Morgan was once marked Lincoln Highway, but "Lincoln" had been painted over.

The 1915 LHA guide included a paragraph on detouring to Denver but did not mention its former Lincoln Highway status. The next year, the guide was not so subtle,

Wishful Thinking

A number of cards were produced as the Lincoln Highway was being planned, none of which shows the final route of the Colorado Loop.

5075. Ute Pass, Automobile Road, near Manitou, Colorado. On the Lincoln Trans-Continental Highway.

9155 Lincoln Memorial Highway near Manitou, Colo.

The publisher of this card predicted the road would run through central Colorado and cross Ute Pass, seen here.

Another from Ute Pass

RUSSELL REIN

BERNIE HEISEY

Davis Drug Company in Leadville produced these cards of a Lincoln Highway that never was. The view to the left is looking south and east from the top of Twin Lakes Hill near Leadville. The card on the right is titled "Along the Beautiful Lincoln Highway coming in to Leadville, Colo."

Looking north to the Old Ford Garage in Julesburg.

reminding drivers to "not be diverted at this point by markers or signs indicating that the Lincoln Highway turns southwest here to Denver." The third edition added, "Numerous red, white and blue markers have been placed at this point to mislead the tourist." By the final edition in 1924, it was even more emphatic: "The Lincoln Highway does not enter Colorado."

At least part of the soon-to-be Colorado Loop had been used by early transcontinental drivers. As Lester Whitman and Eugene Hammond crossed the country in 1903, they drove south from Wyoming over muddy roads through Fort Collins, Loveland, and Boulder. When a front wheel suddenly popped off, Hammond "ran down the hill chasing [the]

The writer of this 1918 letter was a late-night traveler, arriving in Julesburg, via Denver, at 4:30 A.M.

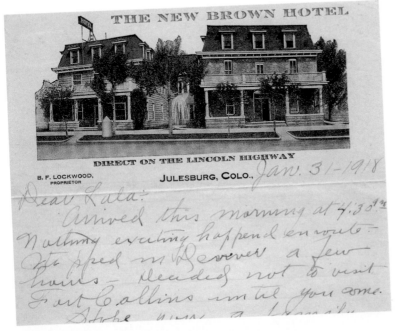

right front wheel as it rolled along." It took them two days to drive from Denver to Julesburg, and then in Nebraska, they found that the Platte had inundated the road, which could be located only by the tops of fence posts sticking out of the water.

The following year, Whitman again took the future loop. In Owl Cañon near Fort Collins, heavy rains had washed out the road, forcing him to take the air-cooled Franklin through the adjacent creek. He jostled for room with twenty-five "emigrant wagons that themselves had to double-team their horses to pull through the rocky water."

Harriet White Fisher wrote that in 1910, she found the roads from Cheyenne to Denver "magnificent," allowing her party to make thirty-five miles per hour. The next day, they drove 150 miles and reached Sterling.

In contrast, Bellamy Partridge wrote in *Fill 'er Up!* that on his 1912 trip across the country, his family avoided the fork into Colorado

for fear of washouts, and once they reached Cheyenne, they took a *train* to Denver.

Some drivers took just a tiny part of the route, following the Union Pacific to Julesburg and then back north. That's what George Wyman did when he crossed the continent in 1903 on his motor bicycle:

Of the 114 miles I made this day, 46 were ridden in the State of Colorado, for the railroad and road both put in a bend from Chappell southward to get to the South Platte River at Julesburg, Colorado and then the road follows the river valley back again into Nebraska; so that 46 miles was all of Colorado I saw. I found one good stretch of road five miles long in the 46, and this was a relief from the railroad ties, so I blessed it and took a snapshot of it for a Colorado souvenir.

Looping to Denver

The Colorado Loop of the Lincoln Highway generally follows U.S. Route 138 toward

Denver. With today's I-76 nearby, traffic on U.S. 138 is light, averaging just over six hundred cars per day. Highway buffs may wonder where the 138 designation comes from, as its number should indicate that U.S. Route 38 is nearby. It *was*, but it was renamed U.S. Route 6 in 1932 in an effort to extend that primary route. U.S. Route 138 could have become U.S. Route 306 (there were already a U.S. Route 106 and 206), but it remains as an orphan and a trivia question.

Two miles into the state is **Julesburg**, the last of four settlements in the region carrying this name. The first grew where overland travelers crossed the South Platte at Upper California Crossing. (The "lower" crossing was northeast of Big Springs, Nebraska.) The town, adjacent to Fort Sedgwick, was named for Jules Beni, who ran a trading post there; he was so disliked that he was murdered, nailed to a fence post, and had his ears cut off. Efforts to change the name nonetheless failed. When the Pony Express was started in 1860, the sole station in the state was established at Julesburg. This first town was burned by Cheyenne Dog Soldiers in 1865, in retaliation for the notorious Sand Creek Massacre, but townspeople simply resettled a few miles east. Both towns were on the south side of the Platte, but two years later, when the Union Pacific dipped south to here, the town was moved north of the river to be next to the railroad. When a branch line was built southwest to Denver in 1881, Julesburg moved a fourth and final time to the new junction.

Fort Sedgwick gained fame again as the setting for the book and movie, *Dances with Wolves*, though the filming was done in South Dakota. The fort is remembered by a 1940 state marker east of Ovid. The first Julesburg is likewise commemorated by a state historical monument, dedicated in 1931, about a quarter mile south of the site.

The nineteen-mile South Platte River Trail traces these places and events. Established in 1991, the rectangular loop is the shortest of Colorado's twenty-four Scenic and Historic Byways. Information is available at the Julesburg Welcome Center, near the I-76 ramp. The loop, which starts and ends there, even acknowledges the Lincoln Highway's role in the area.

U.S. Route 138 passes through Julesburg on 1st Street. The Old Ford Garage at 110 East 1st Street has become a virtual museum, filled with cars and memorabilia from the Oregon Trail and Lincoln Highway, as well as local history. The midteens building opens when the owner is operating his barbershop inside. The restored Hippodrome Theater, built in 1919, is listed on the State Register of Historic Properties and is one of the few theaters left in the country with an arched entryway circled by lightbulbs. At 201 West 1st is the Fort Sedgwick Depot Museum, detailing frontier history in a former 1930s Union Pacific depot.

In *Across the Continent by the Lincoln Highway*, Effie Gladding noted that they had an early supper at the Commercial Hotel here before pressing eastward, making 208 miles on a hot day in July 1914.

After Chuck Anderson biked from Boulder to Chicago in 1993, he wrote an online diary of his adventures. After finding a motel in Julesburg–"a rectangular grid of streets that hung off the main highway like a sheet on a clothesline"–he went out for a ride and was smitten:

I said good evening to folks out for a twilight walk, waved to kids riding around with their buddies, and sighed each time I looked up to see that great bright moon and the luminous sky. . . .

I looked through warmly lit windows as families sat down to dinner. I passed a hobbyist in his garage full of woodcrafting tools, swingsets in the backyards, and kids playing in the clean alleys. I thought how sweet it must be to live in a town like this. I rode past an old brick grade school, churches, and, at the edge of town, the white bleachers of the high school playing field. Tall green corn stalks swayed in the breeze just beyond.

The Lincoln Highway stair-steps its way southwest, passing near the site of Julesburg #3 ("Wickedest City of the West," they called it) and on to **Ovid**. U.S. Route 138 connects the towns along a straighter course. German prisoners of war were held in Ovid during World War II to work surrounding fields; a two-story brick building standing at the corner of Main Street and Monroe Street housed the men.

The road continues southwest through **Sedgwick**, where a 1919 garage sits along U.S. Route 138. The original section-line road into town is now blocked by the town's welcome sign. **Crook** sports a similarly old stucco, canopied Sinclair station at 224 2nd Avenue. The town was platted in 1907 but burned in 1924 and was rebuilt; by 1928, it sported five filling stations.

Three miles west of Crook is the Harmony Ditch Bridge, circa 1925, a solid-rail, concrete span. The road continues through **Proctor** and then **Iliff**, named for a cattleman who owned fifteen thousand acres and controlled ten times that amount of adjacent

Looking north on U.S. Route 138 in Sedgwick.

lands. The town pump, installed in 1890, remains in the center of town, although the water is no longer drinkable.

The next medium-size town since Julesburg is **Sterling**, named for a town of the same name in Illinois, coincidentally also along the Lincoln Highway. U.S. Route 138 comes into town on Broadway, which meets 3rd Street and 4th Street, a one-way pair. Cross streets except for Main Street are named for trees. A vaguely Spanish Colonial garage at 4th Street and Main Street was built in 1926 as a Chevy garage. It was converted about 1930 to Bill's Motors, which sold Kellogg cars. Sterling Motor Lodge on North 3rd Street offers eighteen rooms. Sterling also has an old Fox Theater on Poplar Street near 3rd Street, and another 1920s Spanish Mission-style gas station at 3rd Street and Cedar Street.

The Kozy Kort still operates in Brush.

Going East or Going West
Kozy Kort is Always Best.

34322

The former Cole Hotel on Main Street dates to about 1913 and retains stained-glass transoms and an iron balcony. In 1914, Effie Gladding stopped at the Southern Hotel on Main Street: "We exhorted our host and hostess to put out a Lincoln Highway sign, so that none should miss their excellent table."

U.S. Route 138 ends here, as U.S. Route 6 enters town from the east and turns southwest. East of town on U.S. 6, the Overland Trail Museum documents nineteenth-century migration along the South Platte. The replica stone fort opened in 1936 and has grown to include a village of relocated buildings, such as a schoolhouse, granary barn, barbershop, and blacksmith shop, as well as a new building that traces the history of rural electricity.

About seven miles southwest of Sterling is **Atwood**. This is sugar beet country: The town once had a beet dump, where farmers left their beets until they could be hauled to a factory, and a pickle station where cucumbers similarly waited to be sent for processing. Beet processing produces sugar, and the pulp is used as animal feed.

Six miles farther along U.S. Route 6 is **Merino**. A circa 1930 gas station survives, but more amazing is a bridge over the South Platte River. The circa 1925 abutment is marked "DLD" for the Denver-Lincoln-Detroit Highway, which shared its route with the Lincoln Highway between Sterling and Denver. The town was first called Buffalo, as one of the settlers supplied buffalo meat to pioneers and railroad workers. When the railroad line arrived in 1881, the town was renamed for the breed of sheep just introduced. Today Wisdom Manufacturing makes carnival rides here.

The highway mostly follows U.S. Route 6 to **Hillrose**. The circa 1915 Trout's Garage, right on U.S. 6, was a blacksmith shop converted to auto repair. The road then heads west, leaving U.S. 6, and stair-steps to **Brush**, another town settled on cattle grazing but changed to farming with the advent of irrigation. East of **Fort Morgan** on U.S. Route 34 West, at the southwest corner of Barlow Road, is the Morgan Manor Motel. Right next door is the Valley Drive-In Theater, one of only a dozen remaining in the state.

Brush and Fort Morgan are as close as you can get to the fictional town of Centennial, which by writer James Michener's map lay at a bend in the South Platte to the northwest. The beet industry, portrayed in *Centennial*, was the leading cash crop in this region until 1985, production having peaked in 1930. The Fort Morgan Museum, at 414 Main Street, explores the history of local Indians and the 1864–68 fort. It also includes a 1920s soda fountain and a Glenn Miller exhibit.

The exact route of the Lincoln Highway here is conjecture, but a good guess is that it stair-stepped through **Wiggins**, **Hoyt** or **Prospect Valley** (where a 1940s gas station survives on CO Route 52), and **Bennett**. From there, the Lincoln turned west toward Denver. The original route nearing the city is overlain by I-70. You can exit to **Aurora** and take Colfax Avenue westbound. This also was, and still is, the course of U.S. Route 40; you'll find decades of mid-twentieth-century roadside services, many still basking in the glow of their neon signs. Travelers on that blue highway had just crossed five hundred miles of prairie, and locals were ready to serve their needs.

Among the notable motels is the Manor House at 12700 East Colfax, the Ranger at 11220, and the LaRue at 8828. The Dutch Mill Cottage Court is gone, but a mid-1930s building in the shape of a windmill survives. Pete's Kitchen at 1962 East Colfax has a guy in neon flipping flapjacks.

The Fort Laramie Treaty of 1851 legally gave most of eastern Colorado, including **Denver**, to the Cheyenne and Arapaho Indians. It's hard to believe that 150 years ago the Queen City of the Plains had but twenty cabins. Within two years of the 1858 discovery of gold, the area changed from a native encampment to thousands of (mostly) men looking to make their fortune. Despite its relative isolation, the new riches led the railroads to make the city a regional hub starting in 1870. The sudden, explosive growth also led to numerous problems between the Indians and whites.

Colfax Avenue (the equivalent of 15th Avenue) is also U.S. Route 287 to midtown. The capitol complex, along East Colfax at Lincoln Street, features a century-old Neo-

The Valley Drive-In Theater, Fort Morgan.

Dutch Boy Donuts closed in the 1990s, and the building now houses a Mexican restaurant. Mark Wolfe helped rescue the sign for the American Sign Museum in Cincinnati, Ohio. Many neon signs, however, still line the route east of downtown Denver.

classical state capitol building. In front of it along 13th Avenue (between Lincoln and Broadway) is the Colorado History Museum, with exhibits on emigrants, Indians, mining, and the Cheyenne Dog Soldiers. Adjacent to the west is Civic Center Park, and across Colfax on the west side of Broadway, the 1911 Pioneer Monument honors the region's gold seekers and features Kit Carson on horseback. From there, streets to the northwest are diagonal to Colfax, a result of the town growing out from the South Platte River.

The state's WPA guide, published in 1941, noted the city had 150 hotels, auto camps on the main highways, and accommodations for blacks, intended as a progressive attitude in that era. A few blocks north on Downing, the Black American West Museum and Heritage Center tells the story of black cowboys, the Buffalo soldiers, and other African American contributions to the West. A few blocks west and south is the Museo de las Americas.

About sixty miles to the south is Colorado Springs, scene of the 1913 governors' conference that caused the LHA so much pain. Nearby Manitou Springs retains a bounty of 1950s motels, cafés, and neon signs.

Heading North

In 1906, Denver built a welcome arch in front of Union Station. When it was dedicated, the mayor proclaimed, "It is to stand here for the ages." But feelings—and transportation patterns—changed, so as cars eclipsed trains, the arch was demolished in 1931 as a traffic hazard.

Tourists had a number of options including camping at Overland Park, originally known as Jewell Park, which was also used as a racetrack and airstrip. Twin towers at the entrance supported a canopy—all with a tile roof—and a gas station was adjacent.

A couple blocks north of the Civic Center on Broadway is the triangular Brown Palace Hotel. Another of its Colorado red granite and Arizona sandstone walls faces 17th Street, which runs a dozen blocks northwest to Union Station. Begun in 1888 and opened on August 12, 1892, the Brown Palace is famed for its Italian Renaissance design and Victorian style. It still dazzles visitors with an eight-story atrium with stained-glass skylight. As motorists replaced rail passengers, it remained one of the city's elite hotels. Today it has a rare four-star AAA rating, with rooms running to $1,200 a night.

In *A Frenchwoman's Impressions of America*, Comtesse Madeleine de Bryas wrote that she and her sister were told a story of how the Brown Palace got its name: A shaggy gold miner named Brown had asked for a room, and when turned away, he went and bought the place that day so he could have the room he wanted. In reality, Henry Cordes Brown made his fortune selling land on what became Denver's Capitol Hill. He conceived a grand hotel for the city and spared no expense. It has hosted presidents Theodore Roosevelt, Woodrow Wilson, Warren G. Harding, and Dwight D. Eisenhower, as well as the Beatles.

East Colfax Avenue becomes West at Broadway; there, again at Civic Center Park, the Lincoln Highway bears right on 15th Street. Denver's automobile row was south of here on Broadway; several old car dealerships remain with original signs. To the left is Six Flags Elitch Gardens, opened in 1891 (at a different site) by Mary and John Elitch. It developed into a theater, dance pavilion, and amusement park. The park used to advertise, "Not to see Elitch's is not to see Denver." To the right is the city's current hot spot, the LoDo district, which runs between Larimer Street and the South Platte River from 14th Street to 22nd Street, centered around Union Station.

The Lincoln crosses the river and bears left on 29th Avenue, then turns right to head north on Federal Boulevard, rejoining U.S. Route 287, which had continued west on Colfax Avenue to Federal. U.S. Route 40 stays on West Colfax past a few more neon signs such as the Pig and Whistle restaurant (painted over sign) and motel (sign reading both Hotel and Motel). Farther west, at 6715 West Colfax is Casa Bonita, a wacky all-you-can-eat Mexican restaurant featuring cliff divers, gunfights, mariachis, tunnels, puppet shows, and meals handed out through secret passages. In **Lakewood**, Davie's Chuck Wagon Diner, a 1957 Mountain View (#516) at 9495 West Colfax Avenue, is one of the few East Coast–manufactured diners that ever made it west of the Mississippi.

The road north to Cheyenne was part of the Yellowstone Highway, which connected Denver to the national park–not to be confused with the cross-country Yellowstone Trail.

About a mile after the turn onto Federal Boulevard is Lakeside Amusement Park, a small, family-owned operation, smaller but much more affordable than its big neighbor,

Elitch's. It opened in 1908 and, like Saltair in Utah, was billed as the "Coney Island of the West." The park still has classic rides, such as a small steam train from the 1904 St. Louis World's Fair, a 1940 wooden roller coaster, and lots of Art Deco details. You can buy a ride-all-day pass or pay general admission and buy individual ride tickets; parking is free. Lakeside also holds a place in LHA history: Carl Fisher and his Hoosier Tour visited here in July 1913 while being feted in Denver. To reach the park, turn left (west) at West 44th Avenue. It's at 4601 Sheridan Boulevard, Exit 271 of I-70.

Any sense of the old Lincoln is lost in the urban tangle of interstates and modern commerce. Almost ten more miles north, the Lincoln Highway and U.S. Route 287 turn left on West 120th Avenue at what was once known as Cozy Corner. Continue another three miles through **Broomfield**, named for the broom corn that early settlers grew.

U.S. Route 287 turns right on South 112th Street and goes north for four miles. At **Lafayette**, once a prosperous coal-mining town, the road makes a couple S-curves to the left and proceeds on North 107th Street. Note that streets are numbered eastward from the city of Boulder. One bypassed section of the old highway is still gravel just a block east of U.S. 287. Some ten miles on, the road is Main Street through **Longmont**. A mid-1930s, two-story service station with canopy was along U.S. 287; it has been moved away to save it from demolition.

The highway goes straight north again on North 107th Street. Throughout this drive, the eastern front of the Rocky Mountains is to the left. About nine miles from Longmont, U.S. Route 287 turns east at the old Bert's Corner onto Mountain Avenue and toward **Berthoud**. The Colorado Central Railroad came through in 1877 and built a depot and section house where the tracks crossed Little

Bimson's blacksmith shop—with a rare surviving curbside gas pump—is now part of the Little Thompson Valley Pioneer Museum in Berthoud.

MARK WOLFE

C & W Service Station + Cottage Camp - Loveland - Colo - 1
Location North Part of City on Lincoln Highway

This postcard of C&W Service Station and Cottage Camp shows that the Lincoln Highway was taken seriously by businesses along the Colorado Loop.

Thompson River. The settlement was named in honor of E. L. Berthoud, who surveyed the route. The town was located in a valley, and the railroad asked the inhabitants to move it so the engines could avoid the climb. Late in 1883, the buildings were towed a mile north, and the area prospered from the combination of agriculture and a rail depot.

After a mile and a half, U.S. Route 287 turns left (north) on 1st Street. (A U.S. 287 bypass circles the town to the northwest.) At 224 Mountain Street, A. G. Bimson's Blacksmith Shop has a curbside gas pump; these were popular for decades, but very few remain in place. Next door, a colorful mural graces the facade of the Little Thompson Valley Pioneer Museum in the 1893 Bimson Building and Annex. The museum includes a doctor's office, drugstore, Victorian parlor, and photo studio among other exhibits, and admission is free.

Floyd Clymer, later a noted racer, magazine columnist, and writer-publisher known for his scrapbook-style books, lived in Berthoud at the time of the Lincoln Highway. He was a boy then, but not an average kid.

Clymer's father was a doctor and, like so many, a pioneer in automobile use. In *Treasury of Early American Automobiles*, Clymer said that his father had helped him learn design and construction, "which could be had only by ownership and association." He told how in 1902, at age seven, he fell in love with his dad's curved-dash Olds. At ten, he owned a Reo, and by the next year, he was a dealer for one-cylinder Reos, two-cylinder Maxwells, and one-cylinder Cadillacs. President Theodore Roosevelt called him "the world's youngest automobile dealer." Young Clymer sold twenty-six cars in his first two years. "Ford was not very stout competition then, although in 1905 he built the Model N Roadster at the competitive price of $500. . . . Four cylinders for half a thousand, though a considerable sum, was a recognizable bargain that began to make a dent in my sales."

Treasury pictured a car with huge balloon tires made in Laramie, Wyoming, by Elmer Lovejoy in 1905, and Clymer recalled how, in 1910 at age fourteen, he visited Lovejoy's garage. When he met Henry Ford in 1907 in Denver, Ford told him he hoped he'd someday sell Fords. As there was already a regional Ford seller, Clymer stuck with the E.M.F. "30" and then the Flanders "20," both cars built by the E.M.F. Company in Detroit and distributed by Studebaker wagon company of South Bend, Indiana. But by 1910, Clymer was losing even loyal customers every day to the Model T, which was cheaper to buy and maintain. When his father decided to move to Walla Walla, Washington, Clymer, now just fourteen, and his eleven-year-old brother Elmer cooked up a promotion with Studebaker to sell more Flanders by driving one to Spokane as a publicity stunt. After a grand start, repeated breakdowns led Studebaker to abandon the trip in western Wyoming.

In Walla Walla, Clymer worked for a Studebaker dealer, but by the end of 1910, he'd switched to working at a Ford dealer. In 1911, his family returned to Colorado, and he took the Ford agency in Louisville, Colorado. Ford liked him, but not the idea of a sixteen-year-old salesman, and instead employed him as a broker for established dealers. Clymer was on his way to making lifelong connections that would serve him well in his multifaceted career.

As the Lincoln Highway heads to **Campion** and north, land use starts changing from beets to orchards. U.S. Route 287 becomes Lincoln Avenue heading into **Loveland** (through downtown U.S. 287 jogs left to take Cleveland Avenue north). An old postcard from C&W Service Station and Cottage Camp at Loveland reads, "North part of city on the Lincoln Highway." Surviving along the highway is a mid-1930s, Spanish Mission-style gas station. Rocky Mountain National Park, to the west via U.S. Route 34, was and remains a popular draw for tourists.

North Lincoln Avenue heads north from town, then the road jogs left and U.S. Route 287 follows Garfield Avenue toward **Fort Collins**, where the road becomes College Avenue. A roadside diversion is the Holiday Twin Drive-In Theater, opened southwest of town in 1968 and made a twin-screen in 1976. To get there, turn left on Drake Road, go almost three miles to South Overland

Trail, and turn right—you can't miss the sign with its old Holiday Inn–style logo.

Fort Collins takes its name from a small military post that moved here in 1864, which was itself named for the commander of Fort Laramie. The fort was abandoned within seven years but the settlement kept the name. As Effie Gladding drove south here in 1914, she called it "a very pleasant town in the midst of alfalfa fields." The Northern Hotel, at 72 North College Avenue, was built in 1936 and is listed on the National Register of Historic Places. Five years later, the state's WPA guide noted that the town had two hotels plus tourist camps.

Fort Collins is also home to radio station WWV, a service of the National Institute of Standards and Technology, which broadcasts time and frequency information, plus geophysical alerts, marine storm warnings, and Global Positioning System status reports. The time signal is used for atomic clocks and computers and is accurate to less than a one-second deviation every million years.

U.S. Route 287 heads north from Fort Collins, but then veers left and heads northwest to Wyoming, joining the main Lincoln Highway at Tie Siding and pressing on to Laramie. Meanwhile, the Colorado Loop of the Lincoln Highway turns right onto CO Route 1. It curves left around a lake—one of many in the area—and heads north. After a couple miles, it bends right, then in a couple more, it bends left at Meyer's Corner. It soon enters **Wellington**, CO Route 1 curving right onto West Cleveland Avenue. It crosses tracks and half a dozen blocks later, it meets I-25/U.S. Route 87. The road roughly follows this some twenty miles into Wyoming. There

Honda Doctor occupies a classic 1930s Spanish Mission style gas station in Loveland.

often are parallel lanes that could be original, marked Frontage Road or Service Road. There is at least one break in these as it crosses the interstate. The land is a mix of beets and fruits, plus cattle grazing. Sheep also are brought here for winter fattening.

A quarter mile into Wyoming is the Terry Bison Ranch. If you're on I-25, take Exit 2 onto Terry Ranch Road; that goes north to Cheyenne, but turn right on I-25 Service Road East and go two miles south. There you'll find the ranch's thirty thousand acres of grassland, so much that it crosses back into Colorado. Visitors can stay overnight in a cabin, bunkhouse, RV, or even a tent. The ranch is home to twenty-five hundred American bison, plus horses, camels, llamas, ostriches, emus, peacocks, goats, and even a couple crossbreeds: turkins (half turkey, half chicken) and beefalo (half buffalo, half steer). It also has a restaurant, gift shop, and the state's first winery.

Leaving the ranch and heading back north to Cheyenne, the service road meets Terry Ranch Road/WY Route 223 and can be followed to U.S. Route 85. That road then goes north into downtown Cheyenne.

During their 1915 trip, Emily Post and her son and friend drove the road from Cheyenne to Denver and found it to be "uneventfully excellent all the way," quite a contrast to the mud they'd complained of in the Midwest.

Greetings from Wyoming

When Congress authorized the building of the first transcontinental railroad, it allowed the Central Pacific and the Union Pacific to lay track toward each other until they met, essentially getting paid per mile. It became a race to build as many miles as possible while trying to get as far as possible. The Central Pacific quickly hit the Sierra Nevada and complained as its pace slowed, so increased subsidies were granted for difficult terrain. The Union Pacific therefore made no effort to avoid long, sweeping curves around mountains, such as found in eastern Wyoming.

Once the two railroads were joined, the situation was reversed: Now they wanted to move goods, people, and mail as quickly as possible over the most direct grades. Work gangs ripped up the rails and ties and reused them on straighter, flatter alignments, leaving behind only the granite ballast quarried from the nearby Sherman Mountains. By the turn of the century, most of the line in eastern Wyoming had been relocated.

When LHA officials came looking for a road across the state in 1913, the abandoned railbeds were there for the taking. The Lincoln Highway adopted portions through the Sherman Mountains and west of Rawlins. The railbeds were fairly level and already graveled, though the Sherman granite was rough on early tires and tubes, and conversely, tires crushed the gravel into powder. Worse were the indentations left by the ties, which made it truly like driving on a washboard road.

On most stretches, no railbeds were available, and that's where the early Lincoln Highway could be even more troublesome. Alice Ramsey wrote that in 1909, the paths she followed weren't even roads, by her definition: "They were wagon trails, pure and simple; at times, mere horse trails. . . . With no signboards and not too many telegraph poles, it was an easy matter to pick up a side trail and find oneself arrived at the wrong destination." And as Henry Joy related, he had to take down ranch fences to proceed through the West; "there were no fences, no fields, nothing but two ruts across the prairie." In this landscape, motorists made their own way using imprecise guidebooks, common sense, and luck. Randy Wagner wrote in the spring–summer 1995 *LHA Forum*: "Until about 1917, the Lincoln Highway across Wyoming was defined by the towns it passed through more than by the road itself. How a traveler got from town to town, and by which route, was pretty much left up to the imagination."

Looking at the state on a national scale, LHA directors chose Wyoming for its low crossing of the Rocky Mountains via South Pass. That was indeed the primary passage across the northern Rockies, discovered by fur trappers and adopted as the Oregon Trail, but the Lincoln Highway actually passed fifty miles to its south, following South Pass only in spirit.

The Lincoln, and the first transcontinental railroad before it, mostly followed a path

	WYOMING	U.S.
Population in 1910	145,965	92,228,496
Population in 2000	493,782	281,421,906
Persons per square mile in 2000	5.1	79.6
Approximate miles of Lincoln Highway	427	3,389

across the state called the Overland Trail, blazed in 1862 by mountain man Jim Bridger. It was facilitated by a natural land bridge between the Great Plains and the mountains in southeastern Wyoming called the Gangplank. At mid-state, the trail crossed the Great Divide Basin, a high, flat plateau that's the center of a split in the Continental Divide.

The building of the railroad spawned a dozen towns in the state, but boomtowns had a habit of fizzling as track laying proceeded west. Those that survived—Cheyenne, Laramie, Rawlins, Rock Springs, Green River, and Evanston—would become Lincoln Highway towns. The trails that grew between them were first collectively named the Trans-Continental Highway in 1911 by Good Roads advocate Ezra Emery. He mapped a route across the state, had logs printed in the Cheyenne newspaper, and the next summer, organized its marking with yellow, black, and white bands on fence posts.

The Lincoln Highway generally followed this route, passing through Cheyenne before climbing the Gangplank to Sherman Hill. There, the highest point on the Lincoln Highway, was erroneously labeled the Continental Divide in LHA guides. It was somewhat corrected by the last guide in 1924, with the hill being called a "climb to the divide"; another mention placed the divide at Wamsutter but failed to note that there were actually two crossings on each side of the Great Divide Basin.

The Lincoln stayed with the railroad on an arc northwest from Laramie through Medicine Bow to Rawlins. As the road faded to ruts in the grass, motorists followed ranch fences. "When we came to one of these," wrote Bellamy Partridge about his 1912 trip, "we found a gate across the road, which had to be opened and closed. It said so right on the gate. And some days we would open and close dozens of these gates." He recalled that west of Laramie, they even "drove directly through a large herd of cattle." The 1913 Packard guide to the Lincoln Highway listed eighteen gates between Laramie and Rawlins alone.

Across the Great Divide Basin from Rawlins to Rock Springs, the Lincoln Highway again took to a railbed. Then, in about 1920, a new twenty-four-foot-wide road was built—still narrow, but more than adequate considering the low amount of traffic. The LHA used $20,000 from its Willys-Overland Trust Fund, helping the state complete 105 miles of graded gravel.

In western Wyoming, LHA planners looked ahead for the best place to surmount the Wasatch Mountains along the Utah border. The most feasible pass was east of Salt Lake City on a trail blazed by the Donner party in August 1846 and followed by the Mormons the following summer.

The corn and grain elevators of the Midwest were now far behind, replaced by ranches and mountains. Frederic Van de Water wrote in *The Family Flivvers to Frisco* that Nebraska's tan western end was just "a foretaste of the sun-soaked, wind-brightened immensity of brown empty land that is Wyoming." But it was the pungent aroma of sagebrush that left the biggest impression on him:

Pictures of Wyoming may stir us now and make us vaguely desirous of seeing the original again, but let the smell of sage come to us, let us even smell the faintly akin odor of crushed daisy stems, and we have only to close our eyes to review the

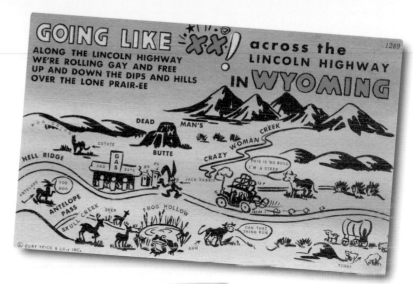

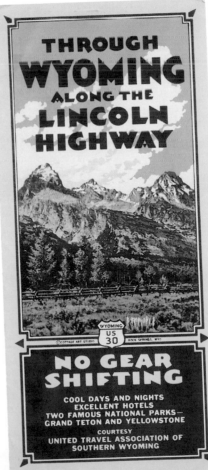

A 1939 promo card and map show the Lincoln Highway name was still strong in Wyoming.

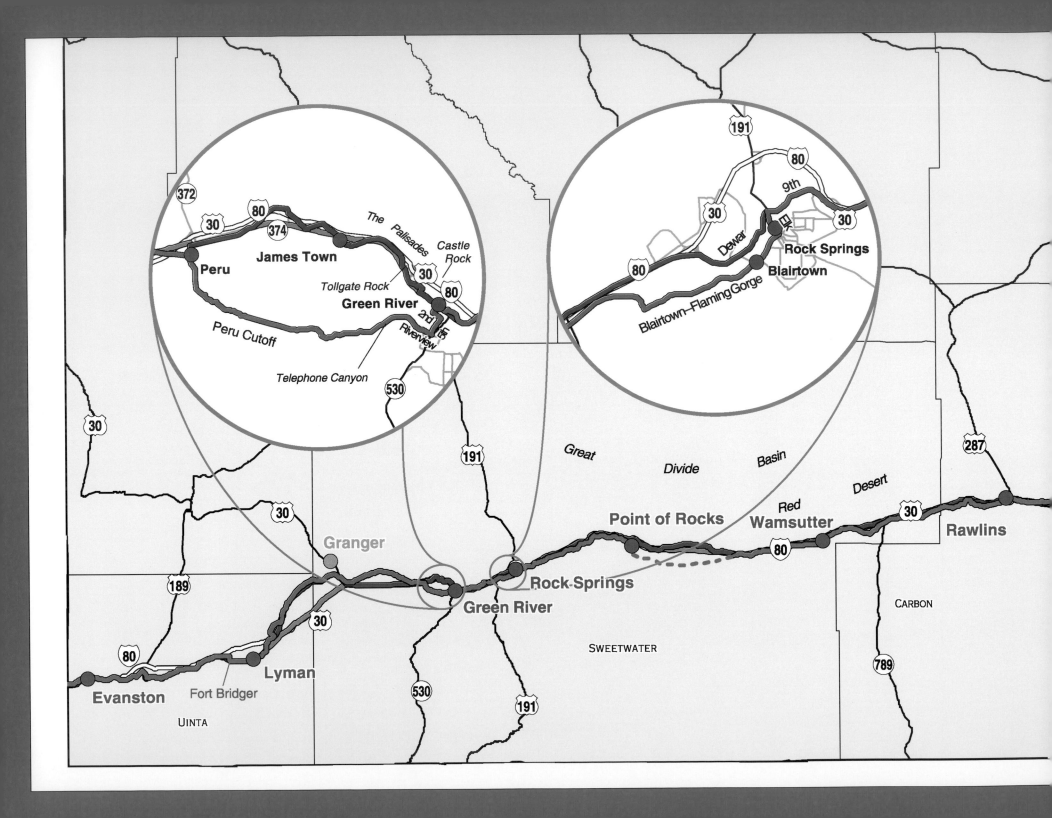

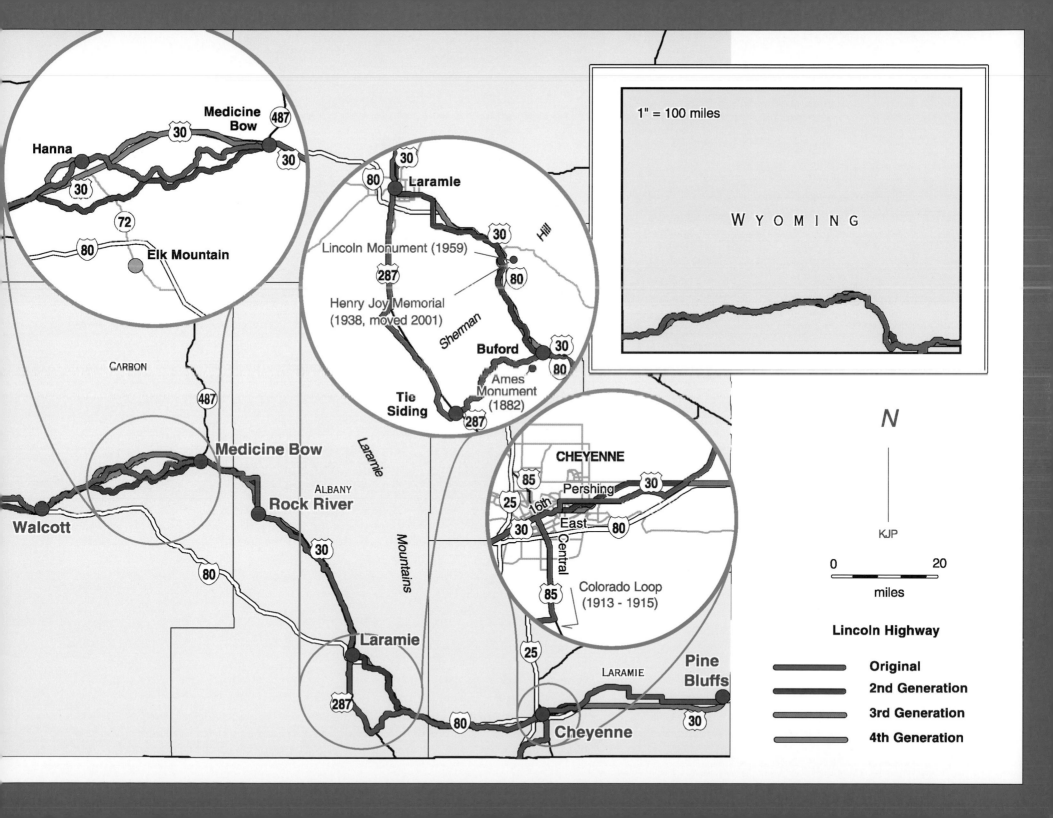

tawny and dusty olive of houseless land running away to the horizon, the sharp untempered angles of the buttes.

This state probably embraces western mythology more than any other—the sagebrush, the cowboys, the log arches over ranch driveways. Wyoming's official logo, a bucking horse and rider, shows up everywhere, and even if the state has fewer working cowboys than it did a century ago, horse riding and hat wearing are still the norm. So are rodeos and western-wear stores.

Although it's the ninth-largest state in size, Wyoming remains the least populated per square mile. In *Across the Continent by the Lincoln Highway*, Effie Gladding recalled waiting for a long freight train to pass near Wamsutter: "'It's good to see you' said the conductor; 'you motor people are about the only signs of life we fellows see out here on the desert.'"

Into Cheyenne and over Sherman Hill to Laramie

The Lincoln Highway enters the state from the east on U.S. Route 30 and skirts the northern edge of **Pine Bluffs**, which was the Union Pacific's leading cattle shipping point in the 1880s. Straddling the border is the shuttered State Line Service Station. The truck stop once was easy to spot by its tower with the words "State Line" on it, but the tower fell in 1996. To the south, along I-80, is the forty-foot-tall Our Lady of Peace Shrine, the tallest statue of the Virgin Mary in the United States. The cast-iron Lincoln Highway marker that stood here, as at every state border after 1917, has been moved to the Wyoming Department of Transportation (WYDOT) office in Cheyenne.

Nebraska-Wyoming state line marker.

The Texas Trail Museum and Monument at 3rd Street and Market Street honors the cattle drive trail that terminated at the railhead here. The High Plains Archeology Museum in town and the University of Wyoming Dig Site to the east explore ten thousand years of local geology and history. On Fridays during the summer, stop by town for the Outlaw Saloon Rodeo.

While I-80 and U.S. Route 30 join and curve west, the original road takes a jagged course through small settlements. It makes a straight shot along the section line to **Egbert**, where it crosses the Union Pacific tracks, jogs one section north to **Burns**, heads west again, then turns north and goes two sections into **Hillsdale**. There it joins the Union Pacific and bends southwest, reaching the abandoned settlement of **Archer**. In 1903, Horatio Jackson and Sewall Crocker, making their cross-country journey, got stuck at this small rail stop just east of Cheyenne. It snowed on July 2, and they camped and ate with a grading gang of fif-

teen men. The 1915 LHA guide noted that its fifteen townsfolk owned three automobiles.

When Harriet White Fisher drove through this part of Wyoming in 1910, she noticed an interesting road repair method: The farmers used fertilizer to fill in holes in the roads.

Alt.-U.S. 30 and Business-80 leave I-80 and, with the Lincoln parallel, head into **Cheyenne**, the first of the five state capitals on the Lincoln to rename the route through town Lincolnway. The equivalent of 16th Street, it once again goes by Lincolnway.

Cheyenne is named for the Native Americans who once inhabited the area. The town grew quickly with the arrival of the Union Pacific Railroad in 1867 and the resultant roundhouse and yards.

A few blocks east of downtown is Holliday Park, home to Lake Minnehaha but dominated by Big Boy, one of a line of monstrous steam locomotives. Only twenty-five of these 354-ton giants were built; this one, #4004, from 1941, was the fifth. It was needed for the rugged freight run from Cheyenne to Ogden, Utah, especially through the Wasatch Mountains.

Central Avenue naturally marks the center of town; here the western end of the Colorado Loop of the Lincoln Highway branches to Denver. About nine miles south, near the Colorado border, is the Terry Bison Ranch, a working ranch detailed in the Colorado chapter. I-25 now makes it a short trip to the Mile High City.

Astride Central Avenue and Lincolnway is the Union Pacific Depot, built in 1887 and just restored. Its 1920s-style lobby features a visitors center, restaurant, and the Cheyenne Depot Museum, which explores regional rail heritage. Between the station and Lincolnway is Depot Plaza, once a bus station but now a small urban park that hosts festivals.

Across the street is the Plains Hotel, built in 1911 and considered—at least by locals—to be the best lodging between Chicago and San Francisco. The entrance walk facing Central Avenue has a mosaic of Chief Little Shield; across Central is the Lincoln Movie Palace, with a stunning 1950s facade. Seven blocks north is the Wyoming State Museum, which has an Auto Club of Southern California–sponsored Lincoln Highway sign.

Cheyenne had a free municipal campground along a lake at the north end of town, probably at Frontier Park. In his *History of Wyoming*, T. A. Larson quoted a figure of forty thousand campers there in 1920, of whom three thousand, from thirty-two states, came to town for Frontier Days. Such a busy camp had a store and police protection in addition to more common amenities such as electric lights, showers, and laundry tubs.

Frederic Van de Water wrote that it was a "big and modern camp set beside a lake. We found no better from Coast to Coast." In 1923, an upscale section could be secured for 50¢ a night, but as Larson pointed out, some locals protested that "to charge money was contrary to the spirit of the Old West." Of course, this trend would only accelerate: "Why let riff-raff stay for free," towns and entrepreneurs asked themselves, "when you can make a few dollars and thereby limit your customers to a better class of motorists?" By World War II, cabin camps were quite common, and trailer courts were increasing too.

Cheyenne is the town where most travelers expected to find the Wild West in full flower. Alice Ramsey found a fine hotel here in 1909, the Inter-Ocean, perhaps named to attract the growing numbers of cross-country motorists. Otherwise, she found it "a true frontier town . . . a typical one with a conglomeration of Indians, cowboys and cattlemen on its streets."

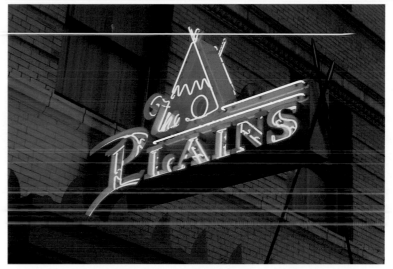

The Plains Hotel, in the heart of Cheyenne since 1911.

In contrast, "you will be much disappointed," wrote Emily Post in 1915, "though it may be well not to show the progressive citizens of that up-to-date city that you hoped they were still galloping along wooden sidewalks howling like coyotes!" Nowadays, during June and July, the Cheyenne Gunslingers

Cheyenne's municipal campground, 1924.

Lincoln Way in Cheyenne has lots of neon, including that of the Firebird Motel and the Red Wood Bar.

By 1942, Lincoln Court spanned forty acres and sixty units.

perform free western skits at Depot Plaza each weekday at 6 P.M., Saturdays at high noon. And Cheyenne's Frontier Days, held every summer since 1897, is the state's biggest annual draw; the first featured Buffalo Bill and his Congress of Rough Riders.

The 1924 LHA guide had some advice for those heading west from Cheyenne: "Always fill your tank at every point gasoline can be secured, no matter how little you have used from your previous supply. This costs nothing but a little time and it may save a lot of trouble." It also recommended carrying a spare gas can and a full water canteen from here west.

A few blocks west of Central Avenue, on the corner of Pioneer Avenue, is Dinneen Lincoln-Mercury, in a 1927 Art Deco dealership. The corner showroom was once a filling station. Lifts operated by city steam are used to take cars to the body shop on the second floor.

Along Lincolnway east and west are a number of older motels still sporting their neon signs. West of town, along a curve parallel to the Union Pacific tracks, you'll find the Lincoln Motor Court and the Hitching Post Inn. Pete Smith built the twenty-four-unit Lincoln Court, along with a service station and grocery. When he died in 1938, his son Harry took over and added garages and thirty-six more rooms. Harry married in 1941; he and his wife, Mildred, eliminated the kitchen units, enlarged the rooms (probably by remodeling the garages), and built what is said to have been the state's first outdoor, in-ground swimming pool. They also built a new motel office with an apartment upstairs that the family used briefly. In 1946, they added the Hitching Post restaurant, which expanded over time to include meeting rooms, a package liquor store, a bar, and motel rooms. Paul A. Smith, having climbed the ladder from bellhop to busboy to most every other position, now runs the large operation. Lincoln Court is still next door, with sixty-four rooms and that outdoor pool. If you like to hear trains day and night, you'll love it here.

I-80 and U.S. Route 30 head west from here, but the original Lincoln went southerly along the railroad, the route marked by its stations: **Corlett**, **Borie**, **Otto**, and **Granite Canyon**. A quarry here, seen just north of the Lincoln Highway and I-80, was the source of all that Sherman granite track ballast, then and now. The Remount Ranch, named for the remounts it supplied for cavalrymen who needed fresh horses, was also once home to Mary O'Hara, who wrote here, among other novels, *My Friend Flicka*. Six miles west, **Buford** was another rail station, but with a school and a business (unspecified in the LHA guides). Not all of the original route can be followed today, and some of it has been erased by the interstate, so I-80 is a convenient way to progress west, exiting to travel parts of the old route. *LHA Forum* articles and Gregory Franzwa's state guide are essential for finding the numerous intertwined routings.

"Gumbo roads" brings to mind Iowa's sticky mud, but Thornton Round wrote in *The Good of It All* that his family encountered gumbo west of Cheyenne in 1914. It was as if, he said, the road was topped by "slick grease. But only for a depth of about one-half inch." Still, that was enough to maroon them. It took an ax and a crowbar to dislodge the mud from the fenders, and the men became covered with the sticky substance in the backbreaking process. "On this day," he wrote, "the gumbo caused us so much trouble we thought of a few new and more apt names for the stuff."

The landscape is changing from rolling grasslands to rocky hills. Approaching the Sherman Mountains, the road ascends the Gangplank, a ten-mile-wide grade that climbs from the plains into the mountains. This grade reportedly was discovered by Gen. Grenville Dodge in 1866, as he scouted a route for the transcontinental railroad through the Laramie Mountains (at the time called the Black Hills). He'd spent two years looking for a practical grade; the challenge was not just finding a low pass, but one whose approaches were also manageable.

There are numerous scenarios explaining the route's discovery. In one version, Dodge was returning from Yellowstone, where he was commanding troops during the Indian campaigns of 1865, when he encountered the grade. When he took charge of the Union Pacific, he reported it and even named the summit for his former commander, Gen. William T. Sherman. Another story goes that his engineering crew, cut off by Indians, stumbled upon the grade while searching for a high place from which to signal for help. But it's not as though the land had never been seen. In 1850, Capt. Howard Stansbury reported on what essentially became the route from Lodgepole Creek to Green River. Or perhaps Jim Bridger, whose Overland Trail opened in 1862, should get the credit. Nevertheless, it was Dodge who recognized the advantage of the long, sloping ridge from the plains to its summit, realizing that the railroad should turn from Lodgepole Creek to follow the ridge between Crow Creek and Lone Tree Creek,

past Cheyenne, up to Sherman Summit at Evans Pass. This is the path the Lincoln Highway would follow half a century later.

From Buford, the Lincoln Highway lies beneath the westbound lanes of I-80. A rest area at mile 333 in the median surrounds Tree Rock. Here the famous limber pine shoots from a crack in a boulder of Sherman granite. It's said that surveyors of the Union Pacific altered its course to pass by the tree, and that firemen on the trains would throw it a drink from their buckets. That lasted thirty-four years, until the railroad was relocated a couple miles south. The abandoned grade became a wagon road, and then in 1913, the Lincoln Highway adopted the old railbed. Faint traces of the old roadbed can be seen southeast of the tree.

The original Lincoln Highway curved west here to follow the old railroad grade for twenty-five miles to Laramie. The ties had indeed been removed, but many noted the incessant bumps, and it was possible that a stray spike or bolt might be encountered. The circa 1920 alignment weaves back and forth along I-80, while the 1940s alignment switches from being beneath the westbound lanes to mostly being under the eastbound lanes.

About two miles west of Tree Rock, the 1913 and circa 1920 branches split, the original bearing left and passing half a mile north of the Ames Monument. This sixty-foot-tall, hollow pyramid marked the highest point on the Union Pacific line, at 8,247 feet. It was designed by Henry Hobson Richardson and built in 1882 using pink granite from the nearby Sherman Mountains. The monument honors U.S. congressman Oakes Ames and his younger brother Oliver, third president of

The road west from Cheyenne included numerous roadside businesses, including Indian Village Motor Lodge. The 1946 United Motor Courts guide located it at 110 West 16th Street (Lincolnway). The forty rooms were steam heated and had phones and showers. Rates on this 1940 postcard begin at $2.50 for two.

Another attraction was Dutch Mill Camp, which advertised "tourist apartments."

The Lincoln Highway at Tree Rock followed the former alignment of the Union Pacific.

TREE-IN-THE-ROCK, THE FAMED LANDMARK OF WYOMING

BERNIE HEISEY

Looking north to Tree Rock, now between the lanes of I-80.

the Union Pacific Railroad. Both were financial backers of the line, though their luster faded with accusations of corruption. (Oakes sold stock in the construction company to twenty-two fellow congressmen; he was found guilty of giving bribes, but somehow the other senators and representatives were found not guilty of having accepted bribes.)

The pyramid was built to be seen by passing trains, but when the railroad abandoned this route in 1901 for a more favorable pathway to the south, the monument was abandoned too. The Lincoln Highway's adoption of the railroad grade introduced the landmark to a new generation, but the Lincoln itself was rerouted half a mile farther away in 1920, and yet another half a mile in the 1930s, leaving the monument alone again in the sagebrush.

The road built in 1919–20 from Tree Rock to Laramie eliminated some of the difficult and dangerous grades. The 1924 LHA guide proclaimed it a twenty-four-foot-wide graveled "boulevard" between the two cities (and for three miles beyond).

Traveling north from Tree Rock on I-80, take Exit 329, Vedauwoo Road, and make two left turns to follow a gravel road to the Ames Monument. Almost a mile from the exit, the 1920 Lincoln goes straight (southeast), back almost to Tree Rock, while the road to the monument bears right (south). Half a mile past that, it crosses Hermosa Road/WY Route 222, the old railbed/1913 Lincoln Highway heading southwest to Hermosa. It's become a faint, rough road. The *Auto Log* pictured in the Introduction gave its sharpest warning for the road two miles west of the monument: "LOOK OUT! Bad down grade."

Three miles later, the Lincoln Highway reached **Hermosa** (called **Sherman Hill** in the 1916 LHA guide; it was listed as offering a store and blacksmith shop but no accommodations). Just past **Tie Siding**, the Lincoln turned north and roughly followed today's U.S. Route 287 through **Red Buttes** and then due north into Laramie. The original route came into town along the railroad and onto Second Street.

Back at Exit 329 (Vedauwoo Road) off I-80, the service road on the west side is the 1920 Lincoln Highway and is drivable. About five miles to the north is the summit of Sherman Hill, at 8,835 feet, the highest point ever on the Lincoln Highway. LHA guidebooks called the summit the Continental Divide, but that's wrong; the route crosses the Continental Divide—twice—about one hundred miles west.

In 1882, the Union Pacific honored brothers Oakes and Oliver Ames with this pink granite monument. The nearby tracks were abandoned in 1901, but the Lincoln Highway used the railbed and once again brought travelers past the spot until it, too, was rerouted in the 1930s.

The Summit Tavern began as the tiny log structure buried in the middle and grew to include a restaurant and overnight rooms. It was located at the highest point on the Lincoln, at 8,835 feet.

Two roads now cross the summit: the 1920 route, mostly a gravel trace, and U.S. Route 30, built in the 1930s and maintained as a service road to I-80.

The first building at the summit was a log house that can be seen in old LHA photos. Photos show a plaque on the chimney that read, "Grenville Dodge Summit Inn, erected by William C. Deming and Leslie A. Miller in honor of General Grenville Dodge the pass finder." Signs there incorrectly noting the Continental Divide were perhaps the source of the LHA's misinformation. Later, a much enlarged Summit Tavern was a must-stop for early drivers. It's long gone, but look for the original concrete foundation to a Lincoln monument that has been relocated.

Today I-80 crosses the summit less than half a mile to the east and 195 feet lower in elevation, although it is the highest point on I-80. If following the old road, turn right just ahead to cross I-80 to the Summit Rest Area at the Happy Jack Road interchange, Exit 323. This is a must-stop for Lincoln Highway fans. The monument to President Lincoln—a blocky sculpture topped by his thirteen-and-a-half-foot bronze bust—was constructed in 1959 to commemorate the sesquicentennial of Lincoln's birth. It was designed and created by Robert Russin, then an art professor at the University of Wyoming. It took ten tons of clay and eleven months to complete. To work in a constant favorable climate, the bust—cast in thirty pieces—had to be formed in Mexico City, transported, and bolted together. It was set atop a thirty-five-foot-tall, cut-granite base, which is hollow with ladders and lightning rods inside. It sat upon the foundation at the Lincoln Highway summit, then was moved here when I-80 was opened in 1969. A visitors center has a small exhibit about the bust and the Lincoln Highway.

The rest area gained another Lincoln Highway landmark late in 2001 when the Henry B. Joy Monument was moved here from the Continental Divide interchange, about one hun-

This 1959 bust of Lincoln, once at the Lincoln Highway's highest summit, was moved here to a lower point along I-80 in 1969.

dred miles to the west. The original location was being vandalized, so the LHA arranged with WYDOT to move the granite monolith, fence, and 1928 concrete LHA posts. This is discussed further on pages 195–96.

The original Lincoln Highway is to the west, following U.S. Route 287 into Laramie; the second-generation Lincoln continues through Telephone Canyon, named in 1882 for the first phone line over the mountains. Most of the original route has been straightened, though bits of old road appear on the right. Even on the interstate, it's still a steep descent, dropping one thousand feet in five miles. The Lincoln then gets lost beneath I-80 as the roads make an S-curve through the canyon on their course northwest toward **Laramie**. I-80 goes south around the town, while the 1920 Lincoln Highway/U.S. 30 enters Laramie from the east on Grand Avenue.

The state's third-largest city is home to the University of Wyoming, whose influence is exhibited by the trendy stores behind Old West facades. As the state's only four-year institution of higher learning, it attracts students from many hundreds of miles. The campus itself has several museums.

Laramie was named for trapper Jacques La Ramee. The Union Pacific came through in 1868, and within three months, there were five thousand residents—the usual mix of workers, soldiers, and troublemakers who followed the rails as they pushed west. Three years later, the town gained notoriety as the first place in the world to let a woman vote in a general election.

One of the early auto pioneers was Elmer Lovejoy, who had a garage at 412 South 2nd Street. He is noted in T. A. Larson's *History of Wyoming* as building the state's first horseless carriage in 1898—with iron tires, ouch!—and the same year brought the first car into Wyoming, a Locomobile steamer. During the 1908 New York–to–Paris race, he opened his shop all night when the Thomas Flyer needed an overhaul. Largely because of his influence, the town of nine thousand already had sixty automobile owners, notably ranchers, who could make a fifty-mile-or-so round-trip to town and back in one day.

Dermot Cole offered this telling anecdote in *Hard Driving*: "Wyoming saw so few tourists in automobiles that as late as 1913 the only map available of the route to Utah was a hand-drawn sketch by Lovejoy. He would loan it out to travelers with the understanding that they would mail it back to Laramie." Indeed, Bellamy Partridge wrote in *Fill 'er Up!* that Lovejoy "loaned me his personal copy of a hand-drawn map from Laramie to Ogden, asking me to check the mileage and mail it back to him, which I was very happy to do, giving him at the same time a brief report on the condition of the roads for other travelers." Lovejoy appears in various diaries and his garage became the Control Point for Laramie.

When Thornton Round's family stayed in town in 1914, he noted that the "men, for the most part, were dressed in true cowboy style, and the women and girls were dressed as cowgirls." Round went fishing the next day with his dad and brother, catching fourteen trout; their hotel restaurant cooked the fish and they shared them with other guests.

For families passing through, stop at the Wyoming Children's Museum and Nature Center at 412 South 2nd Street to try panning for gold and other hands-on fun.

Arcing Northwest from Laramie

At the restored Wyoming Territorial Prison and Old West Park, west of town, you can tour the 1870s prison or visit Frontier Town for saloon shows, stagecoach rides, puppet shows, and ranch animal petting. It opened for visitors in 1987, with tours leaning toward the lighthearted. "There's a place behind bars for you," it advertises, offering nighttime prison tours in complete darkness three times a week.

The Lincoln Highway from Laramie to Medicine Bow has been called the best in the state; straying from I-80, it is little changed from the days of the Wild West, let alone the era of early automobiles. During his family's 1914 trip, Thornton Round noted that the land was excellent for grazing sheep and cattle: "I can attest to this because we drove along roads which were choked with animals slowly moving in huge packs." Once, what appeared to be a white field turned out to be a flock of ten thousand sheep; the animals opened a path to let the cars through then closed behind them.

Early LHA guides offered an alternate route to Rawlins via Elk Mountain. Bellamy Partridge took part of this road on his 1914 trip and forever had fond memories of his accommodations at Elk Mountain. The 1915 guide almost favored it, saying that it was well marked and "offers many attractions to the tourist, sportsman and photographer. The distance to Rawlins being about eighteen miles shorter than via Medicine Bow." According to other guides, it also had thirty-two ranch gates that needed to be opened and closed. The 1935 LHA history summed up what was apparently a significant issue: "A bitter local struggle over the routing between

Laramie and Rawlins, Wyoming, was finally settled only when Governor Joseph M. Carey issued a formal proclamation establishing the route as the Association laid it out and as it now stands."

There was good reason to choose Medicine Bow over Elk Mountain. The latter's much higher elevation brought earlier, heavier snows. Half a century later, I-80 was routed through Elk Mountain against the advice of locals. (The nearby "Snowy Range" mountains should have clued the road planners.) Until a massive snow fence was built, I-80 often closed in winter, its traffic routed on the Lincoln Highway through Medicine Bow.

Heading north into the Laramie Plains, the original Lincoln Highway again took to the abandoned Union Pacific grade at times. Almost the entire Union Pacific route was rebuilt from 1899 to 1902 because of increased traffic and the weight of the railcars, in addition to the desire to build it on a less winding course. Curves and grades were smoothed, and tunnels were built to dodge mountain passes.

The railroad's chief relocations were west of Omaha, the western border of Wyoming, and Sherman Summit–Laramie–Rawlins.

A letter from Grace Carmody reprinted in the winter–spring 1995 *LHA Forum* recalled how rough it was riding the railbed west of Laramie when her dad drove them in an open Studebaker touring car in 1920:

> The ties has been removed but it was still bump, bump, bump for it seemed hours. Mom said, "Jay, we have to be on the wrong road." Dad replied, "I don't know how there has been no place to turn off!" Eventually we saw the red, white, and blue marker painted on a post out there in the desert. It was a relief to know we were still on the Lincoln Highway.

U.S. Route 30, which locals still call the Lincoln, closely follows the older path across the Laramie River and through **Bosler**. What was once a small cluster of roadside businesses now looks mostly abandoned. Twenty miles west is **Rock River**, a quiet gathering of cross streets with vestiges of early auto-era businesses. The Union Pacific helped establish the town in 1901 as a livestock and oil shipping point. The 1916 LHA guide noted a hotel, garage, telephone company, and nine more businesses besides the railroad and express company. By 1924, the town had three hotels and three garages, including its LHA control point, a Lincoln Highway Garage.

A couple gems still line U.S. Route 30: Hostler's General Store (the former Red Top Service) and the Longhorn Lodge, both run by Roy and Betty Hostler. Roy retired from a factory job in York, Pennsylvania—where he

You can get just about anything from friendly Roy Hostler at his store in Rock River.

A gathering of roadside services at Rock River in about 1940.

had to cross the Lincoln Highway daily—and came looking for a business away from noisy cities. He got it. Few travelers stop now, having already gassed up in Laramie or Rawlins. When we stopped in the summer of 2004, Roy said he could pump gas cheaper in the city than he could buy it from his distributor. Reg-

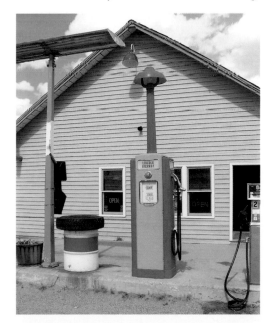

A 1940s Lincoln Highway pump at Hostler's General Store.

THE STRANGEST BUILDING IN THE WORLD MADE OF
DINOSAUR BONES
"MILLIONS OF YEARS OLD" — FOSSIL MUSEUM
COMO BLUFF, WYOMING
— WHERE CREATION PETRIFIED ITS HISTORY —
ON U.S. HIGHWAY 30 — FEATURED BY RIPLEY

FOSSIL CABIN

THE BUILDING THAT MADE THE FOSSIL FAMOUS

A freshet in what was ordinarily a dry wash thirteen miles west of Rock River posed a dilemma for motorists in 1922.

Fossil Cabin claimed to be the only building made entirely of dinosaur bones—almost fifty-eight hundred.

Note Medicine Bow's Lincoln Highway Garage at center, just right of the tall Virginian Hotel.

MEDICINE BOW, WYOMING—VIRGINIAN HOTEL IN BACKGROUND

Sanborn
Y 1062

ular unleaded was going for $2.08 in Laramie; Roy's was $2.36. He said it would cost him $15,000 to pull the tanks out, but it only runs him $10,000 a year for the upkeep. He traded for a 1940s pump that has a Lincoln Highway name insert. It no longer meets codes required to pump gas but the canopy bulb still lights; he especially likes it on winter evenings when the circle of light falls on a blanket of snow.

Turn left on Avenue C and proceed a couple blocks to the long First National Bank building turned Rock River Museum. It advertises dinosaur exhibits but looks closed. On the next block is the two-story Lincoln Hotel, once the town's only lodging, but long since a private home. There is a shortened 1928 concrete Lincoln Highway marker out front.

A mile north of town is a fork in the road at a monument honoring those "who passed this way to win and hold the West." The Lincoln Highway continues straight for about five miles, then turns left; U.S. Route 30 bears left and curves into a valley. It rises back up and rejoins the original route at the Fossil Cabin Museum, a shuttered 1930s tourist attraction. Ripley's Believe It or Not named it "the oldest house in the world," because what looks like stone walls from afar are petrified dinosaur bone fragments—5,796 of them, according to one ambitious counter—from the nearby fossil quarries at **Como Bluff**. This rich "Dinosaur Graveyard," discovered in 1877, became the first dinosaur quarry in the United States. More than a dozen complete dinosaur skeletons have been unearthed, along with twenty-six new species dating back eighty million years, and archaeology teams still make discoveries here.

Seven miles west is **Medicine Bow**, named for the land where Indians were able to craft "medicine" (that is, good) bows. The village grew with the arrival of the Union Pacific in 1868, and by 1880, it had become the leading shipping point for range livestock; twenty years later, it was likewise a major shipping point for wool. Today it's a little gathering of businesses stretched along U.S. Route 30, a quiet town and a meeting place for livestock ranchers from north of town, not much different from Effie Gladding's observations in 1914: "It is only a railroad station, a tiny cluster of saloons, a still smaller cluster of shops, a big shearing shed, and a substantial stone hotel called The Virginian."

The three-story, concrete-block Virginian Hotel took its name from Owen Wister's western novel, *The Virginian: Horseman of the Plain*, which he wrote while in town and published in 1902. Wister had come west for his health in 1882 and spent fifteen years crisscrossing the state, absorbing the life of ranchers, rustlers, and saloonkeepers. His diaries formed the basis of his novel, most famously depicting a sheriff who, when insulted, replied, "When you call me that, smile." Wister used the line in his book, and it's been showing up around town ever since. The book's legacy has endured through three movies and a 1960s TV series.

The Virginian Hotel opened on September 30, 1911, priding itself on being the largest hotel between Denver and Salt Lake City. More notably, it had the town's first electric lights and sewer system. The hotel was built by the town's first mayor, August "Gus" Grimm, and his partner George Plummer. It was listed on the National Register of Historic Places in 1978; in 1984, the hotel was renovated in a Victorian, Gay Nineties saloon look straight out of western movies. The twenty-six rooms start at $20, more for the four suites, including an Owen Wister Suite. Rooms are small and the bathroom is down the hall, but it's as close as you'll get to Old West accommodations.

Gus Grimm was mentioned in the 1913 diary of Hiram Shaw Kneedler, as recounted in the Spring–Summer 1995 *LHA Forum*: "This entertaining individual had 'blown in' as a hobo a few years before, got hold of a saloon

without a cent to his name, and made a lot of money. He owned the hotel, the electric light plant, saloon, and everything else in town."

In *A Woman's World Tour in a Motor*, Harriet White Fisher wrote that her party stopped to get directions to Cheyenne from Gus Grimm, having seen his name on "many sheep trails and roads giving directions, but the hand always pointed toward Gus Grimm's place of business, telling the traveller where he could get fine whiskey."

Heading east to Laramie, Fisher said, the road "was pretty well cut up and filled with the holes made by prairie dogs." They also saw more of Grimm's signs, pointed west now, but were glad for the break from mirages, which had become disorienting.

Across from the Virginian is the former Union Pacific depot; the original burned in the summer of 1913, so the first Lincoln Highway travelers got to see a new depot being built. It closed in 1981, was listed on the National Register of Historic Places in 1982, and reopened in 1983 as the Medicine Bow Museum. There's a 1928 concrete marker out

A 1928 concrete Lincoln Highway post faces the road and the Virginian across it at the Owen Wister Memorial in Medicine Bow.

front, and behind the museum are Wister's cabin from Jackson Hole, transported as a Bicentennial project, and a petrified wood monument to the writer built in 1939.

From Medicine Bow west to Rawlins, railbeds were again used by the original Lincoln Highway until a new gravel grade was opened to the south in the early 1920s. Counting 1931 and 1942 realignments that arc north, there are four parallel generations of Lincoln Highway/U.S. Route 30 spreading west from Medicine Bow.

The original road went to **Carbon**, a Union Pacific coal supply depot that had four thousand residents in 1890 but was abandoned by 1902, when the mines played out. Hiram Shaw Kneedler noted in his 1913 trip diary that it was deserted. It's difficult to reach by the original route, and nothing remains but foundations, though these are well marked by local historians. As this faint original route nears Hanna, it jogs across U.S. Route 30; at the

Looking west from Hanna on the 1940s Lincoln Highway alignment/U.S. Route 30, one of four parallel generations: 1913, 1922, 1931, and 1940s.

OCT. 8, 1971
Medicine Bow, Wyo.

Dear Aunt Mary and family:
Wish you could see the difference out here. Wouldn't want to be buried out here.
Love Emily Lou.

intersection are the abandoned gas station, restaurant, and motel rooms of **Home Ranch**.

Just over two miles to the west is **Hanna**. The 1918 LHA guide cautioned that care should be taken from Carbon to Hanna: "There are stretches that are very rough and many chuck holes." It also warned of the road west of Hanna: "Watch culverts and bridge approaches, it may save your springs and temper." The remnant of that road can be seen if you enter town from the south via WY Route 72 (from U.S. Route 30, built in the 1940s). The 1920s route passes south of Carbon and Hanna. Along the road is the first of three markers noting the contribution of Willys-Overland Motor Company to the 1923 improvement of twelve miles of roadway. (Another marker is along the old road six miles ahead, and the last one is six miles further.) The 1931 realignment brought the road back through the center of Hanna. All the routes meet about five miles west of Hanna.

The various fading generations (some on private property) all roughly follow U.S. Route 30 southwest through **Coyote Springs** to **Walcott**, which is half a mile north of the Lincoln Highway along the Union Pacific but was nonetheless listed in the 1915 guide as having a 125-room hotel, a public school, and two automobiles owned in town. U.S. Route 30 rejoins I-80 here at **Walcott Junction**. George A. Wyman, in the series of articles called "Across America on a Motor Bicycle," described his 1903 journey through this area:

> I reached Walcott, a "jerkwater" settlement, composed of two saloons, a store and a railroad station. It is made important, though, by the fact that two stage lines come in there. . . . I found some interest in automobiles here, and, after inspecting my machine, the natives fell to discussing the feasibility of running automobiles on the stage lines, instead of the old Concord coaches, drawn by six horses, that are now used. One of the stage drivers said that if anyone would build an automobile that would carry 12 or 14 persons and run through sand six inches deep, he would pay from $3,000 to $5,000 for it.

About five miles west, the outpost that was the namesake of **Fort Steele** was one of three forts built to protect the Union Pacific workers in 1868 from Indian attacks. Named for Civil War general Frederick Steele, it was abandoned in 1886 and its buildings sold to the public. Most have since burned, and being adjacent to the rails, some even burned while the fort was occupied, ignited by sparks from locomotives.

The original highway crossed the Union Pacific and passed a quarter mile north of the fort site. The New York–to–Paris racers avoided the flimsy bridge across the North Platte River in March 1908; the Italian Zust chattered over the Union Pacific bridge across the water, while the American crew, driving a Thomas, chanced the iced-over river. A few weeks later, LHA friend Jacob Murdock tried the bridge in his heavy Packard and made it, but by the time Alice Ramsey passed through the following year, the bridge had washed away. She noted that the locals weren't too concerned, as most drove wagons that could ford the river. Her car, however, could not, so she had to secure permission to cross via the Union Pacific trestle. Her description of crossing it is vivid:

> BUMP!
> BUMP!
> BUMP! Three quarters of a mile of this, one bump at a time. There are more bumps in that distance than you would imagine. As if living one day at a time in periods of stress, I lived one bump at a time.

As she crossed, a sharp stomach pain became excruciating: What she thought was acute appendicitis she finally concluded was "*jolt*-itis." In 1931, the Lincoln was rerouted nearly two miles south (adjacent to today's U.S. 30) and a steel truss bridge was constructed—you can see it to the immediate right from I-80/U.S. 30, just east of the exit ramp.

The original route went through **Lakota** and **Granville**, but after 1922, the highway went to a planned community, now called **Sinclair**; U.S. Route 30 angles slightly northwest as it skirts the southern edge. The "Wonder Town of Wyoming" was first named **Parco**, for the Producers and Refiners Corporation, a Denver-based oil company. The refinery and model town for fifteen hundred was built in 1922 to serve the company's employees. In *Boulevards All the Way—Maybe*, James Montgomery Flagg called it "a sort of benevolent tyranny, as the employes [*sic*] are forced to lead a sanitary and uniform existence." Sinclair Oil bought the company in receivership in 1934 and promptly changed the town's name too. The refinery still produces tens of thousands of barrels daily.

At the center of this oasis is the Spanish Colonial style Parco Hotel, its elegance once exemplified by the Fountain Room restaurant, where water poured from statues into a goldfish-filled fountain. The hotel is listed on the National Register of Historic Places but sits closed. In 2004, it was being used partly as a Baptist Youth Mission.

Even if you're driving on I-80, you can take Business I-80 through Sinclair and Rawlins, six miles ahead. The road enters **Rawlins** on Cedar Street (for a while, it was Lincoln Way). It turns right (north) on 5th Street, goes three blocks, then turns left (west) on Spruce. The streets were gravel, but paving was promised in the 1924 LHA guide.

Rawlins is another Union Pacific town, sprouting when the tracks were laid through here in about 1868. It was named for Gen. John A. Rawlins, chief of staff of the U.S. Army, who is rumored to have said, after taking a drink from a spring here, "If anything is ever named after me, I hope it will be a spring of water." The town is still the center of the region's sheep and cattle industry, and a major station on the railroad.

In 1927, Frederic Van de Water wrote that the town had two camps, one free and one pay: "We stopped at the latter for the free camp was packed to the limit with road tramps of all varieties. Their cars were battered. Their equipment and their persons gave the place the drab and defiantly squalid look of a gypsy encampment."

In her 1936 book, *Green Mountains to Sierras*, Zepphine Humphrey wrote similarly that at Rawlins, she and her husband found "the crudest cabin we had yet occupied. No running water (which was just as well, for it would surely have frozen), the minimum of furniture (which was also just as well, for the room was two by four), no "conveniences" of any kind except in a communal bath house. A gas stove, however, and a fairly comfortable bed."

Every July, folks come to Rawlins for the annual Wyoming State Cowboy Poetry Gathering. As in Laramie, a regular tourist stop is at a former prison: the Wyoming State Penitentiary at 5th Street and Walnut Street. It operated from 1901 through 1981 and has not been remodeled. You'll feel the dankness as you tour dark cell blocks, and visitors are even invited to sit in the gas chamber.

West of Rawlins, the routes parallel each other, the original a bit south in the old railroad grade, the later routes intertwined with I-80. Until a new road was built in the 1920s, the original was notorious for its frequent arroyos where storms had erased the road. In his 1913 diary, Hiram Shaw Kneedler wrote that west of town, the road was "good except for transverse ditches that cut across it where rains had washed them out. They were narrow and deep and could scarcely be seen until one got right on them. . . . About fifteen miles out of Rawlings [*sic*] we dropped into one of those ditches with a terrible crash, smashing the windshield, tearing the trunk rack loose, and starting a leak in the gasoline tank."

In *Fill 'er Up!*, Bellamy Partridge wrote, "Some of these washes were as deep as a cellar with almost perpendicular walls. I would not have believed they were passable had they not contained the tracks of automobile tires."

The various routes continue parallel. About twenty-four miles west of Rawlins, Cherokee Hill offers a grand view of the Lincoln Highway and I-80. A couple miles west, at WY Route 789, is Creston Junction. The original route bent south toward **Creston** or **Creston Station**.

Past this area, drivers make the first of two crossings of the Continental Divide. Precipitation east of this ridge flows to the Mississippi River and then the Atlantic; rain west of it *should* flow to the Pacific. But, in a geological

Parco, Wyo. Lincoln Hiwe—looking west.

The hotel in the center of this postcard dominated Parco, now renamed the town of Sinclair. Long closed, the building now houses a youth mission.

quirk, the divide splits to encircle the Great Divide Basin, which is about thirty-five miles wide here. Water falling into the basin flows to neither ocean, but stays there until it evaporates. The peak of Sherman Hill one hundred miles east was erroneously called the divide in LHA guides. As *Westward Hoboes* author Winifred Dixon commented, "There are about as many Continental Divides in the West as beds in which Washington slept in the East."

It was near the Continental Divide exit of I-80, Exit 184, that a monument to Henry Joy stood until 2001. Joy, president of Packard Motor Car Company and first president of the LHA, was also an avid outdoorsman. During a 1915 trip across the Lincoln Highway with LHA secretary Austin Bement and mechanic Ernie Eisenhut, and after almost two weeks of muddy roads, they camped near the Continental Divide. Joy saw what he considered the most beautiful sunset he had ever seen, inspiring a wish to be buried there. His wife, Helen, instead dedicated a monument here on July 2, 1939, three years after his

BERNIE HEISEY

CONTINENTAL DIVIDE SERVICE AT CONTINENTAL DIVIDE (ALT. 7,178 FT.) ON U.S. 30 IN WYOMING

The Continental Divide Lunch in Sweetwater County grew to include a Streamline Moderne gas station.

death. (The date on the monument is 1938, but various problems delayed it a year.) The tall stone tablet was surrounded by a fence and eight LHA concrete posts. The monument was never marked at the interstate but was vandalized repeatedly.

You can reach the site by exiting and turning south toward a T; on the left is a state marker for the divide, and past that, the 1920s Lincoln Highway stretches east. To the right (west) is the gravel 1939 Lincoln Highway. (The original 1913 route of the Lincoln Highway is a mile to the south.) Turn right, and at .3 mile, you'll find the earthen scar still visible on a rise to the left. The monument was moved east in 2001 and now sits at Exit 323, at the Summit Rest Area on I-80.

Bellamy Partridge recalled stopping at a headstone in this area to eat lunch: "We had approached it so gradually that we did not realize we were there until we saw the monument marking the grave of Frank Yort, the surveyor who determined the line. We thought it a rather lonely spot either to start a cemetery or to await the Judgement Day."

The 108 miles from Rawlins to Rock Springs, which includes the Great Divide Basin, traverse high, flat desert land. Wildlife abounds, particularly pronghorn antelope, but also coyotes, bobcats, rabbits, sage grouse, and even eagles.

It's four miles to **Latham Station**; as the 1918 LHA guide explained, "to Wamsutter the Lincoln Way follows the grade of the old Union Pacific road bed." It's another eight miles to **Wamsutter**, originally called Washakie; to avoid confusion with Fort Washakie in Fremont County, the town was renamed for a bridge builder on the Union Pacific Railroad. It's a small settlement, but Thornton Round's family was glad to buy some ice cream here during their 1914 trip, perhaps at the Wamsutter Hotel, the town's only accommodations.

Cyclist Mark Junge stayed overnight here in July 2004. He was following the Lincoln Highway cross-country with the aid of a Helios portable liquid oxygen container to promote the product and show people the freedom it offers. He wrote for the *Wyoming Tribune-Eagle* that the motel here was a bit scary:

This place is a great location for a remake of "Psycho." The front door doesn't lock. But then why should it? There doesn't seem to be anyone around to steal our stuff. There is no screen on the window, but I don't see

a single mosquito or creepy-crawler. No phone to bother us. The hot and cold faucets in the shower are switched, and the showerhead is not too far above waist level. The bathroom fan whines pitifully.

Still, he didn't want to complain too much, as he did have electricity, plumbing, and (intermittent) air-conditioning; it was, he wrote, "a wonderful night of rest below twinkling desert stars."

The trace of the original Lincoln Highway is lost along the Union Pacific tracks. I-80/ U.S. Route 30 is a quarter mile north, with the town in between the railroad and the highway. All head west, the interstate atop some of the old alignments.

In 1913, Hiram Shaw Kneedler was surprised at the conditions west of Wamsutter: "Such roads!—deep narrow gullies or trenches across them every twenty feet or so into which the wheels would drop with a sickening thud."

Effie Gladding found the situation here similar: "We were tormented by the plague of these roads of the plains; namely, gutters made across the roadway by running water in time of freshets. . . . They give the machine a frightful jar and if one comes upon them suddenly they are likely to break an axle."

Floyd Clymer later wrote in *Henry's Wonderful Model T* of his drive across here in 1910 at age fourteen with his eleven-year-old brother:

Jack rabbits played in the beams of our headlights as we neared the Continental Divide. At night the sheepherders would pass us in their covered wagons, if they weren't busy pulling us out of ditches, or a cowboy would stop to talk or wave at us.

The generations of roads stay intertwined over the next sixty-five miles to Rock Springs. At **Red Desert Station**, about seven miles west, you can see three of them: Starting to the south is the original, then just north is the 1920s reroute, and then the 1937 route of U.S. Route 30, all squeezed between today's I-80/U.S. Route 30 and the Union Pacific tracks a quarter mile south.

Eleven miles west, just before **Table Rock**, drivers make the second crossing of the Continental Divide, leaving the Great Divide Basin behind.

Point of Rocks was described by Hiram Shaw Kneedler in his 1913 trip diary as "a few houses by the railroad clustered in a deep ravine." Today it's an I-80 exit, but little of old remains except a stone stage station from the Overland Trail (also called the Cherokee Trail here for when the Cherokee left the Midwest for California gold fields in 1849–50). The station was opened in 1862 by Ben Holladay. He had a stage business and had just gotten a U.S. mail contract and needed a quicker way west. The trail was a shorter and safer alternative to the Oregon-California-Mormon Trail to the north. The station is one of a chain built during that first year. It lasted only until 1869, when the Union Pacific replaced stagecoaches as the way west. The main part of the stage station has been restored, its barn stabilized.

Lester Whitman traveled this section in 1904 and later wrote about the barren landscape (as quoted in Curt McConnell, *Coast to Coast by Automobile*):

From Rawlins to Rock Springs is another 150-mile stretch without gasoline, town, hotel, horse, trail. The section houses of the Union Pacific will have to be used for meals and lodging, but the occupants along this desert are as poor as Job's turkey, and ham and eggs and coffee without milk will comprise the lay-out.

For overnight accommodations, Whitman recommended section houses, which came every six to eight miles. If you arrived just before a meal, the wife of the section boss might even feed you for 25¢.

In 1914, Effie Gladding found only the station, grocery, and a few cottages at Point of Rocks:

The young groceryman has fitted up the rooms over his grocery for passing travelers. We established ourselves in the front one, lighted by one little window. . . . The floor was bare and our furniture consisted of a bed, a chair without a back, a tin wash basin resting upon the chair, a lamp, a pail of fresh water with a dipper, and a pail for waste water. We had two fresh towels and felt ourselves rich in comfort.

It was in this stretch that young Thornton Round collapsed the front end of the Ford he was driving. While the rest of the family took their accompanying Winton to Rock Springs for help, Thornton and his dad stayed here as night fell:

We were surrounded by the blackest of nights and some of the queerest noises I have ever heard. A blood curdling scream came from somewhere out on the prairie. This was followed by a loud cry that might have been made by a loon or some other large bird. A coyote joined the eerie chorus. Several road runners (large birds about the size of pheasants) ran around the car, and as they moved they gave funny little squeals. Whippoorwills called, and we fancied that we could hear a wolf baying.

At 10:30 P.M., his brother returned with a mechanic and a radius rod, plus a reinforcing rod. Thornton's dad said, "Let's put the thing on and get out of here. This is the most scary [*sic*] place I have been in, in a long while."

The 1924 LHA guide noted that the seven-mile stretch from Point of Rocks to **Thayer Junction** was soft, but the road was expected to be graveled soon. As Harriet White Fisher was driving east to Rock Springs in 1910, she "found long stretches of deep sand with high centres."

Postcard collectors know **Rock Springs** they've seen many a view of its arch announcing, "Home of Rock Springs Coal: Welcome." Erected over the Lincoln Highway late in 1928, the $3,000 sign—with one thousand bulbs—spanned C Street north of the railroad until 1941. It was relocated a couple times, then actually junked, before locals raised the funds to restore it. In 1997, it was rededicated close to the original spot.

The restored and relocated welcome arch at Rock Springs.

Dear Mom & Dad,
We just ate supper at the
place on the front and were
never so put out in all our
lives. We had to pay $3.57
for our meal. Once we were
in couldn't walk out but
sure wished that we could.
Love, Dottie & Harold

The town has had various lives as an Over-land Stage station, coal-mining community, and supply point for the railroad, attracting immigrants from around the world to work in its mines. A historical downtown walking tour includes sites visited by Butch Cassidy and Calamity Jane.

The 1916 LHA guide noted that the local speed limit—enforced—was eight miles per hour, one of the lowest along the route.

If you're following I-80/U.S. Route 30, exit to Business I-80 through town, which partially follows the 1926 alignment of the Lincoln. At a Y on Bridger Avenue, turn left onto Elk Street. The original route became C Street—this is where the arch was built in 1928—and crossed the tracks. Once across, it turned right on Spruce Street, possibly today's Blair Avenue. Between B Street and C Street is the former Western Auto Transit garage, which served as an LHA Control Point. The arch can also be found on this side of the tracks at C Street and Main Street. The town has a number of 1928 LHA concrete markers: one at Center Street and Thomas Street, and a pair at the WYDOT building on Elk Street.

Harriet White Fisher wrote that Rock Springs was mostly "a railroad station, a hotel and pool-room, the restaurant containing three rooms, kitchen, dining-room, and bed-room." Adjacent to the hotel, "in an enclosure, were a couple of mules, and we were informed that [two] men made their living by waiting here to pull the heavy caravans and automobiles through the sand with these mules." The pair were disappointed that Fisher's Locomobile did not need their services.

Today the Natural History Museum at Western Wyoming Community College has

Looking west to the Palisades, just west of the town of Green River. The waterway is also called Green River.

at least sixteen dinosaur castings on display throughout the school, said to be the largest collection of dinosaurs along I-80 between Chicago and San Francisco. Boulders from different geologic eras are also scattered around the campus.

Showing up in the 1940 *Travelers Motor Court Service* guide is Hillside Auto Court, at the west end of the city on U.S. Route 30. It was the largest court in town and featured steam-heated garages, though only fifteen of the forty-plus rooms were so heated.

Business I-80 passes straight through town and rejoins I-80, which has circled north. The 1913 highway continues west from Blair Avenue, staying south of the railroad for a couple miles.

From I-80, take Exit 91 and follow Flaming Gorge Way into **Green River**. This town was established before the Union Pacific came through, but it became a division point where trains switched cars. It was named for the river, which explorers also called Rio Verde, but the town is also known as the "Trona Capital of the World" for the natural ore that yields soda ash, a basic ingredient in baking soda, detergents, and glass. Logs floated here from the north were cut into ties for the railroad. The river continues southward some five hundred miles and joins the Grand River to form the Colorado River, which flows south to the Grand Canyon.

From 1913 to 1924, the Lincoln turned south from Green River and followed the Overland Stage road through Telephone Canyon (another canyon with the same name as the one west of Sherman Summit) westward for some seven miles before meeting up with the post-1924 route near I-80 and today's WY Route 372. That's also the site of **Peru**, and the route has come to be called the Peru Cutoff. It's a rough trail today. The post-

1924 route through the Green River Valley can be followed as it parallels the interstate, which lies to the north.

West of town, don't get on I-80; rather, continue straight onto a 1920s alignment of the Lincoln through the Green River Valley, known as the Palisades, for the high rock wall. Rising high above the road and the Green River is Toll Gate Rock. Roadside advertisements were often painted onto the boulders and rock ledges. Three miles west of town, the highway crosses the 286-foot-long Green River Bridge, built in 1924 for the new alignment. I-80 meanwhile tunnels through the rocks.

When the 1906 Franklin trip led by Lester Whitman tried to cross the river, the group had to wade in waist-high, ice cold water to shove the car across while the current pushed it downstream.

Thornton Round noted that in 1914, his family likewise had to ford the river but won-dered how it was crossed in winter: "When we asked this question, we received a very simple and logical answer—'No one travels during the winter.'"

On Monday, July 30, Boy Scout Bernard Queneau wrote of his adventures: "We then went on to Rio Verde, Green River, the real starting point of the Colorado. We gave a life-saving demonstration there, but nearly passed out on account of the cold and the current."

In a renovated 1931 post office, the Sweet-water County Historical Museum has local archaeology and history displays. One artifact is an Auto Club of Southern California–sponsored Lincoln Highway porcelain enamel sign indicating the mileage to Green River and Rock Springs one way, and Granger and Evanston the other.

I-80/U.S. Route 30 heads west, as does an earlier alignment, with a 1940s Sinclair station deteriorating on the right side. After

rejoining the Telephone Canyon route, the original road again breaks off north, skirting **Bryan**. A fine piece of the 1940s alignment (now WY Route 374) closely parallels I-80 right into Little America some twenty miles west of Green River, an oasis in these high plains. Originally Covey's Little America, it was named for Adm. Richard Byrd's camp at the South Pole. The story goes that in the 1890s, the founder was herding sheep and was stranded in a blizzard, dreaming of a place of shelter. Then in the 1930s, he saw a picture of Admiral Byrd's "Little America" camp, likewise far from base camp, inspiring him to build the refuge he once dreamed of. By 1960, Little America was advertising that its fifty-five gas pumps made it the "World's Largest Service Station."

The original complex at the turn to Granger, five miles ahead, burned down about 1970; the business relocated to the just-built I-80. Today you'll find a mix of service bays, cafés, motel rooms, and gift shops drawing

Looking east to the Palisades, with Toll Gate Rock towering over all. U.S. Route 30 slices through the center; the original Lincoln can be discerned at the base of the mountain to the left and curving into the foreground.

SPECIAL COLLECTIONS LIBRARY, UNIVERSITY OF MICHIGAN

A bridge over Green River, three miles west of the town of Green River, 1924.

LITTLE AMERICA
HOTEL · LODGE · CABINS · BAR · COFFEE SHOP · FOUNTAIN · GAS & OIL
Wyoming's Newest Travel Center on U.S. Hiway 30, Wyoming

BERNIE HEISEY

Covey's Little America, circa 1960.

I-80 travelers to Exit 68. In the lobby is Emperor the Penguin; the owners had him shipped here in hopes of making him a live mascot, but his death on the way led to his position since then, stuffed and encased. Little America has expanded to about half a dozen locations and operates one of the largest petroleum production and distribution systems in the West.

Three miles ahead is an I-80 exit called Granger Junction. Two miles to its northwest, the original Lincoln Highway, which has been to the north, has its own important junction, the traditional turning point for

tourists wanting to head northwest to Yellowstone and an outpost of accommodations and services, albeit minimal. The town of Granger is actually a couple miles north of the split. When the federal route numbering system was established, U.S. Route 30 followed the road north, misleading drivers ever since into thinking the Lincoln went that way too. The Lincoln does not go through Granger, nor Idaho to Oregon, but heads to Salt Lake City.

Both Alice Ramsey and Bellamy Partridge took the right branch here, passing through Opal on a route that never was the Lincoln Highway. In fact, after Partridge landed in a gully, a big Pierce Arrow came by, but it was "making a fast run from Denver to Ogden" and only stopped long enough to take a picture. Interestingly, when Partridge's companion walked for help, they soon lost sight of him in the shoulder-high sagebrush. They rejoined the future Lincoln Highway in Evanston.

Zepphine Humphrey and her husband approached here on their drive east, as she recalled in her 1936 book, *Green Mountains to Sierras*: "There were very few traces anywhere of human habitation. We can even at times enjoy downright desolation. But this stretch of southern Wyoming will always spell dreariness to us." That is what led them into town:

> At noon we turned aside from the main road for lunch in a tiny place called Granger. It consisted mostly of a big hotel, apparently empty except for a few men in the echoing dining room. What manner of guests had ever been, or could be, expected to fill it we had no idea. Not tourists surely. Prospectors perhaps, cattle rangers, men traveling on spacious Western errands, escaping convicts and lunatics. . . . The

hotel itself seemed to be run by women, however; and the simple meal of ham and eggs, coffee and pie, was good.

Church Butte, a rock formation towering over the road ten miles west of Granger, was once the site of a gas station and general store, all long gone.

The Lincoln stays north of I-80 until near **Lyman**, when it crosses the interstate near Millersville and heads southwest another five miles toward town. On the west end, a 1928 concrete marker sits astride a picturesque grazing field. On the second floor of the Lyman Town Hall is the Trona Mining Museum, which has preserved the history of trona mining and has expanded into regional history. A concrete Lincoln Highway post stands outside the building. John's Bar—easily identifiable by its windows shaped like the suits of playing cards—was once the town's Lincoln Highway Garage. A picture above the bar inside shows it as just that. Originally, it was a stable, and afterward a theater and an appliance store.

In *Across the Continent by the Lincoln Highway*, Effie Gladding recalled staying overnight here at the Marshall, "half home and half hotel, kept by Mrs. Marshall." They enjoyed their supper and slumber, and even took a picture for the book. It was also near here, she was told, that the "dead line" ran, an imaginary but deadly boundary set by cattlemen forbidding the encroachment of sheep. The conflict stemmed from the way sheep graze so closely and tear up the earth, leaving land unfit for cattle.

The road heads west some five miles to **Fort Bridger**, named for a trading post turned fort. The log and mud post was built in 1843

Looking west in 1927; the road to the right leads north two miles to Granger. About the time this picture was taken, the intersection became the point where U.S. Route 30 split into northern and southern branches. U.S. 30 South followed the Lincoln Highway (left) into Utah, then took the old Lincoln Highway north to Ogden. U.S. 30 North (right) continued to Idaho, never following any part of the Lincoln Highway. The southern designation eventually was removed, and today's U.S. 30 follows the northern branch.

A 1928 concrete marker points the way on a curve east of Lyman.

Casto's Place at Fort Bridger, 1915.

You can get most anything at this store outside Fort Bridger.

During Lincoln Highway days, the fort was home to a prominent local judge, who again ran it as a store and community center. Bridger's original post building was long gone, and only some decaying buildings of the army post remained. The state acquired it in the 1920s; a number of structures from its military era remain, and the state constructed a replica trading post–fort and a museum in the 1888 stone barracks. Archaeologists have discovered foundations from many structures over time: the trading post, a rock wall built by the Mormons for defense, army buildings, and a barn. Every Labor Day weekend, the site hosts the Mountain Man Rendezvous; more than two hundred lodges and tepees are set up in this modern re-creation of the old annual event. Across the road, some buildings also remain outside the state park; a ghost sign reading "Tourist's Supplies" aimed at eastbound motorists slowly fades on the northernmost stone building.

by Jim Bridger and Louis Vasquez, former fur trappers who decided to catch travelers along the Oregon Trail, which had just begun and dipped briefly south at this point. Though it was an important post—one of the first to serve emigrants more than it did the fur trade—it was bypassed by the opening of a shortcut. The owners sold out in 1855 to the Mormons, who operated it for a couple years but burned it as federal troops approached. It became a U.S. military post in 1858 and served the Overland Trail and Pony Express. It was abandoned during the Civil War, but then the nearby gold rush in 1867 and the coming of the Union Pacific boosted business. The fort was abandoned again in the 1870s, and the U.S. government finally sold it in 1890.

This 1928 concrete post was rededicated at Depot Square in Evanston in 1996.

Just outside the entrance, still in the park but hidden in the trees, are the crumbling cabins and attached garages of the Orange and Black Tourist Court. Adjacent is the Jim Bridger Trading Post, selling a mix of gifts, groceries, fireworks, and appliances. Across the road are the Wagon Wheel Café and the Wagon Wheel Motel and RV Park.

An undated postcard from this area reads: "This gives an idea of the desolate appearance of Wyo. The hill is covered with Sage brush. Travelled across the state from east to west and saw hardly a foot of land fit for farming."

Effie Gladding struck a more positive tone, calling the land "delightful desert country, open and rolling, grey-green and blue in its coloring."

James Montgomery Flagg described the roads by recalling that at Ogden, Utah, "smiling and lying natives promised a 'boulevard all the way' to Rock Springs. That was the 'bull' in boulevard, if you will pardon me. It was a scenic railway of a road, sun-baked humps and gullies and loose gravel."

Oregon Trail emigrants headed north from here, but when the Donner party came through in 1846, it chose to go south of Salt Lake (there was no Salt Lake City yet). The Mormons would follow this route the next year.

While today's main road through town continues west, the Lincoln Highway went due north for almost a mile. It gets tangled with I-80, then breaks away south for about twenty miles.

The terrain gradually climbs into the foothills of the Wasatch Mountains. Along the pleasant drive is a railroad underpass, including an original adjacent concrete tube, and Eagle Rock, a rise that the road curves around. The Lincoln comes back to run immediately north of I-80, approaching **Evanston**. Just east of town on the old road is the four-gabled Pete's Rock and Rye Club, along the old alignment. Also on the east end are the Sunset Motel, dating to 1932, and Hablin Park, a municipal campground of the early 1920s.

Like so many small settlements, the former Bear River City blossomed when the Union Pacific came through in 1869; the town celebrates a part of its heritage with an annual Chinese New Year celebration.

The downtown lies west of the railroad tracks. After crossing under them, the Lincoln follows Front Street north two blocks past two restoration efforts that culminated in 1996. The Evanston Hotel (the LHA control point) was built in 1912 on Front Street and carries a circa 1960 sign for Hotel Freeman's. Across the street is a 1928 concrete post at Depot Square, with four plaques that relay the highway's story. The post had originally stood somewhere in Uinta County, was stored for a time at a WYDOT facility, then stood along the Bear River south of town until a Boy Scout project brought it back to the route in 1996. The 1900 station has been beautifully restored.

To see an old Auto Club of Southern California sign from Evanston, you have only to drive west a few hundred miles; the still-functioning club has one at its headquarters' courtyard in Los Angeles. The sign gives the mileage to Coalville and Salt Lake City, Utah.

The Lincoln Highway turned left from Front Street onto 11th Street; at the corner only a portion remains of the Trans-Continental Garage, an advertiser in LHA guides.

After three blocks, the highway curves left onto Harrison Drive. Half a mile ahead, the Lincoln Highway bends right onto Wahsatch Road and goes west. It then begins curving to the southwest. A mile and a half later, a right turn across the railroad is assumed to be the original crossing to the northwest side of the tracks. From there, traces of an older road head west, but stay on Wahsatch Road, which is now a frontage road to I-80.

It's two miles to the state border. The landscape has been changing, and more changes are yet to come.

The Cowboy Chuck Wagon on the west end of Evanston offered "range gourmet food, cooked in giant Dutch ovens."

Painting the Lincoln's red, white, and blue bands west of Evanston during the 1915 trip of Henry Joy, Austin Bement, and Ernie Eisenhut.

Greetings from
Utah

Overland emigrants had blazed a trail north of the Great Salt Lake. The first transcontinental railroad followed suit, despite pleas from Brigham Young for a route through Salt Lake City. But Lincoln Highway officials barely considered that corridor; it diverted too far from the straight line they envisioned across the country. They were aiming for Reno, and although the railroad went there too, it zigzagged its way through Nevada's Humboldt River valley. The LHA instead pieced together a route that went around the southern edge of the Great Salt Desert and

	UTAH	U.S.
Population in 1910	373,351	92,228,496
Population in 2000	2,233,169	281,421,906
Persons per square mile in 2000	27.2	79.6
Approximate miles of Lincoln Highway		
via Fish Springs	273	3,389
via Fisher Pass & Goodyear Cutoff	232	3,389
via Wendover	225	3,389

hooked to a fairly straight trail across central Nevada. It made sense, but it would cause the LHA a lot of grief.

The most feasible crossing of the Wasatch Mountains was through Echo Canyon, and from there, the original Lincoln Highway ran south through Parley's Canyon and into Salt Lake City. This was announced at the Conference of Governors in Colorado Springs in August 1913, and was part of the Proclamation Route, signed on September 10 and publicly announced on September 14.

Utah governor William Spry apparently approved the routing in August, but by September 12, 1913, he sent a telegram to the LHA saying he understood the route would go through Ogden before Salt Lake City and that he could not endorse it otherwise. The road through Ogden did avoid the steep climb to Parley's Summit, and there was already two miles of concrete road between Ogden and Salt Lake City near Farmington. Within days of the proclamation, LHA directors relented, following their own rule of "accepting the dictates of state executives in such matters." The Ogden leg became the second Lincoln High-

way generation between the forks at Echo and Salt Lake City. When Packard published its *Lincoln Highway Route Road Conditions and Directions* in October 1913, it detailed the Parley's Canyon route but noted, "Since this survey was made, the official route has been changed to pass through Ogden."

Ogden interests weren't satisfied with having the route come through their town; they also wanted it to go north of the Great Salt Lake along the path of the railroad to bypass their competitor to the south, Salt Lake City. Ogden boosters apparently made a habit of diverting traffic north around the lake. This and the thirty-six miles the Ogden leg added to the Lincoln Highway led LHA directors to revert to the Parley's Canyon route before the group's first guidebook was published in 1915, making the Parley's route generations one and three.

Until then, the Ogden route brought travelers into Salt Lake City from the north past Temple Square, a must-see for almost every tourist. After 1915, the Parley's Canyon route brought motorists into Salt Lake City from the east, twenty-one blocks south of the square.

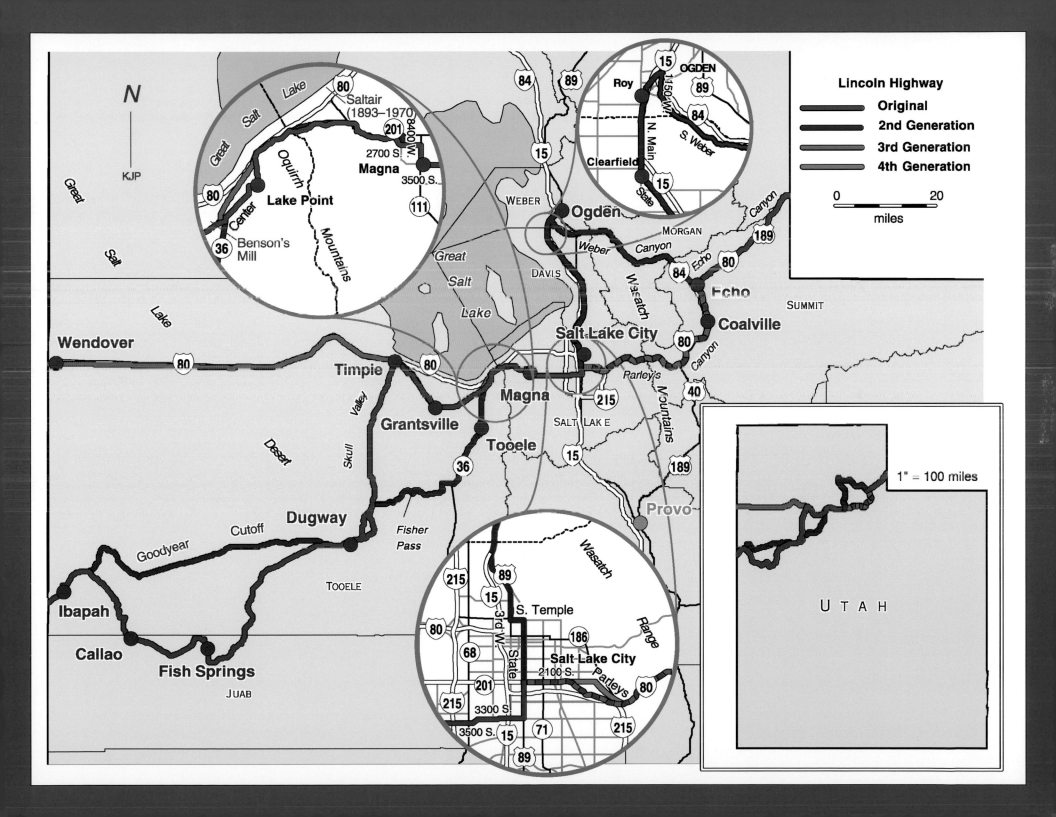

This large (21.5-by-17 inch) westward-looking map examined the challenges of spanning Utah. The original Lincoln Highway turned south at Timpie Station and skirted the Great Salt Lake Desert via Fish Springs. The proposed shortening broke south earlier through Tooele and Fisher Pass, and then across the desert via the Goodyear Cutoff. When Utah failed to finish work on this route, LHA directors grudgingly moved the Lincoln Highway to a road the state would build parallel to the Western Pacific Railroad to Wendover. At far right is the first transcontinental railroad, after it was shortened to cross the Great Salt Lake.

The streets of Mormon-built towns usually count outward from the temple and sometimes carry two names; for example, the 1915 Lincoln Highway enters Salt Lake City on 2100 South or 21st South.

The path west of Salt Lake City was also contested, but this time by interests from San Francisco and Los Angeles. They knew that the route chosen to cross the desert would be a huge determinant in the destination of cross-country travelers.

In 1913, no good roads existed west of the Great Salt Lake. LHA president Henry Joy was familiar with the various desert crossings, having spent years mining in southwest Utah. The LHA also turned to Col. Sidney Waldon for routing advice, who was quoted in the organization's 1935 history: "From Salt Lake we had a choice of going north or south of the Lake. The terrain dictated selection of the southern alignment. We realized that the road must lie in the place where we put it for a number of years. We knew the Pony Express had taken the southern route but that didn't decide us; it only confirmed our judgment that that was the best."

LHA directors chose to skirt the southern edge of the lake and desert by taking a sixty-mile path via Fish Springs. It met the old trail of the Pony Express and crossed into Nevada, where, at Ely, motorists could take the Lincoln to San Francisco or the Midland Trail to Los Angeles. This made the road more valuable and efficient, an important consideration in a state with a sparse population and therefore fewer funds to improve one road, let alone two.

Neither of the California cities wanted a road that could equally serve the other, and Utah preferred no road west at all. It favored the Arrowhead Trail, which cut south from Salt Lake City, where Utah had better scenery and more towns where travelers might spend money. Of course, the Arrowhead would lead drivers through 220 miles of the Mojave

Desert, but Utah leaders cared not once drivers had left their state. Los Angeles didn't mind either; traffic, parched as it may be, would come its way and not San Francisco's. But the LHA knew that was no way to reach the Pacific.

If Utah *had* to choose a route west, it favored building a new road to Wendover, figuring the LHA fight that ensued would delay improvements to either and thereby benefit the Arrowhead in the end. Utah got strong support for this from San Francisco, which preferred that traffic go to Wendover instead of Ely and possible diversion to Los Angeles. Interests in both states cared little how their decisions affected Nevada, which inevitably bore the impact of their crusades.

The leading champion of the Wendover route was William D. Rishel, secretary of the Utah Auto Association and reknowned for his detailed road guides called *Rishel's Routes*, published annually from about 1917 to 1930 by the *Salt Lake Tribune*. About 1922, LHA field secretary Gael Hoag led a party of California interests to Salt Lake City and back, accompanied by Rishel back west to Wendover. Although he bogged down in sand and water on his favorite road, Rishel later wrote spitefully to others on the trip, as quoted in the 1935 LHA history, that he too favored *no* road west, as any such road would only help Nevada. He wrote that he likewise would improve the Arrowhead Trail to keep tourists in Utah longer.

Meanwhile, a shortcut had been attempted across the southern Utah desert, then left to waste. The idea was suggested by Gael Hoag: Run a road through Tooele by widening a wagon trail through the Onaqui Mountains at Johnson Pass, then build a causeway across the Great Salt Desert. The former would trim ten miles from the route, the latter forty-eight. The LHA enthusiastically adopted the plan, with Carl Fisher donating $25,000 to build the road through the mountains, and LHA president Frank Seiberling putting up personal and business funds from his Goodyear tire company to span the desert. Utah signed on to do what it might take to complete both projects, but eventually reneged to concentrate on the road to Wendover.

With the state building the Wendover Road and no funds going to the deteriorating Lincoln Highway route, the LHA grudgingly accepted the new route late in 1927. The story of the Goodyear Cutoff and its relation to the Wendover Road is among the most notorious in Lincoln Highway history. It is explored further in this chapter in the sections on the Goodyear Cutoff and Wendover.

The Goodyear Cutoff has been off-limits to the public since 1942. The cutoff and a tiny bridge over Government Creek are within the Dugway Proving Grounds and Deseret Test Center and can be visited only by special permission, making them tantalizing portions of the road for Lincoln Highway fans.

Those retracing the Lincoln Highway in western Utah must circle around the desert on the 1913 road through Fish Springs or take the 1927 alignment across the salt flats to Wendover. Either option might intimidate drivers or lead casual readers to believe the land is barren, but as John T. Faris wrote in his 1931 *Roaming American Highways*, "It is true that the 246 miles to Ely, Nevada, include a long stretch of desert. Fortunately, this desert cannot be escaped, for it is a place of fascination and real beauty."

1. Echo Canyon

In *Across the Continent by the Lincoln Highway*, Effie Gladding noted the shabby wooden sign marking the Wyoming-Utah state line, hoping that the Lincoln Highway would inspire the states to improve it. By 1917, cast-iron signs marked each state border, with a Lincoln Highway logo and mileages in each direction. This one was moved to WYDOT headquarters, some 380 miles east in Cheyenne, along with Wyoming's other state line marker.

The original highway here later hosted U.S. Route 189 (as does I-80 today) and U.S. Route 30 South, which is no longer used as a designation.

As the Lincoln Highway enters Utah, it is just north of I-80, winding through sagebrush. A fence stops livestock as well as modern-day explorers; the land is owned by the Deseret Land and Cattle Company. Three small but distinctive bridges can be spotted within their land.

The word *deseret* is seen often. It is a word in the Book of Mormon meaning "honeybee" and is used as a symbol of industriousness. The beehive symbol is found everywhere, from the state seal to newspapers to business logos.

Wyuta Station was a railroad stop at the border, named for the adjoining states. The road stays north of the interstate into **Wahsatch**, another rail stop five miles to the southwest (and spelled differently than the mountains). The state's 1941 WPA guide described it as "a sun-beaten, treeless railroad town" dominated by a "black wooden water tower."

The Lincoln Highway enters Echo Canyon in the Wasatch Mountains, the eastern wall of

The second of three identical concrete bridges located just west of the Utah-Wyoming border, all on private property. They were probably constructed in the mid-1920s. Each one had six posts, one on each corner and one in the middle on each side.

the Great Basin, which extends five hundred hot, often barren miles west. The canyon has high red walls of rock and a brush-filled, boulder-strewn streambed. The Lincoln weaves around and beneath the modern road and Echo Canyon Creek.

In *Coast to Coast by Automobile*, Curt McConnell quoted Jacob Murdock, who found the steep road with deep, washed-out ruts extremely slippery when driving east in 1908: "In fact, we tried all the traction makers such as ropes, canvas, etc., that we had. Eventually we got up by short jerks, consisting of speeding up the engine, throwing in the clutch, jumping a few feet, stopping, blocking the rear wheels and doing it over again."

The railroad strays north for a few miles, then rejoins the road near the railroad town of **Castle Rock**, named for one of the many formations in the red sandstone. For about the next fifteen miles, the Lincoln Highway mostly stays north of the railroad tracks and the interstate. As the Union Pacific double-tracked its line through the canyon in the

A Union Pacific limited train climbs Echo Canyon.

early 1920s, it often helped rebuild the Lincoln Highway in spots where the road was being displaced.

About thirty-one miles from the state line, the Lincoln Highway reaches what the 1915 LHA guide called **Main Forks**, a.k.a. Echo Junction. A left-tilted T is formed by the intertwined lanes of I-80 and I-84, the railroad, and roads north and south. Lincoln Highway travelers in 1913 couldn't stay on the north side of the tracks to the T, as they do today, because the road was blocked by a rock outcropping known as the Pulpit. Near today's I-80 underpass, westbound drivers had to jog from the north side of the railroad to the south. Once across, they headed west again. Upon reaching the T, the road north led to Weber Canyon (pronounced WEE-ber) and Ogden. Just before the T, a road turned south to Coalville; that was the Proclamation Route of the Lincoln Highway.

About 1920, the state removed the Pulpit, allowing Ogden-bound traffic to stay north of the tracks. The railroad also then built an underpass so that Coalville-bound traffic no longer had to cross the tracks at grade.

IIa. 1913: Weber Canyon to Ogden and Salt Lake City

The Lincoln Highway, as listed in the Proclamation Route, went through Parley's Canyon, but only on paper. Within a month, the Lincoln was rerouted through Weber Canyon and Ogden. That route will be discussed in this section. In 1915, the Lincoln reverted to Parley's Canyon, which will be explored in the section following this one.

The Lincoln Highway to Ogden turned northwest through a series of small towns in Weber River Valley. The transcontinental railroad was routed through the canyon in 1869, and I-84 came through a century later. Immediately to the right is a smattering of service buildings making up **Echo**, including the Echo Café. Originating as a stagecoach stop, the town also had quite a wild period, as did most that sprang to life during the construction of the transcontinental railroad.

A few businesses remain in Echo on U.S. Route 30 South, a quarter mile west of Main Forks and UT Route 189, including the Echo Café, a gas station, and the Kozy Café and Motel.

UT Route 86 approximates the Lincoln going north. The road crossed the interstate into **Henefer**; you can cross at the overpass for Exit 115. It was here in August 1846 that the Donner Party decided to hack its way over the dense Wasatch Mountains, adding to what would become a tragic delay. The Mormons easily followed their path the next year. A 1927 monument in front of the Daughters of Utah Pioneers' Museum notes the intersection of the pioneer trail and Lincoln Highway.

The Lincoln continues northwest, roughly following UT Route 86, which meets I-84 at Exit 112. Here you must again follow the interstate. About two miles north, on the left, is Devil's Slide, two lines of limestone twenty feet apart and forty feet high. There's a pulloff on I-84 past mile 111. Alice Ramsey noted the slide during her 1909 trip as the first woman to drive across the country: "The declivity was terrific. It would have made more of a *drop* than a *slide* for the aforementioned Devil."

Thornton Round likewise mentioned it in *The Good of It All*. He also noted that the terrain to the west was "a series of long climbs up the mountains and through the canyons that seemed to us to be endless."

The next interstate exit is at **Taggart**, a small community that was once a thriving settlement, as retold in the Winter–Spring 2001 *LHA Forum*. The highway continues winding around the interstate and often can be accessed only by going between modern exits. In **Morgan**, the county seat, the highway passes the former train station on Commercial Street, crosses the interstate, and again heads northwest through **Stoddard**, **Peterson**, and **Mountain Green**.

Craggy rocks must have brought forth visions of the netherworld to early travelers; a horseshoe-shaped bend in the road to the north is known as Devil's Gate. George A. Wyman described it in his 1903 diary, *Across America on a Motor Bicycle*: "The waters of the river fall from a great height and thrash around a sharp bend that has been obstructed for ages by a helter-skelter fall of great blocks of stone from above. It is a seething cauldron of water that rushes with insane, frothing fury."

You can follow I-80 to Exit 87-B, then proceed west on UT Route 60/South Weber Drive six miles to **Riverdale**. Hill Air Force Base is to the left (south). At a turn to 1050 West Street, the Lincoln Highway becomes 1150 West Street; I-84 abruptly stops that street, so you'll need to backtrack to 1050 West Street. At the intersection is the Motor-Vu Drive-in Theater, featuring four screens and Sunday swap meets. Follow 1050 West Street north to UT Route 26/Riverdale Road; the Lincoln was a block to the west, and it

Every one from 50 miles around was bound for Echo City or Evanston on that day, May 29, to see President Roosevelt, whose train stopped in passing long enough for him to make a speech at all the towns of any size. For this reason there was an unusual amount of travel on the roads, and I was repeatedly forced so far over to the side that I had to dismount to escape an upset. The farmers seemed to think I had no right on the road when they wanted to use it, and several swore as they called to me to get out of the way. One man abused me roundly, and told me I ought to get off the road altogether with my damned "bisickle." I did an indiscreet thing in answering him in kind, and he pulled up his team with the intention of getting off and horsewhipping me or to get a steady position to take a pot shot at me with a revolver.

I don't know which—I didn't stop to learn. I let out my motor and quickly got around a bend in the road out of sight.

—George A. Wyman, "Across America on a Motor Bicycle," The Motor Cycle (1903)

Devil's Slide, a pair of limestone outcroppings on the steep walls of Weber Canyon.

LHA member Alan Stockland visited the Motor-Vu Drive-In Theater in Riverdale with his 1935 Hudson.

went about another half mile toward **Ogden** before apparently angling back southwest.

Ogden is the state's oldest city and one of its largest. It was founded by Miles Goodyear in the 1840s at the deltas of the Ogden and Weber Rivers, where they once emptied into prehistoric Lake Bonneville. It's named for fur trapper Peter Ogden (just as the river and canyon are named for trapper John Weber). Mormons bought the town from Goodyear; the streets are broad, revealing the Mormon penchant for wide streets laid along compass points.

About fifty miles northwest of Ogden is Promontory Summit (not Point), site of the joining of the Union and Central Pacific Railroads on May 10, 1869, to form the first transcontinental railroad. Central Pacific stretched 689 miles over the Sierras, the Union Pacific 1,086 miles across the plains. The rails west of Ogden were partly abandoned when the Lucin shortcut was built across the Great Salt Lake in 1904. (There *is* a Promontory Point along the shortcut, and Amtrak trains still go through it.) Promontory Summit was used until 1942, when the rails were salvaged for the war. The National Park Service's Golden Spike National Historic Site re-creates the joining site at Promontory Summit.

An emigrant trail–turned–road paralleled the railroad west and was the route taken by many early motorists, including Lester Whitman and Eugene Hammond as they drove an Oldsmobile east in 1903. As reported in Curt McConnell's *Coast to Coast by Automobile*, Whitman declared upon reaching Ogden, "The only thing fit to use in crossing from here to Reno is a flying machine."

Thornton Round wrote in *The Good of It All* that as his family returned east in 1914, they turned north at Wendover toward Lucin and crossed north of the Great Salt Lake to Ogden; they had to, as there was no road yet from Wendover to Salt Lake City. When they stayed overnight in Ogden, Thornton and his brother stopped at a restaurant with a big aquarium in the front window. They feasted on trout picked right from the water—two apiece—plus German-fried potatoes, cole slaw, apple pie, and milk.

Though the Lincoln Highway was rerouted by 1915, Ogden still attracted auto tourists. Beatrice Massey wrote in *It Might Have Been Worse* that they stayed at the Reed Hotel on her 1919 trip: "The hotel is old, but well kept up. We had a room large enough to hold a convention in, with a smaller bedroom and

bath adjoining, and eight large windows altogether."

In *Green Mountains to Sierras*, Zepphine Humphrey wrote in 1936 that an Ogden tourist camp brought cheer amidst their snowy drive:

One of the best, perhaps the very best, we had found anywhere: with seven (yes, seven; count them yourself!) electric lights, with two gas stoves, and a porcelain sink, and a complete kitchen equipment. All the woodwork and furniture had been freshly painted, and there was a new linoleum rug on the floor. Also a patchwork quilt on the bed. After a trip to the grocery store in the neighborhood, we cooked a good supper and ate it luxuriously by a western window beyond which flamed a brilliant sunset promising better weather tomorrow.

The 1990s saw the establishment of the Ogden River Parkway, three miles along the Ogden River paved for walking or biking, from Washington Boulevard to the mouth of Ogden Canyon. Another attraction is Dinosaur Park and Museum, at 1544 East Park Boulevard, opened in 1993 on six acres at the mouth of the canyon and featuring lifelike sculptures of more than one hundred dinosaurs. Sound effects of the dinos in action complete the effect.

Peery's Egyptian Theater, on Washington Boulevard, was built in 1924 like so many others in the wake of the discovery of King Tut's tomb. The interior was decorated to look as if the audience were sitting between two Egyptian buildings. Closed in the 1980s, it was restored and reopened in 1997. Along with performing arts, it shows occasional movies, including some Sundance Film Festival screenings.

The evocative sign at City Creek Inn, 230 West North Temple, Salt Lake City, is a block west of Temple Square and just a few feet from the Lincoln Highway.

Ogden's Union station is also worth a stop. The original Victorian station burned in 1923, but its 1924 Spanish Colonial replacement thrives as a cultural and retail attraction. A model railroad housed at 25th Street and Wall Avenue re-creates the first transcontinental railroad through Weber Canyon.

The Lincoln Highway's change of direction at Ogden is lost beneath I-84 and I-15. From here, the route headed south to **Roy** and is again beneath I-15 to about 2300 North Street. A parallel alternative is Main Street/ 1900 West Street. This continues south, parallel to the lake. About seven miles south, **Sunset** was named for the view across the lake. To the east is Hill Air Force Base.

The route, which is not certain, can generally be retraced by following UT Route 126 through **Clearfield** and **Layton**, and then Main Street through **Kaysville**. South of town it becomes UT Route 273, crosses U.S. Route

89, and changes to UT Route 106. The route jogs through **Farmington** and heads south on UT Route 106/Main Street/200 East Street. Along the lake is Lagoon Amusement Park, opened in 1896 to encourage ridership on a rail line between Ogden and Salt Lake City, much like that era's trolley parks. It has grown from a picnic resort offering swimming, boating, dancing, playground, and carnival concessions to thrill and water rides. It also has relocated historic buildings at Pioneer Village. Two of the older amusement rides are a carousel and 1921 wooden coaster.

The 1913 Lincoln Highway continues south, following UT Route 106 through **Centerville** and **Bountiful**, and then picks up U.S. Route 89 into **North Salt Lake**. The Lincoln enters **Salt Lake City** on 300 (3rd) West Street. At South Temple Street, the Union Pacific Railroad depot is a block to the west, but the Lincoln turns left (east) and goes four blocks past Temple Square to State Street. It turns right on State Street and follows it (and U.S. Route 89) south. This 1913 route meets the 1915 route coming from Parley's Canyon at 2100 (21st) South.

On July 24, 1847, Brigham Young and a small group emerged from the Wasatch Mountains to see the Great Salt Lake Valley and declared, "This is the place." Finally the Mormons had land no one else seemed to want, where they could practice their religion without persecution. (In the East, their ways, particularly polygamy, were considered too unusual.) This was Mexican territory until the Treaty of Guadalupe Hidalgo the following year ceded much of the Southwest to the United States. Soon the land was crisscrossed by explorers, miners, and federal troops. Today

Old Deseret Village, in the hills southeast of downtown Salt Lake City re-creates a nineteenth-century Mormon village, with more than a dozen transplanted vintage buildings.

The city extends outward from Temple Square on a grid pattern. High-walled Temple Square is not only the heart of downtown, but also the mecca for members of the Church of Jesus Christ of Latter-day Saints (the Mormons). The square attracts both Mormons and tourists from around the world. The temple was started in 1853 but not completed for forty years. Only members of the Mormon faith are permitted inside, but the 1860s tab-

The Utah Hotel now serves as the Joseph Smith Memorial Building

Utah Hotel, Temple and Tabernacle, Salt Lake City, Utah.

ernacle and other buildings, including two visitors centers, are open, and volunteers give tours of the square and offer to explain the history and doctrine of the church. The 11,623 pipes of the Mormon Tabernacle organ along with 360 choristers can be heard at least once a day in a free half-hour performance. Across Main Street to the east is the former Utah Hotel, built in 1911 by the Mormon Church in French Renaissance style, but converted in the late 1980s to the Joseph Smith Memorial Building. Two rooftop restaurants remain open. Genealogists and historians are drawn across West Temple to the famed Family History Library, which serves an important role in the Mormon faith.

Beatrice Massey wrote, "The Utah Hotel is one of the finest in the country. It is owned and run by the Mormons and does them great credit. We dined in the roof-garden, which compares favorably with that of any hotel in New York." James Montgomery Flagg wrote in *Boulevards All the Way—Maybe* that he

stayed here and enjoyed the hotel's "spacious rooms and a marvelous kweseen [cuisine]!" Effie Gladding commented on the rooftop beehive that glowed at night.

When Harriet White Fisher arrived in Salt Lake City on her 1910 trip east (after driving north of Great Salt Lake), she "was anxious to see a real Mormon, and several were pointed out to me, but I could find no marks of identification that made them any different from other men in the East." The road back north to Ogden was bad: "They were building a new one and had it torn up for miles, leaving the soft dirt. As our engine pulled us through, we passed four cars standing there, waiting for teams to come and haul them out of this dirt."

11b. 1915: Parley's Canyon to Salt Lake City

In April 1915, the Lincoln was rerouted to a more direct alignment to Salt Lake City, following the path it briefly took as the 1913 Proclamation Route. At the "Main Forks" at

Echo, the revised Lincoln headed south. If you are following the old highway in Echo Canyon, turn left under I-80 at Exit 169 to get on Echo Dam Road, which is the 1915 Lincoln once it heads south. A stone slab marker at the mouth of the canyon features a Lincoln Highway descriptive plaque, a medallion from a concrete post, and an incised map of the route.

While I-80 curves west and towers above Echo Reservoir, and the former Union Pacific railbed (now a recreation trail) skirt the water's eastern shore, the 1915 route is buried beneath it. Near its southern end, a small concrete bridge is the only sign that the old road came through here. It served the highway until 1930, when the road was relocated for the reservoir. A mile south is **Coalville**, one of many picturesque towns along this section. Effie Gladding had lunch at the Coalville Hotel and praised the "many yards where old fashioned yellow rosebushes were laden with bloom."

The road led to **Wanship** and then through the winding Silver Creek Canyon; the 1918 guide noted that in wet weather, it was dangerous to attempt the canyon without chains. The road is lost beneath I-80; a trail between lanes is the former railbed, now a recreational trail. At Exit 148 of I-80, U.S. Route 40 joins the highway. Less than a mile ahead was Kimball's stage station. Another mile and a half farther is Kimball Junction, site of **Kimball's Ranch** and the Snyder Pony Express Station; nothing survives except two houses and a barn. A mile beyond that, the old road runs south of the interstate, past the Hi Ute Ranch, a tepee and small lake in front of a long barn. South of here is Park City, a favorite of skiers and home to the Sundance Film Festival.

This Buick and Chevy dealer, with adjacent used-car lot, sits quietly in Coalville.

A stream, railroad, and road all squeezed through Silver Creek Canyon, south of Wanship. Today I-80 dominates the landscape.

Three miles farther you'll reach Parley's Summit, at more than seven thousand feet and surrounded by the Wasatch National Forest.

The old road crosses to the north side briefly and descends into Parley's Canyon, according to the 1918 guide "a splendid macadam road" but filled with sharp turns: "It is well to sound your horn and have your car under control, as it is down grade for 15 miles." The guide did say, "There are many beautiful camp sites at every turn."

The rugged gorge got its name from Parley P. Pratt, among the first Mormons to come west with Brigham Young. In the late 1840s, Pratt surveyed the Big Kanyon Road and then made it a toll road. A statue of him and a Lincoln Highway monument can be found at Parley Plaza on 21st South at 23rd East Street in Salt Lake City.

Just over two miles from the summit is Exit 137 of I-80, Lamb's Canyon; the 1915 Lincoln Highway spanned the gap a quarter mile up the canyon. Exit and head south to find the little Lamb's Canyon Bridge, built in 1914, perhaps anticipating the return of the Lincoln. Pebbles on the top of one concrete rail spell out "New State Highway 1914."

Continuing on I-80, less than ten miles later, take Exit 129 (129-B eastbound)/Foothill Boulevard to enter **Salt Lake City**. The 1915 route was a little to the south, lost now to a golf course. A 1924 rerouting follows Parley's Way a few blocks, then bends left to become 2100 South Street. About four miles later, it meets U.S. Route 89/State Street, rejoining

the 1913 route. Turn left (south) on State Street, one of the city's main thoroughfares.

The state's WPA guide, published in 1941, noted that the city had twenty-four hotels and thirty-eight tourist camps. It also listed parking meter rates, starting at 1¢ for twelve minutes. State Street still has a number of older motels with great neon signs, including one with a state capital dome, another with a golden spike (a nod to the completion of the first transcontinental railroad), and one featuring the spires of the Mormon temple. The city's oldest accommodations, the Peery Hotel, at 110 West Broadway (300 South), once again serves travelers.

SPECIAL COLLECTIONS LIBRARY, UNIVERSITY OF MICHIGAN

This little bridge survives in Lamb's Canyon, just off I-80.

JULY 15, 1935
Utah Motor Park,
Salt Lake City

Sunday—
We rested here over Sunday—
Leave for the desert trip
tomorrow. Hot—100° &
98°—This is a fine place,
bath tub, kitchenette, gas
stove, sitting room, very well
fixed—Between cottages is a
roof for the cars—Lola

Lincoln Garage, Salt Lake City, from the 1918 LHA Road Guide.

On the west edge of town, the former Denver and Rio Grande Railroad station is now home to the Utah State Historical Society Museum, which displays the 1917 cast-iron marker that once denoted the Utah-Nevada line. The station was built in 1910 in response to the Union Pacific depot three blocks north.

III. West from Salt Lake City

Salt Lake City lies along the southern shore of the Great Salt Lake, the largest body of water between the Great Lakes and the Pacific. It's a remnant of the ten-times-larger Lake Bonneville, which receded twelve thousand years ago as the last ice age ended. It is a terminal lake: With no outlets, water leaves only by evaporation. Left behind, however, are minerals—chiefly salt—making it at least six times saltier than ocean water. This also makes swimmers more buoyant, allowing them to float easily. Companies have dikes near the shore that harvest about two million tons of salt annually. With so much salt, fish can't

survive; two of the few life-forms are brine shrimp and tiny but annoying brine flies.

With the lake having no outlets and being relatively shallow, small changes in the water level from rain, or lack thereof, cause drastic changes in the lake's area and shoreline. Its size fluctuates from thirty to fifty miles wide and seventy to seventy-five miles long. Rainy weather in the mid-1980s saw beaches, causeways, and even Salt Lake City threatened or flooded by the lake. The changing levels leave algae and brine shrimp on shore and a strong odor in the air.

The name of the prehistoric lake honors Capt. B. L. E. Bonneville, who in 1832 came west on an expedition that continues to be somewhat of a mystery. He established a post at Green River, Wyoming, but never entered Utah. He met Washington Irving and had the writer pen an account of his travels, even naming the Great Salt Lake for himself; that didn't stick, but he got the next best thing.

The Lincoln Highway follows State Street south to 3300 South Street, where the route turns right (west). After a couple miles, the route crosses the Jordan River, then 3300 South Street jogs south to become 3500 South Street. The road makes its way around the southern reaches of the city, then heads northwest to circle around the northern reaches of the Oquirrh Mountains at Garfield Junction.

After eight miles, turn right (north) onto 8400 West Street, then left (west) onto 2700 South Street into **Magna**. The town was called "Pleasant Green (East Garfield)" in early LHA guides. In 1999, an Eagle Scout restored a 1928 concrete marker and planted it at the Magna Veterans' Memorial Park at this intersection.

The town was built on ore-concentrating plants that opened here in 1906. Concentrated ore is then sent to a smelter, such as the one two miles ahead at Garfield, where it's turned into blister copper, which can then be sent to a refinery. Many workers lived in a gathering of tents and shacks at the base of the mountain west of Magna, called **Ragtown**. When Effie Gladding came by, someone had "written facetiously 'Mosquito Park' over the entrance to a swampy district with its little settlement of cottages." The "Italian Miner Settlement," as the LHA guides called it, was bypassed when a concrete road was built in the early 1920s.

Turn right onto 9180 West Street, a 1924 bypass of the original route, then turn left onto UT Route 201. The road west of town winds back and forth across UT Route 201 and onto Kennecott Utah Copper Corporation property. The company even preserved a section of rock retaining wall along the road in the mid-1990s; the Utah LHA chapter presented the mining company with a preservation award, cementing a positive relationship between Kennecott and old road fans.

About a mile ahead is a smelter operation at **Arthur**, then the road curves around what Gael Hoag called a "point of bluffs" in a road guide he compiled in 1913. In the base of the cliffs is a cave used for camping by early motorists. Formally Black Rock Cave, it's popularly known as Dead Man's Cave; a body is said to have been found inside hanging by suicide, but there was also a 1931 archaeological discovery of a seven-thousand-year-old child's skeleton.

A road here branches to the lake and Saltair, but the Lincoln goes west into what

The ridge halfway up the mountain at left was the shore of ancient Lake Bonneville. The Lincoln Highway appears on this 1932 card at lower right, passing beneath a trestle.

GARFIELD SMELTERS ON THE SHORES OF THE GREAT SALT LAKE

LINCOLN AND VICTORY HIGHWAYS ENTERING SALT LAKE CITY FROM THE WEST

2A117

was once **Garfield**. The 1924 LHA guide listed six hundred residents and stated that the Company House of Utah Copper Mines would "furnish meals and lodging if necessary." The town was erased as the ore complex grew in the 1950s. About ten miles to the south is the Bingham Copper Mine, the world's largest open-cut copper mine, now more than half a mile deep and two and a half miles wide.

An even larger collection of industrial buildings and a copper smelter at **Garfield Junction** are against the mountain. The Lincoln passed under railroad tracks that carried the smelter's molten slag to a dump, where the nightly dumping of hot slag lit up the sky.

The old road winds into the property, while UT Route 201 goes straight west and joins I-80. A natural attraction, Black Rock, is along the shore. Beaches east of here include Sunset, Silver Sands, and Saltair, once the lake's largest bathing, dancing, and amusement resort. A mile north of the Lincoln Highway, it was a regular side trip for cross-country motorists.

Amusement resorts began to appear on the lake in the 1870s. The Mormon Church, in response to the perceived reputation of the resorts, formed the Saltair Beach Company in 1891 to build a more wholesome venue, though curiously, the Mormons hoped to make it the "Coney Island of the West." A rail link to the city was started, and on June 8, 1893, Saltair officially opened. The Moorish-influenced pavilion and attractions were set on a platform supported by twenty-five hundred wood pilings. The resort featured a bathhouse, merry-go-round, picnic areas, and the "world's largest" dance floor. Investors took over in 1906 and added games and attractions

such as a Ferris wheel, pool halls, shooting gallery, and roller rink in the Hippodrome. Alice Ramsey squeezed in a visit to Saltair during her 1909 drive. By the time the Lincoln Highway arrived, trains ran daily from Salt Lake City every forty-five minutes from morning until midnight.

Unimpressed, James Montgomery Flagg wrote in *Boulevards All the Way—Maybe* that he and his wife took a trolley here in 1924. "There were thousands of coral-legged water birds screaming about the lake and a sort of dinky Coney Island going on feebly near the bath houses."

A mysterious fire in April 1925 took twenty-six hours to extinguish and devastated the park. The pavilion was rebuilt in similar style, though it differed in its newly striped roof and zigzag-decorated domes. Bernard Queneau and the three other Boy Scouts visited during their 1928 cross-country safety demonstration tour: "After dinner in Hotel Utah, a wonderful building, we drove out to Saltair and took a swim. We found it would cost us 95¢ each so by finding the Manager we only had to pay 35¢ each. However we did not stay long in the water since it was real torture to us who had cuts, etc. from travelling. It is 22% salt. We had great fun however on the roller coaster and watching Mr. Lombardi [the tour's director of demonstrations] in the barrel of fun."

The Depression and another fire in 1931 hurt business, but the biggest impact was the receding water level. By 1933, the resort was half a mile from the water, and the surrounding mudflats were filled with garbage and flies. A miniature railroad had to be built to take guests from the resort to the lake. New rides

Looking north at Point of Bluffs, paved with concrete in the early 1920s. The concrete Lincoln bends left around the rocks and passes Dead Man's Cave, a makeshift stopping place for early motorists. The distant mountain is dirt taken out of the huge Kennecott open-pit copper mine, about ten miles to the south.

The Saltair pavilion, as seen here, had been rebuilt in 1926. It housed 1,250 bathrooms with shower-baths.

15577. New Saltair Pavilion and Bathers, Great Salt Lake, Utah

and concessions were added in the 1940s and 1950s but problems continued. A dike was built in the 1950s to create a swim area, but in 1957 the roller coaster blew over, and Saltair closed after the 1958 season. It was given to Utah in 1959 but still lay abandoned when it became the inspiration and setting for the 1962 film *Carnival of Souls*. Taken by Saltair's elegant ruins, the director and a fellow maker of industrial and educational films used it for the climax of this, their first fictional film. It is not widely remembered but has gained a cult following. The $30,000 film recently got a high-quality DVD repackaging that includes a photo gallery and history of Saltair.

Another fire in 1970 again burned Saltair to the ground. In 1982, Saltair III opened about five miles farther south along the shore of the lake toward Tooele. It was a renovated airplane hangar with a facade reminiscent of the classic structures, but a violent storm in 1984 washed away most of its interior, and the lake's then-high levels left the main floor under five feet of water. Closed once more, it again made a brief appearance on film in the futuristic *Neon City* (1991). New owners restored it and reopened on the one hundredth anniversary, June 8, 1993. It has since closed but again reopened, now totally enclosed for year-round operation. It has a large dance floor, concessions, and a gift shop. Visitors also can swim or go on a speedboat tour. The new Saltair is about sixteen miles from Salt Lake City at Exit 104 of I-80, Great Salt Lake State Park/Saltair Drive.

I-80, railroad tracks, and the old Lincoln Highway converge a mile west of the Garfield Junction smelter on UT Route 201. They head southwest and then bend south around huge salt evaporators that line the lakeshore. The Lincoln Highway jogs through **Lake Point**, south of the interstate, then takes Center Street southwest. The road climbs a small hill and comes to a point that is unofficially called **Main Forks** or **Grantsville Junction**. Two Lincoln Highway routes diverge here: The road southwest to Grantsville was used from 1913 to 1919, and then again starting in 1927, when the Victory Highway to Wendover was adopted. The road south to Tooele was used from 1919 to 1927.

IVa. 1913: Skull Valley and around the Desert via Fish Springs

The 1913 route bears right to follow UT Route 138. In half a mile, it passes Benson's Mill on the right, a restored 1850s gristmill now open to the public. In 1985, local historian Ouida Blanthorn interviewed Oscar Cecil Jones, whose father operated the mill:

> The Lincoln Highway, which then hugged the mill closer, was crowded with families leaving the desert for possible employment on the coast during the Depression. Hungry, they bought for 25 [cents] a sack of bread crumbs. Mrs. Hobson, an old woman who lived where Noall Clarke's home is, had me bring from a Salt Lake bakery day-old bread which she dried on her rooftop and then distributed to the emigrants along with a soup she made from the heads of carp found in the Mill Pond. . . . During this same period of time, many sheep trailed by the mill on their way to the western Tooele County desert.

It's about nine miles to **Grantsville**, a town strung out along its Main Street. The 1915 LHA guide lists three hotels in town. The Lincoln Highway turns north on Center Street, then west on Clark Street. The Donner-Reed Pioneer Museum at Clark Street and Cooley Street is housed in an 1861 adobe schoolhouse. It contains guns, tools, and other artifacts found across the desert in the years following the fateful trip of that emigrant party. A 1928 concrete marker is there too. The museum is open Saturday afternoons or by appointment. An 1866 adobe church is across the street.

Edward D. Dunn wrote of driving across the country and back in his 1933 book, *Double-Crossing America by Motor*. Coming east here, "we followed the road through the barren country to the very pretty Mormon town of Grantsville. It was a relief to enjoy the shade of trees and see the well-irrigated gardens and fields after the hours on the white desert."

The Lincoln angles sharply northeast and is called Old Lincoln Highway, parallel to today's UT Route 138. At **Flux**, UT Route 138 turns northeast, but old U.S. Route 40 continues northwest. The Lincoln Highway is still parallel and to the left. As the road nears the lake, it skirts an outcrop of the Stansbury Mountains, named for Capt. Howard Stansbury, who surveyed the Great Salt Lake in 1849. A pristine piece of the original Lincoln crosses a small rise. The settlement of **Dolomite** once was here, probably named by the Italian miners who worked the area's quarries; the Dolomites are part of the Italian Alps.

The road passes Timpie Spring, then, at the northern tip of the Stansbury Mountains, at **Timpie Point**, various trails again converge: I-80, old U.S. Route 40, the railroad, and the Lincoln Highway. This is also where the 1913 and 1927 routes diverge, the original Lincoln Highway turning south, the later route pointing west to Wendover.

Those traveling I-80 can take Exit 77 and head south on UT Route 196 to follow the 1913 Lincoln Highway south around the desert. Note that much of this route remains unpaved. To follow the Wendover route, go to page 224.

From Timpie Point south to Orr's Ranch, the 1918 LHA guide repeatedly warned drivers that they would find a "poor natural road" and "many chuck holes." The original route here is parallel to and east of UT Route 196. The Stansbury Mountains loom east of that. You can see the old dirt road in the sagebrush parallel to Skull Valley Road and access it near the interstate ramp.

The roads enter the north end of Skull Valley, reportedly named for the many Indian skeletons found by pioneers. These Indians likely were small bands of Goshute (or Gosiute) who lived here despite the arid climate. The state's WPA guide quotes a sobering 1843 description of them as wearing no clothes,

having no shelter, eating roots and lizards, and being hunted every spring to be sold in Santa Fe as slaves.

The Lincoln and UT Route 196 rejoin, and the first sign of any settlement are some gravestones at **Iosepa** (yo-SEP-uh), the Hawaiian name for Joseph in honor of Mormon faith founder Joseph Smith and missionary to Hawaii Joseph F. Smith. In 1889, forty-six members came from the islands to live near the Latter-Day-Saints' temple, but because of a lack of land with water in Salt Lake Valley and their desire to live as a group, the church bought them property in Skull Valley. Effie Gladding stayed here in 1914, when it was still called Kanaka ("South Sea Islander") Ranch. Other Polynesians joined them over the years, but the lure of their lush homeland was too much when a Mormon temple was built on the islands in 1916. The town was abandoned, and today only the distinctive name, a cemetery, and monuments remain to remind visi-

Northwest of Grantsville, various passages can be seen. From the top: old U.S. Route 40, a railroad, wagon rute, and the Lincoln Highway, graveled with very fine black limestone chips that came from the nearby quarry. The view is to the southeast; I-80 is to the left, and the city of Tooele lies directly under the snow-capped peaks in the background.

tors of its interesting heritage. In recent years, festivities and services have been held here every Memorial Day weekend.

Just past **Brown's Ranch**, the old road bends left and runs parallel to the east as both roads go south. The old road enters the Skull Valley Indian Reservation, which retains approximately thirty members of the Skull Valley band of Goshute Indians on land that was theirs in the early historic period. The Goshute are similar to the Shoshone in language and culture. The 1938 statistics for the reservation, as charted in the state's WPA guide, show thirty-eight Goshute Indians there. Only a few farmed the land and the rest of it was rented to

Looking south along the old Lincoln Highway to Skull Valley.

ranchers. Today barbed wire fences it off, except at cattle guards. There is a small village, and you must obtain permission to see the old Lincoln Highway. Their land has been the focus of a long-running dispute over whether or not to build a temporary nuclear waste storage facility. By time it leaves the reservation, the Lincoln is a mile east of the current road, which was built around World War II. Another Goshute reservation is along the Lincoln Highway at the state border.

Other outposts serving early motorists were **Indian Ranch** and, five miles farther on, **Indian Farm**, or **Severe Farm**. The 1913 Packard guide noted that travelers had to pass through a gate at each end. The 1915 LHA guide said that Mrs. Minnie Schepers served the meals at Indian Ranch, and the 1918 edition still listed it: "Garage and eating house.

Orr's Ranch, a favorite stopover for early motorists.

Good food. Comfortable sleeping quarters. Limited supply of accessories. Camp site."

Three miles farther south, a road coming from the east marked "Lincoln Highway" is the 1919 route from Tooele. Together they go south, still just to the east of UT Route 196, and immediately enter **Orr's Ranch**, a well-known outpost that LHA guides repeatedly noted had "excellent ranch meals and lodging." Matthew and Mary Ann Orr had settled here in 1890. After Matthew's death the next year, Mary Ann and their three sons operated it, serving an increasing number of travelers. They took fifty-five-gallon barrels to Tooele and brought back gasoline to sell; two barrels remain as reminders. Son Hamilton became the LHA's local consul. Son William's wife, Pearl, helped cook meals. William and Pearl's daughter Shirley still lives there with her husband, Dennis Andrus, carrying on the tradition of welcoming Lincoln Highway travelers.

Alice Ramsey stopped at Orr's Ranch for repairs in 1909. She'd seen a number of prairie dog holes—and the animals themselves—but she missed one that was "right in the wagon tracks" that she and her group were traveling. A bolt came out of the tie rod, leaving the wheels to splay and causing front axle problems. They wired the front end together and limped to Orr's, where forge work helped better repair it. James Montgomery Flagg wrote in 1925 that his party wished to stay at this ranch, but there was no room.

Orr's is at the east edge of the desert, and the LHA always directed tourists to stop and inquire about road conditions ahead. By the third LHA guide in 1918, a long paragraph had been added to warn of the perils on the way to Fish Springs. The first eighteen miles

were said to be good, "natural desert adobe soil, which makes a splendid speedway," but the following twenty-four were said to be near impassable after rain. Another addition to this guide touted the forthcoming shortcuts through Johnson Pass and across the desert.

The Lincoln Highway heads southwest from Orr's Ranch and crosses UT Route 196/Skull Valley Road. Here it briefly splits, the original route heading south, the alternate Cedar Mountain Cutoff heading southwest. Both head into the U.S. Army's Dugway Proving Ground. (*Dugway* is a Mormon word describing a road that is basically a deep rut cut into a hill, but also came to mean any road dug around the side of a mountain.) In 1942, the Department of Defense took over this huge piece of land, which includes the original route and the Goodyear Cutoff built in 1919. The guarded entrance is where UT Route 196/Skull Valley Road meets UT Route 199. The area is closed to the public except by special permission.

The original Lincoln Highway and Cedar Mountain Cutoff wind unmarked and nearly unseen, and then meet inside about five miles west of the gate, south of the main road into the facility. About another five miles in, the Lincoln crosses that road in an area the military calls Ditto. This was likely the site of **County Well**, a water source dug for teamsters that later served motorists as well. It eventually dried up, and no trace remains. The two generations of the Lincoln again diverge here: the original route around the southern end of the Great Salt Lake Desert, and the 1919 route across the Goodyear Cutoff.

The original route immediately crosses a cedar log bridge over what is now Govern-

This cedar pole bridge carried the early Lincoln Highway across what is now Government Creek, near the middle of Dugway Proving Ground. It is being preserved by the U.S. Army.

ment Creek. There is conflicting information on whether it was built by the Army Transport Convoy in 1919 or sometime before that year. It was rebuilt in the 1930s by the Civilian Conservation Corps and now has stone and concrete abutments. Its significance was first recognized by Lyn Protteau, the self-proclaimed "Lincoln Highway Lady," who drove a truck across the country for years. When she finally got permission to visit the government facility, she learned that the bridge was going to be used for training exercises, and she spearheaded efforts to preserve and restore it. It was listed on the National Register of Historic Places in 1975. You must obtain permission in advance to visit Dugway, and though the army allows vistis, security is understandably tight.

The remainder of the route angles southwest for almost twenty miles, parallel to Lima Road, before reaching the southern Callao Gate of the proving grounds. It then winds another dozen miles around the Dugway Mountains on its way south to Black Rock, though the trail by then is barely visible.

With Dugway off-limits, drivers must detour around to the east and south. At the entrance, where UT Route 196/Skull Valley Road meets UT Route 199, go straight south on a dirt road for nine miles. Then turn right (west) onto Pony Express Road, which generally follows the path of the old Overland Stage and Pony Express. It's a dusty drive full of sagebrush and grasshoppers. (Remember,

The John Thomas Ranch at Fish Springs.

Looking east to a copse of trees marking the spot of the Thomas Ranch. The sagebrush in the foreground gives way to marshes and mirages beyond.

this is not the Lincoln Highway.) The road passes Simpson's Spring, site of a replica Pony Express station, and crosses the Dugway Mountains. At about forty miles, look for Navy Road, which leads back north to Dugway's Callao Gate. Half a mile west of that road, in the sagebrush on the right, is the faint trace of the Lincoln Highway coming from the gate. Another tenth of a mile farther is Black Rock, site of a Pony Express station.

From here west, Pony Express Road closely follows the original Lincoln Highway, though you can sometimes see ruts fanning away where drivers of who knows how long ago made their own way. It's about eight miles to **Fish Springs**. There the faint Lincoln can be seen turning north; Pony Express Road does so too in three-tenths of a mile. Ahead is the office of Fish Springs National Wildlife Refuge, overseen by LHA director and local historian Jay Banta. Actual springs make the marshy land a contrast to the surrounding desert, and the area is home to migrating waterfowl in the spring and fall.

The forty-two-mile stretch from County Well to Fish Springs was described in the 1918 LHA guide as having some rough stretches in the middle and being "impassable in wet weather." The 1915 LHA guide noted that Fish Springs was also the John Thomas Ranch, run by one of the road's most colorful characters. The guide directed motorists: "If trouble is experienced, build a sage brush fire. Mr. Thomas will come with a team. He can see you for 20 miles off." John Thomas built his ranch for Overland stagecoaches but soon began

serving motorists. It was also rumored that he diverted a stream to help his enterprise. Still, visitors found him welcoming. Alice Ramsey wrote that after leaving Orr's, with the advice of friends weighing on them that they should cross the desert, her group drove on until three o'clock in the morning. They rested but three hours, then drove until they reached Fish Springs. There they inquired about a meal, but only dry cereal, canned tomatoes, and coffee were available.

In *The Good of It All*, Thornton Round recalled stopping here in 1914 and being entertained by John Thomas, though he does not name him. But it undoubtedly was Thomas who cooked their dinner, "a fine repast in spite of his eighty-four years. We had salt pork, eggs, baking powder biscuits and Elberta peaches. It was all very tasty." Thomas had just built sleeping quarters. "Quarters" was right; sheets could

be hung from two wires strung between opposite walls to separate up to four guest parties at night. Round was most peeved at paying 50¢ a gallon for gas, when it was selling elsewhere for 14¢. Thomas had the five-gallon cans brought in by hay rack from Ibapah.

Effie Gladding had many kind words for Thomas: "Our host was very hospitable. 'Have some of them sweet pickles, folks.' 'Do we raise cattle here? You bet we do.' 'I have had this ranch over thirty years.'" He said that near the main ranch house was a small stone and log house in which they cooked, and that they kept it because it had been a station on the Wells Fargo stage route. He also offered the advice he was best known for: "He told us that if we got into trouble we should start a fire and 'make a smoke.' 'I'll see you with my glasses,' he said, 'and drive to your rescue with gasoline and water.'"

Nothing remains from the Thomas ranch site. The Lincoln Highway continues around the north end of Fish Springs Mountain, straying a bit from Pony Express Road. Eleven miles from the site of Thomas's ranch, the old and current roads meet at Boyd's Station, a Pony Express and Overland stage station now reduced to rubble.

The roads diverge again for a few miles but rejoin, and nine miles from Boyd's is the small community of **Callao**. It was once called Willow Springs but was renamed in 1895 after a town in Peru. It was also listed in early LHA guides as Kearney's Ranch, and on the north side still sits the abandoned Kearney Hotel. Alice Ramsey and her group stopped just past here at Willow Springs Ranch, having "dinner at a large building where they served us on the second floor." The town still has its one-room schoolhouse.

Pony Express Road turns north, as does the Lincoln Highway. After three miles, the Lincoln veered left. Stay on Pony Express Road another mile; it turns left, then after a mile and a half it turns right. Here is **Six Mile Ranch**, mentioned in all the early road guides. Now heading north, Pony Express Road intertwines with the original Pony Express trail and the Lincoln Highway. About seven miles later, the roads enter Overland Canyon, formed between Clifton Hills and the Deep Creek Mountains. The rubble of an Overland stage station is on the left. After 3.3 miles, at a Pony Express marker, the current road veers right while the Lincoln veers left. You must take the modern road another 2.2 miles to a T, where you can make a left turn. The road to the right of the T is the 1919 Lincoln Highway rejoining from the Goodyear Cutoff.

Heading west from the T, at .8 mile, is **Overland Summit**.

The old and new roads bend around the north end of the Deep Creek Mountains. The old road strays to the south, then, in seven miles, the Lincoln crossed the current road to reach **Sheridan's Ranch**, a quarter mile west. The town of Ibapah is a mile and a half ahead, but Owen Sheridan's ranch was also known by that name. Like many of the ranchers, he was friends with LHA directors. He ran an ad in the 1918 LHA guide that called his place "A Desert Resort of Merit" and noted, "Latchstring Out Day and Night." Effie Gladding had kind words: "Ibapah consists of a very pleasant ranch house and of a general supply grocery, both house and grocery owned by Mr. Sheridan. We had a comfortable night at the ranch house and purchased some beautiful baskets made by the Indians and brought by them to Mr. Sheridan for sale. The air was so fine and the evening so delightful that we reluctantly retired."

A number of structures survive. The main building is now a store; the hotel is used for hay storage and has a incongruous modern lean-to attached.

The small town of **Ibapah** (Goshute for "deep water down") was settled in 1859 by a Mormon missionary to teach agriculture to the Indians. The 1915 LHA guide, which made a habit of listing the number of automobiles owned in each town, noted three in Ibapah (with a population of 350, triple the number of today's residents). In town, at Bateman Ranch, an Auto Club of Southern California sign on display shows mileages to Gold Hill (6), Orr's Ranch (75), Tooele (111), and Salt Lake City (151). After passing through town, the road

Henry B. Joy, sitting, visits Owen Sheridan at his ranch, 1915.

turns right and crosses Deep Creek. Three miles later, some log buildings at a home remain from Weaver's Ranch. Another three-quarters of a mile west is the state line. A Goshute reservation astride the border encompasses 108,000 acres in both states. The 1918 guide noted that the road west was fair for eight miles, then, in Nevada, there were five miles of "bad white sage flat." The drive would not be getting much easier.

IVb. 1919: Tooele and across the Desert on the Goodyear Cutoff

A major shortening of the Lincoln Highway in western Utah was made in 1919. The new route went through Tooele (too-WIL-uh), Fisher Pass, the Goodyear Cutoff, and Gold Hill to Overland Summit. Still, the anonymous writer of "Motoring across America," in the April 25, 1925, *Literary Digest*, commented, "West of Salt Lake City the Lincoln Highway has very little improved road, and while the latter is passable it does not make a comfortable trip."

In a 1918 agreement between the LHA and the state, a $25,000 donation from Carl Fisher helped improve a road through Johnson Pass. (It was to be renamed Fisher Pass, but apparently that was never made official.) Another improvement was funded when LHA president Frank Seiberling donated $25,000 and his Goodyear company $75,000 to build a seventeen-and-a-half-mile causeway from Granite Mountain to Black Point, the so-called Goodyear Cutoff. The state completed the grade and about seven miles of graveling, then stopped under the pretext that it had to remove its machinery for repair. The next season, it claimed it had run out of money for the work. With the Federal Highway Act pending, the LHA thought perhaps Utah was waiting to get federal funds for the road, but after the act passed in 1921, the state chose the route to Wendover as its federal aid road. It became apparent that the state had no intention of ever finishing. A planned direct road to trim six miles from Black Point to Ibapah was never even started, nor was one on the eastern end. The LHA claimed that its contract was broken, but a state cannot be sued unless it permits it.

By 1924, years of no maintenance had left the cutoff rutted and mired, especially the nongraveled eastern end. The LHA guide that year recommended that travelers check at Orr's Ranch or at Gold Hill, at each end, before attempting the cutoff.

At least the LHA completed a mile-long pipeline as part of the project to bring water to Granite Mountain. Still, that left two long stretches between water: thirty-seven miles

An artist's conception of the Goodyear Cutoff included a lighthouse on Granite Mountain and an inn below.

from Orr's Ranch to Granite Mountain and thirty-two more to Gold Hill, plus there was no gasoline for the full seventy miles. Little has changed on this route; keep in mind that you may not find gasoline between Tooele and Nevada.

Back at **Grantsville Junction**, the 1919 route heads south, following UT Route 36 through **Erda**, where the Motor-Vu Drive-In has been showing movies since 1949. UT Route 36 continues to **Tooele**. The town name's origin is unknown, but perhaps it was named for a Goshute Indian chief. The land here was used in the 1850s by the Mormon Church to graze cattle and gather timber. The highway passes through on Main Street, then at the southern end, it bends southwest, still mostly following UT Route 36.

Five miles to the southwest is **Stockton**, the first community in the state to have electric lights. Mining has played a big role, the first claim filed in 1865. Five miles farther

south, UT Route 36 bears right at a fork with UT Route 73. A mile and a half later, the road makes a mild S-curve at **Saint John Station**, a railroad outpost, and heads due west two miles. It turns south and passes through **Saint John**, listed in the 1924 guide as having a small general store and campsites. Half a mile south, the highway turns right through the village of **Clover**, not even listed in the 1924 guide; instead, **Bush's Ranch**, was listed, which was likely about half a mile west of Clover.

The Lincoln Highway follows UT Route 199 uphill to Fisher Pass, with the Stansbury Mountains to the north, the Onaqui Mountains to the south, and the road winding between them. The highway tops the summit at 6,529 feet, then it's two and a half miles to **Willow Springs**. Tom and Rose See ran a tavern on a large spread of the beautiful mountain until the end of 2003, entertaining many Lincoln Highway fans. Rose is also involved with the Fisher Pass Monument Committee,

which is seeking grants and donations to build a memorial to Carl Fisher. The drive is led by Rollin Southwell, "the man from Utah," as he's known to Lincoln Highway friends. The $10,000 monument will feature three large stones blasted from the pass when it was widened in 1918. A tablet on each stone will have the stories of Fisher, the pass, and the Lincoln Highway.

Two miles to the southwest is the settlement of **Terra**, then the 1919 route banks right and intersects Lincoln Highway, a county road. Eight miles from Willow Springs, the 1919 route meets the 1913 route just north of Orr's Ranch. The state was also to build a connector from here to Granite Mountain. Instead, the two routes overlap into the ranch and for about fourteen miles to the Government Creek Bridge inside the U.S. Army's Dugway Proving Ground. Whereas the 1913 route crossed the bridge to the south, the new route skipped it and headed west, generally following modern Burns Road, which became Goodyear Road just before reaching the north end of **Granite Mountain**.

Here the LHA planned to build a lodge-like oasis for travelers ready to surmount the desert crossing. A lighthouse, to be named for Fisher, was to be perched above. Only the pipeline and a water trough were built by the LHA on the south side to bring spring water down to the road. Three miles later, the mud-flats—and the Goodyear Cutoff (Seiberling Section)—begin. For the next seventeen and a half miles it runs straight to the west-south-west, a white stripe through a barren landscape, made all the more daunting now that it's a bombing range. Remember that this seemingly endless expanse was chosen as the

narrowest part of the desert to traverse. The graveled section held up even without maintenance, but the ungraveled part quickly reverted to a mess without a surface or upkeep. The army now maintains it.

In 1919, even as the causeway reached its most completed state, the First Transcontinental Army Truck Convoy bogged down here on its way to the West Coast. The men had to use ropes to pull the trucks across much of it. Wendover Road booster William Rishel, who had hoped just that would happen, said that after the convoy, the rutted road "looked like a plowed field."

In his 1925 book, *Boulevards All the Way— Maybe*, James Montgomery Flagg described the cutoff: "It was built up above the flat expanse of sand and alkali and was once a fair road but now in a terribly cut up condition, the edges strewn with busted tires and twisted mudguards and here and there a wrecked flivver."

At the far end is **Black Point**, the former staging and camp area for the roadbuilders.

The highway leaves Dugway by way of locked gates and then curves north toward the old mining town of **Gold Hill**. The causeway can be viewed along the road by looking back eastward. Gold Hill, named for nearby gold deposits, has had a series of booms and busts, often from other minerals, such as copper,

Looking east along the Goodyear Cutoff from the site of the Black Point work camp.

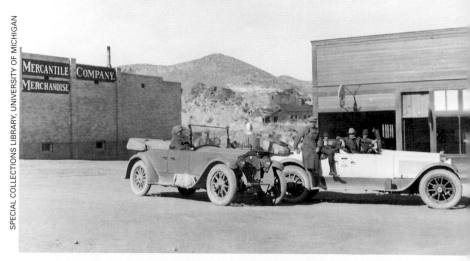

The LHA Packard and camp car, Gold Hill, September 27, 1920.

arsenic, and tungsten. It was past its prime when the Lincoln Highway came through, but according to the 1924 LHA guide, it still boasted garages, restaurants, and a hotel. A number of old stores and homes survive.

The 1924 LHA guide directed travelers to ask Gold Hill garageman and LHA consul K. C. Davis about the condition of the cutoff and whether they should follow it or the original route via Fish Springs. The guide also noted that the road through Gold Hill was temporary until a direct road was built from Black Point to Ibapah. That day has yet to come.

James Montgomery Flagg wrote of arriving here as they drove eastbound: "We went thro Tippet and Ibapah (whatever that means) steadily up thro the rocks–nothing but rocks and heat–to a station called Gold Hill which was a dozen shacks crouched between blistering hills without a single leaf of vegetation to relieve the poached eye."

The gravel road continues–Effie Gladding said it was "practically nothing but the bed of a stream"–to Overland Summit, where it rejoins the 1913 route.

V. 1927: Wendover Route

The Lincoln Highway in western Utah was rerouted yet again at the end of 1927, after a contentious battle with the state. It would now follow the Victory Highway west from Salt Lake City to Nevada.

The Wendover Road was long favored by Salt Lake City leaders. Having both this road and the southerly Arrowhead Trail enter the city would make it, instead of Ely, Nevada, on the Lincoln Highway, the gateway for traffic to both San Francisco and Los Ange-

les. Finally, in 1917, the LHA persuaded the state to invest in the Lincoln and Utah entered into an agreement to build a short-cut across the desert at its narrowest point. Frank Seiberling, president of the LHA and Goodyear, committed $100,000 and the state agreed to finish the road, known as the Goodyear Cutoff, but the July 1919 deadline passed and it was only partly completed. As described earlier, the state finally admitted that it had decided to concentrate its efforts elsewhere.

Meanwhile, interest in the Wendover Road had been revived by the Victory Highway Association, established in 1921 to honor American soldiers killed in World War I. According to George Clark, who produced a brochure about that highway in 2002, little documentary evidence survives from this road, which, like the Lincoln Highway, connected New York to San Francisco. A twelve-foot bronze doughboy was to mark each end, state borders were to have seven-foot dough-boys, and each county line would have a bronze eagle in its nest atop a memorial to that county's fallen troops. It is suspected that no doughboys were produced, but five eagle monuments survive: two in Kansas and three in California (one along the Victory/Lincoln in Truckee).

The Victory Highway followed a trail across the Great Salt Desert that was no more than the faint traces made by overland emigrants, later paralleled by the Western Pacific Railroad. San Franciscans were pleased that motorists would have no chance to divert to Los Angeles, while Southern Californians were incensed. Utah's other road to the coast–the Arrowhead Trail–headed south from Salt

Lake City through Las Vegas to Southern California, keeping tourists in Utah much longer than the Lincoln Highway. The LHA championed its route as a reasonable way to reach San Francisco *and* Los Angeles, serving both cities, but pleasing neither.

So of the three roads from Salt Lake City to the coast, the Lincoln was the least desirable to Utah. In 1921, when the Federal Highway Act directed states to designate 7 percent of their roads to receive federal funding, Utah chose the Victory Highway west of Salt Lake City, leaving the Lincoln Highway unfunded and with no hopes for improvement or even maintenance.

Among the LHA's loudest complaints was that "the so-called 'Wendover Road'" (as per its 1924 guide) crossed the desert at its widest and therefore most dangerous point. The hard surface became flooded with the least precipitation, and when dry, it looked deceivingly safe when it was often a salty mire topped by a thin crust. The LHA's 1935 history says that the state and Salt Lake City interests tried building the Victory Highway three different times before the federal government had to come in and employ new methods–and relaxed standards, the book claims. The road finally opened in 1925 using a mud-filled trench under an oil-surfaced gravel roadbed.

When the LHA cried foul, the Bureau of Public Roads formed a committee to resolve the conflict; it concluded that although the Lincoln Highway was better, circumstances dictated that the Wendover route had the best chance for improvement and therefore was the better choice to receive federal aid. With the committee having no power to change the route, only to comment on it,

LHA directors grudgingly accepted the recommendation. On December 2, 1927, they also "agreed to designate the Ely-Wendover route, when constructed, as a formal part of the Lincoln Highway." And so for the next two years, there was no Lincoln Highway from Wendover to near Ely, Nevada. That "Wendover gap" was not completed until 1930, after the LHA had ceased operations, but it was then marked as the Lincoln Highway.

By then, drivers habitually stuck to the Victory Highway across Utah *and* Nevada, leaving much of the original Lincoln Highway through Utah unpaved. It's also no coincidence that the Lincoln Highway across Nevada (now generally U.S. Route 50) became known as "the Loneliest Road." There are lonelier, but none that are a federal route.

In his 1953 book, *U.S. 40*, George Stewart examined the debate from when the first overland emigrants crossed the desert up to its designation as U.S. Route 40 and determined that two psychological factors were likely influencing the people of Utah: "First, the flat offered a magnificent high-speed roadway, in dry weather. Second, a road across it paralleled the railroad, and during two generations the people of the West had come to look upon a railroad as something that a road naturally followed."

From the north end of the Stansbury Mountains, it's seventy-eight miles to Wendover, with little in between. U.S. Route 40 was later built on or alongside the Victory/Lincoln Highway and even shared its road with U.S. Route 50 (from about twenty miles west of Salt Lake City to Wendover) until a new routing opened across southern Utah. Once I-80 was built parallel to the roads and railroad

in the late 1960s, maintenance stopped on U.S. 40; in an ironic twist, it now sits abandoned and deteriorating, as does the original Wendover Road. Of those seventy-eight miles of the Victory Highway, about sixty miles have survived, forty-five of those drivable.

Recall that the 1927 Lincoln Highway diverged from the original route at Timpie Point, just north of a small lake called Big Spring. The Victory Highway (also third-generation Lincoln and U.S. 40) has been paved over by I-80. Exit 77 is just west of Timpie Point. Parallel roads apparently are later frontage roads. I-80 and the railroad south of it run to **Delle**, about seven miles west, with only a hint of the old roads emerging to the right just before Delle.

Today there are interstate exits at most of the old railroad stops. At Delle, which has a twenty-four-hour gas station–minimart, the railroad, Lincoln Highway, U.S. Route 40, and I-80 all bend right so that eight miles later, they can go around the north tip of the Cedar Mountains. There, at **Skunk Ridge** and Exit 62 of I-80, they all curve left and head southwesterly. The original road to Wendover broke away to the north. The circa 1926 rebuilt version used by the Lincoln Highway bends south before the exit and rejoins two miles to the west. A railroad overpass survives on this segment, reachable from the exit.

At Exit 56, **Aragonite**, the Victory/Lincoln breaks away to the south; to the north are the **Grassy Mountains**. About a mile west of the exit, there are rest areas on each side of I-80. The Victory/Lincoln curved south of the eastbound oasis, then is again mostly buried by the lanes of I-80 past **Clive** and to Exit 41, **Knolls**. The town site was about a mile west of

the interstate exit. The WPA guide described it as a cluster of buildings on the eastern edge of the desert, the last settlement until Wendover. A couple businesses survived into the 1980s, but they've closed and were demolished or moved away. From here west, U.S. Route 40 was built atop the Victory/Lincoln. That makes for a good road to drive for the remaining forty miles to Wendover, though the surface toward the western end is buckled and requires very cautious driving.

The salt desert really begins east of Knolls, as does the Wendover Air Force Range, which parallels the road all the way to Wendover on the south side. To the north is the smaller Hill Air Force Range. The speed limit on I-80 is seventy-five miles per hour, strictly enforced. For more than thirty miles, there is almost no change in the landscape with the exception of a 1981 sculpture standing twenty-six miles east of Wendover. The eighty-three-foot-tall *Tree of Utah* is made of six balls on a spindly rock-coated trunk. Its concrete foundation is just as deep.

The morning after visiting Saltair in 1928, Bernard Queneau's caravan headed for Wendover. The sixteen-year-old wrote in his diary, "We drove all day in this terrible country. . . . We went 55 miles without turning and during this time we saw mirages extending over 100 miles on both sides."

The salt flats are the dried-out bed of the prehistoric Lake Bonneville, the much larger predecessor to Great Salt Lake. The land is mostly hard and dry, but the receding water has not completely disappeared, often resulting in a hard crust but mush underneath. The first recorded crossing was by Capt. John C. Frémont in 1845, with a party that included

SPECIAL COLLECTIONS LIBRARY, UNIVERSITY OF MICHIGAN

Joe Walker and Kit Carson. Walker wrote that others shouldn't follow, but the next year, Lansford Hastings took their path and lured others to follow too. The Donner party attempted the "Hastings Cutoff" of the California Trail in the late summer of 1846. They believed it to be only forty miles across the salt flats, but the true distance was twice that, too long for oxen to go without water. Once the Donner party realized the deadly distance, it was too late to turn back, and they lost cattle, oxen, and four of their wagons.

Frank Mullen Jr.'s *Donner Party Chronicles* (1997) quotes Virginia Reed: "It was a dreary, desolate alkali waste; not a living thing could be seen; it seemed as though the hand of death had been laid upon the country." They suffered, she wrote, "from thirst and heat by day and piercing cold by night." The losses and approaching detour around the Ruby Mountains had tragic, infamous results.

The Victory Highway roughly followed the Hastings Cutoff from Salt Lake City to Timpie, but then the Victory continued straight west, while the Hastings trail turned south for a dozen miles, crossed the future Victory near Grassy Mountains, and they stayed north until they again met in Nevada.

In his 1933 book, *Double-Crossing America by Motor*, Edward D. Dunn described the desert during an obviously dry period: "There is a fine paved road that rises several feet above the level of the salt . . . it is amusing to turn and run [parallel to the road] fifteen or twenty miles right on the hard surface of the desert. The weight of our heavy car made no impression as we drove for miles on this roadless expanse. We scraped some of the salt with a knife, and it was exactly the kind we have on our tables at home."

The Great Salt Lake Desert is lifeless from the salt and alkali preventing the growth of vegetation. The land is so flat that you can see the curvature of the earth on the horizon. The road is so straight that without trees or towns, it's easy to become disoriented as to speed or even direction. Roadside explorer Doug Pappas described the corridor as "the dullest miles in the known universe."

Eight miles east of Wendover, **Salduro** was a railroad stop that grew into a town as a result of the nearby salt and potash mining.

It was abandoned in 1944, after the local potash plant closed and a fire ravaged the settlement, but the potash industry continues to thrive at Wendover.

Just north of there lies the Bonneville Salt Flats Speedway, one hundred square miles of salt flats that, when dry, are rock hard. The potential for a raceway was recognized, and in 1914, an unofficial record of 141.73 miles per hour was set. Wider fame came in 1925, when Ab Jenkins raced and beat a steam engine between Salt Lake City and Wendover. Jenkins became the raceway's most celebrated record holder. Other records include a reported 167 miles per hour on a bicycle, 301 miles per hour on a motorcycle, and 622 miles per hour by a rocket car in 1970. If you visit, stay on paved roads; the surface looks hard, but it may be just a salt crust and mushy beneath. For $75, you can drive on the official course and they'll clock you in your car. Customers have to provide their own car numbers and crash helmets. The speedway is accessible from Exit 4 of I-80.

Bonneville Salt Flats is a state park, as is Danger Cave, which has provided some of the region's earliest evidence of human habitation, stretching back eleven thousand years. The cave is closed to the public, and it takes a few turns to find it, but it is located on state maps and locals will give directions. Nearby but harder to find is Juke Box Cave, used by the Wendover base during World War II; it stayed cool and its lights could remain hidden for blackout rules.

Wendover was founded in 1907 as a supply stop along the just-built Western Pacific Railroad and was named for a surveyor of the line. The railroad piped water here for its steam locomotives; after switching to diesels, it sold the piping to the town. Potash was a leading commodity in the early twentieth century and continues to supply the fertilizer industry, but tourism now dominates. The Nevada side (incorporated as West Wendover in 1991) is filled with casinos, while the Utah side provides gas, food, and lodging. The two towns have cooperative arrangements for schools, firefighting, and law enforcement. Together, they also offer hiking, biking, golf, and scuba diving at nearby Blue Lake.

Wendover Army Air Field was selected by the military in 1940 as a site for bombing and gunnery ranges. It became a training ground for the crews of B-17, B-24, and B-29 aircraft, and home to thousands of airmen. Wide-ranging tests were conducted here prior to the dropping of the first nuclear bombs, and the crew of the Enola Gay trained here. The field was renamed Wendover Air Force Base in 1947, and three decades later, it was turned over to Wendover, Utah, as a municipal airport and renamed Decker Field. It now serves private, commercial, and military aircraft, making

it the world's only surviving fully operational World War II–era airport (though at this time, there are no regularly scheduled carriers). It can be seen to the south; the large hangar housed the Enola Gay. A welcome center ahead has a memorial outside to the 509th Composite Group, which supplied the atomic bomb crews.

After the Victory Highway was completed through here in 1926, there was little traffic, but enough that Bill Smith, a mechanic at a potash plant, opened the Cobblestone Service Station with a partner on the south side of what today is Wendover Boulevard. They attracted motorists with a lightbulb on a pole—pretty simple, but all that was needed in the barren land—and their place became known as "the light in the desert." They added a hotel, and when Nevada legalized gambling in 1931, they expanded it into the State Line Hotel Casino. When a disagreement divided the partners, they tossed a coin for the business. Bill won. In 1935, Bill married Anna Sorensen, a worker in the State Line Coffee Shop. In 1938, they built a new hotel with then-novel air-conditioning. The influx of airmen during World War II brought more prosperity, and in 1952, the State Line got a mascot to replace the lightbulb: Wendover Will, a ninety-foot neon cowboy standing right on the state border and named for the founder. Will was built by Young Electric Sign Company of Salt Lake City, which also made Vegas Vic, a smaller twin who went to Las Vegas. The *Guinness Book of World Records* named Will the "world's largest mechanical cowboy." He has two moving arms, one pointing to the casino, the other waving "hi." His pedestal proclaiming, "Where the West Begins," was replaced in

The Western Service Station in Wendover, Utah, also had a café and "modern court."

1973, when the casino was rebuilt. The family also built Jim's Casino across the street, itself replaced with the Silver Smith Casino in 1994. The casinos were sold to different companies in 2002. The Silver Smith was redone as Montego Bay, owned by Peppermill Casinos, and the State Line Nugget Hotel Casino received a $30 million upgrade—all started with a light bulb on a pole.

Gambling brings overnight visitors from Salt Lake City, and the towns' isolation makes it a must-stop for cars and buses coming through. The Utah town's population is mostly Hispanic, drawn by steady work at Nevada's 24/7 casinos. In the 1960s, the time zone change was moved from near Tooele to the state line, but the casinos on the Nevada side keep to Mountain Time, as most customers come from Salt Lake City.

Once in Nevada, the Victory Highway continued west, but the Lincoln Highway finally got its road south in about 1930. Today's U.S. Route 93 Alt. follows that corridor—110 more lonely miles to Ely, Nevada.

Victory Highway Garage in Wendover, 1924.

Greetings from
Nevada

Motorists heading for the Pacific Coast had crossed the Great Plains and the Great Salt Desert, but a few challenges still awaited in Nevada.

Thousands of wagons on the California Trail had followed the Humboldt River Valley across northern Nevada. The same path was also used by the first transcontinental railroad. This fairly level corridor must have tempted LHA directors, but to reach it, motorists would have had to circle north of the Great Salt Lake. However, there was another possibility.

	NEVADA	U.S.
Population in 1910	81,875	92,228,496
Population in 2000	1,998,257	281,421,906
Persons per square mile in 2000	18.2	79.6
Approximate miles of Lincoln Highway		
via Reno to Verdi	450	3,389
via Reno and Carson City	497	3,389
via Lahontan and Carson City	485	3,389

In 1859, an army survey team led by Capt. James Simpson was sent to find an alternative to the Humboldt route, one that would be shorter yet offer more food and water. Simpson chose a central trail being used by a pack mail service. The Pony Express chose this route too, as did mail and stage lines that followed. The same factors of directness and better conditions drew LHA directors to the central path half a century later. Though the route had mostly languished after the nineteenth-century mining booms played out, it still connected the most prosperous towns across the length of the state.

The main obstacle on the central route was a series of ranges with steep grades. This route passed through the Great Basin, which stretches from the Wasatch Mountains in eastern Utah to the Sierra Nevada Mountains at the California border. In Nevada, it was more like crossing a dozen basins separated by north-south mountain folds. Effie Gladding noticed them as she crossed the state in 1914: "We were passing from one great valley into another, hour after hour. . . . descending into a valley, crossing its immense width, coming

up on to a more or less lofty pass, usually bare, and descending into another valley."

Bellamy Partridge also noted them in *Fill 'er Up!*: "One day in the parched lands of Nevada was much like another. Uphill, downhill; alkali dust, sand dunes."

Early motorists in the East were given driving directions by street name, and in Wyoming by its towns, but in Nevada the Lincoln Highway often consisted of wagon roads between ranches. The 1913 *Lincoln Highway Route Road Conditions and Directions* provides a solid list of ranches, especially in eastern Nevada.

With so few people and so many miles, the LHA stepped up with grants from General Motors and Willys-Overland to fund improvements. In the 1920s, a new alignment between Ely (E-lee) and Eureka bypassed White Pine Summit. A new road over Carroll Summit bypassed the original between Austin and Eastgate (though four decades later, U.S. Route 50 reverted to the old route).

The LHA discouraged alternate routes, so branches such as the Colorado Loop were quietly dropped, but between Reno and Sacramento, the LHA had two official routes. The more direct branch went north of Lake Tahoe and over Donner Summit; the scenic Pioneer Branch went south to Carson City, then southwest around Lake Tahoe and through Placerville, California. (The eastern division point was later moved east of Leeteville near Fallon to bypass Reno.) Both branches received Lincoln Highway concrete posts in 1928. Gael Hoag's 1928 marker log said twenty-eight posts were set aside in Fallon for the road from Leeteville to Carson City "when constructed." One post is in Carson City in front of the Nevada State Museum, and three more are along Donner Lake in California, east of the pass (not at their original locations). Why the LHA favored two routes in this instance remains a mystery.

The discovery of both gold and silver at the Comstock mines in 1859 brought the first rush of settlers to what became Nevada. Towns along the Lincoln Highway, such as Ely, Eureka, Austin, and Carson City, were built on mining—and faded with it. In 1933, Edward D. Dunn wrote of them, "The cities of Nevada, with the exception of Reno, are like small frontier villages." The state has seen repeated booms and busts. In fact, the Newmont Mine near Carlin, to the north in Humboldt Valley, is the best-producing mine in the country today.

The economic swings of mining and agriculture in Nevada led the state to embrace otherwise illicit activities as a means of income. The legalization of gambling in 1931 has made tourism the state's leading industry. Nevada's easy divorce law attracted another niche group to wait out the required period, some in motels catering to the trade. As Bert Bedeau and Mella Harmon explained in their SCA

The Loneliest Road

In his 1953 book, *U.S. 40*, George Stewart compared U.S. Routes 40 and 50 across Nevada. He thought U.S. 50 the more scenic: "It is, however, a comparatively lonely road, with few chances for meals or lodgings."

Three decades later, *Life* magazine ran a short article calling Route 50 through Nevada the "Loneliest Road in America." Richard Moreno, now publisher of *Nevada Magazine*, saw public relations gold. Here he recalls his role in starting the Loneliest Road promotion:

> I was the director of public relations for the Nevada Commission on Tourism from 1985 to 1992 and created the "I survived Highway 50, the Loneliest Road in America" promotional campaign in July 1986. That was the month that a photo and story appeared in the July 1986 issue of *Life* magazine (not *Trailer Life*) that depicted a cowboy on a horse riding across a lonely stretch of U.S. 50 in Nevada. The text to the photo described the 287-mile stretch of U.S. 50 between Ely and Fernley as "the Loneliest Road in America" and cited an unnamed AAA advisor as saying that a traveler would need "survival skills" to make the trip.
>
> The towns along the route were initially upset about the characterization of their region but our office quickly convinced them of the public relations possibilities. In response, we developed a tongue-in-cheek "Highway 50 Survival Kit," which contained useful information about the various towns along the route and included a little game travelers could play; they could take a cartoon map with a tear-off card and have the card stamped with "I Sur-
>
> vived" next to the names of the five major towns along that stretch of road. If the traveler returned the card to us, we would send him or her an official "I Survived Highway 50" certificate signed by the Governor, a pin, and other prizes. We printed 500 of the kits to determine the interest and those were gone in less than a month. To date, the campaign is still going on and more than 40,000 Survival Kits have been sent out by the state. Our office also succeeded in getting the state legislature to officially designate U.S. 50 as the Loneliest Road in America and in having the state highway department erect Loneliest Road signs along the route.
>
> During 1986–89, I promoted the heck out of the Loneliest Road, working with CNN, CBS, the *Los Angeles Times*, the *Chicago Tribune*, etc. to produce features about America's Loneliest Road. I also worked with local businesses in each town to develop t-shirts, bumper stickers, pins, etc. Since that time, there have been a couple of books about the Loneliest Road, a song (for a BBC play), thousands of newspaper and magazine articles from around the world, and probably lots of other stuff I'm not aware of. I also did make a visit to the offices of *Trailer Life* magazine in Southern California in 1987 to promote the Loneliest Road story. The magazine did follow up with a nice story sometime later that year but that was not where the Loneliest Road article first appeared.

The promotion continues to draw tourists looking for life off the interstates. The Nevada Commission on Tourism has taken to calling the corridor Pony Express Territory, but it plans on updating and relaunching the Survival Kit.

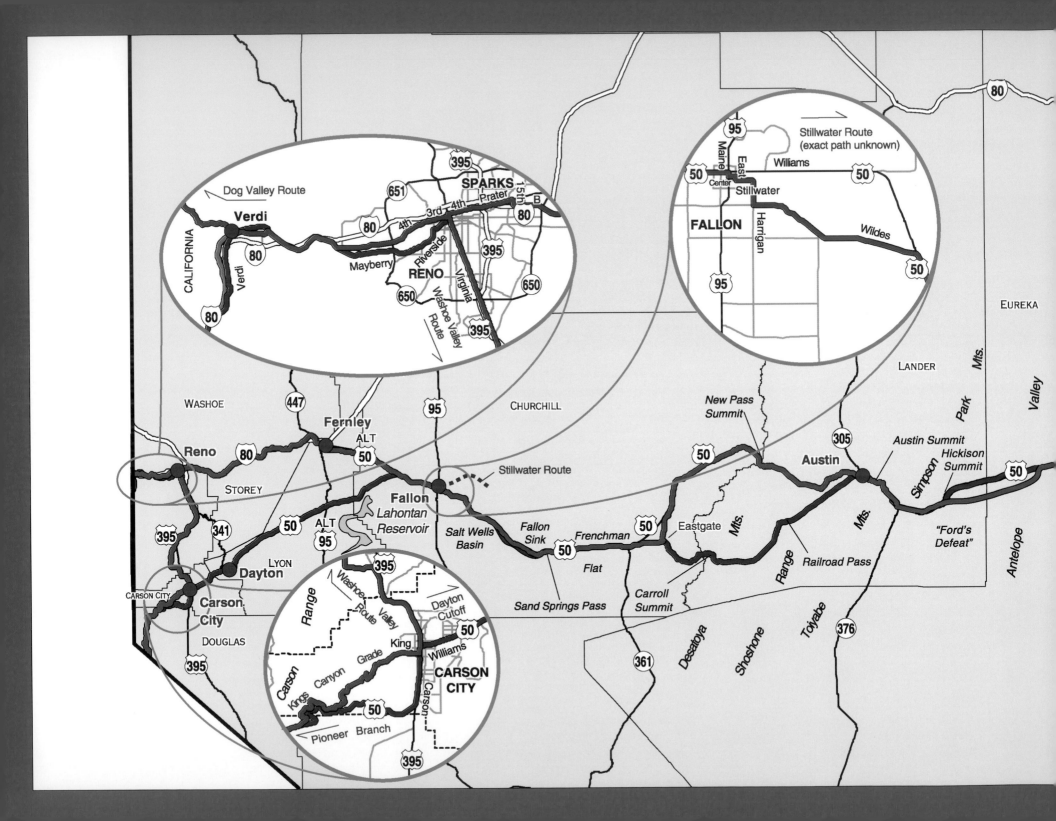

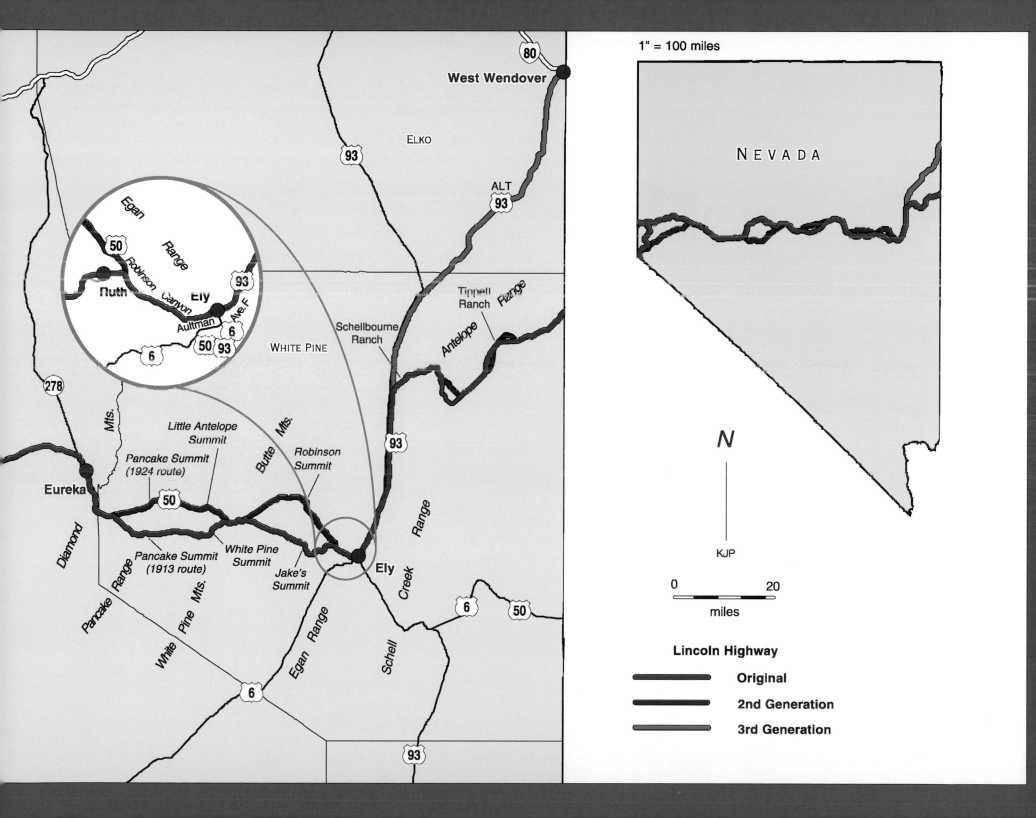

West of Ibapah, Utah, on the original route in 1927. The cast-iron state line marker, left in the picture, is now at the Utah State Historical Society at Salt Lake City.

conference tour guide, "Nevada's sin solutions of legalized gambling, prostitution, prize fighting, and quickie divorces and marriages helped temper the boom-and-bust cycles."

With the fading of mineral riches and the rerouting of the Lincoln to Wendover, the Lincoln Highway across Nevada remains rather isolated. What has been nicknamed the "Loneliest Road" may not be *the* loneliest, but few major east-west federal highways are so sparsely driven.

Effie Gladding didn't call it lonely, but she certainly found it distinctive: "The trail across Nevada could be marked by whiskey bottles if by no other signs."

1a. Utah to Ely via Tippett's Ranch

The original Lincoln Highway enters Nevada about four miles west of Ibapah, Utah. This road served both of western Utah's early routes: the original around the south end of the Great Salt Lake Desert via Fish Springs, and the 1919 reroute across the desert via the Goodyear Cutoff.

The dusty road is hardly used to this day, a result of conflicts with Utah about the rerouting of the Lincoln Highway north through

Tippett's Ranch, a welcome respite in eastern Nevada.

Wendover. In its 1924 guidebook, the LHA couldn't resist one last jab at that state for reneging on its contract: "A sign to mark this border is hardly necessary, as the change in road surface is apparent immediately." The road has never been paved on either side of the border, though the gravel does become smoother in Nevada. You'll want to refer to Franzwa and Peterson's 2004 Nevada book to keep you on the right road and guide you to bypassed outposts.

The Lincoln Highway immediately enters the Goshute Indian reservation, established in 1914. The time zone also changes here from Mountain to Pacific. Sixty miles to the south can be seen snow-capped Wheeler Peak, at 13,083 feet. It sits within part of the Humboldt-Toiyabe National Forest and Great Basin National Park, both along U.S. Route 50.

About twenty miles west of the Utah border, early Lincoln Highway travelers may have stopped at the **Tippett Ranch**, a control station on the Lincoln Highway. On her 1914 drive eastward, Effie Gladding stopped at Tippett's; she reported that the owner had to travel thirty-six miles for his mail and supplies. A general store, with "Tippett" in concrete above the door, remains, as do sod-roofed buildings and corrals, but all are deserted. It's marked now on maps as Tippett.

The Lincoln Highway continues west on Whiskey Road, formerly NV Route 2, and winds its way some thirty miles to U.S. Route 93, crossing Antelope Range and Schell Creek Range. It's a stark but plant-filled land of sagebrush, grasses, and wildflowers, populated by birds, jackrabbits, and pronghorn antelope. Along the way, early guides led motorists between ranches. In the twenty-nine miles between Tippett's and a ranch at Schellbourne were **Pearce's** (or Bednark's), **Stone Cabin**, and **Anderson's**, where good buttermilk could be found, according to the 1918 LHA guide. The original road between Anderson's and Schellbourne was bypassed in the 1920s; the old road could often be seen down in the adjacent wash.

Effie Gladding wrote that at Schellbourne Pass, her party passed both a car from Detroit and "some men with their laden burros taking supplies to the sheepmen in the mountain ranges." Driving east, Gladding lunched at Anderson's Ranch, "where they treated us very hospitably."

At **Schellbourne** (or Fort Schellbourne, as it was once a government post on the emigrant trail) was another ranch. A large stone monument honors the Pony Express.

As Jacob Murdock crossed the country in 1908, he noted, as quoted by McConnell in *Coast to Coast by Automobile*, that lodging in the West had become very uncertain: "In Nevada, at many places, it is necessary to supply one's own provisions. We stopped at some road houses, where they were able to give us accommodations, but we had to furnish all our meals."

It was this road that Boy Scout Bernard Queneau wrote about in his diary on August 3, 1928: "On and on and on over the worst U.S. route I ever hope to see."

About three and a half miles past Schellbourne, the original Lincoln Highway meets U.S. Route 93, the connector route of the 1928 Lincoln through Wendover.

1b. Utah to Ely via Wendover

It took years to build a road from Salt Lake City to Wendover that would not sink into the salty mire. Once completed, the Victory Highway's straight shot to Nevada lured drivers away from the more circuitous route of the Lincoln Highway in western Utah. Drivers then continued down Nevada's Humboldt River Valley through Wells, Elko, Battle Mountain, Winnemucca, and Love-

lock to Fernley, east of Reno. They had no choice.

The LHA acquiesced to the Wendover route in 1927, but directors refused to follow the Victory Highway any farther into Nevada. There was no road to reconnect south to the Lincoln, however, only a rough trail. This left an eighty-mile gap in the Lincoln Highway.

According to Russell Rein, who has researched Gael Hoag's 1928 marker log, the log seems to indicate that the Utah route ended at Wendover and did not pick up until Ely:

The last Utah marker description says "2 L P [left pointing], 1 R P [right pointing] left with Connelly for new junction W of State line." That means three markers were left for some Nevada road improvement. . . . Since Gael Hoag revisited the log in 1930 to accommodate marking the Blair Bridge route, he still didn't include the Nevada route so it probably represents a gap that was never marked.

Indeed, Bernard Queneau wrote in his diary that when the Boy Scout safety tour came through in August 1928, it left the Lincoln at Wendover, "since the old way had been abandoned and the new one was not finished." They picked their way south to Ibapah, Utah, and the old Lincoln Highway.

The LHA was already securing funds to improve the connector, chief among them fifty-two miles of highway from Ely back to where the old road converged from Tippett's. That paved road was finished in April 1930. Celebrations began on June 4 in Ely, where Aultman Street was lined with flags, banners, and bunting. Dignitaries spoke, a symbolic chain was broken, and a parade celebrated the advance of transportation. Festivities

continued for three more days with carnivals, rodeos, dances, circus acts, and visits from other state reps, including the governor of Utah. The town of McGill got in on the fun by blowing up an old smokestack. After three years, the Lincoln Highway gap was closed.

But by then, the advent of numbered highways had already decommissioned named roads like the Lincoln. The Utah road to Wendover became U.S. Route 40. For a time, U.S. Route 50 shared this road, but while U.S. 40 continued west along the Humboldt, U.S. 50 followed the Lincoln Highway connector to Ely. U.S. 50 later was moved to southern Utah and didn't meet the Lincoln Highway until Ely. It then followed the Lincoln across central Nevada, as it still does. The connector south from Wendover is now U.S. Route 93 Alt. and U.S. Route 93.

Those along the Victory Highway were not pleased that a connector had opened to Ely. In *U.S. 40*, George Stewart reported, "The rivalry between the roads was at one time so intense that the towns along U.S. 50 hired an agent to frequent service-stations in Wendover, engage in conversation with westbound tourists, and encourage them to turn left."

Still, the connector probably lured few motorists on an eighty-mile diversion south, and the opening of I-80 in the 1960s only cemented the preeminence of the Wendover Road–Humboldt corridor. Since the mid-1920s, the original Lincoln Highway from Salt Lake City to near Reno has reverted mostly to local traffic and fans of old roads.

Wendover developed in Utah but has grown westward into Nevada since the state legalized gambling. The Nevada side was

The State Line in the 1960s.

BERNIE HEISEY

The bar at the McGill Club in Cyprus Hall was transported from the East Coast by way of the southern tip of South America to the West Coast, taken by wagon to Ely, and brought here in 1907.

incorporated in 1991 as the city of West Wendover. Most growth occurs here around the casinos. The landscape changes here, too. Though the land on the Nevada side was at one time as deep underwater as the Utah flats, the lumpier terrain let the water drain away rather than evaporate. Instead of plant-choking salt, this region has sagebrush.

Little remains from the highway's old days except perhaps Wendover Will at the State Line Hotel and Casino and the Rancho Sierra Motel, with a mountain profile on its neon sign.

I-80 and U.S. Route 40 continue west and then turn northwest toward Wells and the Humboldt River valley. The Lincoln turns left (south) to follow U.S. Route 93 Alt. Many drivers describe this as a bland and boring drive. It certainly is straight for a long time. Pieces of parallel roads could be early versions of the Lincoln Highway, the earlier trail, or simply farm lanes.

About twenty-five miles from Wendover the old Lincoln Highway, almost half a mile west of U.S. Route 93 Alt., passes through Ferguson's Springs, a watering hole that was a stopover for cattle herders and early motorists.

About fifty miles south, at **Becky's Springs** or **Lages Station**, U.S. Route 93 Alt. ends when U.S. Route 93 joins it from the northwest. The Lincoln Highway continues south through Steptoe Valley, a very straight corridor through unpopulated country.

About seventy miles south is the junction with the original Lincoln Highway. About ten miles south of this intersection is **Magnuson's Ranch**, where early motorists could find meals, lodging, fuel, drinking water, and a campsite.

Another seventeen miles south is **McGill**, founded by the Nevada Consolidated Copper Company in 1908 as a company town for its employees. The town name, and the water for the operation, derived from the Adams McGill Ranch, to the northeast. On her 1914 trip east, Effie Gladding visited the smelting works, where she was fascinated by the hundreds of concentrators, which shook the copper from the sand and earth.

You'll spot the McGill Drug Company at U.S. Route 93/11 4th Street by the oval "Rexall Drugs" sign hanging from its wooden front. Built a century ago, it was bought and changed to its current name at the end of 1915. It served the town as a pharmacy until 1979 and still was like a general store for a few years after that. In 1995, no longer in business, the store and its contents were given to the White Pine Public Museum. The inventory is intact, many of the products dating back decades. It also still has a 1930s soda fountain, and the front of the counter is decorated with terra-cotta tiles. Tours are available by appointment. The White Pine Public Museum, documenting the county's history, is at 2000 Aultman Street. Out on the highway is a Frosty Stand from the 1950s.

South of McGill on U.S. Route 93 stands the closed Highway 50 Club, a roadside bar with a neon sign shaped like a federal highway shield.

James Montgomery Flagg wrote in his 1925 book *Boulevards All the Way—Maybe* that

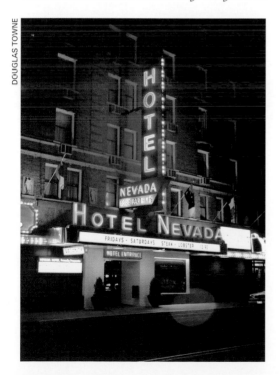

DOUGLAS TOWNE

Hotel Nevada, Ely, 1995.

the road was terrible, with "dust covering the chuck holes that made the tonneau bang in spite of springs and snubbers. We had to drive out into the sage at times to avoid deep morasses of dust, moving at ten miles and thro almost impenetrable clouds of it."

A dozen miles from McGill, drivers enter **East Ely**, which grew as the maintenance depot of the railroad owned by Consolidated Copper. East Ely now flows seamlessly into **Ely**, but its roots as a company town led to a long period of division. Ely, though only a mile to the west, is more constricted by the encroaching canyon walls. It is perhaps the largest settlement until Reno or Carson City. U.S. Route 50 now enters from the south and generally follows the Lincoln Highway across the state.

II. Ely to West of Fallon

The Ely area is rich with billions of tons of copper ore, much of it unearthed at Kennecott copper mines. It is also rich with roadside relics. A 1940s gas station and motel complex has corner glass-block windows and a rooftop sign. The former Lincoln Highway Garage at 1120 Avenue C had been the Ely Garage and Supply Company but rode the wave of Lincoln Highway enthusiasm. It also became a regular advertiser in LHA guides. Like so many early facilities, the garage was multifaceted, repairing cars, pumping gas, and selling Ford, Reo, and Franklin cars, as well as tires and parts. Souvenir metal cups that appear regularly at auction are embossed, "Free road information supplied by highway officials Lincoln Highway Garage Co. Ely, Nevada the auto supply house est. 1912." The building

Ely's Lincoln Highway Garage and Northern Hotel shared an ad in the third LHA road guide, 1918.

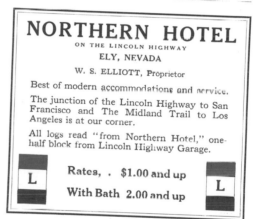

now houses school district offices. When Gael Hoag was state consul, he had an office in Ely at the Northern Hotel.

West of the junction where U.S. Route 6, U.S. Route 50, and U.S. Route 93 leave the Lincoln Highway to the east, Aultman Street is filled with neon signs for motels and restaurants, including Club Rio, Ely Hotel Bar, Plaza Hotel, and El Rancho Motel. The six-story Hotel Nevada and Gambling Hall at 501 Aultman was the tallest building in the state when it opened in 1929, and it remains

At the Eureka Pit near Ruth, in the summer of 1915, the Lincoln Highway Motion Picture Caravan crew pauses with a full-size image of Lincoln. This is now part of the Liberty Pit.

one of the state's oldest hotels. It served celebrities over the years and still offers sixty-five rooms starting around $40 a night. The first-floor walls are filled with artifacts and photos of local scenes, miners, and entertainers. Its casino and restaurant operate twenty-four hours a day. The outside wall has a four-story mural of the hotel's mascot, a donkey-cowboy created by a Walt Disney artist.

The Midland Trail broke away to the southwest on the west end of town, generally following today's U.S. Route 6 to Tonopah. It was the Midland Trail that San Francisco most feared, as this route could divert a great deal of traffic to Los Angeles instead. The 575-mile route went via Tonopah and Goldfield, Nevada, then through Big Pine and Mojave, California, avoiding high Sierra passes where snow closed the Lincoln many months of the year. A June 3, 1917, article in the *San Francisco Chronicle* accused Southern California interests of wanting signs from Salt Lake City to Ely directing traffic to the Midland Trail. The LHA never wished to be part of

this rivalry, and instead provided information on both routes; in its 1924 guide, it listed mileages from Ely to Los Angeles via the red-white-red markers of the Midland Trail. It also gave a complimentary description that went so far as stating that the Midland in Nevada was in better shape than the Lincoln Highway. In *The Good of It All*, Thornton Round

reported that his family took this route as they headed west in 1924.

West of town, the canyon continues to narrow. As it ends, the Lincoln Highway turns to the northwest, and the remains of the mine tailings can be seen. Effie Gladding noted a mountain rich in copper as she drove east toward Ely in 1914: "The Lincoln Highway signs take one to the right on a short detour in order that one may see this mountain of ore, which is being cut away by immense steam shovels, tier above tier."

Five miles west of Ely, around **Keystone**, the original Lincoln Highway turned left toward **Ruth**, the mine headquarters of Nevada Consolidated; its Liberty Pit is the largest open-pit copper mine in the state, said to be two miles long and a mile wide. It had been combined with the Eureka Mine in 1916 to form a single giant pit. Motorists in

The road is realigned through Robinson's Canyon west of Ely to avoid the rail crossings.

1913 could have stayed at the Star Pointer Hotel, named for another nearby mine. This road across Jake's Summit was bypassed in the early 1920s by a new road—today followed by U.S. Route 50—to eliminate railroad crossings. That highway heads northwest to **Robinson Summit** (7,607 feet), then bends back southward toward Illipah, a distance of some twenty-seven miles.

The Lincoln went through **Copper Flat**, **Reipetown**, and **Kimberly**. These settlements, and even the road itself, have been lost to piles of tailings from still-operating mines. It's too bad; early LHA guides said that Kimberly was "an interesting point to tarry." That's no longer recommended; not only is it dangerous to look around, but this also is likely now private property. When Kimberly did exist, it was about seven more miles to **Jake's Summit**, but with the road gone, researchers must approach it from the west. The 1918 LHA guide commented on the road west: "On the eight miles of so called white sage flats west of the summit care should be exercised. Ten miles an hour is about the best these rutted flats of powdery dust will allow."

The road west from here is drivable to **Illipah**, formerly a cattle operation known as **Moorman's Ranch**. Just after the Lincoln Highway was established, Moorman's had expanded by acquiring the adjoining, abandoned Rosevear's Ranch. Captain and Mrs. Moorman were from Missouri; when Effie Gladding drove east in 1914, she found "unforgettable hospitality" when her party stopped here for lunch:

Mrs. Moorman soon had a laden table ready for us, and we sat down to fried bacon and eggs, potatoes, lettuce, radishes, preserved cherries, stewed prunes, milk, tea, and pie. How refreshing it all was! And how pleasant was the soft Southern accent of our hostess which she had not lost in the years on the plains.

Gladding ended up here after trying to get lunch at two other places. First her eastbound group had stopped at Six Mile House, but the rancher's wife said she had limited supplies; however, she phoned ahead to the Hamilton House. Gladding turned right at a fork "and climbed through a narrow, rocky canyon road." But a broken water line forced them to turn around and take the other branch of the fork. They again climbed, this time to 8,115 feet, where they saw another road to Hamilton, but they chose to push on and came upon Moorman's.

The 1920s route rejoins the original road at Illipah, and they press west together as U.S. Route 50 through a gap in Moorman Ridge. On the other side was **Rosevear's Ranch**. It made the LHA guides, but it was no longer open and was listed as a Control Station only. By the 1924 guide, it wasn't listed at all, but the small stone house survives, open to the elements.

James Montgomery Flagg, writing in 1925, reveled in the route from Ely to Austin: "All day thro rocky gorges around snaky precipitous trails such as you see in the movies where the devil-may-care bandits ride, then across sagebrush mesas for hours at a stretch, and at the base of rocky mountain ranges where desperate rustlers hide in screenland." Flagg soon came upon a Ford sedan, which brought him back to present. The driver was having car trouble, and just the night before, the fellow's suit, watch, and food had been stolen at an auto camp.

As before, U.S. Route 50 breaks to the right to follow a 1924 bypass. The newer road crosses **Little Antelope Summit** (7,433 feet) and **Pancake Summit** (more than 900 feet lower).

The original road bears left to **White Pine Summit** then dips south to **Hamilton**. These narrow dirt roads originally served the lead and silver mines nearby. Turning back north, the road went to **Six Mile House** or Coyle's Ranch. A large stone house and outbuildings remain, as do corrals and a dried-up reservoir—all deserted. West of there are four ranch fences with unlocked gates, just as motorists encountered a century ago. LHA past president and researcher Jess Peterson wrote for the *LHA Forum* about his encounter at one of these gates: "There are two kinds of gates in the West: those that you can go through without a problem, and those that can get you in a lot of trouble. The thing is, you can't tell which is which just by looking at them."

While he and sidekick Marvin Wolfe were trying to decide what to do, a truck approached, and the rancher, his son, and two dogs got out. "The rancher was very congenial and let us know that in this particular part of the country there is no problem with going through gates as long as you close them up again. Much relieved, we closed the gate behind us and continued on our way."

The road continues over the Pancake Mountains; like the newer road, the original tops **Pancake Summit**. Part of the original route is gone, but a parallel road reconnects with the 1924 bypass just east of NV Route 892, site of **Fourteen Mile House** or **Maryland Wells**. LHA guides noted that the house was deserted and that the water was not fit to drink,

When this bottle is filled with water and suspended from a handy knob or projection on the automobile, the gradual seepage of the moisture through the canvas cools the contents. . . . It is an easy way to provide cool drinking water as well as refills for the radiator.

—*Alice Ramsey on using a canvas desert water bag between Ely and Eureka, 1909,* Veil Duster, and Tire Iron *(1961)*

usable only for radiators. U.S. Route 50/Lincoln Highway turns north and crosses Pinto Summit (7,376 feet). Just before it, LHA guides listed **Pinto House**, which had camping and water for both drinking and filling radiators. From here, it's seven miles to Eureka.

As Alice Ramsey drove through this part of the state in 1909, she suddenly found a dozen Indians on horseback, bare from the waist up, riding parallel to her car with drawn bows and arrows. The riders turned toward the car, really frightening Alice and her three female companions, but then the men raced ahead, pursuing a rabbit.

The old mining town of **Eureka** supposedly was named for the cry upon the discovery of lead-silver ore. True or not, by the time Bellamy Partridge came through in 1912, he considered it a ghost town, the hotel appearing to be the only occupied building.

Eureka had been called the Pittsburgh of the West because of the heavy black smoke that filled the town from the lead smelters.

This theater and hotel, here in the mid-1950s, still overlook Eureka's Main Street.

RUSSELL REIN

Silver was discovered here in 1864, but the high lead content made it uneconomical to mine until 1869, when the first smelter was built. Eventually fifty mines were producing lead, silver, gold, and zinc. In 1878, Eureka had sixteen furnaces and ore refineries, and their need for charcoal consumed every tree for dozens of miles. David Toll wrote in *The Complete Nevada Traveler* that Eureka had "dozens of saloons, gambling houses and bawdy houses, three opera houses, two breweries, five volunteer firefighting companies, and two companies of militia." Production peaked in 1882, then rapidly declined.

Effie Gladding described her arrival here in 1914: "We were glad indeed when the lights of our lamps flashed on the stakes with their familiar red, white, and blue markings, the friendly signs of our beloved Lincoln Highway. It was nearly nine o'clock when we came into Eureka, and drew up at the dim lights of Brown's Hotel." The hotel restaurant had closed, so they went out to the only eatery open at nine at night, the Venezia, named for the hometown of its Italian proprietor. He and his wife also owned an adjacent hotel. There were no Italian dishes here; the travelers ate fried ham, buttered bread, and tea.

Gladding could tell that the glory days of mining had passed long ago: "Eureka is a most forlorn little town, perched high and dry. . . . As we walked along its silent and dimly lighted main street, we saw the quaint wooden porches in front of the shops and houses, some high, some low, making an uneven sidewalk. Practically all of the shops were closed, only the saloons being open."

Today Main Street is a mix of stores with many old and restored facades. With just

four-hundred-some residents, and only about twenty-one hundred cars taking U.S. Route 50 each day, according to the Department of Transportation, the street can be very quiet at times. In winter, antelope sometimes wander into town. That's why Eureka bills itself as the Loneliest Town on the Loneliest Road. Still, it does offer traveler amenities.

A fire in 1879 destroyed several buildings and accounts for the many surviving structures that were built in that period. The *Eureka Sentinel* building was rebuilt after the fire and now serves as a museum. The Eureka Opera House on Main Street dates to 1880. The Jackson House Hotel, built in 1877, was restored in the 1990s and again offers nine overnight rooms. Across from them is the red brick Eureka County Courthouse, built in 1879. Out front are two bells that served for fire alarms, a 1928 concrete marker, and a diminutive General Motors Section Monument. The small marker and plaque, moved from their original location southeast of town, commemorate twenty-two miles of Lincoln Highway built with GM funds in 1919. The World War II–era Owl Club Bar and Steak House, a dark saloon with deer racks on the wall, is a favorite food stop for locals.

One peculiarity is that the town had brick-lined tunnels, most since collapsed, to ensure beer deliveries from breweries to saloons on Main Street during winter. Children also used them to get to school.

The road from Eureka to Austin was sixty-nine miles, according to the 1915 LHA guide, but required five hours to drive it, with "some hard road, some gravel, a number of washes, some rough spots and some mountain grades." A contract was let in 1922 to improve just

The Eureka Hotel and Café, Eureka.

over twenty-one miles west of Eureka, which was nearly complete by 1924. Where the original and new roads rejoined, drivers encountered Devil's Gate, a tight fit in the Fish Creek Range.

Five sections funded by General Motors and Willys-Overland provided crucial links in central Nevada. Just east of Eureka, $100,000 improved a 21.7-mile stretch; immediately west of Eureka, $45,000 improved 5 miles; from Eastgate to Westgate, $105,000 improved 15 miles; west of Westgate through Frenchman's, $50,000 improved 5 miles; and from Sand Springs west toward Fallon, $125,000 improved 17.3 miles.

The 1913 Packard guide gave numerous warnings between Eureka and Austin of dangerous descents and creeks to cross. The 1915 and 1916 LHA guides had no listings at all.

Finally, the 1918 guide listed some outposts, and the 1924 had even more. **Rigley Ranch**, about thirteen miles west of Eureka, had meals, lodging, and camping. (The 1924 guide had the **Hay Ranch** here.) Twenty-one miles further was **The Willows**, offering nothing but water. The 1924 guide warned that to the west were "some stiff hills . . . be sure your radiator is full." It was six more miles to **Grimes Ranch**; its 1918 listing of "meals, if necessary" was hardly inviting. The 1924 guide warned not to depend on getting water from Floyd Grimes: "He frequently has to haul water for the ranch and may be low."

The road crossed the Monitor and Toquima Ranges, though at much lower elevations than the summits to the south. Effie Gladding met up with two female drivers who warned of a mud hole that her party was bound to hit in Monitor Valley, west of the Monitor Range. "They cheered us, however, by telling us that a nearby settler had a sturdy draught horse and that he would in all probability pull us out for the sum of $2.00 a motor car." Sure enough, when they came upon the morass, the adjacent land was too spongy to go around.

Meanwhile, the farmer, "working with his wife and baby near at hand in his newly cleared field, kept an eye on us." The Gladdings and a Ford traveling with them sank immediately. "After a little pleasant dickering he agreed to pull the machines out for $1.00 apiece." The farmer and his family had just recently arrived and were only living in a small tent, but the farmer said he'd never seen richer land than that which he'd just cleared of sagebrush. Gladding was "secretly glad" that the farmer had the chance to earn extra money . . . but not enough to pay him his asking price.

As the road heads west, white sage and purple stinkweed dot the landscape, and it's not uncommon to see dust devils of all sizes. The original Lincoln Highway branched south, while the 1920s route stays with U.S. Route 50. About ten miles west of Floyd Grimes Ranch on the original route was "Ford's Defeat," named for the cars that had to be hauled by horses over the four-mile-long climb. The new route on lower grades was built in the early 1920s, topping Hickison Summit at 6,564 feet. To the north on the newer road is the Hickison Petroglyph Recreation Area, a walking trail with dozens of petroglyphs in sandstone. It's just north of U.S. 50, where the 1920s route briefly separates.

The road generations rejoin and make some hairpin turns on the way to the 7,484 foot-high **Austin Summit**. The road also has entered another portion of Humboldt-Toiyabe National Forest. A couple miles later is **Austin**, some seventy miles from Eureka

Everyone puts a dollar on the wall at the International Hotel's cafe and saloon in Austin.

and just twelve miles from the state's geographic center.

Austin, named for the Texas hometown of one of its founders, is among the oldest of the state's mining towns. Silver is said to have been discovered when a Pony Express rider knocked a stone off a metal-rich cavern. The population jumped to ten thousand, but the lode played out after ten years. Most of the surrounding towns it spawned have become ghost towns.

As in Eureka, U.S. Route 50/Main Street passes through Austin on a slope. Also as in Eureka, the street can sometimes be very quiet; even more so, as Austin has about 250 residents to Eureka's 400. The 1915 guide lists three hotels: the International, the Hogan, and the Silver State. The speed limit then was six miles per hour.

The International Hotel is one of the oldest buildings in the state. It was dismantled in Virginia City and moved the hundred miles by wagon. It opened here in 1863. "Hotel" has been dropped from its name and it no longer rents rooms, but food and drinks are still served through its swinging doors. The International was a Control Station on the Lincoln Highway, and proprietor William Easton was an LHA consul. Effie Gladding stopped here for lunch in 1914, reporting "a good luncheon prepared by a Japanese cook and served by a natty and very debonair Japanese waiter." James Montgomery Flagg spent a number of pages detailing the hotel in his 1925 book, *Boulevards All the Way–Maybe.*

Bernard Queneau and his three companions spent the night of August 4, 1928, in Austin. He wrote in his diary, "After eating a terrible canned cow breakfast at the cafe, we left at 9:30."

On U.S. Route 50 are the Lincoln Motel and the 1920s Austin Garage, with a gable front. On a hill at the far end of town is the three-story, stone-slab **Stokes Castle**, built in 1897 by two brothers named Stokes, who invested in local silver mines. They only lived here for a month, and it has been empty since. The first floor contained a kitchen and dining room, the second floor a living room and bath, and the third floor bedrooms and another bath. Balconies on the upper floors have disappeared, as has much of the building. To reach it, take Castle Road south from U.S. 50 about a quarter mile.

It's a long one hundred miles from Austin to Fallon, the next major town. The 1915 guide warned of a number of washes, two alkali flats, and cut-up roads as a result of the double teaming of ore wagons. The 1918 guide described the road as "fair to good natural gravel [with] some chuck holes and short bad spots." James Montgomery Flagg found it made for "a nerve twisting afternoon thro mountains and deserts, seeing few cars. The ruts were so deep we had to drive a little to the right or left of them to in order not to scrape the poor car's abdomen entirely off. Between the ruts was a continuous deep line about two inches wide that I discovered was the trail of the crank case nut of many cars!"

In 1920, LHA directors donated $44,500 to the state to either improve the sixty miles to Eastgate or build a new road to the south over Carroll Summit. The latter option was chosen, and work began in 1924. Today, about a mile west of Austin, three roads diverge: U.S. Route 50 goes straight west, the original Lincoln Highway goes to the right, and the 1920s Lincoln Highway (NV Route 722) goes to the left.

The original road, which rejoins and mostly follows U.S. Route 50, went twenty-six miles to New Pass, at 6,348 feet, and then through **New Pass Canyon**, also called Devil's Gate. It was another twenty miles to **Alpine** or **Shoshone Indian Ranch**, then another dozen miles to Eastgate. Effie Gladding stopped for the night at Alpine Ranch, marked by tall cottonwood trees. She was told it was "part of the big Williams estate," run by a Mr. and Mrs. Dudley. She wrote:

> We ate our supper at a long table filled with ranchmen, and took part in an animated conversation on the merits of the present Administration. . . . The master of the ranch told us something of his difficulty in keeping men steadily at work on the ranch. He said that they came and went constantly in spite of good pay, steady work, and kindly treatment.

The problem was chalked up to western wanderlust. And indeed it was named the Williams Ranch in the 1913 Packard guide.

The original route passes numerous Overland Stage stations. The 1925 bypass over Carroll Summit (elevation 7,452) was itself bypassed around 1960, when the original route was rebuilt for U.S. 50. Carroll Summit Road (now marked NV Route 722)—sometimes straight for miles, other times twisting—has hardly changed over the decades: The Nevada-Sierra Chapter of the LHA has proposed that it be designated a Scenic Byway. One of the few structures along the 1920s road is the long-abandoned Carroll Summit Texaco, a deteriorating frame building with a hip roof. A mile to the west, the 1920s Lincoln makes a horseshoe curve, and seven miles later, the road cut through tall cliffs

Eastgate Ranch in busier days.

to arrive at **Eastgate**, then also known as Williams Ranch and part of the large estate owned by a state senator.

Eastgate is the western junction of the original Lincoln Highway over New Pass and the 1925 route over Carroll Summit (NV Route 722). The state's WPA guide has numerous stories about Eastgate's history. One tale was of local buckaroos staging a fictitious murder and lynching, then stringing up the culprit not for the killing, but for rustling cattle, all to teach easterners what they considered the worse offense. The buildings were made of tufa, a soft rock quarried just four miles to the west. Today the remains of some guest cottages survive.

U.S. Route 50 and the original Lincoln Highway split just north of Eastgate; U.S. 50 cuts to the southwest, bypassing the old ranch. It rejoins NV Route 722 five miles west of Eastgate. In between, on NV Route 722, is the Buffalo Creek Bridge, a reinforced-concrete span. A mile west of where the routes rejoin is the famed Shoe Tree, a huge cottonwood with as many shoes as leaves. Russ and Fredda Stevensen, owners of the Middlegate Station bar, restaurant, and minimart, two miles to the

west, played a role in the Shoe Tree's story. A newlywed's spat a few years ago led to the first shoes being thrown in the tree; the Stevensens helped the couple get back together and get on their way. Since then, tossing shoes into the tree has become a tradition. The original Middlegate Pony Express and Overland station was across from the tree.

Middlegate is now two miles west, at NV Route 361. This former Overland Stage station is also a century old. It is along the original Lincoln Highway, which runs a quarter mile south of U.S. Route 50. The Stevensens have owned the former station since 1984, welcoming cowboys, miners, aviators, and travelers alike. They also run a small motel. The 1915 LHA guide noted that Eastgate offered meals, lodging, gas, and camping, but that Middlegate was deserted.

U.S. Route 50 overlays an improvement built in 1924 between Eastgate and Westgate. The original Lincoln rejoins U.S. 50 here. In the 1915 guide, **Westgate** had meals, gas, and camping—no lodging but it *did* have a telephone. It also was a former Overland Stage station; it later became a Civilian Conservation

RUSSELL REIN

The Pony Express Stop at Eastgate Station was one of the original overland mail outposts.

Until it reaches Fallon, Highway 50 cuts through what Nevada natives like to call Real Nevada. In Real Nevada, the range is still open, the air is pure and the cattle graze right out on the highway. During windstorms, the sky can become so choked with dust that the only thing a traveler can do is park his car on the highway and wait until it stops.

–Jim Lilliefors,
Highway 50: Ain't
That America *(1993)*

Corps camp. The three "gate" names derive from the 1859 survey of the route by Capt. James Simpson, who referred to mountain passes as "gates."

The 1918 guide gave multiple warnings that travelers between Westgate and Fallon should top off their radiators and carry extra water. More importantly, it should have warned that the road west of Frenchman's Flat was among the worst sections along the entire highway. The route from Westgate to Fallon was even changed for a number of years to bypass the mud and sand. The 1918 LHA guide explained that late in 1916, the LHA chose to move the highway north through **Stillwater**. The new route, three miles longer, was itself winding and little improved but "vastly better than the old sink route which was always very much cut up due to heavy teaming of ore and supplies." The main route was finally improved in 1922 with partial funding by the LHA through donations made by General Motors.

In the middle of Dixie Valley, a reminder that you're not really in the Old West is the sound of jets overhead using the Fallon Naval

Target Range, situated on both sides of the road. This is where travelers once found gas, food, lodging, and a telephone, at **Frenchman's Station** or Bermond's Ranch, just a dozen miles from Westgate. Effie Gladding wrote, "We passed Frenchman's Flat, where there was a little restaurant and where a Frenchman came out to pass the time of day." By 1924, the LHA guide was boasting, "This was originally a freighters' station, but M. Bermond (the 'Frenchman') the proprietor, has built and fitted up splendid rooms, and will serve such a meal as you might expect on Fifth Ave. in New York." No longer will you find such elegance: The Fallon Naval Air Station purchased the surrounding flats for its target range and demolished the old roadhouse.

The highway tops the Silver Range of the Stillwater Mountains, then drops back down to **Sand Springs**, an old stopover. Effie Gladding described Sand Springs as "simply a lodging place for the teamsters and their horses for the night. We could look down from the plateau on which the little house and the barns stood, upon the white and clay-colored, desolate spaces of the salty val-

ley below. The landlady welcomed us cordially and gave us a plain but hearty lunch."

The Carson Desert loomed ahead, and the road passed right through a white morass, not unlike the Great Salt Lake Desert, which came to be called the Fallon Sink. When Effie Gladding came through in 1914, heavy rains had wrecked the road. Wagons piled high with bales and boxes had to be pulled by up to sixteen horses and mules, their bodies caked with mud. Gladding kept "well to the left of a long stretch filled with salt water holes and with a fairly large salt lake. A new road had been made by travelers, far away from the regular road, which ran close to this small inland sea and which was a hopeless quagmire."

The LHA had long lobbied for an improved road, but things were kick-started after William Durant, vice president and general manager of General Motors, drove from New York to Oakland. GM had a plant along the route in Oakland, and Durant's son, R. C., was chairman of the Lincoln Highway Committee of the Oakland Chamber of Commerce. The chamber, Oakland Commercial Club, and LHA hosted a Lincoln Highway Fiesta on November 12, 1916, to raise money for fixing the Fallon Sink. They made a mock sink along their portion of the Lincoln Highway using mud and soap; when motorists slowed to avoid it, "Lincoln Highway Girls" asked for a $1 donation, and in return, they'd get a Lincoln Highway Flag that said, "I helped build the road over the Fallon Sink." More than eighteen thousand cars were stopped, for a take of $11,000. Durant also contributed $100,000 to improve the sink and nearby portions. The new twenty-foot-

Looking west at Frenchman's Station, 1922.

SPECIAL COLLECTIONS LIBRARY, UNIVERSITY OF MICHIGAN

wide road was built up three feet above the alkali flats and topped with five inches of gravel.

Bellamy Partridge wrote that in 1912, he crossed the sink just fine on chunks of lava that had been laid on the road, but then he got lost west of it in the tire tracks spreading out from workers on a nearby irrigation project:

I stopped at the cabin of a forest ranger to ask directions. He gave them with numerous turnings right and left to take us over the ditches. We went on for a while but did not seem to be getting anywhere. Then I happened to see another ranger's cabin. I drew up in front—and out came the same man. There were no signs of recognition between us. I asked the same question. He gave the same answer, being too well mannered to humiliate me.

I would probably have driven away and, likely as not, would have come back again. But my wife leaned out and handed him an envelope. "Would you please write it down?" she asked pleasantly.

Today you've got help by the side of the road. The solar-powered "Loneliest Phone on the Loneliest Road in America" can be found at a right turn that leads to Sand Mountain, a high ridge known for its "singing." When the wind blows, the shifting mixture of minerals makes a deep booming or humming sound (though today the singing competes with the buzz of dune buggies). Nearby are the remnants of the Sand Springs Pony Express Station. The Bureau of Land Management now operates it as an interpretive site.

Ahead is **Salt Wells** where a refinery processed deposits from the surrounding salt flat. The salt was more than 98 percent pure, but its isolation led to the concern's demise.

The 1916 guide also listed a ranch and saloon. At Grimes Point Historic Site and Hidden Cave, eleven miles east of Fallon on the north side, petroglyphs date back eight thousand years, and you can walk a trail past hundreds of the etched images in the rocks. Nevada was once under Lake Lahontan, and this would have been the beach. You can see the various water levels carved into the hills above the cave.

After so much barren land, **Fallon**, one of Nevada's larger towns, is an oasis, sporting casinos, strip malls, and chain stores unseen for many miles. It's also the site of the Fallon Naval Air Station, east of town, most famous for its "Top Gun" pilot-training program.

U.S. Route 50 enters Fallon on Williams Avenue, but the original Lincoln Highway breaks away from U.S. 50 and jogs in from a few blocks to the south. At least one part, Wildes Road, is overlain by the Fallon Naval Air Station. **Grimes Ranch** (not to be confused with the Grimes Ranch near Ford's Defeat) was a regular stop, but by 1924, the owners were no longer offering accommodations. It was immediately southeast of the air station; a private home, it became the May Ranch, but has since been acquired by the air station and serves as the residence of the station commander.

From 1918 to 1924, the Lincoln east of town strayed to the north, then entered on U.S. Route 50/Williams Avenue. In 1924, the Lincoln was switched back to a southern entrance, nearly identical to the original, which included Harrigan Road, Stillwater Avenue, and Center Street. In late 2004, Center Street was getting a makeover, with ornamental lightpoles, benches, and trees, as

well as plans for markers noting its place on the Lincoln Highway.

First called Jim Town for an early settler, Fallon was renamed when Mike and Eliza Fallon built a store and post office on their ranch in 1896. The 1908 completion of the Truckee-Carson Irrigation Project brought water to the region and spurred settlement. Alfalfa is the main crop, but 'Hearts of Gold' cantaloupes were popular enough to inspire an annual Cantaloupe Festival. The water comes from two rivers, which then feed two dams, one of which—the Lahontan—is ahead on the Lincoln Highway's Pioneer Branch. The naval air station was opened during World War II and also helped the local economy. In 1958, it was dedicated to Lt. Cdr. Bruce Van Voorhis, local Medal of Honor navy pilot. Its fourteen-thousand-foot runway is the navy's longest.

The town was laid out with a wide main street, which today has some casinos and a wood-frame 1903 courthouse that is on the National Register of Historic Places and still in use. The Churchill County Museum, in an old Safeway supermarket at 1050 South Maine Street, calls itself "the Best Little Museum on the Loneliest Road in America." It includes "tales of emigrants crossing the dreaded 40-Mile Desert in the 1850s" and has a 1928 concrete Lincoln Highway marker. The Roper Drive-In Theater was opened in 1954 by a sheep rancher; it lasted until 1978, and its screen stood until 2004. The Overland Hotel was used by LHA officials during the 1915 Motion Picture Caravan and by the 1919 First Transcontinental Army Truck Convoy. Owner George Machado spent three years restoring the hotel back to its 1908 glory, culminating in its addition to the Nevada Register of His-

GOD
BLESS
AMERICA

The Lariat Motel in Fallon sports an amusing neon sign.

toric Places in 1999. It has a restaurant and saloon, and seventeen guest rooms upstairs. Machado still wants to rebuild the balcony that once sat atop ornamental columns in front of the building.

The Lariat Motel, U.S. Route 50/850 West Williams Avenue, has one of the best neon signs in the state: a horse-mounted cowboy swinging a lariat. Bob's Root Beer Stand, also on U.S. 50, has a root beer mug–shaped sign.

The road continues west, following today's U.S. 50. Ten miles from downtown was the deserted town of **Leeteville**, once a resort oasis to wagon trains but reduced to a lone farmhouse by the 1924 LHA guide. The Lincoln Highway splits here. The northern (Donner) route, now U.S. Route 50 Alt., meets I-80 and heads to Reno. Starting in 1921, the southern (Pioneer) route split away here, generally following U.S. 50 southwest toward Carson City. For modern travelers, both branches qualify as great Lincoln Highway routes. As John T. Faris wrote in his 1931 *Roaming American Highways*, "Now it is so difficult to choose between the routes that a wise man takes both."

IIIa. West of Fallon to California via Reno

The 1918 LHA guide mentioned that a road went southwest to the Lahontan Dam and then on to Carson City. It was not yet an official route, but it was said to trim thirty-one miles from the trip. By the 1924 LHA guide, it not only had become part of the Pioneer Branch, but was now the preferred Lincoln Highway route. Directions via Reno were moved to the back of the book.

Until then, all Lincoln Highway travelers headed northwest to **Hazen**, which began as a railroad junction and became a small trading center for ranchers. The 1918 guide recommended that tourists visit a large sampling plant where ores were separated. The road passed just north of the Truckee-Carson Irrigation Project, which was damming water from the Truckee and Carson Rivers to irrigate the dry land.

It was in this area that Effie Gladding stopped for lunch in June 1914 and captured a slice of life quite different from our romantic view of earning a living from the road:

> We stopped at a little roadside place where there was a small grocery next to a tiny dwelling, to ask for some luncheon. The groceryman was very dubious and noncommittal and referred us to his wife. I had noticed that at our approach she fled to some improvised chicken coops back of the little dwelling. So I tracked her to her lair and found the poor little thing really standing at bay. She was a small woman, overshadowed by an immense Mexican straw hat. She said to me somewhat defiantly and almost tearfully that she couldn't possibly do another drop of work. She explained that she had the railroad men to care for when they came in from the road, and that

she had two hundred chickens to look after. . . . I looked around at the hot, dusty little settlement, with no spear of grass, and felt sorry for her.

The modern highway skirts south of Hazen, past the Hazen Market. The store opened in the 1930s on the original route through town, but was relocated in 1944 when a bypass was built. A neon sign has hung above the gas pump canopy since 1949, and a sign next to the door calls the place "a lighthouse in the desert." It is listed on the National Register of Historic Places.

A few miles west of Hazen, the Lincoln Highway bears left away from U.S. Route 50 Alt. The roads head west, parallel but a mile apart, to **Fernley**, where the Victory Highway came south to rejoin the Lincoln. Today I-80 does the same. As the original road stair-steps into town, it passes a new Lincoln Highway monument—a cut-stone base with a narrative plaque, topped by a 1928 concrete post head. Just a couple miles northwest is **Wadsworth**.

LINCOLN HIGHWAY
HAZEN 6.5 Miles
FALLON 21.7 "
AUSTIN 137.1 "
ELY 263.2 "
SALT LAKE 568.1 "

Henry Joy points to a directional sign west of Hazen, 1915.

James Montgomery Flagg, driving eastbound in 1924, had heard of the highway split and inquired here about which road to take. "The clerk told me that the two trails, the Lincoln Highway and the Victory, were a toss-up," he wrote, "the only advantage being better hotel accommodations on the Victory! That little word ONLY was the catch. His information was false—worse than that—criminal."

Flagg learned this firsthand by taking the Lincoln Highway's competitor: "The Victory began immediately to be the worst trail in the world and kept on getting more so every mile we crawled. . . . It wasn't driving—it was crawling and straining, slipping, boiling over and using up the precious water in the desert bags. . . . We had to pass over a wide, dead, alkali lake that was splotched with poisonous green scum." Finally, they met a party coming west, who told them, "'No matter how bad the road you have just come over, no matter what you have been told about this being the best way, turn back!" Among this other party's woes was that in Winnamucca, they had been forced to give the hotel manager the water from their desert bags to cook their dinner.

That was enough for Flagg. He turned around—of course, getting stuck in the sand and needing to be towed—and headed back to the Lincoln Highway. They arrived hours later and stopped at a shack selling gas and soft drinks: "I sat down on the running board and gazed through dust-caked eyelashes and with depressed spirits at the most miserable collection of hovels that ever had the impudence to don a resounding name like Wadsworth." The owner of the soft-drink shack cheered him: "He said if I would take the Lincoln Highway (very bad for a few miles) it would bring

me to a real road into Fallon within a short time." It must have been true—Flagg's next sentence described the hotel at Fallon. As Flagg departed around 6 A.M. the next morning, Fallon's only reporter ran after him to ask about his trip.

Flagg afterward wrote to the LHA about his troubles, and LHA vice president Austin Bement responded:

The Lincoln Highway this year is in the worst condition in Nevada I have ever seen it. This is due primarily to the many sections of road under construction, the new grade in many places cutting the old trail and while the work is going on, making both practically impassable. I noted the same situation of which you speak; i.e., the lack of adequate markers along the Lincoln Way in Nevada. I am glad to say arrangements have been completed with the California State Automobile Association for a complete new marking of the route this fall and early next spring.

A couple years later, the Victory Highway edition of the *Mohawk-Hobbs Grade and Surface Guide* stated, in numerous ways, that the Victory was "the best and fastest route" between Salt Lake City and the coast. The company didn't even publish a guide to the Lincoln Highway west of Salt Lake City.

At Wadsworth, NV Route 447 heads north to Pyramid Lake, the state's largest natural lake and source of the Truckee River. The surrounding land was home to the Paiute Indian tribe and has been a reservation since 1874.

The Lincoln Highway follows the Truckee River and I-80 westward. The original road winds around or is subsumed by the interstate. Two dozen miles later is the interchange for **Vista**. Alice Ramsey found the name appropri-

It was a quarter past two in the afternoon when I left Reno . . . toward Wadsworth and the great Nevada desert. For about 18 miles the road was fair, and then it began to get sandy. Sand in Nevada means stuff in which you sink up to your ankles every time you attempt to take a step. To further enliven matters, it began to rain. Every now and then I had to dismount and walk for a stretch of a quarter of a mile. Several times the soft sand threw me because I did not respect it enough to dismount in time. A bicycle with a six horsepower motor could not get through such sand. The wheel just swings out from under, and the faster you try to go the worse it is. Walking and riding. I managed, however, to make the 36 miles from Reno to Wadsworth in four hours, and there I pitched camp for the night.

—George A. Wyman, "Across America on a Motor Bicycle,"
The Motor Cycle (1903)

ate when approaching Sparks in 1909: "I think I shall never forget the surprise of that vista bursting upon us in the darkness. Here was a hollow in which lay a community brilliantly lighted with electricity!"

Just east of Reno, Thornton Round and his family stopped in 1914 when they came upon a miner walking his burden-laden donkey. When they asked where he was going, Round wrote, "He snapped back at us with, 'Back in the hills, you young scalawags. Now get along with yah, or you'll scare my animal, and if he runs away I'll lose everything I got in the world.' We went on, sorry that we had attempted a conversation in the first place." A mile later, their Ford got a flat, and soon the miner caught up: "'I allus knowned them high-falutin, fan-dangled things would make a heap of trouble. Get a mule like mine so's you'll be sure to get whare you wanta go.'" They fixed their tire and left the miner behind, only to have a horseshoe puncture a tire a mile later. This time, the miner just watched, then told the mule, "'You might have to pull

this here contraption to the city so these folks can get the darned thing fixed.'" They finally departed, by then on friendly terms.

The state's WPA guide noted that a growing industry in this area was the raising of wild game, such as pheasant, for hunting ranges. A local delicacy was stuffed bird: "When the waiter removes a large silver service cover he brings into view two birds erect in a field of wild rice. The meat has been cooked and cleverly inserted into the original skin without disarranging a single feather."

The Lincoln Highway turned southwest, running close to today's I-80 and never far from the railroad. Just west of Sparks, the 1913 Lincoln crossed to the south side of the tracks, bypassing that town to instead go through **Glendale**. It crossed back north just before present-day U.S. Route 395, then turned left

The Farris Motel, built in 1949 at 1752 East 4th Street, retains an interesting tower above the office entrance.

Cremer's Auto Court, built in the early 1930s at 2406 Prater Way in Sparks, became an annex of the famous Harold's Club in 1951 and was renamed the Pony Express Motel. It can be spotted by this fabulous neon sign.

(west) on Prater Way. By 1915, the LHA guide listed **Sparks**. Researcher Leon Schegg believes that the Lincoln was rerouted to cross the tracks back at Standard Way in Glendale, then turned left (west) on B Street (now Victorian Way), then right (north) on 15th Street, and a few blocks later went left on Prater Way, the main street through Sparks.

The old cabin camps, such as Coney Island and Twin City Cottage Camp, are long gone, but many classic motels with neon signs line the road here and into Reno; in fact, the divide between the two towns is hard to discern. Toward the east end is the Rancho Sierra Motel. At 2406 Prater Way, Keshmiri's Pony Express Lodge has a large neon sign from the early 1950s with a horseback-riding Indian chasing a cowboy. The motel was founded in the early 1930s as Cremer's Auto Court, then was renamed in 1951 when it became an annex of the famed Harold's Club. At 1500 Prater Way, the Park Motel has had a neon sign topped by a waving bellboy since 1947. At 1356 Prater Way, Scoopers Drive-In restaurant opened in 1961 as an A&W Root Beer stand. Just to the north, near the municipal line, the El Rancho Drive-In Theater opened in 1950 and has grown to four screens.

The Lincoln Highway becomes 4th Street upon crossing into **Reno**. 4th Street hosted both the Lincoln and Victory Highways. U.S. Route 40 later followed it through town, as Business I-80 still does. Auto-related businesses grew here early and often; by the end

The Sandman, 1755 East 4th Street, at twilight.

of the 1930s, the WPA guide counted eighty-nine hotels plus apartments and auto courts.

East 4th is still lined with vintage businesses; Casale's Halfway Club, a 1937 gas station and roadhouse at 2501 East 4th Street, was considered halfway between Sparks and Reno. The Restwell Auto camp was in the same block, but only the sign remains.

The 1750 block has the Everbody's Inn and Highway 40 Motel, the Farris (with wedding cake–style entrance pylon), and the well-known Sandman, with a neon sign topped by a little car. The rooms are right out of 1950, with rabbit-ear TV antennas and no phones.

Also on East 4th Street are the 1951 Sutro Motel, at 1200; Alturus Bar, at 1044; Abby's Highway 40 Bar and the Morris Hotel, built in 1929 and still sporting nice signs, in the 400 block; the Marion Motel, opened as a rooming house in 1908, at 306; and the Lincoln Hotel, opened in 1922 and now housing Louis' Basque Corner restaurant, at 301. A pole on the street corner once held an early traffic-regulation device: a horn.

In the mid-nineteenth century, what is now the Reno area was home to Washoe and Paiute tribes. It was known as the Truckee Meadows, named for the Indian who directed the Stephens Party out of the Humboldt Sink in 1844. The grassy land along the river became a welcome camping area for overland travelers, and it was here that the Donner party stayed perhaps one day too many before climbing the Sierra Nevada. The town grew with the nearby silver boom and as a Central Pacific Railroad depot. It was named in 1868 for fallen Civil War general Jesse Reno. One of its early settlers, M. C. Lake, had a trading post and kept rebuilding and enlarging until his florid Riverside Hotel was ready when Lincoln Highway traffic came to town. After it burned in 1922, an even larger hotel by the same name replaced it. The Nevada Historical Society Museum, the state's oldest museum, is at 1650 North Virginia Street.

The divorce trade boomed after a 1906 scandal publicized that the residency requirement was only six months, short at the time. Business grew as the period was trimmed to three months in 1927, and then six weeks in 1931, to undercut other states competing for the migratory industry.

Bellamy Partridge wrote that in 1912, he rescued a car of four women stuck at a rail crossing just outside Reno. When telling a garage man later, he was told that they were divorcées waiting out their time: "'They get restless around here. Try to go somewhere every day and usually get stuck.'" James Montgomery Flagg likewise made a crack about divorcées. As for the town, he wrote, "Reno is a mean little dump and the Hotel Golden—oh, mama mia!"

At midtown, 4th Street intersects Virginia Street, the main commercial street going south. The National Bowling Stadium, just southeast of the intersection, fills an entire block, soars six stories high, and cost almost $50 million. Its eighty lanes are used strictly for pro and amateur tournaments. It has a 450-foot-long scoring system, a 16-square-foot video wall for instant replays, and seats for twelve hundred spectators. As if its size weren't enough

Louis' Basque Corner, 301 East 4th Street, is in the Lincoln Hotel, built in 1922.

to make it stand out, the stadium is topped by an IMAX theater in a giant silver geodesic dome shaped like a bowling ball.

The Lincoln Highway stepped south to 3rd Street to head west, though it's likely many travelers stayed on 4th, which bent southward after about ten blocks, subsuming 3rd. From 1923 to 1926, the route went south on Virginia Street a few blocks and turned west on 1st Street, then took Riverside Drive and Mayberry Avenue/Drive. In between these two routes west, the West 2nd Street Filling Station is a cottage-style station with a canopy overhang and a Mobilgas pump out front. At 411 West 4th Street is the Spanish Mission–meets–Modern style Rancho Sierra Motel from about 1950.

Reno was as popular for quickie marriages as for its divorce trade. At 600 West 4th is the Candlelight Wedding Chapel, owned and operated in the same location by John Foulk since 1969. A block later is the Chapel of the Bells, a 1940 restaurant converted to its pres-

West of downtown Reno, the Candlelight Wedding Chapel at 600 West 4th Street can satisfy anyone's quickie marriage needs.

SILVER STATE LODGE — RENO, NEVADA

Half Mile West of Business District - On U. S. 40

The Silver State, built in 1927, was a popular retreat for those awaiting a divorce. The sixteen cabins served as low-income housing until 2003, when they were bulldozed.

These distinctive rails from a little bridge were saved and moved to a pull-off along I-80 at Mogul.

ent use in 1960. They supply music, clothing, flowers, even a witness. Why are such weddings still so popular? Not only does it feel spontaneous and a bit mischievous, but neither blood tests nor a waiting period is required for couples of at least eighteen years of age. As long as they appear at the Marriage License Bureau in either Reno or Incline Village and have a ceremony performed at a wedding chapel or church, it is a legal marriage.

At 1791 West 4th, the Silver State Lodge was built in 1927 specifically for those sitting out their divorce waiting period, but the log cabins were also popular with Lincoln Highway travelers. Despite efforts by the preservation community to save one of the most original sites of Reno's early-twentieth-century divorce industry, the log cabins were demolished in 2003.

On the west end of town, along the south bank of the Truckee River, is Idlewild Park, created for the Transcontinental Highway Exposition of 1927 to celebrate the completion of the Lincoln and Victory Highways. The Mission Revival style California Building was a gift from the neighboring state; now operated by the city as a recreational facility, it is the lone architectural remnant of the exposition. The park also has small roller coasters, a miniature train, bumper boats, a large play area and pool, picnic benches with barbecues, and a rose garden. A lighted street arch was

built for the festivities as well. It wasn't the city's first arch, but it became its most famous when a contest was held to add a slogan. A $100 prize went to the creator of "Reno: Biggest Little City in the World." Ceremonial lighting took place on June 25, 1929. When a newer sign displaced this one, it was moved back to Idlewild Park and eventually to storage. After being restored for the 1994 film *Cobb*, public sentiment helped get it placed on Lake Street near the National Automobile Museum (more on the arch and museum follow on the next page).

The route west to Donner Pass was trod by overland emigrants following the Truckee River. Two miles west of town was a cut through rock. Some three miles farther was **Laughton's Springs** (changed about 1915 to Lawton Hot Springs or just **Lawton**), a resort that became a popular training outpost for prizefighters preparing for matches in Reno. Here the 1923–26 route rejoined from the south.

For the next mile, the road squeezed through a narrow passage along with I-80, old U.S. Route 40, and the Southern Pacific tracks at **Mogul**. It also crossed a tiny branch of the Truckee, but early in 1914, a storm washed out the bridge. Washoe County, said to be lagging in marking the route, planned a box culvert replacement that would be the first concrete bridge on the entire Lincoln Highway. Contractor A. F. Niedt, aware of the criticism and wanting to make this stand out, designed the bridge to spell "Lincoln" on one rail and "Highway" on the other. That April, LHA consul H. E. Frederickson saw the new bridge and was so impressed that he proposed all Lincoln Highway bridges be made so. They weren't, but this one's precious rails

CAROL INGALD

CAROL INGALD

were moved to the interstate for safekeeping in the 1970s by forward-thinking locals and the Nevada Department of Transportation. They're at an eastbound pull-off along I-80, just east of Exit 6, about a mile west of the original culvert (which still exists). Guard posts were recently added to each end to protect the rails from being hit when snow piles up.

The Lincoln Highway branches to the north toward **Verdi**, generally following the current entrance into town from I-80. The town was named for Italian composer Guisseppe Verdi, but could easily have been named for the landscape's change to green as sagebrush is replaced by pine trees. Road and rail improvements have erased much of the Lincoln, but entering Verdi from the east, the road is known to stay south of the railroad while U.S. Route 40 ran parallel a few blocks to the north. Once in town, the Lincoln turns right on Bridge Street, which becomes Dog Valley road, then at the state line changes to Henness Pass Road. The Lincoln Highway followed this route into California and Dog Valley until 1926.

In 1919, when improvements were being planned for the Dog Valley route, locals and LHA consuls began pressing for a flatter, more direct route to follow the Truckee River. After years of debate and construction, the Lincoln was rerouted via Truckee River Road (now NV Route 425 from Dog Valley Road west). The governors of both California and Nevada attended its dedication on June 10, 1926. U.S. Route 40 later followed the same course, as I-80 does now. Road fans will like the Truckee River Arch Bridge, a reinforced concrete-arch bridge across the Truckee River just east of the state line.

IIIb. Original Pioneer Branch from Reno to Carson City

LHA directors always promoted the straightest route without diversions, but one exception existed from the start: the Pioneer Branch. The 1915 LHA guidebook listed it as a more scenic alternative to the "main" road over Donner Pass and through Truckee. Its original incarnation turned south in Reno at 4th Street and Virginia Street; headed to Carson City, around Lake Tahoe, and through Placerville, California; and rejoined the "main" Lincoln in Sacramento. In 1921, the branch was shortened to avoid Reno altogether by diverging from the Lincoln west of Fallon and connecting to Carson City. That routing soon was christened U.S. Route 50.

In Reno, Virginia Street is lined with casinos, such as the Eldorado, Fitzgerald's, Harold's Club, and Silver Legacy. The downtown feels like a smaller and more walkable version of Las Vegas, also retaining more vintage neon. Older motels on Virginia include the Co-Ed Lodge, the Savoy Motel, the Heart o' Town Motel, and the Ho Hum Motel farther south. The best-known landmark is the welcome arch, which says in neon, "The Biggest Little City in the World." The city's first arch was built in 1926, spanning Virginia Street in various styles until 1963, when it was replaced. The 1963 replacement was sold to Willits, California, in 1990. The current arch was built in 1987.

The state's WPA guide went out of its way to say that gambling and the divorce trade were just small parts of Reno's many offerings, and that there was more to the town than its "Christmas tree" appearance at night from the neon-lit nightclubs. Edward D. Dunn saw the town somewhat differently in his 1933 book,

Looking south on Reno's Virginia Street.

Double-Crossing America by Motor: "Unlike the suave, luxurious ease of Monte Carlo and Cannes, the open gambling rooms are bare and grim. . . . Guns, knives, desperation, are sensed everywhere."

The southeast part of Reno was an industrial area in 1913, and Virginia Street (Business U.S. Route 395) was the main road south. It crosses the Truckee River; the concrete arch bridge was a favorite spot for the newly divorced to toss their wedding rings. Overlooking the water was the Riverside Hotel. Today a River Walk lines the Truckee. The National Automobile Museum, just south of the Truckee River on Lake Street, holds hundreds of cars, including the William Harrah collection, some displayed in period streetscapes. Among them are the 1907 Thomas Flyer that won the New York–to–Paris race.

A 1923 auto dealership survives in the 600 block. The 1200 block of Virginia Street, built in 1946 in Art Moderne style, has columns of green tile between each unit.

A block south and a year later, "Landrum's Hamburger System No. 1" was delivered by rail from Valentine Manufacturing in Wichita,

AUG. 3, 1960
Virginia Street, Nev.

Dear Bill,
We're just now recuperating from travelling across the Salt Desert last nite—from 6:15 PM to 6:15 AM!
Yours, Judy

By the 1990s, Landrum's had become the Chili Cheez Café, which didn't last long. In 1999, the little Valentine-brand diner was converted to an auto title loan business and painted an overwhelming green.

Kansas. It was the diner company's smallest model—a Little Chef—with only eight stools. The diner's name was an attempt to emulate such chains as White Tower, for which Valentine also made fifteen prefabs. The Art Moderne lines and two-color porcelain enamel exterior helped get it listed on the National Register of Historic Places in 1998, but in 1999, the interior was stripped for conversion to an auto title loan business. Landrum's chain expanded only once: Landrum's Hamburger System #2, on South Rock Boulevard in Sparks, was built to look just like the real Valentine-brand diner in Reno; it survives, looking more like a real diner than the original.

The two-screen Midway Drive-In Theater was located at 2995 South Virginia but closed in 1982. Farther south, at 12901 South Virginia, a large neon sign topped by what is perhaps a smiling Scotsman marks the Merry Wink Motel. It's hard to believe, but this area once was well outside of Reno.

As U.S. Route 395 heads south, it passes a turn to Incline Village, Crystal Bay, and the

King Street heads west from Carson City until it reaches this dirt road, the beginning of the bypassed King's Canyon grade.

state line location of Cal-Neva Resort on the north shore of Lake Tahoe. It was owned by Frank Sinatra from 1960 to 1963, bringing the Rat Pack to Lake Tahoe. Also, there was Ponderosa Ranch, opened to the public in 1967 as a spin-off from the *Bonanza* TV show, which ran from 1959 to 1973. It was located (fictionally, of course) on the burning map at the beginning of each episode. In an interesting spin, the ranch was actually used for filming in later episodes. Tours of the ranch house included its movable walls, which accommodated filming. The attraction closed in 2004, the land being ripe for development.

Back on U.S. Route 395, signs lined the road in the past for "guest ranches." These were really retreats for those waiting out their divorce period. Today signs advertising "ranches" are for legal brothels.

Springs bubble from the ground in places, with steam drifting into the air. Nevada is said to have 312 hot springs, the most of any state. In 1861, the mineralized hot springs here spawned a hospital and bathhouses known as **Steamboat Springs**. These burned down, but the arrival of the Virginia and Truckee Railroad brought a hotel and new bathhouses, while mining brought prosperity. These burned too—

were the springs *that* hot?—and were rebuilt just before the Lincoln Highway was christened. Today Steamboat Hot Springs, at 16010 South Virginia Street, operates as a health spa. A long strip of crumbling concrete on the east side of the road marks the earlier highway. Another stretch is found four miles ahead, also on the left (east) side. Just to the south, the road splits and encircles Washoe Lake.

Many tourists turned left here to visit Virginia City, center of the Comstock Lode mining riches. The Lincoln curves right toward the fertile Washoe Valley, whose hay was once a prized commodity. Early motorists passed railroad stations at **Washoe**, which also had a campsite, and **Franktown**. U.S. Route 395 cuts a straight course south past the lake; the original road is parallel to the west.

About five miles later, U.S. 395/North Carson Street enters **Carson City**, one of the smallest state capitals. The town was established in 1858 along the Carson River; both were named for explorer Kit Carson. When Comstock Lode silver was discovered a year later, thousands poured into the area. The 1915 LHA guide noted that fifty-three automobiles were owned here.

CAROL INGALD

Lahontan Dam, on the Pioneer Branch of the Lincoln Highway, 1921.

The Frontier Motel, at 1718 North Carson Street, still has its 1950s neon sign of a cowboy with lariat. The Nevada State Museum, at 600 North Carson, is in the former U.S. Mint (1870–93), which understandably produced silver dollars; its exhibits include a replica mining operation. Out front is a relocated 1928 concrete marker. At 420 North Carson is a large neon sign of "the Senator" waving a fistful of dollars above Cactus Jack's Senator Casino. Opened in 1971, the business has grown to half a block long.

Alice Ramsey came through here in 1909, before it was the Lincoln Highway. She and her three companions stopped for lunch at a Japanese restaurant before heading to Lake Tahoe.

The state capitol building is at the center of town. The Lincoln Highway turned right (west) from Carson Street onto King Street. Government buildings now obstruct the way; detour a block north or south. Westbound drivers drove right toward the capitol and did well not to crash into it after having heated their brakes in the twisty King's Canyon.

IIIc. West of Fallon to California via later Pioneer Branch bypassing Reno

The thirty-three miles from Reno to Carson City was concrete-surfaced by the 1920s, but in their never-ending quest to shorten the route, LHA directors bypassed it in 1921. The new state road, following an emigrant trail to California's Gold Rush, made the Pioneer Branch the shorter route to Sacramento, even more so when the Kings Canyon Grade west of Carson City was bypassed a few years later. This also became the path of U.S. Route 50, drawing even more traffic away from Reno.

Having crossed the Carson Desert, travelers on this route from 1911 to 1915 could watch the construction of the Lahontan Dam. It was part of the Newlands Reclamation Project to irrigate the land. The reservoir's headquarters was five miles from the split at **Lahontan**. LHA guidebooks recommended stopping at the dam, even for those drivers traveling the northern branch to Reno. The 1913 Packard guide went so far as to route the highway to the dam and then advised drivers to "turn completely around" so that they could make their way back to the road to Reno. The reservoir holds the Carson River plus water diverted from the Truckee River. Surrounding land continues to be fertile, thanks to the irrigation project, which spurred growth after its completion. The road skirts the north end of the reservoir, which has sixty-nine miles of shoreline. The Bureau of Reclamation, which built and maintains the site, permits boating, camping, and year-round fishing.

At the west end of the dam is **Silver Springs**, then it's about thirty-five miles to Dayton. Even when this road was established eight years after the founding of the Lincoln Highway, it still was only gravel.

The Lincoln Highway branches right from U.S. Route 50 to follow Main Street into **Dayton**, a small town with Old West ambiance. The town began as a trading post and way station for westbound wagons gearing up for the mountains; unlike nearby mining towns, Dayton was on a main through route, the Emigrant Trail and Pony Express passing through the valley. It also served as a milling station during the Comstock Lode years and had a Pony Express station. Its biggest claim to fame was the filming of *The Misfits* in 1960. The movie brought Marilyn Monroe, Clark Gable, and other stars of the era, who hung out at the bar of the Odeon Hall on Pike Street. An LHA logo can be found on the side corner of the Bluestone Building (now the municipal county court and offices) at 235 Main Street.

Most tourists make the eight-mile drive north on NV Route 341 to Virginia City, once the epicenter of the Comstock Lode, the richest silver find in the continental United States. Today the town is filled with souvenir shops in restored buildings. You'll find a wooden sidewalk on D Street, an underground mine tour, and a steam locomotive to Gold Hill.

There were no guard-rails to protect Lincoln Highway drivers along Lake Tahoe.

U.S. Route 50 enters **Carson City** on Williams Street, then turns left (south) on North Carson Street. The original route turned right at the courthouse to follow the Kings Canyon Grade through the Carson Range to Sooner Summit. The winding road began as a Washoe Indian trail and was used as a road west during the California Gold Rush. It was the Comstock Lode discovery in 1859 that brought a rush of traffic. Men and freight were on the move, and the need for timber for fuel and underground supports brought logging. Traffic was finally slowed by the opening of the transcontinental railroad in 1869. After many hundreds of miles, the route leaves behind the Great Basin and its deserts.

During her 1909 trip, Alice Ramsey found this section of the route both steep and sandy. "This was in truth no automobile highway. It was an old wagon trail over the mountains and the grades were stiff." Bellamy Partridge climbed it in 1912:

> It was a single-track road with occasional turnouts, a rough and stony surface, and frightening declivities from which the dome of the courthouse below became smaller

and smaller. Several of the turns were too short for our car and we had to go part way around and then back off a few feet to get a new start. Our brakes weren't too good, and the girls refused to stay in the car during these backing operations and walked around a number of the short turns which were invariably followed by a steep upgrade. I would have been glad to join them, but somebody had to stay in the car.

Effie Gladding described it, too, as she drove east in 1914: "The road was a narrow shelf along a barren, rocky mountain side. There were but few trees . . . it was somewhat dreary and forbidding after the rich forest foliage that we had just left along the lake."

The canyon road was later renamed the Ostermann Grade in honor of LHA field secretary Henry Ostermann after his accidental death in 1920 in Iowa. The 1924 LHA guide called this "one of the most scenic drives in the country," but added, "There are many hairpin turns and brakes should be in good condition." It remains a public road, but is twisting, narrow, and strewn with jutting rocks, making driving hazardous.

Finally, in 1928, the Lincoln Highway bypassed this route in favor of the Clear Creek Grade to the south. The rerouted Lincoln follows U.S. Route 50/South Carson Street out of Carson City. At 2180 South Carson Street is the Nevada State Railroad Museum. Then, as U.S. Route 395 continues south, U.S. 50 turns right (west) toward Lake Tahoe. The 1928 route here actually turns a tenth of a mile to the south; it remains south of U.S. 50 but runs parallel to it for the next eight miles or so. The roads climb **Spooner Summit**, its wooded hills a contrast to the lands to the east. Three-quarters of a mile

after the roads converge again, the Kings Canyon Grade rejoins from the north.

U.S. Route 50 tops out at 7,140 feet, then descends toward Lake Tahoe. The change in vegetation is now very noticeable; the western side of the rise captures the moisture from clouds before they cross to the eastern side, leaving Nevada a much drier state than the lands around the lake and California to the west. Just north of the intersection with NV Route 28, called Spooner Junction, is Spooner Lake, where you can fish or walk a one-and-a-half-mile trail encircling the water. The lake was once the site of a Washoe settlement; some of the granite boulders on the western shore have small, shallow holes in which the Washoe women used rocks to grind seeds and nuts into flour. The Washoe were overrun soon after the area was discovered by John C. Frémont in 1844, and the pine forests became a vacation draw following the Civil War.

South of the NV Route 28 junction, the Lincoln Highway—marked Old Highway 50—parallels current U.S. Route 50 as it heads to **Glenbrook**, a private lakeside resort. The road is not accessible through the gated community. The narrow-gauge Lake Tahoe Railway was built in the 1870s to haul lumber from mills at Glenbrook over Spooner Summit, there to be floated down a flume to Carson City, from which they were carried again by rail to the mines of Virginia City. The town boomed in the next decade, as four lumbermills produced more than thirty million board feet every year, eventually leaving the hills barren.

From Glenbrook, the highway skirts the eastern shore of Lake Tahoe as it heads south. Tahoe is the country's second-deepest lake, averaging 990 feet deep. The renowned blue color comes from the reflected sky at 6,225 feet above sea level. (Surrounding peaks top 10,000 feet.) It's twelve miles wide by twenty-two miles long, with a total of seventy-one miles of shoreline. Sixty-three streams feed the lake, but the Truckee River is the only outlet.

In *Roughing It*, Mark Twain described the lake as "a noble sheet of blue water. . . . I thought it must surely be the fairest picture the whole earth affords." Often forgotten is that Twain was there to stake a claim on the lucrative lumber, and that he let a campfire destroy a mountainside of pine.

After years of little growth, development around Lake Tahoe picked up again after World War II, with an increase in skiing and other recreational activities. As resorts and casinos sprouted, so too did supporting industries. The south end of the lake near the state border was especially developed with ritzy hotels, yet you can still find free camp space. Popular summer activities include fishing and swimming.

Cave Rock on Lake Tahoe, just after a second tunnel was completed.

Three miles from Glenbrook, the road originally went around **Cave Rock**, which juts into and above the lake. In 1931, a tunnel was opened through the rock, and a second portal was added in 1957. The original path remains, but stopping to view the old road or the vista is too dangerous. The Washoe always considered the lake a sacred place, particularly Cave Rock. The area is now Cave Rock State Park; a right turn to the south gives access to a boat launch and parking area for viewing the rock formation.

To the southeast is the community of Lincoln Park. The lake is lined with private getaways, but a couple miles south, **Zephyr Cove** is a popular lakefront resort. The original road breaks away from U.S. Route 50 and is even marked "Lincoln Highway." It is surrounded by very tall pines and small condos. The *MS Dixie II*, made to look like an old paddlewheel steamer, offers cruises of the lake. The Zephyr Cove Lodge, built along the Lincoln Highway, was turned about when the current highway was realigned behind it.

RUSSELL REIN

The road bends inland from the lake but beaches and other recreation areas line the shore. A mile before the border you come to **Kingsbury** and then **Stateline**, which has overtaken the old towns of **Edgewood** and **Lakeside**. The area is a glitzy strip of high-rise casinos, hotels, bars, sporting-goods stores, and restaurants. Edgewood was founded when Friday's Station was built in 1860 for the Pony Express; the small white station still stands. Most development occurred in Lakeside, which is contiguous but officially now in California. Stateline is in Nevada, but most visitors come from California.

Boy Scout Bernard Queneau wrote on August 6, 1928, "We reached Carson City then started our climb in first [gear] for ten miles up the Sierras. We reached Cal. at 12:30 and there we had our blankets examined for the Alfalfa [weevil]."

When James Montgomery Flagg drove east, inspectors had different priorities: "When we crossed the border into Nevada, we were held up for inspection by a rangy ranger who asked us for citrus fruits and dogs."

By the time this postcard was published in the mid-1950s, Stateline, Nevada, was trading on "clubs that consistently feature stars of movies, radio and television," plus "gaming tables, good food, excitement and glamour."

BERNIE HEISEY

Greetings from California

Native Americans lived peacefully for centuries in this land rich with flora, fauna, and waterways. When Spaniards arrived, they thought the land barren, but the myth of California took root nonetheless. Perhaps it started with a 1510 Spanish romantic novel about the fictional Queen Califia, which gave the region its name. After Mexico won independence from Spain in 1821, it awarded vast tracts of land to ranchers who were willing to settle what became California. A period of relative calm and prosperity came to the pastoral society, symbolized by *caballeros*, the gentleman ranch owners. A discovery at Sutter's Mill quickly changed that.

Three centuries of exploration by the Spanish, then Mexicans—two leading mining cultures—had failed to uncover the region's abundant gold. The 1848 discovery came just days before Mexico ceded the area to the United States. The resulting gold rush transformed California, attracting tens of thousands of hopeful prospectors. Towns affected by the rush—Truckee, Placerville, Sacramento, San Francisco—became Lincoln Highway towns, and the 1913 route often adapted roads carved half a century earlier to carry men and supplies between mines and markets.

The Lincoln Highway entered California from the east along two paths. The northern route went through Truckee, past Donner Lake, and over Donner Pass, roughly following today's I-80. The southern route—the Pioneer Branch—went west from Carson City, Nevada, around the southern shore of Lake Tahoe, over Echo Pass, and through Placerville, roughly following today's U.S. Route 50. The routes rejoined at Sacramento.

From there, the straightest path to the coast would have been westerly if not for the far-reaching arms of San Francisco Bay. To avoid the rivers and surrounding marshes, the Lincoln Highway diverted south to Stockton, then west over Altamont Pass to Hayward and north to Oakland. The opening of the Yolo Causeway west of Sacramento in 1916 gave drivers the option of going through Davis and Vacaville and ferrying across Carquinez Strait on their way to San Francisco.

The Victory Highway took a parallel route west by staying south of the Sacramento River via Walnut Grove and ferrying across the San Joaquin River at Antioch. When a toll bridge opened across those straits in 1926, the Victory had the better road to the coast. The next year, the same toll bridge company opened a span across Carquinez Strait from Vallejo to Crockett.

In March 1928, LHA field secretary Gael Hoag suggested nine route changes to the LHA executive committee, including one to move the highway between Sacramento and

	CALIFORNIA	U.S.
Population in 1910	2,377,549	92,228,496
Population in 2000	33,871,648	281,421,906
Persons per square mile in 2000	217.2	79.6
Approximate miles of Lincoln Highway		
Truckee leg	132	3,389
Placerville leg	107	3,389
Stockton leg	134	3,389
Vallejo leg	100	3,389

San Francisco to the Carquinez Bridge route. Hoag announced the change at a press conference that August, and the new route was marked with the organization's concrete posts on September 1, 1928. An article in the fall 2004 issue of *Lincoln Highway Forum* discounted the validity of the Carquinez route, as the concrete posts were the only tangible evidence the authors could find for the routing. Indeed, it can be argued that named highways even ceased to exist after the federal highway numbering system was adopted late in 1925; but for this study, the posts are used as an indicator of the Lincoln Highway's route. If nothing else, the move can be considered a snub to the communities that were on the original route for fifteen years.

In his 1933 book, *Double Crossing America by Motor*, Edward D. Dunn described the route that he drove eastward through Vallejo— "almost continuous orchards"—and then via the Pioneer Branch:

> The lovely, well-shaded city of Sacramento, quaint Placerville (formerly Hangtown), reminiscent of the gold rush days of '49, the sudden climb to an elevation of eight thousand [sic] feet to cross the Sierra Nevadas, and the drop on the other side to the sapphire inland sea, Lake Tahoe . . . made the day's run from the Pacific to Reno one of the most beautiful and varied of our memories.

Ia. Nevada to Sacramento via Truckee

The obvious route from Verdi, Nevada, to Truckee, California, is along the Truckee River, but when the Stephens emigrant party attempted it in 1844, they found that the rocky river bottom made for rough going.

The next year, Caleb Greenwood found an alternate route to the north, a sometimes steep climb over the ridge to Dog Valley, but easier than following the river. These two routes would battle for, and each eventually serve, the Lincoln Highway.

The Dog Valley route was improved by turnpike companies during the stampede east to Nevada's gold and silver starting some ten years after California's gold rush. The Central Pacific Railroad took over the turnpikes as a supply route while it labored to build its tracks over the mountains in the 1860s. The route never served any communities.

This was the road the LHA first chose, although starting in 1916, LHA guides noted that the twenty-two miles from Verdi to Truckee had such steep grades that motorists should carry water for overheating radiators. Interestingly, the guides recommended that those heading *east* to see Lake Tahoe should follow the Truckee River, "a beautiful river, over a good road."

From Verdi, Nevada, the Lincoln Highway follows Dog Valley Road west. At the California line, it becomes Henness Pass Road and climbs 1,250 feet in a northwesterly direction to a ridge overlooking Dog Valley. The highway then turns southwest and rises to a summit of about 6,520 feet. The road descends and changes back to Dog Valley Road. The route once crossed Stampede Creek, but it was dammed decades ago, the valley inundated to become Stampede Reservoir. The Lincoln Highway here is underwater, so where the road name changes you must turn left onto Stampede Dam Road, then a right onto Dog Valley Road and past the dam, to rehook

Like so many others before and to follow, the Lincoln Highway Motion Picture Caravan crew symbolically dipped their tires in the Pacific at San Francisco after crossing the continent.

on the south side of the water with the route of the Lincoln Highway.

The Lincoln continues south on Dog Valley Road to Prosser Creek, where the same dam situation has submerged the road. Drivers can detour left on Prosser Dam Road, which continues south as CR 787 toward Truckee. The Lincoln meets CA Route 89, turns left, and goes over I-80. There it meets Glenshire Drive, which became the western end of the rerouted Lincoln Highway in 1926.

The state took over the Dog Valley route in 1919 and began planning for its improvement. Businessmen and local LHA consuls advocated a new road along the Truckee River as more scenic, less snowy, and connecting communities, though it would be two miles longer and cost three times as much. Politics broke the stalemate, and a new road was started along the river. The railroad and river flumes made space in the tight canyon even harder to find, forcing the road to cross five new bridges, four of them

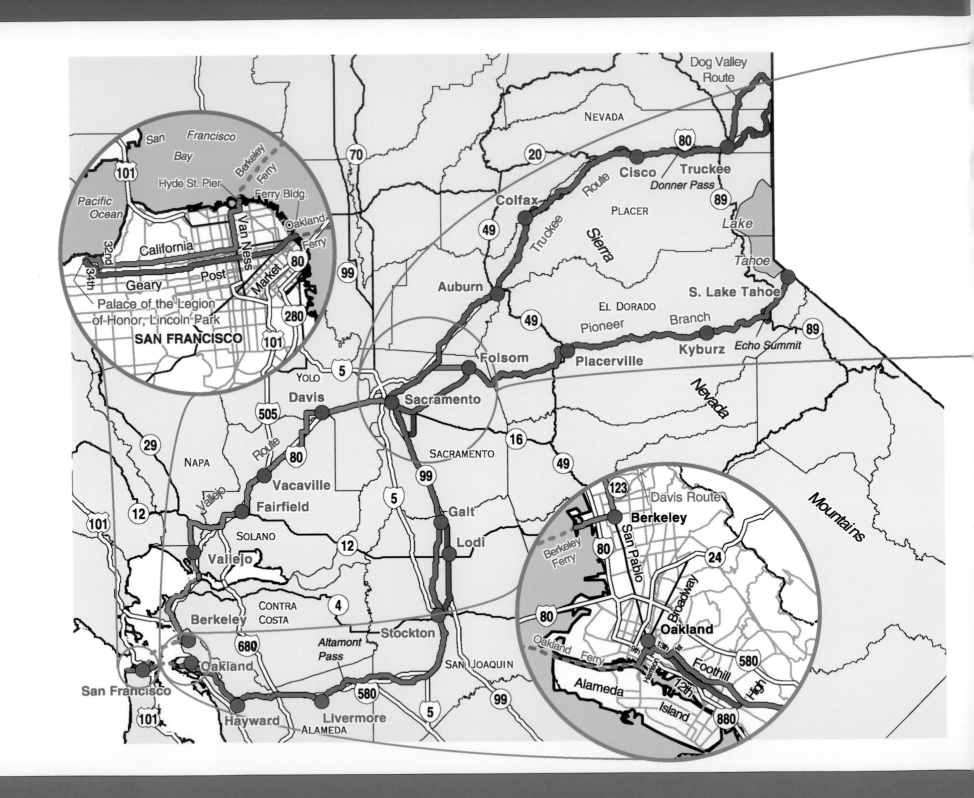

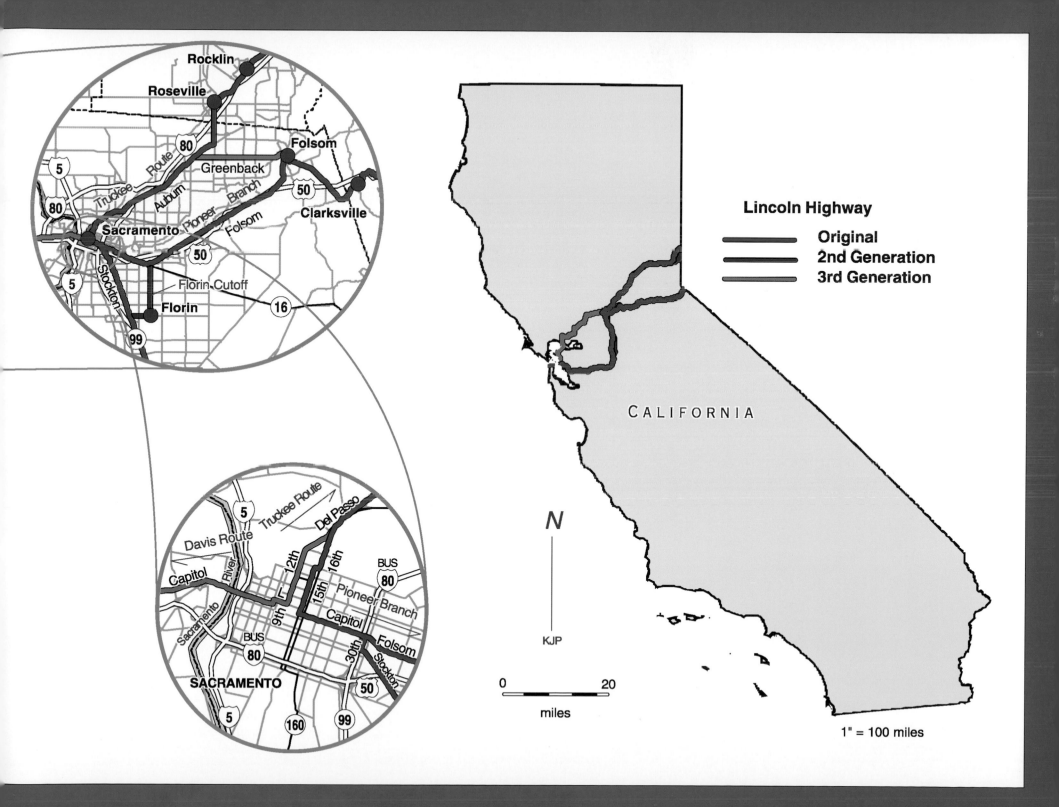

Lincoln Highway

Original

2nd Generation

3rd Generation

CALIFORNIA

N

KJP

0   20

miles

1" = 100 miles

Rocklin

Roseville

Folsom

Greenback

80

Truckee Route

Auburn

Pioneer Branch

50

Folsom

Clarksville

Sacramento

50

Florin Cutoff

16

Florin

Stockton

99

5

80

5

5

Davis Route

5

Truckee Route

Del Passo

Capitol

River

Sacramento

12th

16th

15th

Pioneer Branch

BUS
80

9th

Capitol

BUS
80

30th

Folsom

Stockton

50

SACRAMENTO

5

160

99

BERNIE HEISEY

Truckee's Commercial Row lived up to its name with a string of porcelain enamel and neon signs. Note the rooftop sign for the Riverside Hotel at distant left in this 1940s view.

NORMAN ROOT

over the river, three of those concrete-arch bridges (now gone). The river route was dedicated on June 10, 1926, ultimately costing ten times what it would have to improve the old road.

Decades later, I-80 was overlaid atop much of the 1926 road. Glimpses of the road can be seen from the state line to **Floriston** and

through **Boca**. Exit there to access Glenshire Drive, which heads south, picks up the Lincoln, and heads west to **Truckee**. It rejoins the 1913–26 Lincoln Highway at CA Route 89. Both the original and later routes, heading west together, immediately turn right onto Keiser Avenue and merge into Jibboom Street (some of this lost to modern improvements). The Lincoln soon turns left (south) on Bridge Street; on the right, a stone facade with an arched peak marks the former Truckee Stone Garage. The Lincoln then turns right on High Street—"Commercial Row"—lined with businesses on the north side, and across from them is the town's train station.

In front of the station is an eagle-topped monument to the Victory Highway, relocated from Truckee Canyon, about five hundred feet west of the state line. It's peculiar that it was not on the line; perhaps this was because of the rough terrain. Also, state-line Victory Highway markers were to be doughboys. The memorial was destroyed as the freeway was built through Truckee Canyon in 1962; it took until 1998 for the pieces to be reset and relocated in downtown Truckee. The only change is that the stone base is now brick.

The town grew with the Gold Rush and the first transcontinental railroad. The state's WPA guide described Truckee as surrounded by pine forests but said that it "lacks even a sprig of green." It continued:

> Its ramshackle frame houses and weather-stained brick buildings sprawl over rocky slopes. On Saturday nights the cheap

This circa 1919 Victory Highway marker was rediscovered, restored, and in 1998 placed next to the train station in Truckee.

saloons and gambling halls overflow with lumberjacks, cow-punchers, and shepherds. In winter, when great glistening drifts fill the streets, the nearby snow-clad slopes resound with the shouts of skiers.

In 1993, Truckee finally incorporated, leading to improvements along High Street. Thoughtful planning of roads, parking, sidewalks, and landscaping has led to its listing as one of a dozen leading examples of renewed main streets and downtowns on the Great Streets! website.

The Lincoln heads west, passing under I-80 via Donner Pass Road, then crosses back and stays south of the interstate; both highways skirt Donner Lake, which is to the south. Donner Memorial State Park is southeast of the lake. The 1,750-acre park includes the Emigrant Trail Museum, which explores not only emigrants, but also local history from Native Americans to the first transcontinental railroad. The Pioneer Monument, dedicated in 1918, is near the site of some of the Donner party campsites; its twenty-two-foot pedestal marks the height of snow during the fateful winter of 1846.

The families who would later make up the Donner party left Independence, Missouri, in May 1846. As Frank Mullen Jr. wrote in *The Donner Party Chronicles*, an estimated twenty-seven hundred emigrants made the trip that year. Indian raids were less of a threat than were alkali streams, barren land, the weather, and time. Delays were common on the two-thousand-mile trip, but parties had to keep moving to make it over the Sierra Nevada before snow reached the high peaks. The Donner party bogged down, sometimes literally, by taking a shortcut south of the Great Salt Lake.

The delays—and 125 extra miles—would haunt them as they reached the summit of the Sierra Mountains. An early winter, and one of the harshest on record, buried the Donner-led party in snow and trapped them near the lake that now carries their name. The tales of hardship, especially cannibalism, elevated the story to mythical proportions.

Today the lake and park also offer boating, camping, fishing, cross-country skiing, and snowshoeing. Three concrete Lincoln Highway posts remain in the area, though not in their original locations.

West of the lake, the Lincoln Highway followed the 1864 Dutch Flat and Donner Lake Wagon Road up the Sierras. It was christened CA Route 37 in 1909. A new road was built to the summit in 1924, leaving the wagon road to decay; it's mostly inaccessible today.

Few transportation corridors have as many remnants from different eras as Donner Pass. (Donner Summit is now considered to be two miles north, where I-80 crossed the mountains in 1962.) Indians, emigrants, the transcontinental railroad, the Lincoln Highway, and U.S. Route 40 each carved one or more paths through the pass, which peaks at 7,135 feet. A good book for learning more is George Stewart's *Donner Pass and Those Who Crossed It.*

The Indians who roamed these hills left petroglyphs, little drawings scratched into the granite, and these still line the route. In 1844, the Stephens party surmounted the hills by disassembling its wagons and pulling the pieces up by rope. These efforts gave the spot its name, Stephens Pass, but the appellation was short-lived; two years later, the Donner party tragedy imprinted that name on the lake and the mountain. Travelers often avoided the Donner route not only because of its notoriety, but also because easier routes had been blazed. The Central Pacific Railroad chose it, however, when it began carving a railroad from Sacramento eastward in the 1860s.

As the Central Pacific laid its rails though the pass, it also built a supply road using the old emigrant and mining trails. The Dutch Flat and Donner Lake Wagon Road opened in June 1864; it came to dominate local freight and express business, even drawing Comstock Lode traffic from the road south of Lake Tahoe. The wagon road also allowed the Central Pacific to haul forty train cars and even three locomotives (on log sledges)

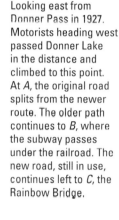

Looking east from Donner Pass in 1927. Motorists heading west passed Donner Lake in the distance and climbed to this point. At *A*, the original road splits from the newer route. The older path continues to *B*, where the subway passes under the railroad. The new road, still in use, continues left to *C*, the Rainbow Bridge.

Looking from the old Lincoln Highway through the subway to the Rainbow Bridge at Donner Pass.

To ride a motor bicycle through the sheds is impossible. I walked, of course, dragging my machine over the ties for 18 miles by cyclometer measurement. I was 7 hours in the sheds. It was 15 feet under the snow. That night I slept at Summit, 7,015 feet above the sea, having ridden—or walked—54 miles during the day. . . . When I sought my motor bicycle in the morning the picture received its first blur. My can of lubricating oil was missing. The magnificent view that the tip top of the mountains afforded lost its charms. I had eyes not even for Donner Lake, the "gem of the Sierras," nestling like a great lost diamond in its setting of fleecy snow and tall, gaunt pines.

Oil such as I required was not to be had on the snowbound summit nor in the untamed country ahead, and oil I must have—or walk, and walk far. I knew that my supply was in its place just after emerging from the snow sheds the night before, and I reckoned therefore that the now prized can had dropped off in the snow, and I was determined to hunt for it. I trudged back a mile and a half. Not an inch of ground or snow escaped search, and when at last a dark object met my gaze I fairly bounded toward it. It was my oil!

—George A. Wyman, *"Across America on a Motor Bicycle,"*
The Motor Cycle *(1903)*

Austin Bement and Henry Joy found high snow in the Sierra Nevada Mountains on June 8, 1915.

SPECIAL COLLECTIONS LIBRARY, UNIVERSITY OF MICHIGAN

up and across the summit. Once the first train crossed Donner Pass on November 30, 1867, the wagon road fell into disuse for four decades, until 1909, when it was made part of the state highway system. Stewart wrote that a highway engineer who traveled the route in 1909 found it "in such abominable condition that one could scarcely call it a road at all." That was essentially the road the Lincoln Highway followed four years later. Only small portions of the wagon road remain on the east slope and to the west near Cisco Grove and Big Bend.

The Central Pacific Railroad required fifteen tunnels over the mountains, the longest and deepest being the Summit Tunnel (#6), at 1,659 feet. It was so long, and was taking so long, that a shaft was drilled to also excavate from the middle. The tunnel took more than fifteen months to build, the mostly Chinese laborers hand-drilling holes in the granite, then blasting it with just-invented nitroglycerin. The Chinese were specifically imported for the job; locals were too tempted by the independent life offered by mining and were pulled away every time there was word of another strike. The tunnel eventually was finished in August 1867.

The snows that trapped the Donner party were worse than normal, but not uncommon. Storms sweep in from the ocean and sometimes drop as much as eighty inches of snow on the mountain, while Truckee gets perhaps only a couple feet and Reno a couple inches. Snowfalls in the winter of 1866–67 and the following year were both very heavy, more than forty-four *feet* of snow falling the first winter. It had been thought that plows could keep the way clear between tunnels, but the bad winters

during construction changed the thinking. The solution was snowsheds, built like a covered bridge with two enclosed sides and a peaked roof. One-sided galleries were also joined to mountainsides to let avalanches slide over the tracks. Protection was built over a combined thirty-seven miles; the twenty miles from Donner Pass to Cisco had nine snowsheds.

The Lincoln Highway passed through four of those snowsheds in the fifty miles between Donner Pass and Emigrant Gap. Wagons and motorists had to stop, slide open a door, check for trains, slide open the opposite door, drive through, then stop again to close both doors. It's likely that motorists often left them open in summer months. These were similar in concept to the ranch gates of the Midwest, but unlike the threat of a cranky cow, a train could and did kill travelers that failed to pass through before the next train arrived.

In *The Good of It All*, Thornton Round recalled that during his family's 1914 trip, they made sure no trains were approaching their snowshed crossing by laying a pencil on the tracks to check for vibrations. They then drove through, only to have their car get hung up on the tracks.

In 1912, the state started a program of eliminating at-grade rail crossings on its highways. Among the first bypassed was where the Dutch Flat and Donner Lake Wagon Road crossed the tracks at the east end of tunnel #6. The new crossing was via a little underpass between tunnels #7 and #8. The Lincoln Highway used this underpass, called the "subway," when it adopted the wagon road the following year. By 1914, the resultant increase in traffic forced its widening.

The 1916 LHA guide advised travelers to pause and enjoy the view: "Just after crossing under the Central Pacific Railroad, the tourist should walk back to the top of the tunnel, where a fine view of Donner Lake and the distant mountain ranges of Nevada may be had."

In 1924, a new road with milder grades was built up the east side of the mountain. Near the point where the new grade joins the wagon road/original Lincoln Highway is a plaque commemorating "China Wall," a steep stone wall supporting the railbed built by Chinese labor. The highway still used the subway, then the new road continued to the west. In August 1926, a new open-spandrel concrete-arch span allowed the road to bypass the subway altogether. The Donner Summit Bridge, also called the Rainbow Bridge, was unusual at the time in that it bridged only dry land. More distinctive is that it not only curves, but also rises at a seven percent grade. The new road was soon marked U.S. Route 40. By the 1980s, the bridge was in danger of being demolished, but local historians and residents helped raise funds for a restoration. The bridge was rededicated in September 1998. Few cross-country drivers noticed; I-80 had bypassed this transportation confluence more than thirty-five years earlier.

Though the climb to Donner Pass could be grueling, descending it eastbound was likewise difficult. A number of recollections can be found in Curt McConnell's account of early transcontinental journeys, *Coast to Coast by Automobile*. Regular transcontinental driver Lester Whitman wrote, "Failure of the brakes or a broken chain could mean a dangerous runaway for our machine, so we stopped,

chopped down a small pine tree and tied it onto the rear axle to be used as a drag."

In *U.S. 40*, George Stewart recalled coming through here in 1920, when the road was still a winding dirt trail: "Its sudden drop-off on the eastern face of the pass was breath-taking in beauty, but also heart-stopping, as one looked at the narrow and plunging road, corkscrewing off to some bottomless nowhere."

Clinton Twiss similarly wrote in *The Long, Long Trailer* that his eastbound climb to Donner Pass was scary, but not as scary as the descent to Truckee:

> Making the big climb to Donner Summit was a thriller, especially so when you have two-and-a-half tons pulling on your rear and urging you back to your starting point. We ticked off the elevation. Auburn 1400 feet. Emigrant Gap 5250 feet. Donner Pass 7135 feet. Then suddenly the top, and the sharp drop down the other side.
>
> It looked like a ski run. The highway lost fifteen-hundred feet in what seemed less than a mile. We went into low—then put on the trailer brakes—then the car brakes. I *longed* for an anchor.

After 130 years of use, the railroad tracks were removed in 1993. Portions of the tunnels and snowsheds remain, as do the petroglyphs and ghosts of advertisements painted on the granite.

Donner Pass Road heads west, parallel and north of the original road, now called Lake Van Norden Road. They rejoin near **Soda Springs**, while I-80 similarly comes back from its northern diversion. The Lincoln Highway/Donner Pass Road crosses to the north side of I-80 at the Soda Springs exit and meets up with the South Fork of the Yuba River, making for a close assemblage of rails and roads.

Soda Springs Hotel, west of Donner Pass, 1949.

A couple exits west on I-80, the Lincoln crosses back south to **Big Bend**. The Big Bend Visitor Information Center is run in association with the surrounding Tahoe National Forest. The center displays a collection of Lincoln Highway artifacts. Across from it, behind the Big Bend Fire Station, is a replica concrete marker, set here in 1999. There's a bit of asphalt Lincoln Highway in

Rainbow Lodge, on old U.S. Route 40 east of Big Bend, has changed little over the decades.

NORMAN ROOT

Baxter's Station, thirty miles east of Auburn, was a popular one-stop; it included a gas station, hotel, cabins, restaurant, post office, and the Old Forty-Nine Trading Post.

the forest, and a trace from the Overland Immigrant Trail; trees remain deformed from when they were used to winch wagons down the slope, and granite rocks have rust stains from being rubbed by wagon wheel rims. The Rainbow Inn at Big Bend is a 1920s ski and hunting lodge that includes a bar and formal restaurant.

The old highway follows Hampshire Rocks Road west, crossing I-80 yet again to **Cisco Grove**. West of here, I-80 has erased the old road, but then it splits off to the south to Yuba Gap. Today it's marked Crystal Lake Road, a private drive. Then it's once again subsumed by I-80 through **Emigrant Gap**, the famed passage from the high Sierra Mountains to its foothills. The first emigrants to cross in 1845 had to lower their wagons by rope to the floor of Bear Valley.

For the next forty miles, the road descends this narrow ridge through wooded canyons: Bear River to the north, the North Fork of the American River to the south. In *The Good of It All*, Thornton Round described it as they returned home driving eastbound: "The road

was narrow, and we had to resort to constant carburetor adjustments to increase the flow of gasoline as we climbed higher. There were dangerous unfenced gaps in the mountains, and no warning signs."

Beatrice Massey wrote in *It Might Have Been Worse*: "One of the finest views is the mighty canyon of the America River, with the timbered gorge and the rushing stream two thousand feet below. You are held spellbound by the scenery as you descend the western slope to Sacramento."

The old road breaks away north of I-80 at **Baxter**, taking Baxter Road. This was the site of Baxter's Station, a regular stop for cars and buses seeking fuel and food. It started as a meat market and grew to include a general store, post office, hotel rooms, and cabin camp. A few buildings and foundations remain, then the Lincoln presses westward via Alta Bonnynook Road.

West of **Alta**, it follows Ridge Road to **Gold Run**. The name is not coincidental. This is sometimes called the Mother Lode country, filled as it was with gold and overrun by hopefuls in the 1860s and 1870s.

It all started with Swiss immigrant John Sutter, who in 1840 had built a fort at today's Sacramento. It was not only a complete trading post, but also included cultivated land and thousands of head of livestock. In 1847, Sutter sent rescuers to bring the Donner party survivors from the Sierra Nevada. A few months later, he sent about twenty men, including James Marshall, fifty miles northeast to build a sawmill on the South Fork of the American River. (This was near Coloma, between the two future branches of the Lincoln Highway.) The mill was almost finished

in January 1848 when Marshall discovered gold as he was deepening a tailrace, but Marshall was more concerned about finishing his sawmill. He didn't want gold seekers bothering him, and Sutter likewise didn't want his ranch overrun, so both kept it secret. Which, of course, meant that the news spread quickly. One of the crew went to San Francisco and bought every mining implement available, then started shouting of the discovery in the streets and made a windfall selling the tools at outrageous prices. Squatters and schemers overwhelmed the fort, and by the end of 1849, Sutter had sold it.

The romantic image is of a miner panning for gold, but the Gold Rush quickly inspired complex operations. At first miners found gold along streambeds, where it had been collecting for millennia, and they used pans. As these sources quickly ran out, other methods, such as the sluice box, were used for less-rich deposits. Towns such as Dutch Flat, Gold Run, Auburn, and the area around Colfax grew as mining camps. By the 1860s, hydraulic mining was greatly altering the landscape. Flumes and pipes carried water, which was then sprayed at banks of gravel; these are called "diggings" despite the method of clearing.

As Stewart described it in *Donner Pass*, "The tops of the ridges were washed away, and gigantic scars of treeless gravel remained." The high red cliffs north of Gold Run were cleared this way, then the displaced gravel—and the topsoil—flowed downhill, clogging Bear River canyon above Dutch Flat to about 150 feet high. The resulting floods pitted miners against farmers. In Curt McConnell's *Coast to Coast by Automobile*, Lester Whitman noted the effect on the roads during his 1904 drive:

"Large boulders had rolled into the road and streams trickling across the trail had cut deep ruts. . . . By Dutch Flat, Gold Run, and other old-time mining centers we climbed. The streams, the banks, the hills themselves show the fierce onslaught of hydraulic mining of early days."

The forest begins changing from pine and cedar to black oak and manzanita. The old highway crisscrosses I-80 near **Magra** and into **Colfax**, which had been called Illinoistown but was renamed for the Speaker of the House of Representatives, who visited the Central Pacific while it was being built in 1865. This area is traditionally known for growing pears, plums (dried as prunes), grapes, and apples.

The road crosses back to the south side of I-80 and follows Canyon Way, then Ponderosa Way, then Paoli Lane. It passes through **Weimar**, then recrosses to the north side of I-80. On the south side of the frontage road at West Paoli Lane and I-80 are the former Lou Labonte Restaurant and gas station, rusty pumps out front, and both in disrepair. A new Lou Labonte Restaurant is in Auburn on Lincoln Way.

The highway crosses yet again to the south side of I-80. The road in this region goes through a number of old railroad underpasses. At **Applegate**, three early subways that separated the Lincoln from Southern Pacific tracks are still in use: Heather Glen Subway and the East and West Applegate Subways, all along U.S. Route 40.

The Lincoln Highway crosses again to the north side at Clipper Gap, then returns back south. Lincoln Way heads southwest into **Auburn** and jogs its way through town. Auburn was first called Wood's Dry Diggings

but was renamed by gold miners for their hometown of Auburn, New York. The Gold Rush of 1849 brought prospectors, who beat paths to surrounding camps. The WPA guide colorfully described these trails as they developed into turnpikes, which became "choked with stagecoaches, mule teams, and freight wagons, where highwaymen often lay in wait for hold-ups." The guide also gave a great description of Auburn's Old Town section: "Here narrow streets twist uphill under wide-branching trees, past crumbling brick buildings with sagging iron doors and shutters and over-hanging balconies."

The railroad and orchards boosted the economy as the mines gave out. Today the Local Merchants Association has marked Lincoln Way through town with colorful signs, and a 1928 concrete Lincoln Highway

post has been moved and set in front of City Hall. The County Courthouse museum has a wooden Lincoln Highway sign. A walking-tour map of Old Auburn can be had at the chamber of commerce in the railway depot at 601 Lincoln Way.

When Thornton Round's family departed from San Francisco for their return drive east, they made it as far as Auburn, where they offered a farmer $1 to camp. In return, the farmer let them eat any of his fruit; they chose sickle pears. Then they cooked pork chops, noodles and gravy, tomatoes, watercress, and a custard pie they had bought along the road. At night, they patched inner tubes by moonlight.

West of town, I-80 is over top of the old road, then it breaks to the north all the way to Roseville. In between, it follows Ophir Road

The "old town" section of Auburn features the distinctively topped firehouse from 1891.

A few miles [east] from Sacramento is the land of sheep. The country for miles around is a country of splendid sheep ranches, and the woolly animals and the sombrero-ed ranchmen are everywhere. Speeding around a bend in the road I came almost precipitately upon an immense drove which was being driven to Nevada. While the herders swore, the sheep scurried in every direction, fairly piling on top of each other in their eagerness to get out of my path.

—George A. Wyman, "Across America on a Motor Bicycle,"
The Motor Cycle *(1903)*

and then Taylor Road into **Newcastle**. U.S. Route 40/Taylor Road tunnels beneath the town, but the Lincoln curves around the south edge, following Old State Highway. Newcastle was the only mining camp in this area to survive as a settlement, turning to fruit packing as output dwindled from placer mines (when the mineral is within a glacial deposit).

The highway turns right from Taylor Road onto Callison Road, then left on Sisley Road through **Penryn**, named for the Welsh town of Penrhyn, but spelled differently. A stretch of original fourteen-foot concrete pavement survives here from the early 1920s. Fruit

Tradewinds Motel, just east of Sacramento.

growing continues along the road to **Loomis** and **Rocklin**.

At **Roseville**, the old highway intersects I-80, then turns north to follow Atlantic Street and Vernon Street. The town continues to be a shipping point for the many fruits grown in the region. The road bends left on Riverside Avenue, crosses I-80, and becomes Auburn Boulevard into Citrus Heights. Auburn Boulevard turns right and heads west; coming in from the south is Greenback Lane, the 1927 route of the Pioneer Branch of the Lincoln Highway.

The highway has entered the suburbs of **Sacramento**. Part of Auburn Boulevard has been erased by I-80, but it picks up again on the north side, with short jogs on El Camino Avenue and Del Paseo Boulevard. Just northwest of downtown is the junction of the American and Sacramento Rivers. After 1915, traffic from the north had a new way into town, the five-arch 16th Street Bridge across the American River (named by John Sutter for the American trappers). It was widened in 1935 and made longer in 1941, and a parallel span was added in 1958. The original was pictured in the 1924 LHA guide, which also had a map of Sacramento showing the Lincoln taking 15th Street south, then turning east on M Street before continuing south to Stockton. The 1916 LHA guide carried an ad for a Lincoln Highway Garage at 15th Street and K Street. The 1916 guide listed it as the town's LHA control point.

Whether on 15th Street or 16th Street, any driver needing tires after 1928 would have pulled up to an impressive Art Deco Firestone tire store at 16th Street and L Street. In 2004, with the lease expiring, the family

that owned the site planned to add a fourteen-story office tower and perhaps residential units to an area of town that was again becoming trendy.

With 16th Street one-way north, most drivers cross the American River and follow the ramp onto 12th Street. This goes south a dozen blocks to the state capitol and Capitol Park.

1b. *Nevada to Sacramento via Pioneer Branch*

The Pioneer Branch headed south from Reno to Carson City, went around Lake Tahoe, and entered California. It was considered the equal of the Truckee route, but its course was not even listed in the 1913 Packard guide except to say, "The Lincoln Highway is divided at Reno, one branch going via Truckee and the other turning south via Lake Tahoe." Drivers depending on this guide were on their own if they took the southerly branch. Worse, in the early years, there were no facilities or accommodations between Lake Tahoe and Placerville, some sixty miles. But LHA guides gave the route increasing coverage until the last edition in 1924 made it the dominant route.

The southern route crossed into California from Stateline, Nevada, where older motels mostly have been replaced by larger chains. U.S. Route 50/Lake Tahoe Boulevard continues west, but the old Lincoln Highway branches left on Pioneer Trail. If you stay on the federal route through **South Lake Tahoe**, you'll find small motels in contrast to the casinos on the Nevada side. At 3058 U.S. 50 is the Lake Tahoe Historical Society and Museum, which features displays on the region's Washoe Indians, pioneer farming, and the logging industry. The El Dorado Recreation Area offers a large sandy beach, picnic tables, and shady parking. Tourists often choose to divert west on CA Route 89/Emerald Bay Road to Tallac Historic Site, which includes three elite estates from a century ago.

Alice Ramsey, mesmerized by California's scenery during her 1909 cross-country drive, commented only briefly on the road surface here: "The road was still narrow and the surface was a powdery kind of sand, but less deep." Three years later, Bellamy Partridge found the roads noticeably changed as he entered California: "We were now on highways that were full width and stone surfaced." He attributed it to the state's preparations for the 1915 Panama-Pacific Exposition.

Pioneer Trail heads southwest about ten miles to **Meyers**. The route briefly joins U.S. Route 50 then turns left on South Upper Truckee Road. It angled right on Meyers Road, but that is now closed to the public. It then turned onto Johnson Pass Road, a path from pioneer days, and crossed U.S. 50. Take U.S. 50, which tops **Echo Summit** at 7,365 feet. Those who drove the original road had to contend with a hairpin turn and 17 percent grade to reach the summit. You can glimpse stunning views of Lake Tahoe as you head east, though there are few chances to pull over.

As Effie Gladding and her party descended Echo Summit and drove through Meyers in June 1914, the "road was very sandy, and as we drove among the pine trees it was in some places so narrow that the hubs of our machine just cleared the tree trunks." The Pioneer Branch remains a rugged, forested route.

The Sierra Nevada is thick with cedar, pine, and fir trees. Westbound drivers should still expect hairpin turns after the summit. The

A hairpin turn near the top of the east slope at Echo Summit, 1924.

SPECIAL COLLECTIONS LIBRARY, UNIVERSITY OF MICHIGAN

1924 LHA guide warned motorists in both directions: Westbound drivers would find the climb of thirteen hundred feet in two miles to be taxing on their radiators. That same grade was a danger to those going east, so second gear and light braking were advised.

The original Lincoln Highway passes through **Little Norway**. The area, not surprisingly, has stunning, alpinelike scenery. The road soon enters the El Dorado National Forest and parallels the rushing South Fork of the American River.

The Lincoln follows U.S. Route 50 through **Phillips**, **Twin Bridges**, and **Strawberry**, where a rock formation called Lovers Leap is seen on old postcards. Only at some places do older alignments peek though; a trace of the original Lincoln Highway can be found near the Lovers Leap parking area.

The road continues along the river, twisting as it does. At **Kyburz**, the Kyburz Lodge has operated since about 1930. The one-stop is named for long-ago proprietor and LHA consul Ralph Kyburz.

At **Riverton**, there's a roadside viewing area at the site of Moores Station and Riverton Hotel.

Abutments of a 1900 stone-arch bridge, which the Lincoln Highway used, are still visible in the river; three of the bridge's four approach-ramp obelisks have been found and are displayed. This was the third bridge at the site, and it's been replaced two more times. This was on the privately run Lake Tahoe Wagon Road.

About three miles west, on old U.S. Route 50 in **Pacific**, Pacific House is another early gas, food, and lodging stop. And yet another roadhouse, the Pine Lodge Club, remains in **Pollock Pines** on Pony Express Trail and is easy to spot by its neon sign. The old road broke to the north just east of town; U.S. 50 becomes a four-lane freeway.

Pony Express Trail continues north of U.S. Route 50 through **Cedar Grove** to **Camino**. It heads west on Carson Road, then shortly rejoins U.S. 50. Just ahead is the El Dorado National Forest Information Center, which

Placerville about 1940.

can supply news on roads and weather from here back to Nevada.

To follow the original road into **Placerville**, exit onto Smith Flat Road, which connects a mile later to Broadway. The Lincoln soon jogs south to Main Street, where a 1928 concrete Lincoln Highway post is embedded in the wall of Tortilla Flat Restaurant.

After the 1848 discovery of gold in California, the town was first named Old Dry Diggins; the dry dirt had to be hauled to water so gold could be washed out. It didn't take long for troublemakers to arrive among the prospectors, and as a result of an 1849 hanging the place was renamed Hangtown. The spot is marked by the Hangman's Tree Historic Spot Saloon at 305 Main Street. Nooses are a pop-

Sutter's Creek, Placerville (once Hangtown), El Dorado, Angels Camp, Coarsegold, Gold Run, Chinese Camp—these names bespeak a romance that has fled, a dead past. There are dead cities up those dry streambeds, just as there are dead cities over the mountains in Nevada. But between the brown heart of California and brown Nevada towers the fresh, fragrant green of the Sierra.

—Lewis Gannett, Sweet Land *(1933)*

ular motif around town. The saloon even has an effigy hanging from its roof.

Realizing that a name like Hangtown might have drawbacks, locals incorporated their town as Placerville in 1854. The current name derives from the placer gold deposits recovered from the South Fork of the American River. Sutter's Mill, site of the 1848 discovery of gold, has been reconstructed at the Gold Discovery State Historic Park in Coloma, nine miles northwest.

Placerville's rush of wealth from gold was repeated as it became the main stop on the road east to the Comstock Lode. Many entrepreneurs got their start here, from butcher Philip Armour, who went on to fame in the canned-meat business, to a family named Studebaker who made miners' wheelbarrows.

In *A Woman's World Tour in a Motor,* Harriet White Fisher wrote of a visit to this town during her 1910 drive east across the country: "We stopped at Placerville for luncheon. We shall never do so again. The meat was tough, the milk sour, the tea cold, and the waitress impertinent."

Effie Gladding enjoyed her drive east from Placerville in June 1914: "The road was in excellent condition and ran on through the forest for miles, flanked by sugar pines, cedars, firs, balsams, and yellow pines. Squirrels darted back and forth in front of us. The wild white lilac was blooming at the roadside." It's quite a contrast to her portrayal of the "decidedly bumpy" route west of town, which she called "uninteresting, the forest being scrubby, the road dry and dusty."

The 1915 LHA guide noted that Placerville's speed limit was ten miles per hour and that there were "85 automobiles owned."

At the west end of town, the Lincoln jogs north on Canal Street then a portion is lost to the west under U.S. Route 50. It then follows Placerville Drive west and then south. Next to the county fairgrounds is the El Dorado County Historical Society Museum, where two concrete Lincoln Highway markers have been moved to flank the entrance. The highway crosses south of U.S. 50 and becomes Forni Road; Weber Creek Bridge, just south of U.S. 50, is still being used. Forni Road weaves south to **El Dorado**; the Lincoln turns right on Pleasant Valley Road, where Poor Red's Barbecue, in a former Gold Rush–era stagecoach station, is a local favorite for lunch, dinner, and drinks.

Heading west, the highway becomes Mother Lode Road at **Kingsville**, then starts jogging back and forth across U.S. 50. At the former site of **Clarksville**, short pieces of Bass Lake Road on each side of the freeway retain the original twelve-foot-wide concrete pavement from 1918. The 1918 Carson Creek Bridge on White Rock Road is also in use, and stone walls from Gold Rush–era buildings still stand.

The highway takes White Rock Road to Placerville Road, crosses U.S. 50 going north, becomes East Bidwell Street, and enters downtown **Folsom** via Riley Street. At the banks of the American River, the Lincoln turned west on Leidesdorff Street, then southwest along Folsom Boulevard.

After 1927, the Pioneer Branch stayed with Riley Street and crossed the American River on a 1915 open-spandrel concrete bridge that the city would like to replace with a wider span. The adjoining circa 1893 Walker Bridge (steel Pennsylvania Petit through truss) was reerected in 2000. On the other side, Greenback Lane then heads west (originally it followed Orangevale Avenue) to join the Truckee route at Auburn Boulevard at **Citrus Heights**, as noted in the previous section. Combined with the rerouting of the Lincoln west of Sacramento, this shortcut helped drivers bypass the city's downtown streets.

The original Lincoln Highway route follows Folsom Boulevard, a straight shot southwest along the railroad, while U.S. Route 50 weaves north and south of the route. The roads go through Rancho Cordova and finally curve right (west) at **Perkins**, with California State University Sacramento on the right.

Just east of the curve, growth has slowly enveloped the Sacramento 6 Drive-In Theater along Folsom Boulevard (on Oates Drive just east of where Folsom Boulevard and U.S. 50 cross). Increased lights affect movie watching, and the land has become extremely valuable. After years of rumors, the drive-in was set to close at the end of the 2004 season. An insightful article in the August 5, 2004, *Sacramento Bee* by Garance Burke said that owner Syufy Enterprises "hopes to raze the eucalyptus-lined lot to build a twenty-screen multiplex and shopping mall." Was the problem low attendance or profits? Not according to the vice president of operations and training for Syufy, which owns six other drive-ins and seventy-five multiplexes: "It totally makes money because we own the land, so we don't have occupancy fees. It's just that the new project will be a better leverage of the corporate investment." A young patron saw the situation differently: "There's no commercialism or any of that stuff like they have at the walk-in theaters. I'm going to be so sad if this place closes."

At Perkins, a cutoff was available to bypass Sacramento. Instead of curving northwest into downtown, drivers could head south via **Florin** to the Lincoln Highway on its original path south to Stockton. To take the cutoff, turn left (south) on what logically enough is called Florin Perkins Road and follow this to Florin, then turn right (west) on Florin Road to Stockton Boulevard. That was the Lincoln Highway from 1913 to 1926 (this is followed in the next section).

Folsom Boulevard continues northwest to **Sacramento**, a fairly verdant city set in the middle of the bountiful Central Valley. At 30th Street, the 1913 route headed south, picking up Stockton Boulevard. Those who missed the Florin cutoff but were not heading downtown would turn left here to continue to San Francisco. Folsom Boulevard becomes Capitol Avenue (formerly M Street). A block north, at 27th Street and L Street is Sutter's Fort State Historic Park, which features a reconstruction of the post that became famous in 1848 when gold was discovered at Sutter's Mill northeast of Sacramento (discussed in the previous section).

The Lincoln Highway took drivers right to the state capitol. Technically, the route backtracked from here between 1913 and 1928. After that date, the route headed west toward Davis on Capitol Avenue.

Called the Gold Creek Bridge, Orangevale Avenue Bridge, American River Bridge, and the Rainbow Bridge (for its arch), this span west of Folsom is threatened with replacement. Built in 1915, it became part of the Lincoln Highway after 1927, when the Lincoln was rerouted west of Folsom to avoid downtown Sacramento and to ease the connection to the new Lincoln which headed west from Sacramento instead of south. Beyond the bridge is the iron truss Walker Bridge.

11a. Sacramento to San Francisco via Stockton

The 1913 Lincoln Highway departed south from Sacramento and generally followed then U.S. Route 99 (now CA Route 99) through the Central Valley to Stockton. (U.S. Route 50 also once followed this route but now ends in West Sacramento, where it meets I-80.) Irrigation made this valley extremely fertile. Effie Gladding described it: "We drove along an excellent asphalt road, through grain fields and orchards, the almond orchards being loaded with their green, velvety fruit."

The highway heads south on Stockton Boulevard. Just past the Florin cutoff, it merges onto CA Route 99 (a service road continues to carry the Stockton Boulevard name). The route passes through **Elk Grove**; the WPA guide noted this was the center of the Tokay grape-growing region and had one of the oldest wineries in the state.

At **Galt**, an area still strong in the poultry, dairy, and fruit industries, the original route branches right to follow Lincoln Way. The town erected a monument in 1998 in

JUNE 6, 1947
99 Tour-O-Tel, Sacramento

Hi Pop,
By golly we made it—crossed
the Calif state line at 6:15
PM your time. This is a
picture of the place where we
are staying tonite. Think
Moms tired.

Love June

NORMAN ROOT

SMUD Park (short for Sacramento Municipal Utility District) on Lincoln Way to commemorate the highway. It includes a piece of the 1924 roadway taken from the old Dry Creek Bridge south of Galt. A time capsule was also buried.

At a fork two miles south of town, two generations of Lincoln Highway diverge. The original bears right, staying with Lower Sacramento Road; the 1924–26 routing bears left on East Woodson Road. The Lincoln is then lost beneath CA Route 99 for three and a half miles before following Cherokee Lane into **Lodi**.

Back on the original route, the road passes through the San Joaquin subway, which carries the Western Pacific Railroad over the Lincoln Highway. It goes through **Woodbridge** and continues south, jogging but staying with Lower Sacramento Road. It then enters **Stockton** and merges onto Pacific Avenue, makes a three-block jog east on Harding Way, and turns right on El Dorado Street. El Dorado is

This monument in Galt's SMUD Park honors the 1924 roadway and the Lincoln Highway, which was switched to it in 1927.

one-way northbound, so turn right from Harding Way onto Center Street.

Agriculture has played an important role for towns on both the original and later routes. Though some farms have disappeared, canning and distribution industries remain. In Lodi, on the later alignment, a grape festival and harvest fair has been held every September for more than sixty years. That route follows North 99 Frontage Road south to the Calaveras River, then after a short gap (you must take I-99 between exits), it picks up Wilson Way (formerly Cherokee Lane and East Street). Wilson enters Stockton and heads south, parallel to the original route, then the Lincoln turns right (west) on Main Street. This intersected the original route at El Dorado Street in the downtown (Main Street now stops a block east of El Dorado Street). A block north on El Dorado Street at Weber Avenue, the Mission Revival style Stockton Hotel opened in 1910 and became the city's leading accommodations. The elegant hotel featured a roof garden with fountain and pergola. A 1950 renovation couldn't stop the inevitable slide, and it stopped renting rooms in 1960. The hotel housed county offices until 1992, and then it sat abandoned for a decade. In 2004–05, it was being rehabbed as a mix of apartments and retail.

The Lincoln Highway, no longer separated, progresses south on El Dorado to Charter Way, where it turns right (west). Three blocks later, it bears left on French Camp Turnpike Road, parallel with and east of I-5. Drivers have to take the interstate between exits, where it has erased a portion of the Lincoln. Then exit onto French Camp Road and take it into the town of **French Camp**, named

The Stockton Hotel was undergoing restoration in 2004.

for French-Canadian trappers who camped and hunted here in the 1830s. This was the end of the trail from about 1832 to 1845 for French-Canadian trappers employed by the Hudson's Bay Company. The 1916 LHA guide noted the area's rich farms and good salmon fishing and duck hunting.

The Lincoln follows a frontage road to Louise Avenue, where it jogs to the west side of I-5 and goes south on Manthey Road. At **Mossdale**, about where CA Route 120 branches south, the Lincoln and I-5 cross the San Joaquin River Bridge. The Lincoln Highway got a new bridge in 1926—a concrete, rainbow-shaped span still in use. The adjacent Mossdale Crossing commemorates the final link in the first transcontinental railroad. The San Joaquin River drawbridge connected San Francisco with the cross-country portion that ended at Sacramento. The first train crossed it on September 8, 1869. Mossdale Crossing Park and Ramp is two miles north of the intersection of I-5 and I-205 in Tracy.

Immediately ahead, about where I-205 intersects, the old highway is lost. You can follow the Lincoln by exiting I-5 onto West 11th Street and then turning right on Grant Line Road into **Banta**. It then jogs to the left on G Street, 7th Street, and F Street, which becomes Brichetto Road. The Banta Inn on 7th Street has been "a cowpokes saloon" (so the sign says) since 1879 and was rebuilt after a 1937 fire. Tales of hauntings surround the inn, involving a mother and child caught in the fire and a former owner who died of a heart attack behind the bar in 1967 and reportedly likes to move things, in particular stacking the coins in the register. Next door is a former general store.

The Lincoln rejoins 11th Street and takes it through **Tracy**. California's WPA guide said of this town, "Its main street, lined with restaurants, cafés, and soft drink stands, is a popular stopping place for truck drivers who pilot big loads through Altamont Pass."

The highway follows Byron Road and Grant Line Road through picturesque **Mountain House**, a community noted by the Mountain House Café. Adjacent is **Altamont**, perhaps best remembered outside this area for the notorious 1969 rock concert at Altamont Speedway, where a young man was stabbed and killed by a group of Hells Angels who had been hired by the Rolling Stones as security. The speedway is located just to the south where I-205 and I-580 meet. Altamont was settled as a Southern Pacific stop; in Lincoln Highway days, it was a crossroads for local farmers. LHA guides noted that its population was eighty, and now the tiny settlement is nearly deserted.

A gray building with "Summit Garage" legible near the roofline is the only roadside service building still standing, partly restored and used as a vocational training facility.

The hilltops in Altamont Pass are dotted with windmills. Rail lines also shared this corridor, and four bridges were built along Altamont Pass Road/Lincoln Highway; the most spectacular was Carroll Overhead, planned and designed in 1917 but delayed by the war and not built until 1921. The massive concrete span provided a grade separation from the Southern Pacific Railroad. The road was bypassed in 1938 with construction of the state highway (now I-580) and has barely changed. As for the Carroll Overhead, it was no longer needed after the rail line was abandoned, so the county demolished the crumbling bridge in 1988.

Livermore is yet another town where drivers must take numerous roads to follow the Lincoln Highway. Detailed maps are required; those published by the LHA California Chapter are recommended. In general, the route followed Gardella Plaza/Old First Street, then turned right onto Junction Avenue. A merge onto Portola Avenue is blocked by Lincoln Highway Memorial Park; jog around it via Pine Street and L Street.

Locals recall the roads of long ago being jammed with vacationers and produce trucks heading to Stockton canneries. Altamont Pass took a toll on radiators, tires, and transmissions; one of the repair stops was the Highway Garage on Portola Avenue at North L Street (next to the Lincoln Highway park). Earl Duarte's father, Frank, built the garage in 1915. Earl was interviewed in October 1997, when he was eighty, for an *Oakland Tribune*

Remnants of the original Lincoln Highway can be seen beneath this railroad trestle at Mossdale.

article on the road. "The garage was open seven days a week," he said. "No one could come from Oakland to here without car trouble." The garage (and service station/Durant, Flint, and Star dealership) was saved and restored by the Livermore Heritage Guild starting in 1976. It was rededicated in 1996, and it is now a Lincoln Highway Museum operated by the guild.

The road west to **Dublin** has been overlaid by I-580. The original narrow stretch followed a creek through Dublin Canyon. The interstate has sliced up the road in town, but

About 1920, my older brother Everett and I made a trip between Bowman (Auburn) and Oakland via Sacramento, Tracy, Altamont, Livermore and Hayward. . . . we had a supply of five tires and tubes as spares. . . . By the time we had crossed over the Altamont Pass and reached Livermore, we had used all five tires. A series of one flat after another depleted all the spares. We had been traveling on well-used tires, and since the Lincoln Highway had only been completed five years earlier, it was not in the best of condition. . . . We had left Bowman at 10 am and it took sixteen hours to reach Oakland. We did not take time to stop to eat—just to change tires!

—*Clyde Hammond, age 101, quoted in Wes Hammond, "Altamont Pass: Travel Memories of Four Individuals," The Traveler (California LHA), Spring 2002.*

Cal 38

Altamont Pass, often misidentified as Dublin Canyon. This is a good example of how tight turns were turned into gentle curves.

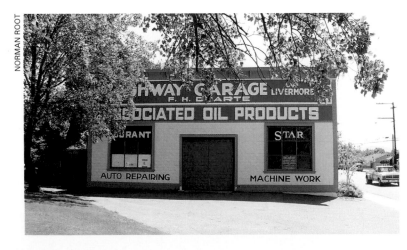

The Highway Garage of Livermore, built in 1915, has been restored and operates as a Lincoln Highway Museum.

Dublin Court, Dublin Boulevard, and Dublin Canyon Road can each be followed. Take the last, now a frontage road, until it ends, then follow East Castro Valley Boulevard, first south, then north, of I-580 into **Hayward**.

The LHA guides explained: "The Lincoln Highway runs through the Dublin Canyon at Hayward. It is one of the main passes through the Coast Range Mountains." Postcards once celebrated the beauty of the area.

Turn left on Grove Way, which immediately crosses I-580. The Lincoln then turns left onto A Street, follows it for a few blocks, then turns right on Foothill Boulevard; here the highway starts its push northward to Oakland and San Francisco. Foothill Boulevard, now also CA Route 238, continues until an interchange at I-580 has erased the old road. Today's drivers must detour right onto East Castro Valley Boulevard, then left on John Drive, which curves around to rejoin Foothill Boulevard heading north. The route then again merges briefly with I-580.

Exit at Estudillo Avenue and take MacArthur Boulevard through **San Leandro**, famous a century ago for its cherries. The annual Cherry Festival, started in 1909, is still held today. That same year, the San Leandro Creek Bridge was built; it likewise survives, located just after turning onto MacArthur. At 98th Avenue, the famed Oakland Zoo is to the east in the 525-acre Knowland Park. The zoo has 440 animals living in naturalistic habitats.

At 73rd Avenue, with Eastmont Mall on the left, the Lincoln bears left to again follow Foothill Boulevard. The mall sits on the site of a Chevrolet plant (noted in the discussion of the Fallon Sink in the Nevada chapter). Ground was broken in 1916, and by 1919, the plant was producing one hundred cars and trucks per day. Several other automakers opened plants here too, earning the city the nickname "Detroit of the West," but that did not last. Chevy operations moved away in 1963.

The Lincoln originally took Foothill Boulevard to 1st Avenue in downtown **Oakland**; several vintage postcards picture Foothill, as does the 1924 LHA guidebook, but it has since gone through various generations of urban sprawl and decline. In 1924—and lasting until the entire route was bypassed in 1928—the Lincoln was realigned to turn left up ahead at High Street, then right on 14th Street (now International Boulevard). At 23rd Avenue, it jogged left to 12th Street, which it followed into town, rejoining the original alignment at Lake Merritt. The saltwater lake, on the right, was an unsightly tidal basin until 1898. It now boasts grassy banks, walking paths, and controlled water levels.

The Lincoln Highway routes rejoined to follow 13th Street at the lake, but that's now one-way eastbound. At 13th Street and Harrison Street is the former Hotel Oakland, the city's leading hotel for early motorists; it's now senior housing. The route went left on Harrison Street, right on 9th Street (another one-way southbound now), and left on Broadway. About ten blocks ahead were the ferry slips, since converted to Jack London Square, an outdoor shopping area named for one of the city's best-known writers. London lived here from 1876 to 1916; his international fame came in 1903 with his book *Call of the Wild*. The upscale retail area includes a log cabin that London supposedly lived in, moved from the Yukon, and the First and

The Hotel Oakland now houses senior citizens.

Last Chance Saloon, built in 1880 from the timbers of a whaling ship. The bar was a favorite of London's; it was indeed the last chance for liquor for those taking the ferry to "dry" Alameda Island, or the first chance when arriving here.

The convergence of rails, roads, and waterways has made Oakland a major shipping crossroads; by 1970, it had surpassed San Francisco as the region's leading port. Accommodating containers is especially critical, as their ability to be transferred among ships, trucks, and train cars reduces cargo handling. Oakland's vast flat land enables containers to be easily stored and allows direct links with overland truck and rail transportation, conditions harder to find in hilly San Francisco.

From 1913 to 1928, Lincoln Highway travelers took the Broadway Ferry across the bay to **San Francisco**. After a six-mile boat ride, visitors landed at Ferry Slip 4, just south of the Ferry Building. Today, just a few blocks south, the San Francisco–Oakland Bay Bridge serves the same purpose, carrying I-80. Travel across it is free eastbound (on the lower level), but $1 westbound. It passes through a tunnel on Yerba Buena Island; an exit takes drivers to the connected Treasure Island, built for the 1939 World's Fair. Take it as fair warning that the Oakland end of the bridge is known as "the maze."

The waterfront northwest of San Francisco's Ferry Building has become known as the Embarcadero, a park with restored trolleys running along its length all the way to Pier 39 and Fisherman's Wharf.

Beth O'Shea described her arrival in *A Long Way from Boston*, which recounts her circa 1922 trip:

MARKET STREET, LOOKING TOWARDS FERRY BUILDING, SAN FRANCISCO, CALIF.

From 1913 to 1927, Lincoln Highway travelers took a ferry from Oakland to San Francisco's Ferry Building.

After a while the boat nosed into its slip beneath the pointed clock tower of the Ferry Building and we drove off into Market Street, the busy main stem that bisects the city all the way to Twin Peaks. The slot, it was called, they told us. Anything south of Market Street was "south of the slot." There were flower stands on every corner, and in Union Square the cable cars with their long open-air seats were starting off on their clanging, perilous journeys up the hills.

The Gold Rush boosted San Francisco's population from 800 in 1848 to 25,000 two years later, and 150,000 by 1870. As boatloads of dreamers arrived, passengers and

"In San Francisco, I saw for the first time that great California institution, the cafeteria. They pronounce this word in California with the accent on the 'i.' To a traveler it seems as if all San Francisco must take its meals in these well equipped and perfectly ordered restaurants."

—*Effie Gladding*, Across the Continent by the Lincoln Highway *(1914)*

NORMAN ROOT

The Ferry Building today.

BERNIE HEISEY

California Palace
of the Legion of Honor,
Lincoln Park, San Francisco,
where the Lincoln Highway ends

WESTERN TERMINUS OF THE LINCOLN HIGHWAY

The end of the Lincoln was marked by a sign and flagpole until 1928, when this concrete terminus marker was added.

SEPT. 9, 1954
Union Square Showing
Garage, San Francisco

Hi Ben!
Well here we are in this fabulous city of S.F. It is chilly tho bright sunshine. We've taken 2 tours so have really done the town.

Mom & Dad.

Like Oakland, San Francisco was home to at least one early carmaker: the California Auto Company, which made gasoline, steam, and electric cars priced from $500 to $3,000. They touted these prices as "from $100 to $300 cheaper than Eastern manufacturers."

San Francisco also was home to the first school in the United States named for President Lincoln–Lincoln School on 5th Street near Market Street. The city erected the first Lincoln statue, dedicated on the first anniversary of his death. Both the school and statue were destroyed in the 1906 earthquake and fire.

The Lincoln Highway ran from the Ferry Building southwest on Market Street about eight blocks to Post Street. This stretch was the last to run horse-drawn streetcars, which were replaced in June 1913. Post is now one-way eastbound; those westbound can take Geary Street, a block to the south. A couple blocks to the west, between the two streets, is Union Square, once the town center and eventually named for the pro-Union meetings held here as the Civil War loomed. The city's Automobile Row stretched eight blocks west from here to Van Ness Avenue. After about eighteen more blocks, the Lincoln Highway turned south on Presidio Avenue for one block, then west on what is now marked Geary Boulevard.

It's some forty-five blocks to the next right turn; the original route took 36th Avenue, but that is no longer a through street, so turn right on 34th Avenue and enter Lincoln Park. The road becomes Legion of Honor Drive and S-curves to the California Palace of the Legion of Honor, a museum of fine arts dedicated to California's soldiers who died in World War I.

At first there was no special marking at the end of the Lincoln Highway. Then, in

1915, the LHA erected a sign, making it a permanent marker on September 14.

On July 4, 1917, the 250th birthday of Betsy Ross, the Native Daughters of the Golden West (NDGW) erected the Betsy Ross Memorial Flag Pole at the end of the road. Plans had begun long before the Lincoln was routed here, but the NDGW struggled with funding; they even began charging members a 10¢ fee. The location was disputed twice before settling on Lincoln Park. As plans were made for 1917, a "godsend" occurred: a 120-foot-tall Douglas fir washed up on a nearby beach, perfect for the pole. The flagpole disappeared in the 1970s. It has been suggested that a similar pole should be mounted on the ninetieth anniversary in 2007.

11b. Sacramento to San Francisco via Vallejo

In 1928, the Lincoln Highway was rerouted (as indicated by concrete posts) to an alignment now paralleled by I-80, from Sacramento through Davis and Vallejo to Berkeley, where a ferry still took drivers to San Francisco. This was made possible with the bridging of the Carquinez Strait. Parts of the new route were soon designated U.S. Route 40.

The Victory Highway stayed south of the Sacramento River by traversing Courtland, Walnut Grove, and Isleton, crossed the east end of Suisun Bay at Antioch (by toll bridge after 1926), and through Pittsburg to Berkeley.

The realigned Lincoln Highway departed from Sacramento to the west via M Street and crossed the M Street Bridge over the Sacramento River. The bridge had been built by a railroad in 1911 so that the tracks went down the middle while traffic was confined

even crews abandoned the ships. Some boats remained at the wharves and were adapted as bars or restaurants; others were salvaged or sunk. As the city grew, the land around them was filled and built atop. Hundreds of boats remain underground, particularly beneath the skyscrapers of the financial district west of Market Street to Broadway.

CAUSEWAY OVER YOLO BASIN BETWEEN SACRAMENTO AND DAVIS, CALIFORNIA.

91682

Until construction of the Great Yolo Basin Trestle in 1916, crossing the marshy Sacramento Valley was nearly impossible. The rutted Tule Jake Road spanned the three miles but was flooded most of the year.

31:- TOWER BRIDGE, SACRAMENTO, CALIFORNIA.

Tower Bridge, Sacramento.

to nine-foot-wide lanes on the outside of the central trusses. The central span rotated on a pier in the channel to let tall ships pass. Even worse traffic backups came from the switching of trains at its east end.

It was replaced in 1936 by the Streamline Moderne Tower Bridge, a vertical-lift span. M Street has also been renamed Capitol Avenue. Immediately north is Old Sacramento, the town's original bustling waterfront. As commercial activity moved east, the area became a slum. Starting in the 1960s, twenty-nine acres were rehabbed, and now the area features shops and restaurants, some in buildings from the mid-nineteenth century. The National Landmark area also includes the Discovery Museum and the California State Railroad Museum.

Half a mile south of the bridge is the Towe (rhymes with cow) Auto Museum, at Front Street and V Street featuring examples of every Ford made before 1952. The museum has a library and archives, and a 1928 concrete marker out front was moved from Van Ness Avenue in San Francisco.

Once across the river, the 1928 Lincoln Highway continues on West Capitol Avenue through **West Sacramento**. The street is lined with postwar motels, a result of serving both the Lincoln Highway and U.S. Route 40. Even the state's 1939 WPA guide mentioned "the roadside clutter of city outskirts—billboards, auto camps, gas stations, fruit and vegetable stands, truck garden plots, and ranchers' shanties." Today the years of prosperity have long since passed; as Andrew Wood of

MotelAmericana.com describes it, Capitol Avenue "becomes a land of chain linked vacant lots, duct taped windows, and drive-in movie theatres turned into trailer parks."

Business I-80/CA Route 99 are parallel to the south, and now I-80 comes in from the north. In 2002, a replica Lincoln Highway concrete post was placed at the bicycle path park at the approach to the Yolo Bypass Causeway. Capitol Avenue merges onto the interstate. It's barely noticeable that the lanes ahead are raised, but the underlying marshland long vexed drivers and was another reason why the Lincoln Highway was not initially routed this way.

The first motorists forging across the marshes followed the rut-filled Tule Jake Road, named for the tule marsh plants it traversed. It was typically unusable in winter and spring, when the Sacramento River flooded the land, which is why most traffic went south to the Lincoln Highway via Stockton. The three-mile Great Yolo Basin Trestle, or Yolo Causeway,

Sweems, north of Davis, included the "Y" Café, coffee shop, service station, auto court, and Greyhound bus depot, seen here in 1944.

finally bridged the quagmire with its March 1916 opening. That month, the *Vacaville Reporter* wrote that, "led by the Davis band, 27 automobile loads of Davis people slipped over the Yolo causeway Saturday night and surprised Sacramento by making the first excursion across the tules." The causeway was widened in 1932, but traffic demands (and its wooden piers) led to its being demolished in 1962. It was completely rebuilt to carry I-80; the original was north of the interstate, and for years, many of the support piles could still be seen. At the west end, the highway bears right onto CR Route 32A; the surviving twenty-foot-wide concrete marks the location of the original roadway.

Part of the abandoned road between I-80 and the railroad is now a bike path, looking not unlike the early days except for new billboards. The old highway joins Olive Drive as it enters **Davis**, which the 1926 *Mohawk-Hobbs Grade and Surface Guide* called a grain and sheep center. The Lincoln turns right on Richards Boulevard and passes under the Southern Pacific tracks via a short 1917 tun-

nel. It immediately turns left on 1st Street, and three blocks later, takes a right on B Street.

B Street goes north a few blocks to an intersection with Russell Boulevard to the left and 5th Street to the right; on the southeast corner, a 1928 concrete marker from the corner of Richards/1st has been moved and reset under a tree in Central Park. The Lincoln turns left on Russell. Along the left (south) side is the University of California at Davis, a leading agricultural and wine research school.

The intersection with CA Route 113 (formerly CA Route 99) is a modern mix of ramps, but this was once the Y where the road coming south from Woodland ended. Numerous photos document the Sweems one-stop: a filling station, coffee shop, soda fountain, café, bus depot, and the Davis Y Auto Court. No trace remains, except a recently reset 1928 Lincoln Highway concrete post on the southwest corner and an adjacent 1986 historical plaque noting that the highway once was lined with black walnut trees planted in the 1870s and known as the Avenue of Trees.

U.S. Route 40 would later make a direct path west, but the Lincoln Highway followed section lines: west on Russell Boulevard, south on Pedrick Road, west on Sievers Road, and south on Currey Road crossing I-80. Entering **Dixon**, the road becomes North 1st Street; at Industrial Way, a replica concrete Lincoln Highway post was placed in front of a Ford dealership in 2000. 1st Street (also marked CA Route 113) continues into downtown Dixon. The *Mohawk-Hobbs* guide called this "a wealthy town in a rich dairy and grain section." The downtown still has many locally owned businesses. Fans of roadside kitsch recall Dixie the Dixon Dinosaur arriving at a

convenience store along I-80 in 1994. The fifty-foot, fiberglass-skinned brachiosaurus was moved to Benicia a couple years later and was renamed Benny. Zoning battles may have followed, as Benny has since been moved to private property. A jog west on A Street in downtown Dixon puts the Lincoln on Porter Street, which it took west from town.

Again following section lines, the highway bears right onto Midway Road, then left on Meridian Road. It bumps into I-80, which has erased part of the old road as it headed south; development has erased much more.

Across from where I-505 meets I-80, Helen Harbison Power began selling fruit to travelers on July 3, 1921, in the shade of a tall walnut tree, and a business called the Nut Tree was born. Helen and her husband, Edwin "Bunny" Power, also became known for selling figs and lemonade, and by 1923, the *Vacaville Reporter* noted that they were employing fifty people to tend their 135 acres. Even in the off-season, fifteen employees were needed to serve motorists, ship fruit orders, or package candy and nuts. The next year, the Powers built a factory in Vacaville, and then they bought another factory that specialized in making fancy containers. Meanwhile, the fruit stand had grown to include a tearoom, restaurant, and soda fountain. The Power children got involved, and by the 1950s, with traffic ever increasing, the family added a toy shop, then a huge addition that used the new method of tilt-up concrete walls, and even an airport. (Talk about competition—on the west side of town, the new Ranchotel motor inn added a twenty-three-hundred-foot-long runway too.)

The Nut Tree restaurant got a brief review in AAA's 1955 *Western Accommodations Direc-*

tory: "This western food is America's newest type of cuisine. Packed with history, shaped by climate, tempered by many nationalities and improved by ingenuity."

The Nut Tree had become an institution, visited by tourists and kings alike, but alas, family differences led to its closure in the 1990s. The land lay bare for years, but now a baseball field has been built there, and the former orchards are now home to the Factory Stores at Nut Tree, which bring more development . . . and traffic.

Just past the I-505 cloverleaf, the Lincoln Highway breaks away along Monte Vista Avenue into **Vacaville**. A century ago, Vacaville was a leading producer of fresh fruit. The town was known for its welcome signs: ten-foot-diameter, orange-and-black billboards showing two grizzly bears on hind legs carrying a basket of fruit between them, and proclaiming, "Eat Vacaville Fruits." As the industry declined, the economy shifted to serving a nearby army air base and navy yard. A great source of information is "A 100-Year Snapshot of Vacaville," an online collection of articles by the *Vacaville Reporter*.

The Lincoln Highway turned left on Mc-Clellan Street and right onto School Street, now closed to traffic. The School Street Pedestrian Walk has two original concrete Lincoln Highway markers, both in their third locations, but each within two blocks of where they were originally set. On the west end is the 1911 concrete-arch Ulatis Creek Bridge. The historical society operates the old city hall and jail across the creek.

At the west end of School Street, the highway joins Main Street for a block. A Mexican restaurant on Main occupies the 1938 post

office and still has its WPA mural. From Main Street, the highway bears left on Merchant Street and heads southwest. A postcard view shows a concrete bridge—with high-arched sides and "Vaca Valley" on a sign overhead—crossing Alamo Creek. The town was a midway point for travelers, but it took until 1920 to open its first hotel, the thirty-four-room Hotel Vacaville on Merchant. It burned in 1936.

West of Vacaville, I-80 has obliterated much of the old road through Lagoon Valley, but a stretch of Cherry Glen Road is beautiful, meandering around fields and orchards, sometimes on vintage concrete pavement. After it ends at I-80, Nelson Road picks up to the south, then after another gap, North Texas Street enters **Fairfield**. The highway makes a right turn onto the similarly named West Texas Street; a 1928 concrete marker sits in front of the Solano County Courthouse. A bronze statue of Francisco Solano along U.S. Route 40 honors an overlord of the regional Indian tribes (though honoring him by his Spanish name). He was a friend and ally of Gen. Mariano Vallejo, who was settling the area, and it was Vallejo who asked in 1850 that the new county be named Solano.

A 1928 concrete marker east of Rockville is less visible; it's in the backyard of a house on Rockville Road. As Texas Street becomes Rockville Road, the marker originally sat along the highway in front of the house at Chadbourne Road. The road, with little change through time, is lined with vineyards. Once in **Rockville**, the highway turns left on Suisun Valley Road. It jogs through the jumble of freeways to **Cordelia** (some sections lost) and

BERNIE HEISEY

NUT TREE · HIGHWAY U.S. 40 · VACAVILLE CALIFORNIA

A roadside business called the Nut Tree grew up around this giant black walnut.

then heads northwest on Jameson Canyon Road, following CA Route 12. At CA Route 29/Napa-Vallejo Highway, the Lincoln turns south; at American Canyon, it leaves CA Route 29 and heads south on Broadway Street.

Vallejo (vie-YEA-ho; Americanized to val-LAY-ho) is located on the north side of the mile-wide Carquinez Straits between Suisun Bay and San Pablo Bay, through which the Sacramento and San Joaquin Rivers flow toward San Francisco Bay. The town was founded by Gen. Vallejo in 1851. He'd come to the area in the 1830s wanting to build a town bearing his name. When California was established in 1850, he willingly cooperated, offering to build museums, schools, and parks, as well as land to build the state capitol. The town briefly hosted it before the capital was moved to Sacramento. The economy was fueled by the Mare Island naval shipyard from 1854 to 1994. The town is now home to Six Flags Marine World/Africa USA wildlife park.

Would you portray yourself as a chicken to help your business?

When built, the Carquinez Bridge was called the largest highway bridge in the world, at 30 feet wide and 4,482 feet long. Such impressive figures did not hold up long in the crush of traffic, and a twin was built adjacent.

Downtown, just before Broadway ends, many cross streets are named for states; a matchbook advertised the Chicken Coop Inn at Alabama Street. The Lincoln Highway jogs left and continues south on Alameda Street. About ten blocks later, the highway bears left onto 5th Street. Just a few blocks back, Benicia Road must have once intersected Alameda Street; another matchbook advertised the Barrel Club next to the Big Barrel on the "Lincoln Hiway" at Benicia Road.

5th Street merges into I-80 and crosses the Carquinez Strait, now on a new span.

Carquinez Bridge between Crockett and Vallejo, Pacific Highway—San Francisco to Sacramento

Until the waterway was bridged, cars crossed by ferry. In 1926, the cost for the ferry to the town of Rodeo was 55¢ per car and 10¢ per passenger. Boats ran every twenty minutes at peak for the fifteen-minute trip. The American Toll Bridge Company built a pair of spans—first the Antioch Bridge, which the Victory Highway adopted when it opened in 1926, then the Carquinez Strait Bridge twenty-six miles to the west. When it opened in 1927, at a cost of $8 million, the Carquinez was the world's largest vehicular span. The state highway moved from the ferry to this bridge, and the Lincoln Highway followed suit. A twin bridge was added in 1958, but by 2004, the original was set for demolition.

Once across, I-80 speeds southward but San Pablo Avenue meanders alongside San Pablo Bay and through the former port towns of **Rodeo**, **Pinole**, and **San Pablo**. Rodeo gets its name from the annual cattle rodeos that were held in the area by Spanish settlers. Legend has it that Pinole was named for the meal Indians made from acorns and grass seeds and gave to a band of starving Spanish soldiers here. An old timber railroad overpass once used by the Lincoln Highway in Pinole was demolished in October 2004.

The road at **Richmond** crosses I-80. The town was a deep water harbor and so became a transfer point for the region's produce and products. At this point, the water to the west is now San Francisco Bay. San Pablo Boulevard pushes south through **El Cerrito**, "the little hill," and **Albany**, originally called Ocean View but renamed for a mayor's birthplace. In the 1920s, the El Cerrito Camp offered fourteen cottages and a laundry room starting at $1.25.

In downtown **Berkeley**, the Lincoln turns right on University Avenue, following it to the Berkeley Pier on San Francisco Bay, now a colorful tree-shaded park. The city is known for the University of California campus and its left-leaning causes. The state's WPA guide had little good to say, mentioning only U.S. Route 40's roadbed as crossing the "brackish mudflats of the bayshore, where the stagnant odor of decay wafts inland. The grayish waters lap half-rotted pilings and sway small dories."

The ferry crossed to San Francisco's Hyde Street Pier, the eastern end of the city's Marina District and the western end of the Embarcadero. Though this is the later route of the Lincoln Highway, the ferry was available beforehand; in 1914, Thornton Round's family crossed to Berkeley on their way to Sacramento.

In 1919, Beatrice Massey crossed on a ferry boat holding seventy-five cars. She marveled at the harbor, surrounded by hills and crowned by Mount Tamalpais. The water was filled "with ships from every land . . . dressed with the flags of every country," plus fifty battleships of the Pacific fleet and a host of smaller craft, "from high-powered motor launches to fishing boats, 'wind-jammers,' or old-time sailing vessels, ocean liners, great freighters, transports, and tramps, all form[ing] a part of the scene along the Embarcadero."

She also wrote that the day after she arrived in San Francisco, so did the First Transcontinental Army Truck Convoy. She even dined with its commander Lt. Col. Charles McClure, who told her the desert sands had been the worst part of the trip.

Frederic Van de Water wrote in *The Family Flivvers to Frisco* that they felt a change in the

THE GOLDEN GATE FROM PALACE OF THE LEGION OF HONOR, SAN FRANCISCO, CALIF.

92

CALIFORNIANS, INC. PHOTO

2A-H799

RUSSELL REIN

Looking east from Lincoln Park across San Francisco Bay, 1932. The
Golden Gate Bridge, sketched-in here, was not completed until 1937.
The flagpole marked the western terminus of the Lincoln Highway.

*You will be weary at night, but you will be ready for the open road and the new
adventure the next morning, particularly if you drive leisurely and really see things
as you go along. . . . And if you are like me, you would feel that you would some
day like to make the entire trip again.*

—*Effie Gladding,* author of Across the Continent by the Lincoln Highway,
in the foreword to the LHA's 1915 road guide

climate long before they reached the bay: "Miles from the coast, the coolness of San Francisco, the assuaging breath of sea and fog, reached overland and touched us. Sunbaked for weeks, we shivered with cold as we took the Richmond ferry across the bay and continued to shiver from another cause when we drove off the boat and into the city." He was referring to the fast drivers and steep hills: "We were grazed by innumerable drivers; we involved ourselves in numerous, notable traffic tangles and we had begun to love this haphazard, ugly, mature city."

The area between the Hyde Street Pier and Municipal Pier is now called Aquatic Park and features docked historic ships, a cable car turnaround, and the San Francisco Maritime

National Historic Park. A year-round visitor center at Hyde Street and Jefferson Street (in a 1907 brick building) has exhibits and rangers who can assist you year-round. The Maritime Museum, inside the Bathhouse Building (a WPA project built to look like a Streamline Moderne ship), has numerous displays and period photographs documenting the region's history.

Immediately to the east is Fisherman's Wharf, the city's main tourist attraction. Street vendors, restored brick buildings such as the Cannery, and seafood restaurants recall its heritage as an important fishing-industry locale.

The Lincoln took Hyde Street a few blocks south, jogged west on North Point Street, then turned south on Van Ness Avenue (also

marked U.S. Route 101). It followed this often-congested street some sixteen blocks to California Street, where it turned right (west). Another Automobile Row was located on Van Ness Avenue from Lombard Street south, past California Street to Market Street, and many of the showrooms survive, readapted.

The Lincoln Highway followed California Street some fifty blocks westward. In between, a marker survives at Park Presidio Boulevard (more precisely, at 14th Street next to the bus shelter). The Lincoln turned right on 32nd Avenue, then left at El Camino del Mar; the westernmost extant marker is hidden here in shrubbery on the southeast corner.

El Camino del Mar curves along the water's edge to the California Palace of the Legion of Honor. The Beaux Arts building traces its roots to the 1915 San Francisco Panama Pacific International Exposition. Alma de Bretteville Spreckels fell in love with the French Pavilion at the exposition, itself a replica of the Palais de la Légion d'Honneur in Paris, an eighteenth-century landmark on the left bank of the Seine. Alma persuaded her husband, sugar magnate Adolph B. Spreckels, to recapture the beauty of the pavilion as a new art museum for San Francisco. At the close of the exposition, the French government granted them permission to construct a

End of the trip, August 8, 1928. Local Boy Scouts gathered in San Francisco's Lincoln Park around the Rodin sculpture *The Three Shades* to greet (from left on the Reo Speed Wagon) scouts Edward Pratt, Carl Zapffe, Bernard Queneau, and Mark Hughes.

BERNARD QUENEAU

In time—in some time to come—the Lincoln Highway will be a real transcontinental boulevard. But don't wish this trip on your grandchildren!

—Beatrice Massey,
It Might Have Been
Worse *(1920)*

Seventy-four years after he last visited Lincoln Park, Bernard Queneau, left, stood in 2002 with Boy Scout Troop 17 and a newly installed replica terminus marker.

CAROL INGALD

permanent replica, but World War I delayed the groundbreaking until 1921. Built on what was then a remote site known as Land's End, the California Palace of the Legion of Honor was completed in 1924, and on Armistice Day of that year, its doors opened to the public. In keeping with the wishes of the donors—to "honor the dead while serving the living"—it was accepted by the city of San Francisco as a museum of fine arts dedicated to the memory of the thirty-six hundred Californians who had lost their lives on the battlefields of France during World War I. The museum displays four thousand years of ancient and European art, including Auguste Rodin's *Thinker*, which sits in the museum's Court of Honor.

The terminus of the Lincoln Highway was marked in the parking lot by two plaques at the base of a flagpole. In 1928, a concrete Lincoln Highway post was set at the foot of a bronze sculpture of the *Three Shades*. All disappeared over the years. Then, in 2002, a replica terminus post was installed nearby.

Attending the ceremony was eighty-nine-year-old Bernard Queneau, who had crossed the country during the summer of 1928 as a Boy Scout to promote the marking of the highway by these concrete posts. He returned yet again in 2003, newly married to LHA past president Esther M. Oyster. The couple was part of a caravan driving more than thirty-three hundred miles across the country on the Lincoln Highway. They were following in the footsteps—and tire tracks—of drivers ninety years earlier who first began looking for red, white, and blue bands painted on telephone poles.

The website www.brianbutko.com includes illustrations, information, and links to some of the places mentioned in this book. Following are some of the key organizations that can help you with further reseach.

One of the strangest of all Lincoln Highway cards. The water wagon humor on the front is matched by an interesting note on the back: "Jim you ought to be here. More jack[rabbit]s than we can kill. . . ."

Curt Teich Postcard Archives (CTPA)

The CTPA is the nation's largest publicly held repository of postcards and related materials, with more than 360,000 cataloged images. The core of the collection is from the Curt Teich Company, which produced postcards from 1898 to 1978. Many postcards in this book were originally printed by the Teich company; their use here is courtesy of CTPA. The archives website includes an invaluable postcard dating guide. CTPA, Lake County Museum, 27277 Forest Preserve Drive, Lakewood Forest Preserve, Wauconda, IL 60084, (847) 968-3381.
www.co.lake.il.us/forest/ctpa.htm

Lincoln Highway Association (LHA)

The LHA identifies, preserves, interprets, improves, and publicizes the routes and businesses of the Lincoln Highway through publications and an annual conference. The headquarters is filled with books, brochures, and collectibles. Annual conferences held in Lincoln Highway states every June offer sessions and tours. A quarterly magazine regularly has in-depth articles, news briefs, and numerous vintage and contemporary illustra-

tions. LHA, P.O. Box 308, Franklin Grove, IL 61031, (815) 456-3030.
www.lincolnhighwayassoc.org

Lincoln Highway Association Collection, University of Michigan

The Transportation History Collection of the Special Collections Library, University of Michigan, holds materials from the original LHA office in Detroit from 1912 to the late 1930s. These include trip logs, board minutes, press releases, the 1928 logbook of markers, strip maps, and drawings by landscape architect Jens Jensen for the Ideal Section. There also are more than three thousand photographs showing construction, bridges, campsites, and directors traveling the route. Thanks to a grant from the university's Friends of the Library, and through the collaboration of staff in the Special Collections Library and Digital Library Production Service, nearly all of the photos have been digitized and placed online. Special Collections Library, 7th Floor, Harlan Hatcher Graduate Library, Ann Arbor, MI 48109-1205, (734) 764-9377.
www.lib.umich.edu/spec-coll

Available at the university's Bentley Historical Library are the Henry Bourne Joy Papers, donated by his wife in 1946, including a scrapbook of his 1915 trip. BHL, 1150 Beal Avenue, Ann Arbor, MI 48109-2113, (734) 936-1333. www.umich.edu/~bhl

Lincoln Highway Heritage Corridor (LHHC)

Pennsylvania's LHHC promotes tourism and preservation along and near the Lincoln Highway in six counties: Westmoreland, Somerset, Bedford, Fulton, Franklin, and Adams. The corridor encourages economic development, intergovernmental cooperation, cultural conservation, recreation, and education. New metal signs mark the original route. An interpretive center with a library, exhibits, and gift shop is planned for the Ligonier area. LHHC, P.O. Box 582, Ligonier, PA 15658, (724) 238-9030.
www.lhhc.org

Lincoln Highway National Museum and Archives (LHNMA)

The LHNMA, briefly located in Galion, Ohio, is for now an online collection of information. www.lincoln-highway-museum.org

Lincoln Highway Special Resource Study

Information about the recent National Park Service study is available online, including the 136-page summary report in PDF format. www.nps.gov/mwro/LincolnHighway

Lincoln Highway Trading Post

The official supplier of Lincoln Highway merchandise; all sales benefit the LHA. Souvenirs include shirts, caps, postcards, signs, flags, CDs, and a variety of new and reprinted publications. P.O. Box 6088, Canton, OH 44706, (800) 454-8319.
www.LHTP.com

The Lincoln Museum

Dedicated to the life and legacy of the sixteenth president, the Lincoln Museum contains thousands of artifacts, clippings, photos, books, and documents, including three hundred signed by Lincoln. A permanent exhibit includes eleven galleries and eighteen interactives. Lincoln Museum, 200 E. Berry Street, Fort Wayne, IN 46802, (260) 455-3864.
www.TheLincolnMuseum.org

The Patrice Press

Founded and operated by Gregory Franzwa, author of five comprehensive Lincoln Highway state guides to date—*Iowa*, *Nebraska*, *Wyoming*, *Utah*, and *Nevada* (see Bibliography)—this press handles a variety of books on the Lincoln Highway and other historic trails. P.O. Box 85639, Tucson, AZ 85754-5639, (800) 367-9242.
www.patricepress.com

Society for Commercial Archeology (SCA)

The SCA is the oldest national organization devoted to the commercial-built environment. Through publications, conferences, and tours, the society helps preserve and document twentieth-century structures and architecture, including diners, gas stations, drive-in theaters, tourist courts, highways, and neon signs. SCA, c/o Dept. of Popular Culture, Bowling Green State University, Bowling Green, OH 43403, (419) 372-2136.
www.sca-roadside.org

Bibliography

General

Alsberg, Henry G. *The American Guide: A Source Book and Complete Travel Guide for the United States.* New York: Hastings House, 1949.

Anderson, Mary Elizabeth. *Link across America: A Story of the Historic Lincoln Highway.* Windsor, CA: Rayve Productions, 1997.

Automobile Blue Book, Official AAA 1908. New York: Class Journal Co., 1908.

Bain, David Haward. *Empire Express: Building the First Transcontinental Railroad.* New York: Viking Press, 1999.

Belasco, Warren. *Americans on the Road: From Autocamp to Motel, 1910–1945.* Cambridge, MA: MIT Press, 1981.

Berger, Michael L. *The Devil Wagon in God's Country: The Automobile and Social Change in Rural America, 1893–1929.* Hamden, CT: Archon Books, 1979.

Bliss, Carey S. *Autos across America: A Bibliography of Transcontinental Automobile Travel, 1903–1940.* Austin, TX: Jenkins and Reese, 1982.

Borglum, Lincoln. *Mount Rushmore: The Story behind the Scenery.* Las Vegas: KC Publications, 1993.

Brimmer, F. Everet. *Autocomping Facts.* Chicago: Outers' Book Co., 1924.

Brinkley, Douglas. *Wheels for the World: Henry Ford, His Company, and a Century of Progress.* New York: Viking, 2003.

Bryson, Bill. *The Lost Continent: Travels in Small-Town America.* New York: Harper & Row, 1989.

Butler, John L. *First Highways of America.* Iola, WI: Krause Publications, 1994.

"Chauffeur." *Two Thousand Miles on an Automobile: Being a Desultory Narrative of a Trip through New England, New York, Canada, and the West.* Philadelphia: J. B. Lippincott Co., 1902.

Clymer, Floyd. *Henry's Wonderful Model T, 1908–1927.* New York: McGraw-Hill Book Co., 1955.

———. *Treasury of Early American Automobiles, 1877–1925.* New York: Bonanza Books, 1950.

Cole, Dermot. *Hard Driving: The 1908 Auto Race from New York to Paris.* New York: Paragon House, 1991.

Copeland, Estella M. *Overland by Auto in 1913: Diary of a Family Tour from California to Indiana.* Indianapolis: Indiana Historical Society, 1981.

Crane, Laura Dent. *The Automobile Girls at Chicago.* Philadelphia: Henry Altemus Co., 1912.

Davies, Pete. *American Road: The Story of an Epic Transcontinental Journey at the Dawn of the Motor Age.* New York: Henry Holt and Co., 2002.

de Bryas, Comtesse Madeleine, and Jacqueline de Bryas. *A Frenchwoman's Impressions of America.* New York: The Century Co., 1920.

Diviney, Ann E. *From Sea to Shining Sea: A Hike Across America on Old U.S. 30.* Self-published, 1997.

Dixon, Winifred Hawkridge. *Westward Hoboes: Ups and Downs of Frontier Motoring.* New York: Charles Scribner's Sons, 1925.

Dreiser, Theodore. *A Hoosier Holiday.* New York: John Lane Co., 1916. Reprint, Bloomington: Indiana University Press, 1997.

Duncan, Dayton, and Ken Burns. *Horatio's Drive: America's First Road Trip.* New York: Alfred A. Knopf, 2003.

Dunn, Edward D. *Double-Crossing America by Motor.* New York: G. P. Putnam's Sons, 1933.

Eisenhower, Dwight D. *At Ease: Stories I Tell to Friends.* Garden City, NY: Doubleday & Company, 1967.

Ellingson, Yvonne. *From Sea to Sea in a Model T.* Boulder, CO: Fred Pruett, 1990.

Faris, John T. *Roaming American Highways.* New York: Farrar & Rinehart, 1931.

Fisher, Harriet White. *A Woman's World Tour in a Motor.* Philadelphia: J. B. Lippincott Co., 1911.

Fisher, Jerry M. *The Pacesetter: The Untold Story of Carl G. Fisher.* Fort Bragg, CA: Lost Coast Press, 1998.

Flagg, James Montgomery. *Boulevards All the Way—Maybe.* George H. Doran Co., 1925.

Flink, James J. *The Automobile Age.* Cambridge, MA: MIT Press, 1988.

Foster, Mark S. *Castles in the Sand: The Life and Times of Carl Graham Fisher.* Gainesville: University Press of Florida, 2000.

Franzwa, Gregory M. *The Oregon Trail Revisited.* St. Louis: Patrice Press, 1972. Revised, 1988.

———. *The Overland Trail Revisited.* St. Louis: Patrice Press, 1972.

Gannett, Lewis. *Sweet Land*. Garden City, NY: Doubleday, Doran & Co., 1934. Very good travelog but not about the Lincoln Highway.

Gladding, Effie. *Across the Continent by the Lincoln Highway*. New York: Brentano's, 1915.

Gunther, John. *Inside U.S.A.* 50th anniversary ed. New York: Curtis Publishing, 1947. Reprint, Book-of-the-Month Club, 1997.

Hamilton, Donald. *The Steel Mirror*. Greenwich, CT: Fawcett, 1948.

Hammond, John S., II. *From Sea to Sea in 1903 in a Curved Dash Oldsmobile*. Egg Harbor City, NJ: Laureate Press, 1985.

Harmon, Craig. *"The Perfect Tribute": The Lincoln Highway Lincoln Bicentennial Celebration, 2003–2009*. Galion, OH: Lincoln Highway National Museum and Archives, 2003.

Hill, Frank Ernest. *The Automobile: How It Came, Grew, and Has Changed Our Lives*. New York: Dodd, Mead & Company, 1967.

Hogner, Dorothy Childs. *Westward, High, Low, and Dry*. New York: E. P. Dutton & Co., 1938. Little Lincoln Highway material.

Hokanson, Drake. *The Lincoln Highway: Main Street across America*. Iowa City: University of Iowa Press, 1988.

Humphrey, Zephine. *Green Mountains to Sierras*. New York: E. P. Dutton & Co., 1936.

Hyatt, Patricia Rusch. *Coast to Coast with Alice*. Minneapolis: Carolrhoda Books, 1995. Juvenile fiction.

Jakle, John. *The Tourist*. Lincoln: University of Nebraska Press, 1985.

Jensen, Jamie. *Road Trip USA: Cross-Country Adventures on America's Two-Lane Highways*. 3rd ed. Emeryville, CA: Avalon Travel, 2002.

Jones, Constance, ser. ed. *The Old West*. New York: Fodor's/Random House, 2003.

Kimes, Beverly Rae, and Henry Austin Clark Jr. *Standard Catalog of American Cars, 1805–1942*. Iola, WI: Krause Publications, 1985.

Lewis, Sinclair. *Free Air*. New York: Harcourt, Brace & Howe, 1919. Reprint, Lincoln: University of Nebraska Press, 1993.

Lewis, Tom. *Divided Highways: Building the Interstate Highways, Transforming American Life*. New York: Viking, 1997.

Lichty, Bob, and Rosemary Rubin, eds. *Lincoln Highway Anniversary Cross Country Tour, Tour Guidebook*. Canton, OH: LHA, 2003.

Lilliefors, Jim. *Highway 50: Ain't That America*. Golden, CO: Fulcrum, 1993.

Lincoln Highway Association. *Achievement on the Lincoln Highway 1920*. Detroit: LHA, 1921.

———. *The Complete Official Road Guide of the Lincoln Highway*, eds. 1–5. Detroit: LHA, 1915, 1916, 1918, 1921, 1924; Reprints, 2nd ed., Sacramento, CA: Pleiades Press, 1984; 5th ed., Tucson, AZ: Patrice Press, 1993.

———. *H. C. Ostermann*. Detroit: LHA, 1920.

———. *The Lincoln Highway: Its Ideals, Plans and Purposes*. Detroit: LHA, 1913.

———. *The Lincoln Highway: The Story of a Crusade That Made Transportation History*. New York: Dodd, Mead & Co., 1935. Reprint, Sacramento, CA: Pleiades Press, 1995.

Mason, Grace S., and Percy F. Megarel. *The Car and the Lady*. New York: Baker & Taylor Co., 1908.

Massey, Beatrice Larned. *It Might Have Been Worse: A Motor Trip from Coast to Coast*. San Francisco: Harr Wagner Publishing, 1920.

Mathison, Richard R. *Three Cars in Every Garage: The Story of the Automobile and the Automobile Club of Southern California*. Garden City, NY: Doubleday & Co., 1968.

McConnell, Curt. *Coast to Coast by Automobile: The Pioneering Trips, 1899–1908*. Stanford, CA: Stanford University Press, 2000.

———. *A Reliable Car and a Woman Who Knows It: The First Coast-to-Coast Auto Trips by Women, 1899–1916*. Jefferson, NC: McFarland & Co., 2000.

National Midland Trail Association. *The Midland Trail: The Shortest Motor Road from Coast to Coast*. [1916]. Reprint, Glorieta, NM: Rio Grande Press, 1969.

National Park Service. *Lincoln Highway Special Resource Study and Environmental Assessment*. Washington, DC: U.S. Department of the Interior, 2004.

Nicholson, T. R. *The Trailblazers: Stories of the Heroic Age of Transcontinental Motoring, 1901–14*. London: Cassell & Company, 1958.

———. *The Wild Roads: The Story of Transcontinental Motoring*. New York: Norton, 1969.

Oppel, Frank, ed. *Motoring in America: The Early Years*. Secaucus, NJ: Castle Books, 1989.

O'Shea, Beth. *A Long Way from Boston*. McGraw-Hill, 1946.

Partridge, Bellamy. *Excuse My Dust*. New York: Whittlesey House, 1943. Fact-based fiction.

———. *Fill 'er Up!: The Story of Fifty Years of Motoring*. New York: McGraw-Hill Book Co., 1952.

Patrick, Kevin J., and Robert Wilson. *The Lincoln Highway Resource Guide*. Indiana: Indiana University of Pennsylvania for the National Park Service, 2002.

Patton, Phil. *Open Road: A Celebration of the American Highway*. New York: Simon and Schuster, 1986.

Post, Edwin. *Truly Emily Post*. New York: Funk & Wagnalls, 1961.

Post, Emily. *By Motor to the Golden Gate*. New York: D. Appleton and Co., 1916.

Rae, John B. *The American Automobile: A Brief History*. Chicago: University of Chicago Press, 1965.

———. *The Road and the Car in American Life*. Cambridge, MA: MIT Press, 1971.

Ramsey, Alice Huyler. *Veil, Duster, and Tire Iron*. Pasadena, CA: Castle Press, 1961.

Ridge, Alice A., and John Wm. Ridge. *Introducing the Yellowstone Trail: A Good Road from Plymouth Rock to Puget Sound, 1912–1930*. Altoona, WI: Yellowstone Trail Publishers, 2000.

Roe, Bill. *All the Way to Lincoln Way: A Coast to Coast Bicycle Odyssey*. Davis, CA: Rowhouse Publishing, 2000.

Round, Thornton. *The Good of It All*. Cleveland: Lakeside Printing Co., 1957.

Scharf, Virginia. *Taking the Wheel: Women and the Coming of the Motor Age*. Albuquerque: University of New Mexico Press, 1992.

Schuster, George, and Tom Mahoney. *The Longest Auto Race*. New York: John Day Co., 1966.

Sears, Stephen W. *The Automobile in America*. New York: American Heritage Publishing, 1977.

Shaffer, Marguerite S. *See America First: Tourism and National Identity, 1880–1940*. Washington, DC: Smithsonian Institution Press, 2001.

Sharp, Dallas Lore. *The Better Country*. Boston: Houghton Mifflin, 1928.

Spears, W. H. *America's Fascinating Highways: Eastern United States and Canada*. Chicago: Osburn Publishing Co., 1941.

Stern, Philip Van Doren. *Tin Lizzie: The Story of the Fabulous Model T Ford*. New York: Simon and Schuster, 1955.

Stewart, George R. *U.S. 40: Cross Section of the United States of America*. Maps by Erwin Raisz. Cambridge, MA: The Riverside Press, 1953.

Thralls, Zoe A. *Keystone Geography Units, Stereographs and Lantern Slides, Unit Seventeen, From Omaha East on the Lincoln Highway*. Meadville, PA: Keystone View Co., 1942.

Trego, F. H. *Hints to Tourists Traveling on the Lincoln Highway*. Detroit: LHA, 1914. Reprint, Franklin Grove, IL: LHA, 2002.

Twiss, Clinton. *The Long, Long Trailer*. New York: Thomas Y. Crowell Co., 1951.

Vale, Thomas R., and Geraldine R. Vale. *U.S. 40 Today: Thirty Years of Landscape Change in America*. Madison: University of Wisconsin Press, 1983.

Van de Water, Frederic F. *The Family Flivvers to Frisco*. New York: D. Appleton and Co., 1927.

Williams, John A. *This Is My Country Too*. New York: New American Library, 1965.

Wyman, George. "Across America on a Motor Bicycle," *The Motor Cycle* (1903). Installments in five issues.

"Zero Milestone Number," *American Motorist* 15:7 (July 1923).

New York–New Jersey

Bianco, Anthony. *Ghosts of 42nd Street: A History of America's Most Infamous Block*. New York: William Morrow, 2004.

Cunningham, John T. *New Jersey: America's Main Road*. Garden City, NY: Doubleday & Co., 1966.

Eliot, Marc. *Down 42nd Street: Sex, Money, Culture, and Politics at the Crossroads of the World*. New York: Warner Books, 2001.

Federal Writers' Project of the Works Progress Administration. *Stories of New Jersey: Its Significant Places, People and Activities*. New York: M. Barrows and Company, 1938.

Genovese, Peter. *Jersey Diners*. New Brunswick, NJ: Rutgers University Press, 1996.

——. *New Jersey Curiosities*. Guilford, CT: The Globe Pequot Press, 2003.

——. *Roadside New Jersey*. New Brunswick, NJ: Rutgers University Press, 1994.

History's Highway: The Lincoln Highway in New Jersey, Lincoln Highway Association Year 2000 National Conference. LHA, 2000. Itinerary and tour guides.

Kahn, Robert, ser. ed. *City Secrets New York City*. New York: Little Bookroom, 2002.

Pappas, Doug, et al. *The Lincoln Highway in New York/New Jersey*. LHA Northeast Chapter, 1997.

Traub, James. *The Devil's Playground: A Century of Pleasure and Profit in Times Square*. New York: Random House, 2004.

Pennsylvania

Bruce, Robert. *The Lincoln Highway in Pennsylvania*. Washington, DC: American Automobile Association and National Highways Association, 1920.

Butko, Brian *The Lincoln Highway: Pennsylvania Traveler's Guide*. Mechanicsburg, PA: Stackpole Books, 1996. 2nd ed., 2002.

Butko, Brian, and Kevin Patrick. *Diners of Pennsylvania*. Mechanicsburg, PA: Stackpole Books, 1999.

Pennsylvania Department of Highways. *Facts Motorists Should Know*. Harrisburg, PA: Department of Highways, 1924, 1926.

Pennsylvania Writers' Project. *Pennsylvania: A Guide to the Keystone State*. New York: Oxford University Press, 1940.

Rowe, James W. *An Historical Guide of the Lincoln Highway*. Scottdale, PA: Mennonite Publishing House, 1935.

West, J. Martin, ed. *War for Empire in Western Pennsylvania*. Ligonier, PA: Fort Ligonier Assoc., 1993.

West Virginia

Cashdollar, Roy C. *A History of Chester: The Gateway to the West*. Chester, WV: Boyd Press, 1976. Revised 1985.

(Also see Pennsylvania for *The Lincoln Highway: Pennsylvania Traveler's Guide* by Brian Butko.)

Ohio

Buettner, Michael Gene. *A History and Road Guide of the Lincoln Highway in Ohio*. 5th ed. Lima, OH: Self-published, 1999.

Roseboom, Eugene H., and Francis P. Weisenburger. *A History of Ohio*. Edited and illustrated by James H. Rodabaugh. Columbus: Ohio State Archaeological and Historical Society, 1958.

Writers' Program of the Works Progress Administration in the State of Ohio. *The Ohio Guide*. New York: Oxford University Press, 1940.

Indiana

Arter, Dixie, Angie Quinn, and Jan Shupert-Arick, eds. *Headlights on Indiana's Lincoln Highway 11th Annual Conference, Lincoln Highway Association*. Fort Wayne, IN: LHA Indiana Chapter, 2003.

Buettner, Michael G. *Lincoln Highway Association 2003 Map Packet*. Fort Wayne, IN: LHA Indiana Chapter, 2003.

McCord, Shirley S., comp. *Travel Accounts of Indiana, 1679–1961*. Indiana Historical Bureau, 1970.

Pohlen, Jerome. *Oddball Indiana: A Guide to Some Really Strange Places*. Chicago: Chicago Review Press, 2002.

Writers' Program of the Works Progress Administration in the State of Indiana. *Indiana: A Guide to the Hoosier State*. New York: Oxford University Press, 1941.

Illinois

Frantz, Ruth, ed. *Main Street to Miracle Mile: Lincoln Highway Association 1999 National Conference*. Rochelle: LHA Illinois Chapter, 1999.

Pohlen, Jerome. *Oddball Illinois: A Guide to Some Really Strange Places*. Chicago: Chicago Review Press, 2000.

Ridge, Ann, ed. *Illinois Visitors Guide*. Chicago: Illinois Department of Commerce and Community Affairs, 1990.

Iowa

Ausberger, Bob, ed. *The Lincoln Highway Iowa Map Pack: "A Great Iowa Tour."* [1994]. Revised [2000].

Franzwa, Gregory M. *Iowa*. Vol. 1 of *The Lincoln Highway*. Tucson, AZ: Patrice Press, 1995.

Henry, Lyell, ed. *On the Lincoln Highway: Iowa's Main Street*. Cedar Rapids: Mount Mercy College, 1996.

"Lincoln Highway Tour" in *The Lincoln Highway Corridor: Design and Conservation of the Roadside Landscape*. Ames: Iowa State University, 1991. Conference materials.

Nebraska

Federal Writers' Project of the Works Progress Administration for the State of Nebraska. *Nebraska: A Guide to the Cornhusker State*. New York: Hastings House, 1939.

Franzwa, Gregory M. *Nebraska*. Vol. 2 of *The Lincoln Highway*. Tucson, AZ: Patrice Press, 1996.

Mead & Hunt and Heritage Research. *Nebraska Historic Highway Survey*. Lincoln: Nebraska State Historical Society and Nebraska Department of Roads, 2002.

"Where Is Nebraska, Anyway?" *Nebraska History* 80:1 (Spring 1999). Theme issue.

Colorado

"Cheyenne Dog Soldiers," *Colorado Heritage* (special issue). Denver: Colorado Historical Society, 1997.

Wiley, Wanda. "Mother of the Lincoln Highway." *The Green Book Magazine* (October 1919). Reprint, courtesy Brian Butko, in *LHA Forum* 5:3 (Spring 1998).

Wolfe, Mark. "How the Lincoln Highway Snubbed Colorado." Reprint, courtesy Colorado Historical Society, in *LHA Forum* 7:1 (Winter 2000) and 7:2/3 (Spring/Summer 2000).

Writers' Program of the Works Progress Administration in the State of Colorado. *Colorado: A Guide to the Highest State*. New York: Hastings House, 1941.

Wyoming

Franzwa, Gregory M. *Wyoming*. Vol. 3 of *The Lincoln Highway*. Tucson, AZ: Patrice Press, 1999.

Laramie Plains Museum Education Committee. *The Old Lincoln Highway: Tracking It Down . . . in the Laramie Area*. Laramie: Laramie Plains Museum, 2004.

Larson, T. A. *History of Wyoming*. Lincoln: University of Nebraska Press, 1965.

———. *Wyoming: A Bicentennial History*. New York: W. W. Norton & Co., 1977.

Writers' Program of the Work Projects Administration in the State of Wyoming. *Wyoming: A Guide to Its History, Highways, and People*. New York: Oxford University Press, 1941.

Utah

Franzwa, Gregory M., and Jesse G. Petersen. *Utah*. Vol. 4 of *The Lincoln Highway*. Tucson, AZ: Patrice Press, 2003.

Galloway, John Debo. *The First Transcontinental Railroad: Central Pacific, Union Pacific*. New York: Simmons-Boardman, 1950. Reprint, New York: Dorset Press, 1989.

McCormick, Nancy D., and John S. McCormick. *Saltair*. Salt Lake City: Bonneville Books/University of Utah Press, 1985. Reprint, 1993.

Powell, Allen Kent. *The Utah Guide*. 2nd ed. Golden, CO: Fulcrum Publishing, 1998.

Writers' Program of the Works Progress Administration for the State of Utah. *Utah: A Guide to the State*. New York: Hastings House, 1941.

Nevada

Bedeau, Bert, and Mella Harmon. *Headin' for Reno or Bust: Sin & the American Roadside*. Reno, NV: Society for Commercial Archeology, 2002. Tour guide booklet.

Evans, Lisa Gollin. *An Outdoor Family Guide to Lake Tahoe*. Seattle: Mountaineers Books, 2001.

Franzwa, Gregory M., and Jesse G. Petersen. *Nevada*. Vol. 5 of *The Lincoln Highway*. Tucson, AZ: Patrice Press, 2004.

Schegg, Leon C. *The Complete Official Lincoln Highway Donner Route Road Guide*. Nevada-Sierra Chapter for the LHA Conference, 1996.

Toll, David W. *The Complete Nevada Traveler*. Virginia City: Gold Hill Publishing, 1993.

Writers' Program of the Works Progress Administration in the State of Nevada. *Nevada: A Guide to the Silver State*. Portland, OR: Binfords & Mort, 1940.

California

Gebhart, Fred, and Maxine Cass. *On the Road around California*. Lincolnwood, IL: Passport Books, 1997.

Gilger, Paul, ed. *The Lincoln Highway in California: From the Sierra Nevada Mountains to the Pacific Ocean*. Sacramento: LHA California Chapter, 2002. A collection of regional and city maps.

Hansen, Harry, ed. *California: A Guide to the Golden State*. Originally compiled by the Federal Writers' Project of the Works Progress Administration for the State of California. New York: Hastings House, 1939. Revised 1967.

Mullen, Frank, Jr. *The Donner Party Chronicles: A Day-by-Day Account of a Doomed Wagon Train, 1846–1847*. Photos by Marilyn Newton. Reno, NV: Halcyon imprint of Nevada Humanities Committee, 1997.

Root, Norman, ed. *Lincoln Highway Association 10th Annual Conference*. Sacramento: LHA California Chapter, 2002.

Stewart, George R. *Donner Pass and Those Who Crossed It*. Menlo Park, CA: Lane Book Co., 1964.

———. *Ordeal by Hunger: The Story of the Donner Party*. Drawings by Ray Boynton. New York: Henry Holt, 1936. Revised, Boston: Houghton Mifflin, 1960.

(Also see Nevada for *The Complete Official Lincoln Highway Donner Route Road Guide* by Leon C. Schegg.)

Population Figures

For 1910 population figures for each state, the source was "Population of Counties by Decennial Census: 1900 to 1990," compiled and edited by Richard L. Forstall, Population Division, www.census.gov/population/cencounts. For 2000 figures, the source was U.S. Census Bureau: State and County QuickFacts, http://quickfacts.census.gov/qfd.

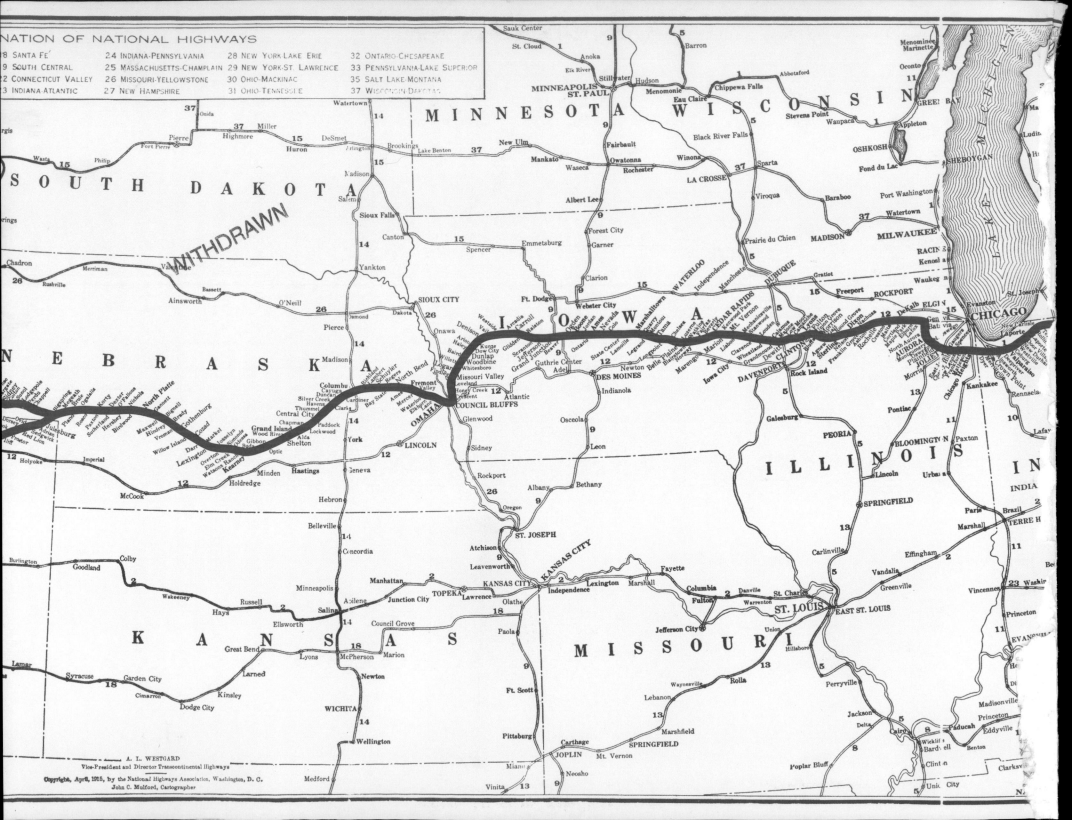

...NATION OF NATIONAL HIGHWAYS

8 SANTA FE	24 INDIANA-PENNSYLVANIA	28 NEW YORK-LAKE ERIE	32 ONTARIO-CHESAPEAKE	
9 SOUTH CENTRAL	25 MASSACHUSETTS-CHAMPLAIN	29 NEW YORK-ST. LAWRENCE	33 PENNSYLVANIA-LAKE SUPERIOR	
2 CONNECTICUT VALLEY	26 MISSOURI-YELLOWSTONE	30 OHIO-MACKINAC	35 SALT LAKE-MONTANA	
3 INDIANA-ATLANTIC	27 NEW HAMPSHIRE	31 OHIO-TENNESSEE	37 WISCONSIN-DAKOTAS	

WITHDRAWN

MINNESOTA WISCONSIN

SOUTH DAKOTA

NEBRASKA

IOWA

ILLINOIS

INDIANA

KANSAS

MISSOURI

LAKE MICHIGAN

CHICAGO

A. L. WESTGARD
Vice-President and Director Transcontinental Highways

Copyright, April, 1915, by the National Highways Association, Washington, D. C.
John C. Mulford, Cartographer